CONTEMPORARY ACCOUNTING THEORY

Dickenson Series on Contemporary Thought in Accounting
John W. Buckley, Editor

CONTEMPORARY ACCOUNTING THEORY

Eldon S. Hendriksen

Washington State University

Bruce P. Budge

University of Idaho

Dickenson Publishing Company, Inc.
Encino, California and Belmont, California

ISBN-0-8221-0116-5
Library of Congress Catalog Card Number: 73-81294

Printed in the United States of America
Printing (last digit): 9 8 7 6 5 4 3 2

Contents

Preface

One of the problems faced by modern accounting educators is the pressure to accomplish, within the college curriculum, all that seems necessary. Accounting theory is often limited to rationalized attempts to explain current accounting practices. An examination of normative theories and a discussion of their implications are often beyond the "traditional scope" of accounting education. This may account, at least in part, for the failure in the accounting profession of theorists and practitioners to communicate with each other.

Accounting, like any field of inquiry, must change and progress as the society it serves changes and progresses. It is important, therefore, that students of accounting be exposed to, and gain an understanding of, the attempts being made to advance accounting theory.

A significant amount of controversy is inevitable if the advancement is to be achieved. Since there are no absolutes in accounting theory, it is possible to use the exposition of controversy itself to provide a better understanding of the theory. This is done by making each position and concept "relative" to some other position and concept.

Without efforts directed toward concepts as well as applications, there can be no real progress toward better serving society. More important, however, is the realization that progress in terms of pure theory is not enough. Accountants who do the world's accounting must appreciate new theory if there is to be significant impact on accounting practice.

For that reason we have selected a group of readings that we believe will be of significant value to students at the intermediate level or above. The book is divided into five sections, and an attempt is made to provide some representation of most of the major controversial positions concerning subjects ranging from basic theory constructs to problems of reporting relevant information for external users in their decision processes.

Eldon S. Hendriksen
Washington State University

Bruce P. Budge
University of Idaho

CONTEMPORARY ACCOUNTING THEORY

1. OBJECTIVES OF ACCOUNTING THEORY

The objectives of accounting theory are to provide a frame of reference by which accounting practice can be evaluated, and to guide and direct accounting practice in new situations. Through theory, accounting procedures must be tested for consistency, logic, and usefulness.

Many theories of accounting may be required to accomplish these objectives. By the use of both descriptive and normative theories it should be possible to draw the basic criteria for making decisions. Ideally, whenever a question of application is raised, accountants should turn to theoretical criteria for assistance in finding the best answer.

Unfortunately, theories of accounting are not well enough developed to fulfill these objectives in all situations. Consequently, accounting has been charged with a number of serious shortcomings, which can be corrected by greater attention to sound theoretical bases.

Developing such sound theoretical bases for accounting is an ambitious task and may be an impossible one. Nevertheless, accounting theorists continue to work toward that end. Their efforts have been aimed in diverse directions; sometimes in the same direction but to different lengths. Any attempt at classification of their work will undoubtedly result in some arbitrariness. Even so, the following discussion is an attempt to identify some distinctly different approaches to the development of accounting theory.

The first approach is a study of what was recently considered to be accounting theory. It has developed over many years through the process of general acceptance. It constitutes a rather formidable body of knowledge which by and large describes current accounting practice. Such a theory (developed by general acceptance) is not constrained by any very basic

1

propositions, but is based primarily on acceptance by those who practice and use accounting. This approach to theory development is still very much alive and continues to grow. It is basically descriptive and is therefore limited in its ability to guide and direct accounting activity, so the need for new criteria persists.

Another growing theory of accounting is based on value. Advocates of this approach see valuation as the basic proposition of accounting. Through a sound method of valuation, it is believed that an adequate theory can be developed. Within this approach are such concepts as service potential value, current cash equivalent, replacement cost and others. Valuation based theories may be either normative or descriptive. All are concerned primarily with the measurement of the value of either individual assets or the firm in total. In some cases valuation may be based on past and current information, while in other cases, valuation must rely on future expectations. This is more forward looking, in many cases, than the traditional approach of the accounting profession.

A third approach to the development of accounting theory involves predictive ability. This represents almost a complete turn-around from the traditional position of looking to the past. Instead of being concerned with accumulation of past data for the sake of reporting past activity, this approach evaluates all accounting information on its ability to aid in making useful predictions. The predictive ability approach is relatively new and will ultimately rely heavily on statistical procedures, many of which are currently being developed.

Having made the preceding distinctions, it is clear that the development of accounting theory is not without controversy. The articles in this section were chosen to help the reader develop an understanding of the controversy and to provide a sense of direction concerning the development of accounting theory.

The first article is by Carman G. Blough. Mr. Blough was the Security and Exchange Commission's principal staff accountant from December 1934 to November 1935, and Chief Accountant from December 1935 to June 1938. He was also the full-time Director of Research for the Institute of Certified Public Accountants from 1944 to 1961. Who could better qualify to discuss the development of accounting principles over the period from the thirties to the sixties? The article is historical in nature. It traces the development of the administrative process which determined accounting principles in the United States during this period. Mr. Blough discusses the American Institute of Certified Public Accountants' attempts to develop authoritative statements of accounting principles, and finally deals with the need for development of a basic foundation from which accounting principles can be derived.

The historical struggle and failure to develop a set of principles or theories of accounting by which accounting practice could be evaluated is traced in adequate detail. One should capture from the article the essence of a theory of accounting developed by a process of general acceptance, and understand more fully what is meant by "generally accepted accounting principles."

The second article, by Robert Sterling, is a review of an important work by a committee of the American Accounting Association, "A Statement of Basic Accounting Theory." Sterling's review provides insights which are not obvious from a casual reading of the Statement itself. He points out the Committee's suggestions on valuation which include the use of current costs as well as the use of data not connected with the traditional transaction. Further, he points up a new methodology used by the committee. Instead of viewing accounting as a process of recording, classifying, and analyzing data, the Committee redefined accounting as a measurement-communication system. From this broader definition the committee developed the standards, guidelines, and specific recommendations included in the Statement. The Statement has had a significant impact on accounting theory.

The third article in this section is by William H. Beaver, John W. Kennelly, and William M. Voss. It attempts to construct a theory based on the predictive ability of accounting information. A hypothetical study is developed to demonstrate how empirical evidence concerning the predictive ability of accounting information could be gathered. Lease capitalization and prediction of loan default are used as illustrative cases.

Carman G. Blough, formerly Chief Accountant of the SEC, was Director of Research for the American Institute of Certified Public Accountants and has taught accounting in several universities.

Development of Accounting Principles in the United States

Carman G. Blough

It is very difficult to decide what should be included in a paper of this kind to be presented to such a well informed audience. Very little can be said that has not already been put in writing. A comprehensive coverage of the subject is out of the question in the time available. Accordingly, only a few of what seem to be among the more significant events will be touched upon.

Accounting is a very young profession. Even double entry bookkeeping is only a few centuries old, and financial reporting is in its infancy.

For a great many years accounts in this country were kept for the primary, if not the exclusive, purposes of management. This was true in the United States long after the Companies Act in England required the recognition of the interests of investors in the financial reporting of companies in that country.

Widespread concern with respect to the significance of accounting principles, as such, began to evidence itself in the United States for the first time during the early 1930's, that period of time commonly referred to as "the depression". Many persons, rich and poor alike, had lost heavily as a result of the crash in the Stock Market in the autumn of 1929. They had bought corporate stocks at unreasonably high prices in relation to their issuer's

Reprinted by permission of the author and publisher from *Berkeley Symposium on the Foundations of Financial Reporting*, (Schools of Business Administration, University of California, Berkeley), 1967, pp. 1–14.

earnings or future prospects. Many, if not most, of those small investors who could least afford the loss had bought, on small margins, shares in companies of which they knew absolutely nothing purely on the basis of rumors or tips from persons who knew no more than they themselves.

As an aftermath of the Stock Market debacle in the fall of 1929 many people became very much interested in learning its causes and what could prevent a re-occurrence. It was only natural that both the conduct of the stock exchanges and the financial reporting policies of the corporate issuers of listed securities came in for severe criticism. The results were serious self-appraisals by the accounting profession and the New York Stock Exchange, and passage of the Securities Act of 1933 and the Securities Exchange Act of 1934. The latter created the Securities and Exchange Commission. All of these were important influences affecting the development of accounting principles.

In starting our consideration of the development of accounting principles with these events of the early 1930's we must, in fairness, recognize that this was not the beginning of constructive thought in the field. Uniform systems of accounts by Federal and State regulatory authorities and the Federal and State income tax laws together with their interpretations had introduced concepts of accounting that were completely new to many companies. As early as April 1917 the American Institute of Accountants (now the American Institute of Certified Public Accountants) had, at the request of the Federal Trade Commission, prepared a "Memorandum on Balance Sheet Audits" which was published by the Federal Reserve Board under the title "Uniform Accounting" for the use of companies seeking bank loans. Also there was a considerable increase in accounting literature during the 1920's. Nevertheless, the first concerted, serious action toward the development of accounting principles took place in the early 1930's.

The New York Stock Exchange, in its efforts to improve the reporting of many of the companies whose securities were listed with it, sought the help of corporate officials, the Controllers Institute and the American Institute of Accountants. The American Institute appointed a special committee to cooperate with the Exchange. Meetings were held and correspondence conducted between this Special Committee and representatives of the Stock Exchange from 1932 through 1934. The release of this correspondence in 1934 as an Institute pamphlet under the title "Audits of Corporate Accounts" is generally recognized as the first milestone on the long road in the development of accounting principles.

This special committee was made up of well qualified and highly respected members of six leading accounting firms. Furthermore, a committee of the Controllers Institute gave its approval to the conclusion reached between the accountants and the Stock Exchange. With these powerful forces behind the final recommendations they carried far more weight than any previous statement that had ever been made on accounting matters.

In addition to stating five principles of accounting which were immediately accepted by all concerned, the correspondence laid great stress on the necessity for disclosure of the accounting methods employed and consistency in their application from year to year. Also, it is interesting to note that the committee, in considering the type of audit report to be furnished with financial statements submitted to the Exchange, recommended for the first time that auditors state whether the accounts were presented in accordance with "accepted principles of accounting." this was the forerunner of our now standard phrase "Generally Accepted Accounting Principles."

It was also the Committee's idea that each listed company should be required to prepare and file with the Exchange a statement of its methods of accounting and reporting which would be accompanied by an agreement that if any material change was made the Exchange and its stockholders would be fully informed. This provision was never put fully into effect, however, probably due to the fact that not long afterwards the SEC came into being and required all listed companies to disclose in their registration statements the accounting methods they followed with respect to certain matters which the Commission deemed important. Since registration statements were open to public scrutiny and copies had to be filed with the Exchange the aims of the correspondence in this respect were actually accomplished.

The next important steps in the development of accounting principles, and probably the most important ones of all, were the passage of the Securities Act of 1933 and the Securities Exchange Act of 1934. The 1933 Act was first placed under the jurisdiction of the Federal Trade Commission but fear of the penalties prescribed by the Act together with the sluggishness of the investment market resulted in few offerings being made. Since few registration statements were filed and the Securities Division was only one of the responsibilities of that Commission, little was done under the Act during its first year except to recruit and organize a small staff and familiarize it with the provisions of the law.

With the passage of the Securities Exchange Act of 1934 in the late summer of that year, however, things began to happen. The Securities and Exchange Commission, created by that Act, was given regulatory authority over all National Securities Exchanges. The administration of the 1933 Act and the staff of the Trade Commission's Securities Division were transferred to it and all companies wishing to have their securities listed on any national securities exchange were required to have them effectively registered with it not later than July 1, 1935.

Major emphasis was given in both Acts to the importance of financial statements to be filed with the Commission by every company wishing to have its securities listed on a national securities exchange and by most companies wishing to sell securities in interstate commerce or through the mails. Accordingly, the new Commission, as an important part of its early activities, quickly took steps to recruit an accounting staff and to develop forms and regulations governing the filing of financial statements and other financial data.

Fortunately, due to the freedom from Civil Service restraints, the determination of the Commissioners, particularly its chairman, to resist the pressures of politicians to hire their favorites, the depressed business conditions that made high grade accountants available, and the challenge which the administration of the laws offered, it was possible to employ a well trained, high grade staff of accountants rather quickly.

In addition to recruiting permanent staff the Commission called upon and accepted offers by prominent members of the accounting profession, teachers, financial analysts and investment bankers to help in developing the forms and regulations that would provide the kind of financial data that would be most useful to investors and prospective investors in whose interests the laws had been passed.

As a result, most of the forms and regulations were completed and available to prospective registrants by the beginning of 1935. During the first six months of that year probably more questions on accounting matters were raised and resolved, rightly or wrongly, than ever before or since in a like period of time. Over twenty-five hundred companies whose securities were listed on one or more of the twenty national securities exchanges filed registration statements which had to be examined and questions raised and answered regarding them. Furthermore, as the result of a relaxing of fears of liability and an increasing market for securities, many more companies filed registration statements under the 1933 Act during that time than had previously been filed. Every registration statement contained Income and Surplus statements for at least three years and one or more balance sheets, all in greater detail than most companies had ever previously issued, and each was accompanied by a substantial amount of supporting financial data. Never before had so much information regarding the accounting principles, methods and procedures of business concerns been made known as that which became public during the first six months of 1935.

Since this information was available for public inspection and copies could be obtained by anyone for ten cents a page, financial analysts, investment bankers, brokerage houses, rating agencies, financial writers and a host of others were soon studying, comparing, criticising and commenting on what these registration statements disclosed. For the first time it was possible to know of the many areas of differences that actually existed among the accounting practices followed by well known business enterprises. These differences soon became the subject of discussion, criticism, defense and analysis. From these sprang much of the impetus for the consideration that has been given to the subject of accounting principles in the years that have intervened.

Mention should be made of the fact that in 1935 the American Association of University Instructors in Accounting changed its name to the American Accounting Association, opened its membership to anyone interested in accounting and broadened its objectives to include the development of accounting principles and standards.

The merger of the American Society of Certified Public Accountants with the American Institute of Accountants under the latter's name in 1936 was also important. It brought all of the leading practitioners into one national body. This made possible the heavy impact which subsequent activities of the Institute have had on the development of accounting principles.

During the year 1936, about a year after the disclosures through the SEC filings, two documents were published which were designed to bring some order out of the chaos. One was a statement prepared by a committee of the American Institute of Accountants and published by it under the title "Examination of Financial Statements by Independent Public Accountants." Although primarily designed to help the auditor in his selection of auditing procedures, it also dealt with some accounting principles. The other was a statement prepared by the Executive Committee of the American Accounting Association and published by it under the title "A Tentative Statement of Accounting Principles Underlying Corporate Financial Statements." This statement was designed to afford a broad base of principles which would function as guides in the selection of procedures to be followed in preparing corporate reports. The Institute's pamphlet was viewed primarily as a helpful audit manual by most practicing accountants, particularly the neophytes. The Association's statement did not create much interest among practicing accountants at the time. However, it was widely studied in academic circles and the extent to which it and its numerous revisions were used by textbook writers and classroom teachers has undoubtedly had a substantial effect on practice as students who studied them became influential practitioners.

During the latter part of 1936, 1937 and the early part of 1938 an increasingly heated controversy was taking place within the Securities and Exchange Commission among the commissioners themselves. Two of the commissioners, both lawyers, were of the opinion that the Commission itself should promulgate a set of Accounting Principles that would have to be followed by all companies required to file financial statements with the Commission. The others were either strongly opposed to that procedure or were not convinced that it was desirable. The then Chief Accountant was very much opposed to the proposal. He argued that the development of accounting principles and the elimination of the areas of differences should be left to the accounting profession, whose members dealt so intimately with the problems in their day to day practice, and that the Commission should cooperate.

During these internal discussions the Chief Accountant took the opportunity, during the fifteenth anniversary meeting of the American Institute of

Accountants in the fall of 1937, to make it clear to the members that unless the profession took steps to reduce the areas of differences in accounting practices the Commission would.

In April of 1938 the Commission decided to give the profession a chance to lead the way and issued a statement of its administrative policy in the form of Accounting Series Release No. 4 issued on April 25, 1938. This statement read as follows:

"In cases where financial statements filed with this Commission pursuant to its rules and regulations under the Securities Act of 1933 or the Securities Exchange Act of 1934 are prepared in accordance with accounting principles for which there is no substantial authoritative support, such financial statements will be presumed to be misleading or inaccurate despite disclosures contained in the certificate of the accountant or in footnotes to the statements provided the matters involved are material. In cases where there is a difference of opinion between the Commission and the registrant as to the proper principles of accounting to be followed, disclosure will be accepted in lieu of correction of the financial statements themselves only if the points involved are such that there is substantial authoritative support for the practices followed by the registrant and the position of the Commission has not previously been expressed in rules, regulations, or other official releases of the Commission, including the published opinions of its chief accountant."

Thus the Commission reserved the right to decide whether a particular accounting principle had "substantial authoritative support" and also to take a position rejecting any principle even though it had substantial authoritative support by issuance of a rule or regulation or an opinion by its Chief Accountant. On the other hand it agreed to accept statements in which the accounting principles had substantial authoritative support unless it or its Chief Accountant had previously taken a contrary position. This gave companies and their auditors a workable basis on which to prepare financial statements for filing with the Commission. It also opened the way by which any recommendations by the organized profession could be given recognition by the Commission as having "substantial authoritative support."

In 1938 the American Institute of Accountants published for distribution to its members and others interested in accounting a report that had been made to the Haskins Sells Foundation by two Professors of Accounting and a Professor of Law. This report, entitled "A Statement of Accounting Principles," was developed by these three distinguished educators at the request of the Haskins Sells Foundation and was financed by it. In its letter of July 15, 1935 to the chairman of the group, the Foundation stated that it wished an independent and impartial study of the subject of accounting principles in the hope "that there may be established a body of principles which will become useful in unifying thought and which by its acceptance will serve to standardize accounting practices."

Without detracting from the great amount of work that went into the study and the comprehensive picture of what the accounting practices were, it must be said that the report did little, if anything, to narrow the areas of differences. However, anyone who read it could not fail to be impressed with the wide variety of procedures that were being followed in accounting for similar transactions and in that way undoubtedly it helped to point up the need for doing something to standardize practices.

About this time representatives of a number of the larger firms that had substantial numbers of clients registered with the SEC got together with a view to meeting the challenge of the Commission. Their idea was to see whether they could agree on a statement of principles which they would all follow. These they believed would be accepted as having "substantial author-itative support" and, because of the many companies upon whose statements these firms reported, would become the accepted principles.

As was to be expected, the persons who were in this small informal group were also active in the affairs of the American Institute. After concluding that it was desirable to work cooperatively in the development of accounting principles, it was a short step to the idea that any recommendations that might be developed in that way would carry a great deal more weight if the group were larger and were organized as a committee of the Institute. Recog-nizing the limited budget of the Institute, each of the firms agreed to contrib-ute equally to a fund sufficient to finance the work of such a committee for several years. A discussion of the idea with officials of the Institute brought an immediately favorable reaction. Accordingly, a small existing three-man Special Committee on Accounting Procedure was used to recommend to Council that the committee be enlarged and given authority to issue state-ments on matters of accounting principles. The recommendation was ap-proved and in the fall of 1938 a wholly new Committee on Accounting Procedure was created composed of twenty-one leading members, including the original cooperators.

The first meeting of the newly formed committee was largely taken up with a discussion of the best way to proceed. At first it was thought that a comprehensive statement of accounting principles should be developed which would serve as a guide to the solution of the practical problems of day to day practice. It was recognized that for such a statement to be of much help to the practitioner it would have to be much more comprehensive and in far greater detail than the "Tentative Statement" of the American Account-ing Association issued two years previously.

After extended discussion it was agreed that the preparation of such a statement might take as long as five years. In view of the need to begin to reduce the areas of differences in accounting procedures before the SEC lost patience and began to make its own rules on such matters, it was concluded that the committee could not possibly wait for the development of such a broad statement of principles. Instead it concluded that it should set to work as quickly as possible to resolve some of the more pressing controversial matters that were responsible for the criticisms leveled at financial reporting and for the concern of the SEC. This decision was described by members of the Committee as "a decision to put out the brush fires before they created a conflagration."

At that same meeting the committee authorized the employment of a Director of Research to develop information for the committee and to assist in the preparation of such pronouncements as it might decide to make. The first appointee to that position was a university professor who was to spend one half of his time on the work of the committee.

The Accounting Research Bulletins that were issued by the Committee on Accounting Procedure with the help of the three men who functioned as Directors of Research and members of their staffs during the years of the Committee's existence from 1938 to August 31, 1959 are so well known to members and students of our profession that no discussion of them will be included in this paper. However, their influence on the development of accounting principles has been one of the major factors in the improvement in accounting practices and in maintaining the authoritative position of the profession.

Because the Commission has refrained from exercising its statutory authority to make rules and regulations governing a broad area of accounting principles in favor of letting the profession lead the way, it must not be assumed that it has taken no part in the development of accounting principles or in the narrowing of areas of differences.

Both the Accounting Procedure Committee and the Accounting Principles Board have been very careful to keep in close touch with the Chief Accountant of the SEC. He has been kept informed as to the subjects under consideration and the progress being made on each. He has been furnished with copies of drafts of proposed Bulletins and Opinions and his comments and criticisms have been invited and received. Efforts have always been made to secure his agreement which were usually successful. When he did not agree his reasons were always given careful consideration. In most cases any differences were resolved by frank discussions of the arguments pro and con. On at least one occasion a subject was dropped from the agenda of the Committee because the arguments advanced by the Chief Accountant convinced members of the Committee that it would be unwise to proceed at the time.

On the other hand, there have been cases in which the Committee proceeded to issue a Bulletin even though the Commission had unresolved objections to the position taken in it.

The Commission has undoubtedly been a force in spurring the Institute on to covering more subjects more quickly than it otherwise would have done.

From time to time members of the Commission or its Chief Accountant have needled the Committee and the Board into accelerating their activities by pointing out that the Commission has a statutory responsibility in this area and will have to exercise its authority if the profession does not make satisfactory progress. In my opinion this has been very salutary and we should be very appreciative of the fact that the Commission has both recognized the qualifications of the profession to take on the task and has prodded it into action that otherwise might have been too long delayed.

Because both the 1933 and 1934 Acts placed a great deal of emphasis on disclosure the Commission did not hesitate to move quickly into that area. There is a general belief that principles of disclosure are accounting principles. Whether that is so or not the SEC did not stand back in that area even though it did defer to the profession on the matter of accounting principles generally.

The very first forms and regulations that the newly formed Commission promulgated required the disclosure of information that had always been considered confidential by many managements. The one that caused the loudest and most angry protest was the requirement that the income statements disclose sales and cost of goods sold. Approximately twenty-five hundred companies had to file registration statements and have them accepted before July 1, 1935 (extended to July 15) or their securities would have been delisted. Of these, over six hundred at first refused to include sales and cost of sales data in the public file. It was filed confidentially under a rule of the Commission that information harmful to the company might be so handled unless and until the Commission made a finding that the company's reasons did not justify withholding the facts from the public. After notice of such a finding, the company had ten days in which to withdraw its registration, as a result of which its securities would be delisted.

Hearings were granted to a substantial number of these companies. After considering all the arguments presented (and there were few new ones after the first few cases) and after hearing extended testimony from security analysts, investment bankers and other users of financial statements as to why the information was necessary, the Commission notified all of the companies affected that the information was necessary for a fair presentation and that this need overcame any arguments that had been advanced against it.

On one matter which everyone recognizes as an accounting principle the SEC took a stand from the very beginning. Because it established its position so early we often overlook the fact that in that area the Commission never gave the profession a chance to even consider the matter insofar as registrants are concerned. I refer to the basis for accounting for assets. As far as I know there have only been two exceptions to the principle that assets must never be accounted for at more than their cost, and they were very special types of situations.

As most of you know, it was common practice in the 1920's for companies to write-up their assets, particularly land, buildings, machinery and equipment. While accountants often encountered situations in which such restated values were based on very questionable appraisals or no appraisals at all, they had usually gone along on the assumption that this was a responsibility of management and required only disclosure on their part. They even accepted the practice of charging income with only the depreciation on cost and amortizing the amount of the write-up of depreciable assets by charges to the appraisal surplus.

One of the first members of the newly formed SEC to be appointed was a former General Counsel for the Federal Trade Commission who had been in charge of that Commission's very comprehensive investigation of the public utility holding companies. During that study the flagrant write-up policies of the holding companies and their subsidiar. s and the havoc they caused when the crash came in 1929 and 1930 kept impressing themselves on the chief investigator to the point that their evil became almost an obsession with him. It was only logical to expect that when he had an opportunity to outlaw write-ups he would do so. So strong were his convictions and so convincing were his arguments against write-ups that all of the other members of the Commission were persuaded to take a positive stand against them from the very first case in which the question arose.

It is interesting to note that, although many corporate officers argued vehemently in favor of recognizing unrealized appreciation in their cases, very few accountants gave more than half-hearted support until nearly fifteen years later after the question of accounting for price-level changes began to intrigue some prominent members of the profession in both the practicing and academic fields. Suffice it to say, however, that the Commission has never appeared to waver. In 1950, at the suggestion of the Committee on Accounting Procedure, the Institute's Director of Research and the SEC's Chief Accountant attempted to work out some criteria setting forth conditions under which assets might be restated upward. When they had reached agreement the proposals were submitted to the Committee and to the Commission. However, they were unacceptable to both, so the matter was dropped.

Although the Committee on Accounting Procedure decided at its inception that it should turn its attention to current problems of pressing importance, it never gave up the idea that it would be desirable to develop a comprehensive statement of accounting principles sufficiently detailed to be a real guide to the practitioner in the settlement of his day to day problems. In 1949 the Committee decided to undertake to prepare such a statement. A subcommittee was appointed and a considerable amount of work was done by it and members of the staff with that in view. However, the results of these efforts were highly unsatisfactory to everyone concerned and the work was ultimately abandoned in favor of a revision and restatement of the bulletins that had previously been issued. This was completed and published in 1953 as Accounting Research Bulletin No. 43.

However, agitation for a codification or comprehensive statement of accounting principles continued with increased force. In addition, rumblings were heard from various sources that other organizations of accountants should participate in the development of accounting principles besides the Institute. Those most often named were the Controllers Institute (now the Financial Executives Institute), the American Accounting Association and the Federal Government.

In the fall of 1957 the incoming president of the American Institute, in his inaugural address, reviewed the progress that had been made toward the development of accounting principles and the narrowing of areas of differences and proposed that the Institute undertake to restudy the research program. Subsequently he appointed a committee known as the "Special Committee on Research Program." In the appointment of that committee the president took into account the agitation for recognition of the other accounting organizations and appointed to the committee the then Chief Accountant of the SEC, the immediate past-president of the Controllers Institute and the immediate past-president of the American Accounting Association. It was this committee's recommendations which were adopted by the Council of the Institute and brought into being the Accounting Principles Board and the Accounting Research Department as they exist today. It was the unanimous opinion of this committee that no other organization should be in a position to veto any proposed statements by the Accounting Principles Board. However, it was its recommendation that other accounting organizations should be kept in close touch with the work and should be given every opportunity to present their views on matters under consideration.

Since the creation of the Board in 1959 at least three members have always been presidents or financial vice-presidents of prominent corporations, three have been well recognized professors of accounting in universities and for a while the Comptroller-General of the United States represented the Federal Government. Since the Comptroller-General is the only accountant in the Federal Government who has the final say with respect to accounting matters in his department and cannot be overruled by a board, commission or cabinet member, no other government representative was selected when he resigned from the Board. However, in this way representatives of the other organizations primarily interested in accounting principles have a voice in the action of the Board. In addition, committees of the American Accounting Association and the Financial Executives Institute and the staff members of the Securities and Exchange Commission along with other interested persons are kept informed on matters under consideration and their views are sought on proposed opinions of the Board before they are issued.

There are those who seem to believe that very little progress has been made towards the development of accounting principles and the narrowing of areas of differences in the principles followed in practice.

It is difficult for me to see how anyone who has knowledge of accounting as it was practiced during the first quarter of this century and how it is practiced today can fail to recognize the tremendous advances that have taken place in the art.

Accounting is an art and not a science. Its principles are not natural laws but rules developed by man to meet the needs of the business community. Accounting evolves as the needs of business evolve. Just as our civil and criminal laws have evolved through trial and error on the part of legislatures and courts, so our principles of accounting have evolved and will continue to evolve. During the past thirty-five years there has been no standing still. Companies were faced with new problems they had to solve, and professional accountants have had to make decisions with no precedents to follow.

It has been my privilege to have watched and participated in a great many meetings in which well-informed men, determined to find the right answer, have honestly struggled long and hard through thousands of man hours to reach sound decisions on matters of accounting principles. In fields of social science, such as accounting and law, honest men often differ radically as to what is best. Basic differences in philosophy motivate people, yet each may be as honest and objective in his approach as another.

Lawyers and judges often differ widely as to the proper decisions under identical circumstances, and in spite of the centuries behind it law still has many, many unsettled areas.

It is very doubtful whether any way can be developed by which, on a comparable basis, changes in accounting principles can be made to meet changes in business or can be developed to meet new situations before companies are required to account for them. It has been suggested that some body might be set up to which new problems might be submitted for solution in advance of the time when they would have to be reflected in financial statements. Whether this would be good for accounting or whether periods of experimentation are desirable before a particular principle is decided upon to the exclusion of others is a serious question, the answer to which is far from clear. Furthermore, new problems often have to be dealt with before there is time for any authoritative body to consider the matter.

Some have advocated that the United States Securities and Exchange Commission should determine which accounting principle or method would be acceptable for particular types of transactions. Others have suggested that a new governmental body be created which would have jurisdiction over the accounting principles to be followed by all companies doing business in interstate commerce. Others have advocated the creation of a Federal Accounting Court which would have authority to settle all accounting matters.

In my opinion, it is not desirable to have a governmental body lay down rules governing accounting principles to be followed by companies of all kinds. It is doubtful whether the staff of any governmental agency could have the breadth of experience which would be needed to prepare such a statement of principles. Only a widely diversified group including certified public accountants of broad experience would have the knowledge necessary to make such a statement of principles that would be practical. Furthermore, rules by governmental bodies have a tendency to become solidified and it is questionable whether there would be sufficient flexibility in such a body to meet the changing needs of business.

So far as an Accounting Court is concerned, it could act only after there was controversy with respect to an accounting principle and could act then only after formal court procedures which would likely take considerable time. Its decisions would most likely be based on the facts in particular cases and would probably not be sufficiently broad in scope to be of a great deal of help until a very large number of cases had been resolved.

It is quite apparent that the need for greater comparability of financial reports has become quite widely accepted in both financial and governmental circles. The question then arises as to how this is to be brought about if we are to avoid having accounting principles dictated by governmental fiat.

In a few of its bulletins the Committee on Accounting Procedure spelled out criteria that should govern the determination of the principles to be applied under transactions which superficially appeared the same but differed in fact. The treatment of long term leases and of business combinations are examples. The Accounting Principles Board has used this method also.

However, in these and in many other opinions the Institute's position has not always been stated clearly and concisely, in terms that left no room for quibbling. Sometimes this has been due to differences among members of a committee which forced compromise and equivocation in order to obtain the two-thirds majority necessary to issue any statement. Sometimes the entire committee thought the time was not ripe to go as far as it would have liked to go. Sometimes it was thought that a contrary position was so well established that a recommendation that it be considered unacceptable might result in the whole bulletin being rejected.

Undoubtedly this lack of clarity and positiveness has been responsible for much of any lack of adherence to the bulletins that there has been. It has seemed to me that in those cases in which the Institute's position has been stated in unmistakably clear and positive terms its opinions usually have been followed almost immediately.

There is evidence that the Accounting Principles Board will act more promptly and positively than it or its predecessor has in the past. It is very important, in the interests of better financial reporting and of the well being of the profession, that accountants who find themselves out of sympathy with the recommendations of the Board will nevertheless get behind them and give them a fair trial. If this is done I firmly believe it will produce far better results than rules by governmental fiat. Moreover, it would leave the way open for further evolution of accounting principles by those most qualified by their day to day activities, their training and their experience to do it.

In conclusion, it is my opinion that true comparability in the accounting principles followed by different companies in the presentation of their financial reports is desirable. For the application of principles to particular facts, criteria requiring intelligent, professional judgment should be established as guides to getting true comparability. Such criteria and the principles to which they relate should be established by a highly qualified group of experienced accountants selected by the accounting profession and not by the government. The profession should accept such leadership and put its recommendations into effect. Governmental bodies should support its recommendations. Such a body should be flexible enough to recognize the need for change or for new principles and their application, and to act as promptly as sound judgment will permit.

Robert Sterling is Arthur Young Distinguished Professor at the University of Kansas.

A Statement of Basic Accounting Theory: A Review Article

Robert R. Sterling

The Committee to Prepare a Statement of Basic Accounting Theory[1] was charged "to develop an integrated statement of basic accounting theory which will serve as a guide to educators, practitioners, and others interested in accounting. The statement should include adequate support for any position taken and sufficient explanation to provide clarity, yet be as concise as feasible." (p. v) This is indeed a large order, so large that hardly anyone would be surprised if the committee failed.

The ideas presented in the *Statement* can readily be traced to the literature but this is not a criticism; instead it is the nature of a committee effort. A committee will report only what is "generally accepted" by its members and often general acceptance of ideas requires previous exposure. We are told that the committee met eight times for a total of twenty days (p. vi) and this lends further support to the previous exposure hypothesis. Radically new ideas would have probably required much longer. Thus, the accounting theorist will find little that is new in the *Statement*. He may disagree with parts or all of it but he will find nothing to shock or stimulate.

Nevertheless, this document is a revolutionary one when its contents are compared to contemporary practice and education. The differences are not

---

[1] *A Statement of Basic Accounting Theory*, American Accounting Association (Evanston, Ill., 1966); hereafter the "*Statement*" and the "committee." Page numbers for quotations without further reference are from the *Statement*.

Reprinted by permission of the author and publisher from *Journal of Accounting Research*, Vol. V (Spring, 1967), pp. 95–112.

only in the specific suggestions on valuation, e.g., current cost, non-transaction data, but also in two more important respects: (1) methodology and (2) world-view.

Methodology

The committee's methodology is self-consciously antithetical to the previous inductive or empirical methods. They imply that such methods do not yield a theory: "... many accountants ... equate 'accounting theory' with the sum total of all accounting practices currently in use." (p. 6) The function of a theory to them is prescriptive, not descriptive. Their standards ". . . provide means of *accepting or rejecting accounting methods. . . .*" (p. 6) "Not only should information that meets the standards be included in accounting; all information that does not meet the standards should be excluded." (p. 3)

This is diametrically opposed to the Paton and Littleton method of weaving together current practices into a coherent whole and to Grady's method of inventorying practices and then justifying them. Also it is a decisive break with the AICPA method of issuing bulletins on current controversial issues which arise in practice.

I agree with this break; I think that the "inductive" approach commits the elementary fallacy of getting *ought* from *is*: to conclude that what *is* is what ought to be. The enthymeme is that there is some natural law or divine hand that makes the *is* good, or perhaps unalterable. I know of no modern science that takes this view. In mechanics, friction *is*, but no one concludes that it ought to be. On the contrary, the physicist continually tries to lessen or avoid it. Sociology and anthropology observe human behavior and generalize about it but no one concludes that it ought to be the way it is. On the contrary, "value judgments" about what people ought to do are carefully avoided. Except for some theologies, I know of no discipline other than accounting which induces what ought to be from what is.

The AICPA bulletins follow a method which has been described as the "crisis" or "fire truck" methodology. They wait for a fire and then rush in to put it out. Often the previous set of generally accepted principles proves to be insufficient for the resolution of the crisis. In such cases a new principle is introduced ad hoc, i.e., the practices cannot be explained by the existing principles and thus a new principle is introduced for the specific purpose of explaining the practice. For example, *Bulletin No. 43* states that cost is the principle (presumably because it fulfils the objective of measuring income by matching appropriate *cost* against revenues). But several different flows are generally accepted and therefore an ad hoc principle needs to be introduced which permits several "costs"; lower of cost or market is justified by introducing costs which "lose their utility"; market higher than cost is generally accepted for some products and thus the ad hoc principle of "immediate marketability at quoted prices" is introduced.[2] It is a commonplace observation that any theory can be saved by the simple expedient of introducing ad hoc principles every time a crisis arises.[3] However, the question is not whether it *can* be saved but whether it *should* be saved. With the introduction of a number of ad hoc principles, soon the theory denies nothing. A proposition which denies nothing affirms nothing. The cost principle for inventory denies very little since it permits net realizable values, replacement prices, standards, and a host of costs. More importantly, if another unknown value were to become generally accepted, we could add another principle to cover it. Thus the theory cannot, in principle, deny anything and, therefore, it is totally useless except as an apology for what is or was.

The committee disclaims this approach, but there is no discussion of why they rejected it nor is there any explicit presentation of the method they employed. I think I know what method they employed but it would have been preferable had they stated it.

The committee redefined accounting and then deductively reasoned to the standards, guidelines, and specific recommendations. "The committee defines accounting as the process of identifying, measuring, and communicating economic information to permit informed judgments and decisions by users of the information." (p. 1) To them accounting is a measurement-communication system. Such a definition is often referred to as "invitational," i.e., a writer or speaker invites the audience to think of the word as he defines it. I will indicate below how readily the standards follow if one accepts the definition.

The committee has invited us to accept a definition of accounting and deductive reasoning, both of which are radical changes from previous official publications (the Moonitz mutation excepted) without justification for either. The deductive method is not new in science, but it is new and radical in accounting and this change requires some persuasive arguments. So does their definition. It might be said that the new definition is "self-evident" and

---

[2] *Accounting Research and Terminology Bulletins*, American Institute of Certified Public Accountants, 1961. It is enlightening to compare the depreciation definition (p. 76) with the lower of cost or market discussion. (p. 30) Assets lose their utility by using up service potential and costs are used to allocate (not value) that loss; but inventory loses its utility because the market declines. "Although the *cost basis* ordinarily achieves the objective of a proper matching of *costs* and revenues, under certain circumstances *cost* may not be the amount properly chargeable against the revenues of future periods." (p. 30) I hardly see how anything other than cost can be appropriate to the objective of properly matching costs and revenues.

Also, compare the Mason dissent on valuing marketable securities (p. 23) with the discussion of inventories valued at market higher than cost. (p. 34) Below I refer to this as "cognitive insulation." Elsewhere I have called it "apologetics" in the strict sense of that term. (*The Theory of the Measurement of Enterprise Income*, Chapter VI).

[3] Philosophers of science sometimes play a parlor game in which someone interprets the new scientific discoveries by use of the older, abandoned constructs, e.g., Aristotle's elements of air, earth, fire, and water or the phlogiston theory. It can always be done if ad hoc principles are permitted.

thus needs no justification. It is not self-evident to Mr. Morrison, who thinks that the *Statement* is only ". . . of certain aspects of . . . accounting. . . . But it offers little in the way of basic accounting theory as a foundation for a body of sound accounting principles. . . ." (p. 97) Knowing Mr. Morrison's propensity to "fairness" one could have predicted this reaction. But that is precisely the point: knowing others' propensity to "conservatism," "matching and attaching," etc., one can predict their reaction. Eventually the battle will have to be fought at this level of abstraction. One will have to present well-formed arguments about what accounting ought to be. Until then one can either accept or reject the committee's definition and deductions. Since they did not make the argument and one practitioner has already reacted, it is doubtful that they have fulfilled the charge to guide practitioners.

It is more difficult to judge how the *Statement* will fare in guiding educators. A long tradition of accounting education has developed from the inductive approach. (Recall that Littleton presented the coherent theory as an aid to education so that students need not memorize rules.[4]) Most undergraduate accounting curricula seem designed solely to prepare the student for accounting practice. The popular textbook trilogies point almost exclusively toward the CPA exam and often the success of a school is judged by the percentage of students who pass. This means training the student for contemporary practice by teaching him what is now done. Thus, the changes in curricula come from changes in practice as do changes in theory. Changes in practice are likely to be cognitively insulated—two practitioners solving the same problem in different ways and both practices becoming accepted—and thus it comes as no surprise that the texts are cognitively insulated, e.g., rejecting appraisal values because they vary in the theory chapter and then laboriously explaining the variations in costs in the rest of the chapters. Students and teachers have done fairly well in accepting this much insulation, but I doubt if they could accept a redefinition. It will take a master weaver to weave "accounting is matching and attaching" together with "accounting is a measurement-communication system."

If educators and textbook authors continue to emphasize practice, the *Statement* will have little impact. I suspect that they will continue because the students need jobs. Thus practice will continue to dominate education and the committee will have failed in its charge.

The committee has, however, fulfilled the less ambitious function of providing an "official" collection of ideas generally accepted by theorists. Previous individual efforts by theorists have not been successful. For the most part, they have not been refuted—just ignored and forgotten. It may be more

---

[4] "Teachers of bookkeeping and later of accounting and auditing found it necessary to supplement the accumulated rules and descriptions of procedure by explanations and justifications. This was done in order that study should be something more than memorizing of rules." A. E. Littleton, *Structure of Accounting Theory* (American Accounting Association Monograph No. 5, 1953), p. 185.

difficult to ignore a committee's official pronouncements, and this might be a first step in reversing the direction of accounting change. Perhaps it will go from theory to practice instead of the previous direction. If so, it will be the most significant development since Pacioli. Like most developments, it will create new problems. The first is the implementation of new ideas from theorists. An analogy can be drawn from technology. At some point the theory needs to be frozen so that an instrument can be built and debugged. The next instrument will embody further theoretical advances, some of which result from the discoveries in the previous one. Accounting is more difficult because it is continually practiced and consistency is desirable, i.e., the time-series needs to be linked. More important, accounting is an institution in the Veblenian sense—a habit of thought by a large group of people—and as such it is inevitably slow to change and Veblen (but not Marx) would argue that it is completely invulnerable to revolution. Under this view, the theory of accounting is subject to revolutionary change but the practice of accounting must be evolutionary. The education of practicing accountants is the connecting link and requires some hard thought and choices from among rather unattractive alternatives.

A final point on methodology springs from the following: "These techniques include generally accepted accounting principles and practices, as well as alternatives which may not meet the criterion of 'general acceptance' but for which there is substantial authoritative support." (p. 6) "Techniques" is not well defined but it includes things ". . . used by accountants in measuring, describing. . . ." (p. 6) I find this an odd proposition in the context of the *Statement*, although it would not be odd under the Paton and Littleton, Grady, or Bulletin 43 methodology. "General acceptance" is a necessary and sufficient condition for the inclusion of a technique under the inductive method, but the committee's proposition indicates that *either* "general acceptance" or "substantial authoritative support" is sufficient. This permits more latitude in selecting techniques and therefore less uniformity of practices. Moreover, reversion to "general acceptance" seems to contradict the committee's position that a theory should be prescriptive. A prescriptive theory implies a criterion of theoretical validity, and neither general acceptance nor authoritative support guarantees theoretical validity.

World-View

The committee has invited us to view accounting as a measurement-information system. This new view precludes some questions but poses others. In their reference frame, it is no longer appropriate to argue about which convention or assumption comes closest to the "actual" cost or income; it is not appropriate to assume that if we carefully describe (fully disclose) the methods used, then the figures will be meaningful, or that only invested costs or transaction data are the subject matter of accounting or that by its very name accounting reflects costs. Under the new view, measurements in accounting are a function of some end. This is a change in "world-view" and is the stuff that revolutions[5] are made of. Given this view, the standards, particularly the relevance standard, are almost too obvious. This is not a detraction; instead it is in the nature of the change in world-view.

To raise the question of measurement is to raise the question of relevance. One never measures all the properties of an object; instead one measures those properties that are relevant to him. Churchman's Crusoe example makes this abundantly clear.[6] When Crusoe sets out to find a flagstone to fit his hearth, the length is obviously relevant. It is equally obvious that the carbon half-life and a host of other properties are irrelevant. However, it is obvious only under this view. Under some other view, one could argue that the carbon half-life was the appropriate measure because it was, say, the truth or perhaps more objective than length.

To raise the question of measurement is to raise the question of communications. Measurement is a process of comparison; one measures the same object at different times to make an inter-temporal comparison, or different objects at the same time to make an instantaneous inter-object comparison. This means that one communicates inter-spatially or inter-temporally. The communication can be inter-personal or with one's self. (The object of Churchman's example was to show that Crusoe had to communicate with his past.) This is commensurate with information theory since self-information is included.

Verifiability and freedom from bias are desiderata of all measurements and thus, they follow readily from the new view. The surprise is not that these are included as standards but that "objectivity" is *excluded*. In one sense, the committee is to be commended for avoiding this quagmire. What is "objective"—the real properties as opposed to our perception of them—has gone through several reversals in philosophy and, as a consequence, it is highly confused. From the measurement literature of the physical sciences one would assume that instrumentation is the requisite for an objective measurement. A pointer reading that all would agree to is considered objective. This view can be confuted by the simple observation that someone must read the pointer and this is, *ipso facto*, a subjective perception. Even more damaging is the ultimate test of the instrument. We might all agree that the butcher's scale points to 50 pounds when one wiener is placed on it but I

---

[5] This is a construct about the formation of constructs and the disputes are legion. For my bias as well as the phrase, see Thomas Kuhn, *Structure of Scientific Revolution* (Chicago: University of Chicago Press, 1962), p. 90 *et passim*.

[6] C. West Churchman, "Why Measure," in *Measurement: Definitions and Theories*, eds. C. West Churchman and Philburn Ratoosh (New York: John Wiley & Sons, Inc. 1959), p. 89.

suspect that we would prefer our "subjective" estimation, i.e., we woul claim that the objective reading was *wrong* and revert to some subjectiv basis such as hefting. In accounting, objectivity is even more confused, so th force of, e.g., Mr. Morrison's comment is lost to me. He denies current cos because no objective method of determining it has been found. (p. 98) I d not know what he had in mind but I suggest the following procedure: (1) Se out the tests of objectivity in as precise a form as possible. (2) Apply thos tests with equal vigor to both historical and current costs. (3) Report th results in comparative form.

I suspect that "objectivity" to accountants is nothing more than an emo tional response to suggestions for other (non-cost) valuation schemes, an we would do well to abandon the term. This may have been the motivation o the committee. However, abandoning the term does not solve the problem that gives rise to the term. Perhaps verifiability and freedom from bias ar attempts to clarify so that meaningful propositions can be formed. If so, it i a beginning but a woefully weak one. If we are to conceive of ourselves a metricians, there is a lot of epistemological spade work to be done before we can proceed.

The last standard of quantifiability is rather puzzling, given the measure-ment view. There are many different meanings attached to measurement bu insofar as I know they all have to do with numerals and/or numbers.

The elaboration (pp. 11–13) of quantifiability seems directed to two ends: (1) Accounting need not be restricted to "value" quantities and (2) "The quantification of data adds usefulness." I agree with the first point since relevant quantities are not necessarily value quantities. The second point is followed by a brief outline of the famous S. S. Stevens school of measure-ment. In some circles this school is considered infamous because in some instances it negates the usefulness of quantification. The best known case is the numbering-of-football-players question. Stevens would claim that the numbering of football players is a "Measurement" (under the nominal scale) while others claim that this does violence to a well established linguis-tic fact and it adds nothing to the names of the players. This violation may cause confusion instead of adding usefulness. An example more germane to accounting is any asset to which a number has been assigned. Stevens would claim that the "assignment of numerals according to a rule—any rule—" is a measurement[7] and *then* he would concern himself with what one could legiti-mately do with that number. Thus, to Stevens all of our current methods—

[7] S. S. Stevens, "Measurement, Psycho-physics.and Utility" idem. p. 19. The chief architect of the physics view says: "Measurement is the process of assigning numbers to represent quantities. . . ." Norman R. Campbell, *Physics: The Elements* (Cambridge: Cambridge Univer-sity Press, 1920), p. 267. In addition to all the other differences in these definitions, the numeral-number distinction causes some difficulty. Cf. C. G. Hempel, "Fundamentals of Concept Forma-tion in Empirical Science," *International Encyclopedia of Unified Science*, Vol. II, No. 7 (Chi-cago: The University of Chicago Press, 1952), pp. 55 and 85.

LIFO, SYD, lower, discounted—and any others would be measurements. Bergmann, for example, and most metricians of physics orientation would deny that it is a measurement unless it is additive and the property of additivity requires some descriptive correlate or empirical meaning. Thus, to Bergmann our current methods would not be measurements unless we could stipulate the descriptive correlates.

The Stevens position makes one question the verifiability standard. Suppose my rule was different from yours. Could you then "verify" my figure? The auditor does verify but it is in the peculiar fashion of accepting management's estimate of the life and salvage value, management's decision on which ancillary costs should be attached to the asset and which should be expensed, and finally management's decision on which depreciation equation should be used. All of these are bounded but they vary widely and thus the auditor has "verified," come up with the same figure, only after the odd procedure of accepting all the decisions which *necessarily* (analytically) lead to that figure. Bergmann would probably say that this is neither a measurement nor a verification. My reading of the *Statement* leads me to believe that the committee would consider a quantity so derived to be a measurement and a verification. If so, I note an exception.

This problem is crucial to the *Statement* because Mr. Morrison has rejected current costs because they are not objective and verifiable; and because the majority of the committee continually concede that historical cost is more verifiable than current cost. "Historical transaction-based information has been verified by a market transaction, and hence is of great usefulness when verifiability is emphasized." (p. 30) This is a contradiction of the primary standard of relevance. A figure may be verifiable but irrelevant and therefore completely useless. On the other hand, an unverified guess at a relevant figure may be quite useful. If the guess is erroneous it may lead to erroneous decisions but that is the category mistake that the committee is making. Different degrees of accuracy, different tolerances of errors, are required for different decisions, but this is covered by the relevance standard. Verification may make us more confident of the accuracy of the figure because the measurement has been repeated and it makes deliberate misrepresentation more difficult. Verifiability is therefore highly desirable but relevance is indispensible.

For these reasons, I do not understand why ". . . the original-transaction data or other valuation will continue to be reported in the current-cost column where current cost is unverifiable because there is no other evidence which meets the minimum requirement of the verifiability standard." (p. 28) Presumably the reason for reporting current cost is that it is relevant, and historical cost, in this context or column, is not. But the above proposition shifts criteria and reports an irrelevancy. This irrelevancy is reported in the current-cost column and added in so that the problem of summing inconsistent figures—figures which represent different dimensions—arises again. Further, it assumes that the original-transaction data or other valuation does meet the verifiability standard. Some of the peculiarities of historical-cost verification were outlined above, but note here that this verification requires a shift in operations. Current cost measurements require a set of operations quite different from those of historical cost measurement. Thus, in principle, one cannot verify historical cost with current cost operations or vice versa. If there are current costs which cannot be measured and verified, then I would opt for presenting non-quantative information in accordance with the quantifiability standard. "When accountants present non-quantitative information in compliance with the other standards they should not imply its measurability." (p. 7) If current cost is relevant but not measurable, we should not imply its measurability by substituting historical cost.

Finally I think the committee concedes too much to the verifiability of historical cost. Elsewhere I have reviewed the operational requirements for determining historical cost.[8] It is sufficient here to note the resemblance between incorrigible statements and some of the things an auditor is asked to verify. An incorrigible statement is a first-person present-tense report of a sensation, e.g., "I feel pain" or "I see blue dots." It is readily seen that such statements are impossible to verify or falsify. Compare these incorrigible statements to statements of estimation or intention. For example, "I estimate that boulder to weigh 50 tons." If you weigh it, you can falsify the predicate "50 tons" but you can never falsify the fact that my estimation was 50 tons. If you estimate its weight without measuring it, you have neither verified nor falsified either the 50 tons or my estimation. Consider "I estimate the life of that machine to be 50 years" or worse "I intend to maintain and use that machine so that it will last 50 years." Ex post there is a way to find out how long it did last but that is too late. Ex ante one might make a separate estimate but that does not help. These statements, particularly the latter report of intentions, are in principle unverifiable and unfalsifiable. Current costs, in many instances, are also estimates, but there is no reason to concede that one kind of estimate is more verifiable than another.

The guidelines presented are also extensions of the measurement notion. The first three may be considered an elaboration of the relevance standard. The last two recognize that measurements are comparisons and that comparisons in two directions are possible and desirable. If one wants inter-firm comparisons, then there must be "uniformity of practices," and we can stop all this nonsense about diversity being good. If one wants to argue for "flexibility" one must deny inter-firm comparisons and replace it with some other desideratum. Accountants have long accepted guideline 5—"Consistency of practices through time"—because it is obvious that one cannot com-

---

[8] Robert R. Sterling, "Operational Analysis of Traditional Accounting," *Abacus*, December, 1966.

pare or link time-series without consistency. Guideline 4 is simply an application of consistency to different firms for the same reasons.

The View Extended

The measurement-communication system presented by the committee may be diagramed as follows:

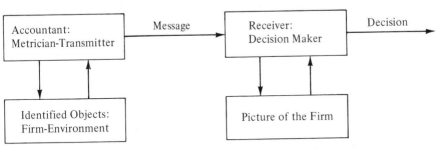

This conforms to the definition of "accounting as the process of identifying, measuring, and communicating economic information to permit informed judgments and decisions by users of the information." (p. 1) The firm or other entity and its environment are identified and measured and then a message is prepared and communicated to the receivers.

The diagram again emphasizes the notion of relevance. Everything about the firm cannot be reported—the modifier "economic" limits the scope—nor should everything be reported. The information to be reported must be relevant to some "decision model." (p. 31 *et passim*). More important, this diagram locates the decision model: it is at the destination that the receiver possesses the decision model.

The diagram also emphasizes the omissions. The model originated by Shannon and Weaver includes a channel with a finite capacity. This omission, I think, is a serious defect in the committee's work. They imply that the advent and increased use of computers obviate this consideration. While it is true that the computer has and probably will continue to increase capacity for gathering and processing information it still has a finite capacity. Even if it did not, we would still want to limit the capacity. Anyone on the mailing list of U.S. Government documents knows very well that it is possible to be inundated with relevant information.

This communication system is a solution to a prior economic decision. Scarce resources have been allocated to the system and it must operate within that constraint. In fact, one could say that information or communication theory is an "economic" problem. It is an attempt to maximize the quantity of information with a given constraint. Without the constraint the problem is trivial. Redundancy would provide a complete solution.

My reaction to the "different incomes for different purposes" proposal is in the same vein. The motivation for this proposal is quite correct: no single statistic is relevant to all purposes. However, to propose that a different statistic be prepared for each purpose overlooks the constraint. It is the trivial solution to the problem and solves nothing.

The committee has not made this proposal but it has proposed that we transmit *more*. Both historical and current costs are recommended and ". . . the committee advocates the reporting of all information that is believed to be relevant to the judgments and decisions of any substantial group of users." (p. 22) In my view, more is certainly needed but the crucial question has not been broached: within a given constraint how do we select the statistics so that we maximize[9] the information?

Reference to the relevance standard will not solve this problem. There are many receivers with a wide variety of purposes, and different receivers with the same purpose may have different decision models. At the formal level of analysis, relevance is an either-or proposition. Either a given statistic is specified by the decision model or it is not, and therefore it is either relevant or irrelevant. Given the variety of purposes and the variety of models for the same purpose, the channel capacity begins to bind at the outset.

This immediately suggests a binary measure of relevance. We could poll the receivers to find out which binits were (1) relevant and which were (0) irrelevant to them. Then we could transmit the binits with the largest value. Suggestions for this sort of thing have been advanced previously, but some rather important problems result from this approach.

Suppose we convince ourselves that any decision model which specifies historical cost is an invalid model, i.e., it will yield decisions consonant with the specified purpose only by chance. Further, suppose that the poll of the receivers showed historical cost to be relevant to most receivers. Should we transmit historical cost?

---

[9] I mean by "maximize information" considerably more than the information or communication theorists mean. They are concerned with ". . . the *choice*, the range of possible messages . . ." and exclude ". . . moral import, scientific significance, artistic quality, even speculative value in business. . . . Not one of these concepts, essential though they are to the usual meaning of 'information' come within the ambit of our definition. . . ." G. T. Guilbaud, *What Is Cybernetics?* (New York: Criterion Books, 1959), p. 59. Guilbaud is quoting Brillouin in part of the above.

Almost all information theorists emphasize this distinction. Goldman, for example, says information theory measures "the *quantity* of information, not its value" (p. 300) and then makes the distinction clear by the following example:

The quantity theory of information which we have been developing may appear incomplete and perhaps disappointing to the reader because it does not treat the *value* of information. There are just as many binits in the information which tells whether John Smith's wife had a boy or girl, as in the information which tells whether your own wife had a boy or girl. Stanford Goldman, *Information Theory* (New York: Prentice-Hall, 1953), p. 63.

In accounting we are primarily concerned with the "value" of the information, not in the choices or the number of binits. Thus, formal information theory has little to contribute to accounting except insofar as the *general* concepts help us to organize our thinking. But this emphasizes the seriousness of the omission of the general concept of a limited capacity.

The force of this question will not be lost on those who have taught decision-making courses. We have known since Jevons that "in commerce, bygones are bygones" but our students rarely know this. In fact, exclusion of *the* cost from a decision seems to be counter-intuitive. I suspect that this is true for the general population as well as our students. Of course, if we have enough capacity we can transmit this data along with others.

The concern of the committee with socio-economic matters or with the "correct" allocation of resources opens this position to question. If we are convinced that the receivers are using the wrong decision model, we have a dilemma. (1) We can transmit the information specified by their wrong model which will yield right decisions only by chance. (2) We can transmit the information specified by the right model which will be irrelevant to their model, and hence right decisions will result only by chance.

Neither alternative is attractive but I would argue for the second, largely on the grounds that communications are not neutral; instead they are educational. Comparative sociologists have often pointed out that our taste in "news," "literature," "music," etc. is largely determined by what was previously communicated to us. If the newscasters poll the populace today they will find that present tastes place football scores high on the list and cricket scores low. However, the very transmission of football scores reinforces this taste and is a major factor in determining the tastes of the coming generation. The accountant is in the same position. He cannot be neutral because his transmissions will be a major factor in determining what the future generations consider relevant. The very definition of information is dependent upon previous information; it is a cause of desires in an on-going process as well as an effect of the present desires.

For this reason I am suspicious of the simplistic idea of polling the receivers. In the present state of accounting, I have no doubt that a poll would improve our current reporting but it does not even approach a satisfactory solution. In my view there is no "final" solution for the following reasons.

The major problem of accounting is to develop a *general* information system. By this I mean a system that supplies relevant data to both specific and unspecific decision models. The point can best be illustrated by the committee's programmed-unprogrammed matrix. (p. 44) If we have a production process with a variable material mix, there is a unique solution by a linear programming model. The capital budgeting model will provide a yes-no solution to simple investment problems. These models clearly specify the relevant data. Therefore, they can be automatized—hooked to the information-computer system—and the output, the "information" that is received by humans, is already a decision. The relevance problem is trivial in such cases. In fact, the computer can be programmed to *ask* for the relevant data.

It is in the unprogrammed areas that difficulties are encountered. There the decision models are not well defined; indeed the problems are often unknown. It is this area of internal reporting that intersects with external reporting. External reporting also has programmed data requirements, e.g., the revenue code specifies the relevant data in tedious detail and thus there is no relevance problem. The difficult task is to make measurements that are relevant to the unprogrammed decisions. Since the problems which give rise to unprogrammed decisions are likely to change over time and since the perceived problems are (partially at least) a function of the information received, it is unlikely that a final solution can ever be found. This is not a note of despair. On the contrary, I think it is a realistic view of the difficult and exciting problems which face us. They have always faced us, we have just failed to recognize them. That is, the change in world-view both permits and forces us to look at a different set of problems. In my opinion, the new view is the correct one and it has the potential to change accounting from a ritualistic and dogmatic tradition to a vital part of the economic process and an academic discipline with problems that would challenge the greatest intellects.

Historical and Current Costs

The committee asserts: "A case was built, on the grounds of relevance, for the communication of a current expression in the form of replacement cost of the economic significance of the resources acquired, utilized, and held by an accounting entity." (p. 73) A perusal of Chapter III does not support this assertion. There is no systematic case presented for current cost although there are a number of individual allegations that it is relevant. The committee summarizes the argument on p. 19: "Evidence of dissatisfaction with extant accounting practices abounds. A principal criticism relates to the deficiencies of historical cost as a basis of predicting future earnings. . . , " and "we find historical cost information not adequate for all purposes." "We accordingly recommend that current-cost information as well as historical-cost information should be reported." Thus, the primary support for current cost comes from dissatisfaction with historical cost. This does not follow. Not-p does not necessarily imply q. That is, the rejection of or dissatisfaction with one alternative does not lead to the acceptance of another without further argument. The second point is that historical cost is deficient in *predicting* future earnings. There is no assurance that current cost will be any better for purposes of prediction. Measurement is commonly confused with prediction. Measurement is a process of discovering an *extant* condition, and prediction is concerned with a future condition. Thus, prediction requires some kind of law connecting the past and present with the future. Measurement does not require the additional step of applying the law. Goodman's simplistic example[10] is "if butter is placed in a 300° degree oven,

---

[10] Leonard Linsky, *Semantics and the Philosophy of Language* (Urbana, Ill., University of

it will melt." One can measure the temperature of the oven without making the prediction. As a second step the prediction can be made if the effects of temperature on butter is known, i.e., if the law connecting the measurement of the extant state with a future state is known. Temperature is said to be relevant to this law and tensile strength is not. However, the fact that tensile strength is not relevant does not imply that temperature is. The deficiencies of historical cost in predicting the future does not imply that current cost is any less deficient. Unless one can demonstrate the existence of some law-like conditional which specifies current cost, the point is moot.

Given these considerations, I am puzzled by the conclusion that ". . . accordingly we recommend that current-cost information as well as historical cost information should be reported." Nothing the committee has said leads me to that conclusion. It may be that they are trying the shotgun approach: by presenting *more* statistics accountants will satisfy more receivers. But the suggestion for *more* neglects the standard of relevance.

It is possible to be just as dogmatic about current cost as about historical cost. It is possible for everybody to jump on the relevance-current-cost bandwagon in the same uncritical way that we attached ourselves to the matching-historical-cost construct. If the new world-view is to be accepted and acceptable, it needs to be applied with rigor and precision. All the details cannot be worked out immediately, perhaps all of them can never be completely worked out. But current cost is not a detail, it is an entire scheme of valuation. Therefore, it deserves and requires more justification than the committee gave it.

In short, my plea is for a demonstration that current cost is relevant. Without the demonstration there is the danger that relevance and irrelevance can be tossed about as "appropriately match" has been in the past. There is already some evidence of this in the cost accounting literature. Direct cost is said to be relevant to managerial decisions and therefore goods ought to be valued that way on the balance sheet and income statement. It is obvious that the historical cost, however defined, of those units already produced is sunk and therefore irrelevant to all decisions about those units. Direct cost may be used as a guide in projecting what the future marginal cost will be but it is only a guide since we may expect various changes and adjust for them. These adjusted costs are the expected marginal costs in the short or intermediate run and are relevant to some short run decisions. The direct costs are relevant only insofar as they furnish a guide to future marginal costs. Moreover, they are a guide to only part of the picture because it is likely that at least part of the "fixed costs" will become variable within the firm's target horizon, i.e., it will be necessary to replace part of the plant. These expectations of indirect costs are also relevant; these future expected outlays are relevant to whether the firm will continue or not. They must be

Illinois Press, 1952), pp. 162–65. In this book Goodman uses the butter example in an exposition of counter-factual conditionals, not predictions. However, the same law-like process holds.

netted against expected future revenue, discounted, and then compared to the present exit value to decide whether to continue or liquidate. This illustrates the economic decision process, albeit in an oversimplified way. The historical costs are never relevant except as one uses them in a projection. Even in a projection, a series of several past prices is desirable; a single cost is not likely to be used for projecting future behavior. Also, current costs, meaning present replacement prices, are not relevant. All replacements, except those already made, lie in the future and therefore the (discounted) future price is relevant. That is, the time adjusted predicted prices are compared in order to select one of the available alternatives but the present replacement price is, at best, only one price in a trend that will be used to predict the future.

The present replacement price may be stated thus: if I were to replace now, then X is the amount I would have to pay. But we never replace *now*. It may be that the committee is working under the tacit assumption of going concern. If so, one can derive a physical capacity or opportunity cost argument. This works best for inventories where the operations are repetitive and there is some discretion over price, i.e., a markup-turnover model. Under this view one must replace (because going concern is interpreted that way), and therefore a unit of inventory has an opportunity cost equal to its replacement price. If the markup is based on the historical cost and prices are rising, *cet. par.*, then the number of units in inventory will decline.

I think there are many things wrong with the going concern view but it is not appropriate to review them here. The pertinent point is that if the committee made the going concern assumption, it was not stated. Instead they simply alleged that current cost "*is* a relevant variable." (p. 34) It may be relevant to some model, like going concern, but that model needs to be exhibited before we can make a judgment.

The committee makes few assertions about the relevance of historical cost. Perhaps the only general claim made is that it is "of great usefulness when verifiability is emphasized" which was discussed above. Otherwise justification of historical cost is limited to fulfilling specific demands such as those from tax authorities and regulatory commissions. Such agencies ". . . not only have special needs but also the power to specify the information to be submitted. . . ." (p. 21) These special needs could be fulfilled by reference to some general ethic such as a Hobbsian edict—one ought to obey the law— instead of a principle peculiar to accounting.

The committee recommends that special needs should be fulfilled but labeled as "not in conformity with generally accepted accounting principles." (p. 16) I am in complete accord with this and also with the proposition that such requirements should not influence accounting principles. One can prepare tax returns without it affecting his theory of accounting.[11]

---

[11] The tax law is a good example of the non-neutrality of information. In my view, the chief

The committee takes note of the marginal analysis for internal management. (p. 60) There would be little distortion if one asserted that the whole of the marginal analysis can be directed to proving that historical cost is irrelevant to economic decisions. Given this, and the committee's position on legal authority, and the lack of cogency of historical cost's claim to verifiability, then one may wonder why there is a historical cost column in Appendix II. What is historical cost relevant to?

Since this is a polemic, I will state the proposition positively so that the reader can demolish it.

(1) "*Relevance* is the primary standard . . . " (p. 7) and ". . . all information that does not meet the standards should be excluded." (p. 3)

(2) Historical cost is irrelevant to all economic decisions (Sterling's allegation).

(3) Ergo, historical cost should be excluded. The quarrel will probably be with (2) and, again being deliberately polemical, I challenge any one to demonstrate that historical costs are relevant to economic decisions. Since (2) includes a universal quantifier it will take only one counter case to falsify it.[12]

Perhaps the committee intended the *Statement* to be transitional. If so, I have no quarrel with the inclusion of historical cost. The difficult problems of transition were noted above and I can sympathize with the committee's dilemma.

Summary and Conclusion

My reaction to the *Statement* is on two levels. First, I agree with the new methodology and world-view. My criticism on this level is directed to the

---

determinant of tax law has been extant accounting practices; that is, the information previously prepared by accountants has determined, to a very large extent, the kind of information specified by the tax authorities. Negative support for this view comes from the almost total lack of effect of the cogent "command over goods" arguments from Simons, Haig *et al*. Positive support is harder to come by but it can be observed that tax law, in the main, has closely conformed to generally accepted accounting principles. It would be circular to now argue that we ought to supply historical costs to taxing authorities because "they want them." To base accounting principles on the tax code makes the circle vicious. As information processors, accountants occupy a crucial position. We can stop beating our breasts about being a profession and quietly accept the almost awesome power and responsibility that is thrust upon us by the very nature of an information system. Another alternative is to let our instrumental function be usurped by another group (statisticians perhaps) while we become a priesthood with nothing but an empty ceremony to perform.

[12] In order to avoid Plutarch's criticism of critics, I will state my suggestion for the replacement of the criticized ideas. I think the current exit value of a held asset is relevant to almost all economic decisions. Further, it has the additional informative characteristic of indicating the direction, but not the magnitude, of the expectations of those in control. Convincing argument for this proposition is too lengthy for this review. In fact, attempts to be definitive, even under simplifying assumptions, are apt to become tedious. However, tedium is sometimes necessary and I go through the exercise in *The Theory of the Measurement of Enterprise Income*.

absence of explicitness and persuasive argument. This gap makes general acceptance less likely.

Second, given the new world-view and methodology, there are errors and omissions. The capacity constraint is the most serious omission because this obscures the crucial problem of developing criteria for the selection of data; it permits the trivial solution of transmitting everything and rejecting nothing. The effect of information, the non-neutrality notion, was also omitted and this is serious because it neglects the importance of the information transmitter's role and allows for the possibility of forming a vicious circle.

The standards and guidelines readily follow from the new view, and the relevance standard is correctly considered to be primary. There are some difficulties, however, with the verifiability and quantifiability standards, particularly when they are vis-à-vis.

The specific valuation recommendations do not immediately follow from the relevance standard. The model in which current cost is relevant was not exhibited. Historical cost seemed to spring from tradition and transitional consideration instead of a deduction from the relevance standard. This is compounded when the committee, erroneously I think, concedes greater verifiability to historical cost and then, on these grounds, permits its inclusion in an additive column where it had previously been excluded on the grounds that it was irrelevant.

There is some evidence that the committee suffered from indecisiveness as to what the *Statement* ought to be. In some places it is pure theory, in other places it takes specific positions on contemporary practices[13] and in other places it is concerned with transition and the future.[14] I would have preferred that it concentrate on theory and would argue that the "basic accounting theory" and "fundamental research" phrases in the charge support my preference. Others have taken the opposite position and are disappointed because the committee did not set out a long series of allocation rules. All of which only proves that it is impossible to please everybody; that different receivers have different constructs and that no single *Statement* is relevant to all.

Most of my criticism can be summed up under the "adequate support" charge. My plea was for more: more support, development, explicitness, rigor, precision. Note however, that the committee was also charged to be as

---

[13] For example on pooling versus purchasing (p.23) they recommend the latter because the former carries forward the historical cost which is irrelevant to "investment decisions." They want to record the new exchange values caused by this "new market transaction" of merging. Why? Current cost as of the date of each succeeding balance sheet is going to be reported anyway. They are quarreling about what goes in the historical cost column and argue for a historical cost as of the date of merger instead of as of the date of original purchase. Is there something inherently more relevant in, say, a 1960 cost than in a 1950 cost?

[14] "Scope of Future Accounting" (pp.64–65) expresses their belief in a trend toward multiple valuations and multi-dimensional reporting. "The committee has taken a first step by recommending two-column reports emphasizing historical cost and current cost."

"concise as feasible"; it also had a capacity constraint. Given this constraint, a historical perspective, the fact that it was a committee and so forth, perhaps this *Statement* is all that one could reasonably expect. In addition, as Kuhn puts it:

> . . . that commitment [to the new world-view or paradigm] must extend to areas and to degrees of precision for which there is no full precedent. If it did not, the paradigm could provide no puzzles that had not already been solved.[15]

Or, if the committee had done everything, there would be nothing left for the rest of us to do.

---

[15] Kuhn, *op. cit.* p. 99.

William H. Beaver is Associate Professor of
Accounting at Stanford University, John W.
Kennelly is Associate Professor at the University
of Iowa, and William M. Voss is Professor of
Accounting and Chairman, Department of
Accounting and Quantitative Methods, Ohio
University.

Predictive Ability as a Criterion for the Evaluation of Accounting Data

William H. Beaver, John W. Kennelly, and William M. Voss

The evaluation of alternative accounting measurements is a problem of major concern to the accounting profession. With respect to this problem, Ijiri and Jaedicke have stated:

> Accounting is plagued by the existence of alternative measurement methods. For many years, accountants have been searching for criteria which can be used to choose the best measurement alternative.[1]

One criterion being employed by a growing body of empirical research is *predictive ability.* According to this criterion, alternative accounting measurements are evaluated in terms of their ability to predict events of interest

---

[1] Yuji Ijiri and Robert K. Jaedicke, "Reliability and Objectivity of Accounting Measurements," *The Accounting Review,* (July 1966), p. 474.

Reprinted by permission of the authors and publisher from *Accounting Review,* Vol. XLIII (October, 1968), pp. 675–83.

to decision-makers. The measure with the greatest predictive power with respect to a given event is considered to be the "best" method for that particular purpose.

The criterion has already been applied in several different contexts. Brown has investigated the ability of models using alternative income measures (i.e., with and without tax deferral) to predict the market value of the firm. Green and Segall evaluated interim reports in terms of their usefulness in the prediction of future annual earnings. Horrigan has examined the predictive content of accounting data, in the form of financial ratios, with respect to bond rating changes and ratings on newly issued bonds. One of the authors has studied accounting measures as predictors of bankruptcy and bond default.[2]

Because the predictive ability criterion is currently being used and is likely to experience even greater use in the future, this paper examines its origin, its relationship to the facilitation of decision-making, and the potential difficulties associated with its implementation. In order to illustrate the issues under discussion, the paper will refer to a hypothetical research project. The project proposes to evaluate the merits of alternative methods of reporting financial leases in terms of the prediction of loan default.

Loan default was chosen as the dependent variable for two reasons. A large body of literature in financial statement analysis suggests loan default is an event of interest to decision-makers (e.g., bankers), and a priori arguments can be advanced that will relate accounting measurements to the prediction of loan default. A cash flow model of the firm, such as that developed by Walter, implies that the probability of loan default is a function of the ratio of total debt to total assets.[3] However the model does not specify how debt and assets are best operationally measured. The financial lease controversy provides two measurement alternatives—capitalization and noncapitalization.

A priori arguments have been advanced, supporting each alternative as the more meaningful.[4] Empirically testable implications can be drawn from

---

[2] Philip Brown, "The Predictive Abilities of Alternative Income Concepts" (an unpublished manuscript presented to the Conference for Study of Security Prices, Graduate School of Business, University of Chicago, November 1966); David Green, Jr. and Joel Segall, "The Predictive Power of First-Quarter Earnings Reports: A Replication"; James Horrigan, "The Determination of Long-Term Credit Standing with Financial Ratios"; William H. Beaver, "Financial Ratios as Predictors of Failure." The last three papers appear in *Empirical Research in Accounting: Selected Studies, 1966* (Institute of Professional Accounting, Graduate School of Business, University of Chicago, 1967), pp. 21–36, 44–62, and 71–102, respectively.

[3] James E. Walter, "The Determination of Technical Solvency," *Journal of Business* (January 1957), pp. 30–43. Extension of the Walter model as applied to financial ratios appears in Beaver, *op. cit.* The lease study need not restrict itself to only the debt-asset ratio. Other ratios affected by capitalization could also be studied.

[4] Arguments for and against capitalization appear in John H. Myers, *Reporting of Leases in Financial Statements* (American Institute of Certified Public Accountants, 1962); and Donald C. Cook, "The Case Against Capitalizing Leases," *Harvard Business Review* (January–February 1963), pp. 145–155.

these arguments if they are interpreted in the light of the cash flow model. If the capitalization of leases does provide a "more meaningful" measure of debt and assets, then a debt-asset ratio that includes the capitalized value of leases in its components ought to be a better predictor of loan default than a debt-asset ratio that ignores capitalization.

The empirical part of the hypothetical study would involve the collection of financial statement data for a sample of default and nondefault firms. The debt-asset ratio would be computed for each firm, under each of the two lease treatments. The object would be to see which debt-asset ratio was the better predictor. An index of predictive ability is provided by the dichotomous classification test, which classifies the firms as default or nondefault based solely on a knowledge of the debt-asset ratio. The classifications are compared to the actual default status of the firms to determine the percentage of incorrect predictions—the lower the error, the higher the predictive power. The lease assumption that resulted in a lower percentage error would tentatively be judged the better, the more meaningful, measurement alternative for the purpose of predicting loan default.[5]

The Origin of the Predictive Ability Criterion

Knowing the origin of the predictive ability criterion is important in understanding what is meant by predictive ability and why it is being used in evaluating accounting data. The criterion is well established in the social and natural sciences as a method for choosing among competing hypotheses.[6] It is our belief that alternative accounting measures have the properties of competing hypotheses and can be evaluated in a similar manner. Consider the following common features of competing hypotheses and alternative accounting measures:

(1) Both are abstractions, which disregard aspects of reality deemed to be irrelevant and retain only those few crucial elements that are essential for the purposes at hand. Because there are many ways to abstract from reality, an unlimited number of mutually exclusive alternatives can be generated. Hence there is a need for a set of criteria for choosing among them.

---

[5] The sample design described here parallels that used in the Beaver study. A more complete description of the classification test is discussed in that study (pp. 83ff.). Another index of predictive power is provided by an analysis of Bayesian likelihood ratios. In many respects, the likelihood ratio analysis is superior to the classification test. However, the classification test was used because it can be more briefly stated and more easily understood. Also both indices ranked accounting measures virtually the same in the Beaver study.

[6] This section relies heavily upon the literature in scientific methodology, especially the following works: Morris R. Cohen and Ernest Nagel, *An Introduction to Logic and the Scientific Method* (Harcourt Brace, 1934); Ernest Nagel, *The Structure of Science* (Harcourt Brace, 1961); C. West Churchman, *Prediction and Optimal Decision* (Prentice-Hall, 1962); Abraham Kaplan, *The Conduct of Inquiry* (Chandler, 1964); and several articles appearing in Sherman Krupp's *The Structure of Economic Science* (Prentice-Hall, 1966). Additional bibliographic references appear in Carl Thomas Devine's "Research Methodology and Accounting Theory Formation," *The Accounting Review*, (July 1960), pp. 387–399.

(2) Tests of logical propriety are one basis for evaluation. Conformity to these tests is a necessary but insufficient condition for selecting the "best." Two or more alternatives may pass the tests, and in that event it is futile to argue which is the "more logical." Ultimately, the choice must be made on the basis of which abstraction better captures the relevant aspects of reality. There is a need for an additional criterion that evaluates the alternatives in terms of the *purpose* for which they are being generated.

(3) A primary purpose is the prediction of events, and hence comparison of alternatives according to their relative predictive power is a meaningful basis for evaluation. Predictive power is defined as the ability to generate operational implications (i.e., predictions) and to have those predictions subsequently verified by empirical evidence. More precisely, a prediction is a statement about the probability distribution of the dependent variable (the event being predicted) conditional upon the value of the independent variable (the predictor). Typically, the prediction asserts there is an association between x and y such that the outcome of y is dependent upon the value of x [i.e., $P(y/x) f(x)$].[7] But merely asserting the prediction does not make it "true." It must be verified by investigating the empirical correspondence between what the prediction asserts and what is in fact observed. Thus the determination of predictive ability is inherently an empirical question.

(4) The use of the predictive ability criterion presupposes that the alternatives under consideration have met the tests of logic and that each has a theory supporting it. The determination of predictive ability is not an indiscriminate search for that alternative which will maximize the R^2 (or any other index of predictive power). Theory provides an explanation why a given alternative is expected to be related to the dependent variable and permits the investigator to generalize from the findings of sample data to a new set of observations. Consequently, a complete evaluation involves both *a priori* and empirical considerations.

The lease study reflects each of the points listed above. Each measurement system (i.e., with and without capitalization) is an abstraction. One basis for choosing between them would be to subject the underlying *a priori* arguments to the tests of logical propriety, but in this case neither argument is inherently illogical. Hence it is impossible to resolve the controversy on solely *a priori* grounds. Note also it would be erroneous to prefer the capitalization of leases merely because noncapitalization abstracts from certain aspects of the lease event. To say one measurement system is more abstract

---

[7] Occasionally, a hypothesis may specify an independent relationship among the variables [i.e., $P(y/x) P(y)$]. For example, the random walk theory of security price movements asserts that the probability distribution of the price change in a given time period is independent of the price change in any previous period. See Eugene F. Fama, "The Behavior of Stock Market Prices," *Journal of Business*, (January 1965), pp. 34–105. In comparing competing predictors, the relative strength of association with the dependent variable becomes the relevant consideration. Strength of association can be measured in many ways, which will vary with the nature of the data and the inferences to be drawn from the data. In the lease study, the percentage error in classification was chosen as the index of association.

than another is not an indictment of that system. The additional data provided by capitalizing leases may be irrelevant for the purposes at hand or may even be harmful in the sense of contributing only "noise" to the system. A choice can only be made by applying some purposive criterion. In the lease study, the purposive criterion chosen was predictive ability—in particular, the ability to predict loan default.

It is possible to generalize beyond the context of the lease controversy. Most, if not all, accounting controversies can be viewed as disputes over the relative merits of one measurement alternative versus another. The inadequacy of relying solely upon *a priori* arguments is generally recognized by the accounting profession. Several recent articles have drawn attention to this inadequacy and have called for more empirical research in accounting.[8] One factor that has impeded a movement in this direction is the inability to specify what the nature of the empirical research should be, although there is a consensus that the research ought to relate alternative measures to the purposes of accounting data. The predictive ability approach provides a method for drawing operational implications from the *a priori* arguments such that the measurement controversies become empirically testable according to a purposive criterion.

Relationship to the Facilitation of Decision-Making

A key issue in accepting this approach is the contention that predictive ability is a purposive criterion. This section will examine that contention in more detail and will relate predictive ability to what is generally regarded as the purpose of accounting data—the facilitation of decision-making.

The idea that accounting data ought to be evaluated in terms of their purposes or uses is one of the earliest and most prevalent thoughts in accounting. In 1922 Paton concluded:

> Accounting is a highly purposive field and any assumption, principle, or procedure is accordingly justified if it adequately serves the end in view.[9]

Recently the American Accounting Association's *A Statement of Basic Accounting Theory* stated:

> In establishing these standards the all-inclusive criterion is the usefulness of the information.[10]

In spite of the obvious appeal to the idea that accounting data ought to be

---

[8] For example, R. J. Chambers, "Prospective Adventures in Accounting Ideas," *The Accounting Review*, (April 1967), p. 251.

[9] William A. Paton, *Accounting Theory* (The Ronald Press, 1922), p. 472.

[10] American Accounting Association, *A Statement of Basic Accounting Theory* (American Accounting Association, 1966), p. 3.

useful, the utilitarian approach has lacked operationality. Chambers has noted:

> For, if accounting is utilitarian there must have been some concept or some theory of the tests which must be applied in distinguishing utilitarian from nonutilitarian procedures. . . . It is largely because the tests of "utilitarianness". . . . have not been made explicit that the body of accounting practices now employed contains so many divergent and inconsistent rules.[11]

One reason for the inability to specify tests of usefulness is the manner in which usefulness is interpreted. Almost without exception, the literature has related usefulness to the facilitation of decision-making. The primacy of decision-making has been stressed by both Paton and *A Statement of Basic Accounting Theory*:

> The purpose of accounting may be said to be that of compiling and interpreting the financial data . . . to provide a sound guide to action by management, investor, and other interested parties.[12] The committee defines accounting as the process of identifying, measuring, and communicating economic information to permit informed judgments and decisions by users of the information.[13]

However, the use of the decision-making criterion faces two problems. The first is to define the decision models (or processes) of potential users of accounting data. This problem has been noted by both Anton and Vatter.

> If we assume an operationalist view—that is, that information ought to be for decision-making purposes—the criteria [sic] is based upon an extension of significance, i.e., for what is the information significant. . . . While this is a purposive criterion it also gives us the dilemma noted above as to who will be the decision-maker and the uncertainty of his context.[14]
>
> Observation, analysis, and projection should be aimed at decision-making. This implies a view of the past and present that permits and facilitates decisions, without making them. How this fine line can be established depends upon what the decisions are, who makes them, and what data are relevant for those purposes. These questions still remain unanswered.[15]

Most business decisions currently are not made within the framework of a formally specified decision model. That is, in most decision-making situations, no model is available with which to evaluate alternative accounting

---

[11] Raymond J. Chambers, "Why Bother with Postulates?" *Journal of Accounting Research*, (Spring 1963), p. 3.

[12] William A. Paton, *Essentials of Accounting* (The Macmillan Company, 1949), p. 2.

[13] American Accounting Association, *op. cit.*, p. 1.

[14] Hector R. Anton, "Some Aspects of Measurement and Accounting," *Journal of Accounting Research*, (Spring 1964), p. 6.

[15] William J. Vatter, "Postulates and Principles," *Journal of Accounting Research*, (Autumn 1963), p. 197.

measurements. Consider the lending decision faced by a loan officer in a bank. The specification of his decision model would require a knowledge of what the decision variables are, what weights are assigned to each decision variable, and what constraints, if any, are binding on the loan officer. It is unlikely that even the decision-maker would produce a formal model that would describe the process he went through in making lending decisions. Rules of thumb, such as "do not loan to any firm with a current ratio below 2," can be found, but it would be extremely difficult to determine the decision model implied by such rules. Specification of decision models, for the most part, is beyond the current state of knowledge. Although operations research and other quantitative techniques offer promise of greater specification in the future, it is not clear how soon, or to what extent, such specifications will be possible.[16]

The second problem is, even after the decision model is specified, it is not sufficient for determining which accounting measure produces the better decisions. Many, if not all, of the decision variables are capable of being measured in more than one way. For example, assume that a loan officer's objective function for the lending decision is a known function of promised return and probability of default on the loan. The lease controversy provides two operational measures for assessing the probability of loan default. The decision model can indicate whether different decisions are produced by using different definitions of the debt-asset ratio as a surrogate for the probability of default, but it cannot indicate which definition (i.e., with or without capitalization) will lead to the better decisions. Additional information is needed as to which ratio provides the better assessment of probability of default (i.e., which ratio is the better predictor of loan default).

At this point the relationship between predictive ability and decision-making becomes evident. Note the distinction between a prediction and a decision. In the context of the bank's lending decision, a prediction states the probability of loan default if the bank loans to a firm with a set of financial ratios. The decision is whether or not the bank should grant the loan, which also involves additional decision variables such as the promised return. The illustration points out an important relationship between predictions and decisions. A prediction can be made without making a decision, but a decision cannot be made without, at least implicitly, making a prediction.

In a world where little is known about the decision models, evaluating alternative accounting measures in terms of their predictive ability is an appealing idea, because it requires a lower level of specificity regarding the decision model. To evaluate alternative lease treatments in terms of their

---

[16] The difficulties encountered in attempting to specify the decision processes of loan officers are well documented in several articles appearing in the text by Kalman J. Cohen and Frederick S. Hammer, *Analytical Methods in Banking* (Irwin, 1966). Of special interest is the article by Kalman J. Cohen, Thomas C. Gilmore, and Frank A. Singer, "Bank Procedures for Analyzing Business Loan Applications," pp. 219-249.

ability to predict loan default, we assume only that the probability of loan default is a parameter of the decision process, even though we may know little about how the bank's loan officers use the assessments of probability of default in reaching their decisions. Hence the predictive ability of accounting data can be explored without waiting for the further specification of the decision models.[17]

Because prediction is an inherent part of the decision process, knowledge of the predictive ability of alternative measures is a prerequisite to the use of the decision-making criterion. At the same time, it permits tentative conclusions regarding alternative measurements, subject to subsequent confirmation when the decision models eventually become specified. The use of predictive ability as a purposive criterion is more than merely consistent with accounting's decision-making orientation. It can provide a body of research that will bring accounting closer to its goal of evaluation in terms of a decision-making criterion.

Difficulties of Implementation

The purpose of this paper is to present the difficulties as well as the benefits of the predictive ability approach. However, none of the potential problems to be discussed are inherent to this approach. They are merely "facts of life" that are likely to be encountered in any meaningful attempt to evaluate alternative accounting measures.

(1) One difficulty of implementation will be the specification of what events constitute parameters of decision models and the specification of a theory that will link those events to the accounting measures in some sort of predictive relationship. The studies cited earlier suggest some of the events that could be predicted.[18] Also, portfolio theory appears to be a productive area for providing dependent variables, although as yet the relationships between the parameters of the portfolio models and the accounting data have not been explored.[19] However, a brief survey of the disciplines from which the dependent variables and the predictive theory are likely to originate indicates that much remains to be accomplished. In large part then the evaluation of accounting data, using the predictive ability criterion, will occur in conjunction with development and testing of predictive relationships in related disciplines, such as economics and finance.

(2) The findings of a predictive ability study are conditional on how the predictive model is specified. The construction of the prediction model in-

---

[17] The relationship between predictions and the decision model is further discussed in the next section.

[18] See footnote 2 for the bibliographic references.

[19] Harry M. Markowitz, *Portfolio Selection: Efficient Diversification of Investments* (Wiley, 1959). William F. Sharpe, "Capital Asset Prices: A Theory of Market Equilibrium Under Conditions of Risk," *Journal of Finance* (September 1964), pp. 425–42.

volves a specification of the functional form of the relationships (e.g., linearity) and also how the variables are operationally defined. In the financial lease study, the findings would be conditional upon the rates used to discount the lease payments and the particular set of financial ratios used in the study. If no difference in predictive ability is found between the two sets of ratios (capitalized, noncapitalized), the finding may be attributed to (a) the particular discount rates chosen were not the appropriate rates, (b) the ratio form is not a meaningful way to express relationships among financial statement items, (c) the particular ratios chosen were not the optimal ratios for the prediction of default, or (d) capitalization does not enhance predictive ability. Additional research regarding the possibility of (a), (b) and (c) must be explored before inference (d) can be drawn. The accounting measure and the prediction model are being jointly tested. Positive results constitute a joint confirmation, while negative results may be due to a flaw in either or both factors. In practice it may be difficult to isolate the source of the negative results.

Another problem arises when positive results are obtained (i.e., when a "significant" difference between alternative measures is observed). For example assume the debt-asset ratio computed under the capitalization assumption predicts better than the noncapitalized debt-asset ratio in a single ratio prediction model. If additional ratios were included in the prediction model, the noncapitalized form of the debt-asset ratio might contribute more to the predictive power of the multivariate model than the capitalized form. If different models suggest contrary conclusions regarding the relative predictive power of the two lease assumptions, additional research will be needed to explain the reason for the conflicting results. Even if consistent results are observed for all of the models tested, there is always the possibility of an untested model which possesses greater predictive power and yet suggests the opposite conclusion regarding the relative predictive power of the alternative measures under study.[20]

(3) A third difficulty occurs because accounting data are currently being used as decision variables. There are two possible reasons for observing an association between the accounting measures and the event being predicted. (a) There is a "true" causal relationship between the measures and the event. (b) Decision-makers perceive there to be a causal relationship, and this perception is sufficient to produce an observed relationship. In the lease study a relationship between financial ratios and loan default may be observed because there is a causal relationship such that a "poor" ratio increases the probability of default. However, a relationship may also be observed merely because bankers believe there is a causal relationship and use

---

[20] There are two other related qualifications regarding a predictive ability study. (1) The findings are conditional upon the population from which the sample is drawn. (2) The findings are conditional upon the alternative measures chosen for study. For example, a third unspecified and untested measure may be better than the two measures under consideration.

the ratios as decision variables. The bank may sever a line of credit because a firm fails to improve its ratios to a respectable level. The severing of the line of credit forces the firm into default. Similarly, the efficacy of capitalizing leases may be diminished or eliminated if loan officers do not incorporate the capitalization of leases into their credit analysis. Any observed relationship may be due to either (a) or (b) or both. It may be impossible to tell from the sample data the extent to which factor (b) is present.

If the objective is predictive ability, do we care what its source is? Yes, if source (b) is not expected to be permanent. Decision-makers' use of accounting data as decision variables may change over time. In fact, the findings of a predictive ability study may cause them to change, and this might change the predictive relationships observed in the future.

(4) The evaluation of relative predictive power may require an assumption about the loss function associated with the prediction errors, which in turn involves additional knowledge of other variables in the decision model. Without this knowledge it may be impossible to conclude which measure is the better predictor.[21]

For example, suppose the capitalized debt-asset ratio predicts the default status of a sample of default and nondefault firms with a lower number of total misclassifications. Can we conclude that capitalization is preferable? Not necessarily. Suppose the noncapitalized debt-asset ratio has more total misclassifications of both default and nondefault firms but fewer errors with respect to the classification of default firms. Since the loss of misclassifying a default firm is likely to be greater than the loss associated with misclassifying a nondefault firm, the latter measure may be the better predictor in terms of minimizing expected loss. More would have to be known about the loss function before one measure could be chosen over the other.

Moreover, even if the capitalized debt-asset ratio performed better with respect to both type errors, additional analysis is needed before capitalization of leases could be recommended, because capitalization involves a greater cost to collecting additional data and making the necessary computations. Capitalization might lead to better predictions, but are they sufficiently better to warrant the additional cost? The answer involves a cost-benefit analysis, which requires a knowledge of the loss function and hence the other decision variables.

The amount of additional knowledge of the decision model that will be required can only be assessed within the context of the empirical results of each predictive ability study. The margin of superiority of one measure over another may be so great that it is obviously the better predictor regardless of the form of loss function. In other situations, perhaps only the general form

---

[21] Every index of predictive ability involves some assumption regarding the loss function of the prediction errors and/or the distribution of prediction errors. If different indices suggest different measures are better, the inability to select which index is appropriate implies the inability to select which accounting measure is the better predictor, until the loss function can be specified.

of the loss function (e.g., linear or quadratic, symmetric or asymmetric) need be specified. In instances where a greater knowledge of the loss function is needed than is available, the role of the predictive ability study may be to present the distribution of prediction errors for each measure and let the reader apply his own loss function in choosing among the measures. In any event the researcher must be constantly aware of this relationship to avoid drawing unwarranted inferences from the data.

(5) The findings of a predictive ability study are conditional upon the event being predicted. Even if a measure is a better predictor of one event (e.g., loan default), it is not necessarily a better predictor of other events. Additional research would be needed to investigate the predictive power of the measure for other purposes. If different measures are best for different predictive purposes, the problem of satisfying competing user needs arises.[22] If this problem exists, it would be difficult to resolve, although the use of multidimensional and special purpose statements offers a tentative solution.[23]

Concluding Remarks

Two implications emerge from the previous discussion: (1) The preference for an accounting measure may apply only within the context of a specific predictive purpose or prediction model. It may be impossible to generalize about the "best" measurement alternative across different contexts. (2) Even within a specific context, the conclusions must be considered as tentative.

The inability to generalize is a possibility, but not an inevitability. We have cited only *potential* difficulties, whose relevance can only be assessed empirically, not by *a priori* speculation. What is important is to know to what extent we can generalize across purposes, and the only hope of acquiring this knowledge is to conduct the predictive studies. If we discover that different measures are best for different purposes, it would be erroneous to believe that the predictive studies are any less important because of that discovery. The inability to generalize, if it does exist, is not a flaw of the predictive ability methodology. It merely reflects the state of the world or the state of accounting theory, but in neither case is it an indictment of the methodology that exposes that fact.

Even within a specific context, the preference for one measure over another is tentative. A measure that performed poorly may not be permanently rejected in the sense that the researcher may refine the measure (and its

---

[22] The decision-making criterion also faces the same potential problem. See comments made by both Devine and Moonitz. Carl Thomas Devine, *op. cit*, p. 397. Maurice Moonitz, *The Postulates of Accounting* (American Institute of Certified Public Accountants, 1961), p. 4.

[23] For suggestions regarding multidimensional reporting see American Accounting Association, *op. cit.*

theory) or redesign the study in the hope that future research will demonstrate that the measure is really better. Also there is always the possibility of an unknown or untested measure that performs even better than the best measure tested. Theory construction in other disciplines is an evolutionary process, where the hypotheses are continuously being revised, redefined, or overturned in the light of new theory and new evidence. There is no reason to believe that accounting theory will be different.

Although it is important that a general awareness of these factors exists, neither the potential inability to generalize nor the tentative nature of the conclusions should be regarded as a deterrent to conducting the predictive studies. Extension of research efforts into the predictive ability of accounting data is necessary for the fulfillment of accounting's decision-making orientation and for the meaningful evaluation of alternative accounting measures.

2. MEASUREMENT OF INCOME AND FINANCIAL POSITION

The Balance Sheet and Income Statement have been the basic reports of accounting for generations. The Balance Sheet has been assumed at times to represent a measure of value while the Income Statement has been assumed to represent a change in value. However, other basic objectives have been proposed from time to time.

Central to either report is some particular process of measurement. It may be possible to concentrate on the measurement process itself, or upon assumed changes in value; but valuation or alternative measurement concepts are an integral part of either emphasis. Traditionally, the valuation process has been based on historical cost. Many accounting questions have been concerned with the allocation of these historical costs among various time periods or among various units of production. The allocation will itself affect both the measurement of financial position and reported income as it assigns part of the historical cost to the Balance Sheet and part to the Income Statement.

Accounting theorists have attempted to focus on different valuation bases for both conceptual and practical purposes. This section exposes the reader to a number of articles dealing with different concepts of valuation and income determination.

Briefly, the controversy in accounting over valuation methods revolves around historical cost and entry value; current cost and entry value; current cash equivalent and exit value; and "economic income" which is neither an entry value nor an exit value. Economic income stems from J. R. Hicks's definition of income for an individual. It involves the discounting of expected future cash flows to arrive at a present value. Unfortunately, many writers assume that there is no question regarding the nature of the cash flows to be involved. It may help the reader to keep in mind that for the firm, future cash flows might mean dividends of the firm, operating cash flows of the firm, funds flows of the firm, or some other benefit stream.

The first article by Harold Bierman, Jr. and Sidney Davidson presents a conceptual definition of income based on the change in value determined by using a dividend model. They recognize that their definition is not operational, i.e., accountants cannot actually measure value and value change in these terms, but they illustrate how this particular concept of income can be used to test alternative accounting procedures.

Stephen H. Penman continues in the second article with a discussion of several contemporary valuation concepts. It is his intention to discover a theoretically sound model of asset valuation by putting each concept to a certain test, thereby rejecting some and, in fact, accepting one. The "economic income" model is accepted. His conclusions may not be as important for our purposes as his discussion of the various valuation concepts.

The third article by Keith Shwayder takes a position opposite to the first two articles. Here one can clearly see the lack of agreement among accountants concerning valuation. Five cases are analyzed in an attempt to demonstrate that the "economic income" model is not only impractical but also an unsound theoretical model for accounting income measurements.

Matthews J. Stephens leads us in a somewhat different direction as he discusses the possible shortcomings of using current cost as a basis of valuation in accounting. He attempts to show that current costing would not overcome the deficiencies of historical costing, but would add other dimensions of confusion to the process of income measurement and valuation.

The next two articles in this section can be studied as a single unit. George J. Staubus evaluates the position taken by R. J. Chambers on valuation and income determination. In his reply Chambers states his basic proposition that the appropriate value for assets, and therefore the appropriate basis for income measurement, is the current cash equivalent for the asset, i.e., the amount the asset will bring into the firm if sold. Staubus examines a number of decision situations in an attempt to show that current cash equivalents do not provide appropriate and relevant information for most decisions. Chambers's reply reaffirms his position arguing that choice (decision) requires both factual information about the firm's holdings and valuation of its prospects on the basis of these holdings. The function of accounting, according to Chambers, is to provide factual information, not to make the valuation.

Inasmuch as the concept of service potentials and future cash flows have been so prevalent in the valuation discussions, George Staubus's discussion of alternative flows seems particularly appropriate. He discusses several asset flow concepts: earnings, working capital, quick flow and cash flow. He concludes that the value of each concept depends upon the relevance to the decision maker, and the choice between the alternatives is not usually obvious.

*Harold Bierman, Jr., is Professor of
Accounting and Managerial Economics at
Cornell University. Sidney Davidson is Arthur
Young Professor of Accounting and Dean of
The Graduate School of Business at the
University of Chicago.*

The Income Concept—Value Increment or Earnings Predictor?

Harold Bierman, Jr. and Sidney Davidson

Many major accounting problems deal with aspects of income measurement. In the analysis of these problems accounting suffers from the lack of a clear-cut, operational definition of income based on a well-defined objective. We propose to indicate how an understanding of two general concepts—income as an increment in value and income as a predictor of earnings—may be useful in resolving some problems of income measurement.

An understanding of these two concepts may also be helpful in deciding questions of presentation of financial position. The theories underlying income measurement and financial position presentation are, of course, completely intertwined. If a firm starts at one position and moves through time to a second position, we can either say that the income of the period will depend on the beginning and ending positions, or we can say that the final position was a logical result of the income of the period being added to the initial position.[1]

In practice, the measurements of income and financial position are also tied together, but not always in a beneficial manner. Too frequently the accountant approaches a transaction and chooses the method for recording it

---

[1] We assume no capital transactions.

Reprinted by permission of the authors and publisher from *Accounting Review,* Vol. XLIV (April, 1969), pp. 239–46.

that better measures income *or* better measures the financial position of a corporation. In this paper we will develop a means of evaluating different ways of recording transactions, without compromising on the quality of either the measure of income or financial position.

Income as a Value Increment

Let us first assume a perfect world of certainty where we can obtain any information we wish and we want to make a decision whether or not to buy all or part of a corporation. The only information we need is the present value of the firm now (V_0), where the present value is based on the firm making the best possible sequence of decisions in the future. V_0 is equal to the present value of all future dividends (including any future liquidating dividends).[2]

$$V_0 = \sum_{t=1}^{\infty} D_t(1+r)^{-t}.$$

One period from now the value of the firm after the first dividend will be V_1. Assuming a dividend of D_1 at time 1, we will define the income of the firm for the first period (Y_1) to be:

$$Y_1 = (V_1 + D_1) - V_0.$$

Assuming a rate of discount of r, in a world of certainty we know that

$$V_0 = \frac{V_1 + D_1}{1+r}, \quad \text{or} \quad V_1 = V_0(1+r) - D_1,$$

therefore

$$Y_1 = (V_0(1+r) - D_1) + D_1 - V_0 = rV_0.$$

With certainty, the income of a period is equal to the rate of discount times the value of the investment at the beginning of the period.

Under conditions of uncertainty, the value of the firm at any future date can only be estimated. The actual value of the firm at some subsequent date will be affected by events which are uncertain at the present. Thus the *ex post* values of V_1 and D_1 will be a surprise to us when one period passes and we can measure them. We can again define the actual income Y_1 as:

---

[2] Sale of our shares to another is, of course, the equivalent of a liquidating dividend. We do not consider tax effects in this analysis, nor changes in the general price level.

$$Y_1 = (V_1 + D_1) - V_0,$$

but now we cannot assume that

$$V_0 = \frac{V_1 + D_1}{1 + r}.^3$$

Nevertheless we can define income to be:

$$Y_i = (V_i + D_i) - V_{i-1}.$$

This equation should be recognized as being the algebraic equivalent of Hicks' definition of income.[4] Income is defined as being equal to the dividend that could be paid and leave the firm as well off at the end as at the beginning of the period. Since V_0 and V_1 both measure the present value of future dividends and D_1 is the dividend at time 1, Y_1 measures the improvement of the economic position of the stockholder during period 1.

One advantage of this definition of income is that it bypasses the difficulties associated with defining realization.[5] Since the income is a function of the values at the beginning and end of the period, the gains that the accountant traditionally considers to be unrealized are included in the income measure. Unfortunately, this introduces the prime operational difficulty of the definition. The income of a period is greatly influenced by errors of measuring the total values of the firm at the beginning and end of the period. Small errors (in terms of percentage) in estimating the value of the firm at either moment in time may result in large errors in the measure of income.[6]

For example, if V_0 were measured correctly and there was an error of 1% in measuring V_1 (where V_1 equalled $100,000,000), the error in income would be $1,000,000. If income actually was 8% of capital, or $8,000,000, this would be an error of 12½% in measuring the income of the period. If the same error of estimation affected both V_0 and V_1 in the same direction, the income of this period would not be affected but the income of one or more earlier periods would have been misstated.

The relationship $Y_i = (V_i + D_i) - V_{i-1}$ is, of course, a value increment measure. It is presented here as a frame of reference that we can use to evaluate accounting practices. It is conceptually satisfactory but is not neces-

---

[3] In this sentence V_1 and D_1 are *ex post* values. Previously, the *ex ante* and *ex post* values were identical.

[4] J. R. Hicks, *Value and Capital*, 2nd ed. (Clarendon Press, 1946), p. 176.

[5] See the report of the 1964 American Accounting Association Concepts and Standards Research Study Committee, "The Realization Concept" in the *The Accounting Review* (April 1965), pp. 312–322.

[6] This difficulty would decrease in importance if analysts shifted from the use of the measurement of income Y_1 to the use of V_0.

arily an operational procedure for computing income. The present distinction between realized and unrealized gains is not clear-cut but it may be a useful means of calling the attention of the user of accounting information to a higher degree of uncertainty associated with the unrealized changes.

Since the conceptually satisfactory definition of income may not be an operational one, the accountant is forced to use measures that are estimators of this approach. One way of judging these estimators is to consider whether or not they tend to be consistent with the conceptually satisfactory measure. This test is not the same as obtaining an income measure that is a good predictor of next period's income.

Enough information should be supplied so that the analyst can adjust the reported income figure to obtain the type of measure that he desires (the characteristics of the best measure are not obvious). For example, there may be better predictors of value than the past period's income. If V_0 were measured correctly (and with perfect certainty) it would be the measure of value of the firm. Lacking certainty an estimator of V_0 is needed.

The Search for a Predictor of Earnings and Value

The investor wants a predictor of earnings or value for decision making. We have argued that with perfect information, the only measure we need is V_0. The income of the first period will be equal to rV_0. When the assumptions are changed, and the future is no longer known with certainty, we would only need to know V_0 and its probability distribution to make decisions. The estimate of V_0 and its probability distribution incorporates all the information about the future of the firm that we have available. While the explicit inputs in the computation of V_0 are the future dividends of the firm, the expected incomes of the future are the basis of estimating the dividends. To say we have obtained a complete estimate of V_0 implies that we have estimated the results of future operations.

To determine the actual income of the first period, in addition to V_0 we need to know the values at time 1 of V_1 and D_1 since $Y_1 = (V_1 + D_1) - V_0$. The actual income is likely to differ from the expected income used as an input in determining V_0 since V_1 at time 1 will be different from the value we expected it to be when we estimated V_0 at time zero. If we define V_{1e} as the value of V_1 estimated at the start of period 1 and V_{1a} as the actual value of V_1 at the end of the period, then the definition of income becomes:

$$Y_1 = rV_0 + (V_{1a} - V_{1e}).$$

All estimates of future incomes will be adjusted in light of the experience obtained by operating in the first period. Thus the actual income of the first period (or any period) is important since it is the basis of the revision of the

estimates of future incomes and the present value of the firm (at time 1 w
have a new V_0 for future calculations, V_{1a}, the actual value as of time 1 of th
previously estimated V_{1e}).

Indirect Measures of Income

Unfortunately the values of V_1 and V_0 may be very difficult to obtain; thus
we may have to estimate Y_1 indirectly. A common estimator that is used is:

$$Y_1 = R_1 - E_1, \quad \text{where}$$

$$R_1 \text{ is the revenues of period 1, and}$$

$$E_1 \text{ is the expenses of period 1.}$$

We could broaden the definition of R_1 to be the measure of any item
tending to increase the present value of the stockholders' equity (and the
ability to pay dividends in the future), and E_1 to be the measure of item
tending to decrease the stockholders' equity.

Applying the above definitions, a $100 increase in the value of an invest
ment that cost $300 is income (increasing by $100 the ability to pay future
dividends). If an uninsured building with a value of $10,000 is destroyed
there is a decrease in the expected ability to pay dividends and thus a
decrease in the income of the period, although the extrapolation of the loss
may result in a bad prediction of the next period's income.

While generally we cannot use the relationship $Y_1 = (V_1 + D_1) - V_0$ in
the real world as the prime means of estimating the income of a period, the
relationship can be used as a means of evaluating the accounting procedure
that is used to measure revenues or expenses. For example, let us apply the
above principles to the choice between LIFO and FIFO using the following
assumed conditions.

At the beginning of the period the ABC Company has $500 of cash and
100 units of product that cost $2 per unit (and have a net realizable value of
$2). During the period it sells the 100 units for $350 and purchases 100 units
of inventory at a cost of $300; these units have a net realizable value of $300
at year end. It has $550 of cash at the end of the period.

This example may be analyzed in terms of the suggested analysis of income measures of this paper. At the beginning of the period the company
could expect to have enough resources to pay dividends of $700. At the end
of the period the amount of dividends that could be paid is $850 and this
amount is independent of the inventory valuation convention employed.
With no dividends having been paid, the income of the period is:

$$Y = V_1 - V_0 = 850 - 700 = 150.$$

Position Statement Items

	Assuming FIFO		Assuming LIFO	
	Beginning of period	End of period	Beginning of period	End of period
Cash	500	550	500	550
Inventory	200	300	200	200
Stockholders' Equity	700	850	700	750

The income statements resulting from the two cost flow assumptions are:

	FIFO	LIFO
Revenues	350	350
Expenses	200	300
Income (loss)	150	50

This does not agree with the LIFO measure of income, though it is equal to the FIFO measure. On the basis of the definition of income developed above, we can conclude that FIFO is a superior measure of income. Also, note that FIFO's position statement gives a measure of the present value of future dividends (the assets of the firm now could result in dividends of $850).

In the above example the liquidating value is assumed to be equal to the going concern value and equal to the cost. When the liquidating value differs from the going concern value we would accept the latter measure of value if we believe the firm will continue to operate. If the inventory of the ABC Company at the end of the period can be expected to be sold to realize $400 instead of the $300 amount that is equal to cost, V_1 would be $950 ($550 of cash plus $400 of inventory) and the income of the period ($V_1 - V_0$) would be $250. Neither FIFO nor LIFO would include this $100 of gain because it is defined to be unrealized. However, the use of FIFO will come closer than LIFO to measuring the income as defined in this section, assuming the price changes after purchase follow a linear trend.[7]

We have defined the financial position at the beginning of the period as consisting of 100 units of inventory and $500 of cash, and the financial position at the end of the period in terms of 100 units of inventory and $550 of cash. One could say that the only change in the period is an increase of cash of $50 and this is the amount of income reported by the use of LIFO.

---

[7] If the prices follow a linear trend the net realizable value of the inventory at the end of the period is closer in amount to the cost of the most recent purchase than the cost basis of the beginning inventory.

But, this interpretation neglects the change in the market value of the inventory. At the beginning of the period we have the resources to pay a dividend of $700. At the end of the period we have the resources to pay a dividend of $850. This improvement of $150 is reported by FIFO. The income of $150 reported using FIFO is *not* a prediction that in the future earnings will be sufficient to support a dividend of $150 a period. Instead, it is a measure of historical events. If we think that this economic process of price change will be repeated exactly in the future—that is, we forecast the same amount of profit will be earned each year in the future, then we might well have an intangible asset of some magnitude. The procedure suggested in this paper relies only on the forecast disposition of the goods on hand and the dividends that could result from their disposition. This is a more modest objective than predicting the results of all future operations and price changes and incorporating these estimates into the accounts.

Considering dividend flows, assume that at the beginning of the period the dividend stream of the ABC Company was expected to be $35 a year extending into perpetuity. Discounted at the investor's time value of money of 5%, a perpetuity of $35 has a present value of $700. The investor is willing to leave the funds invested in the firm since he would receive the same benefits with the funds invested in the firm as he would get if he sold his investment. If he sold, he would receive $700 which he could invest and earn $35 a period. Now assume that at the end of the period he finds that the value of his investment in the firm is $850, equal to the firm's net assets of $850. If the expected dividends were to remain $35 a year he would sell his investment since he can earn $41.50 a year by doing so and investing externally. Thus there is an implicit assumption, if he does not sell, that the investor expects a dividend increase some time in the future as a result of the change in asset values. He has reason to expect this increase since the firm now has more assets (and he has a larger equity in the firm). If the increase in dividends is not expected to be forthcoming he will sell some or all of his equity in the assets (thus receiving a "dividend"). The increase in asset value does not require further price increases, but is a function of the prices that are currently in effect. The value change has already taken place and implies a change in the expected amount of cash that can be distributed to the capital contributors in the future.

It is well known that the FIFO measure of income incorporates some market gains and losses. Since the definition of income being used as a criterion also includes market gains, it is not surprising that FIFO is "proved" to be superior to LIFO.[8] Despite the lack of surprise, the method of analysis may be useful.

---

[8] The American Accounting Association Committee on Concepts and Standards-Inventory Measurement took a similar position relative to LIFO. See *The Accounting Review* (July 1964), pp. 700–714 for the committee's report. Charles E. Johnson's classic article, "Inventory Valuation—The Accountant's Achilles Heel" is also of interest, *The Accounting Review* (April 1954), pp. 15–26.

Extraordinary Items

Assume a situation where V_0 has been reasonably measured by the accountant and an extraordinary event (say a fire, an explosion, or an unexpected change in the rate of economic obsolescence) occurs subsequent to this valuation. To the extent that V_1 is decreased by this special event, we would recognize that a loss has occurred affecting Y_1, the income of period one.

The income of the past period is clearly affected, but our objective might be to predict the next period's income. Another unlikely event might or might not occur in the next period, and there is a variety of possibilities for predicting the income of the next period. We could use:

a. the most likely income (leaving out the unlikely extraordinary item);
b. the expected income (incorporating unlikely events and the probabilities of their occurring);
c. the expected income assuming another extraordinary event will occur.

If it is important that our prediction of next period's income coincide with the actual income of that period, we might use the "a" estimator above since that income has the largest probability of occurring. If we want to make a prediction that will be correct on the average, then we choose "b." If we want to be dramatically correct (though likely to be wrong), then our choice would be "c." The accountant cannot anticipate the analyst's criterion, which in part depends on the consequences of making an error in estimation. However, he can present the income data so that the analyst can entirely exclude extraordinary items when desired (as he will if his choice is "a"). He can indicate the likelihood of the extraordinary items recurring (so the analyst can choose "b"), and since the special items are clearly defined the analyst can choose "c" if he so desires.

The solution suggested above is comparable to that required by the Accounting Principles Board (APB hereafter) in Part I of Opinion No. 9.[9] There the Board calls for a presentation in the form:

Income before extraordinary items
Extraordinary items (listed)
Net income.

This information provides the data for choices (a) and (c). A ten-year summary of earnings would provide help in indicating the likelihood of recurrence of extraordinary items and would facilitate choice (b) if desired.

We can use the above analysis to again compare FIFO and LIFO. FIFO incorporates the market gains and losses, and is a reasonable predictor of

---

[9] Accounting Principles Board, "Reporting the Results of Operations I—Net Income and the Treatment of Extraordinary Items and Prior Period Adjustments," Opinion No. 9 (American Institute of Certified Public Accountants, 1966).

next period's income *if* the price changes of the past period will be repeated in the next period. If prices remain as they are currently, then LIFO is apt to be a better predictor of the next period's income. Thus it is not clear whether the use of LIFO or FIFO will lead to a better predictor of the next period's income. The preference for FIFO in the previous section was based on the fact that FIFO comes closer to measuring income, if income is defined as the difference between the end and the beginning of the period values of the firm, and if the net realizable value of the inventory at the end of the period is closer in amount to the cost of the most recent purchases than to the cost basis of the inventory at the beginning of the period.

To provide the same type of information here as is available for extraordinary items, a dual pricing—LIFO and FIFO—of inventory flows would be required. The LIFO valuation would be used in the calculation of gross margin, and the difference between LIFO and FIFO valuations would be recognized as a separate component of income. On the position statement, inventory would be valued in FIFO terms.

The income component representing the difference between LIFO and FIFO valuations is a holding gain (or loss) validated by the acquisition by the firm of units of inventory at the FIFO price. The holding gain (or loss) reflecting the difference between value at the end of the period and FIFO cost is more difficult to verify. Generally accepted accounting principles would not recognize such gains (or losses) since they are unrealized.

Ideally the LIFO minus FIFO market gain (or loss) component should be shown as an extraordinary item in the income statement. The definition of extraordinary items in APB Opinion No. 9 probably can not be stretched to include components of this type, so under present generally accepted accounting principles it would have to appear above the "income before extraordinary items" line.

Conclusions

The analysis of this paper is based on the basic relationship:

$$Y_1 = (V_1 + D_1) - V_0.$$

It accepts the concept of income as a value increment, as an enhancement of wealth or command over economic resources. The relationship is offered, however, as a method of analysis rather than as an operational tool. The difficulties of measuring the value of a firm are generally too immense for the above equation to become the operational basis of measuring income of a period.

The suggested income measure may not be a good predictor of future earnings since it reflects value changes that might not be repeated in the future. Hopefully, enough information on the details of computation would be supplied so that an analyst could use the detailed income data as the basis for predicting the incomes of future periods.

Despite its limitation as an operational tool, the definition of income presented in this paper is useful as a mechanism for testing alternative accounting procedures. Given two or more alternative methods we should attempt to judge whether they are consistent with:

    a. a reasonable definition of income as the change in value of a firm between two points in time, and
    b. a reasonable predictor of future income.

Frequently the alternative that is consistent with "a" will be inconsistent with "b." There are two escape hatches available. One, we can supply the information that will enable the analyst to make the type of forecast he desires. Second, the income measure of this period does not have to be a good predictor of future income or of a firm's value. By any reasonable definition the historical income measure deals with the events taking place within one time period. The proper predictor of value is not Y_1 but V_0 (and at time one, V_1). The predictor of income for the next period must be consistent with the estimates of V_0, V_1 and D_1. Past revenues and expenses can be used to predict the future income, but this estimate may be improved by incorporating knowledge of the asset structure at the beginning of the period. A chemical company may make a major scientific discovery in 1968; an investor may secure a sharp increase in market value in 1968 of the shares in a new company he backed. Conceptually, the present value of the scientific discovery in excess of cost and the increase in market value of the shares are included in 1968 income; only a normal rate of return on these enhanced values would be included in 1969 income unless there were further discoveries or value changes in that year.

The value of a firm at the beginning of the period, V_0, depends on the market's prediction of this period's income, and we have defined this period's income as depending on V_0. Does this mean that (a) and (b) above are the same test, or perhaps even that the definition is circular? V_0 does depend on estimates of future income (or more properly, on them as proxies for future dividends), as does V_1, but the estimates are made from different vantage points. The estimate of V_0 is made without the knowledge of the events of year one, while the estimate of V_1, reflects the occurrences of the year, including, for example, the scientific discovery of the chemical company and the increase in market value of the holdings of the investor. It is the difference between the two estimates ($V_1 - V_0$), plus dividends, that is the historical measure of income. The income of the present period may be a poor predictor of future income (unless the changes of this period are expected to reoccur), and yet be a good measure of the change in financial position during the period.

Accountants spend much time and effort arguing the merits of different approaches to accounting problems. To make these efforts more fruitful, we should start from a sound conceptual base. The definitions of income and financial position offered in this paper are not completely operational and cannot be the basis of recording all transactions. However, they can be the basis of standards against which present practices might be compared.

Stephen H. Penman is Tutor in Accountancy
at the University of Queensland in Australia.

What Net Asset Value? — An Extension of a Familiar Debate

Stephen H. Penman

Perhaps one subject more than any other has been the subject of debates among accounting theorists in the last decade: the valuation of assets. And so it should, for this is one area of great importance. Traditionally, it has been accepted by accountants, inclusive even of those who maintain the shareholder's equity as the center of accountability, that the legal and economic rights of equities are determined by the list of net asset values in the Balance Sheet. The valuation of the equities of owners is accomplished as a secondary process giving these items the nature of a residuum. This then places upon the process of asset valuation an importance of being the determinant of financial position. The importance of asset valuation in accounting theory is further emphasized by a realization of the articulation of the valuation of assets and income determination. This interdependence of the Balance Sheet and Profit and Loss Statement is obvious, whether a capital maintenance approach or a transactions approach is adopted towards income determination.

The purpose of this paper is to discover a theoretically sound model of asset valuation by reference to the basic underlying concept of Financial Position. It will be shown that several models of asset valuation can be developed from alternative assumptions or definitions of Financial Position, but that the application of certain metaphysical constraints brings about the

Appreciation is expressed to Professor Reg S. Gynther of the University of Queensland, Australia, for his helpful comments.

Reprinted by permission of the author and publisher from *Accounting Review*, Vol. XLV (April, 1970), pp. 333–46.

rejection of some of these models. The paper falls into two parts. Firstly, the Financial Position Assumption (and thus the asset valuation model) considered most theoretically sound and relevant to the environment of accounting will be developed. Secondly, the often avoided realm of practice will be ventured into in order to subject the model to the constraint of objectivity. These two areas, while complementary to each other, should be seen as quite distinct parts—the development of theory and the application of that theory. The need for objectivity in published reports is not a determinant of the theoretical model but rather a constraint on the application of theory.

It is anticipated, then, that responses to this paper will also be at two types: criticism of the theoretical ground underlying the model chosen and criticism of the modification of that model under the constraint of objectivity.

The Financial Position Assumption

Once one has chosen and defined one's assumptions it is possible to set up upon those assumptions a theoretical structure that is completely compact and logical, no matter how related to abstraction and unrelated to reality. It is contended here that the various "theories" of asset valuation currently being expounded in accounting literature are each sound (with perhaps a few minor irregularities) within their own assumptions and framework. The varying assumptions giving rise as they do to different frameworks center, it would seem, about the notion and viewpoint of the essence of Financial Position or the concept of value, the definition of which is a prerequisite to the definition of the nature of an asset. It is the effect of differing viewpoints as to what is meant by this basic concept of Financial Position which makes the various "theories" irreconcilable. Those varying assumptions will now be discussed in order to provide a base for what follows.

The Historical Cost Assumption

It might be thought that the application of historical cost to Balance Sheet figures is hardly a method of asset valuation. However, this is the "valuation" (so called) currently being used by most practicing accountants and thus demands recognition and exposition. Let it be emphasized, however, that historical cost is not a valuation concept. It is just here that we can discern the concept adopted by traditional accounting of Financial Position. A Statement of Financial Position (Balance Sheet) is not meant to show values but rather unexpired costs[1]—a bridge over which the unexpired costs of one period are carried to the next accounting period. Professor W. T. Baxter expresses this well when he says that conventional accounting

tends to dismiss the Balance Sheet as a mere appendage of the revenue

[1] William A. Paton and Ananias C. Littleton, *An Introduction to Corporate Accounting Standards* (American Accounting Association, 1967), p. 25.

account—a mausoleum for the unwanted costs that the double-entry system throws up as unregrettable by-products[2]

Hence the Balance Sheet is literally a sheet of balances.

The Economic Worth (or Wealth) Assumption

Many accounting theorists have adopted an assumption of Financial Position as the economic wealth of an entity at a specific point of time in relation to its continuing activity, given the intentions of the direction of that continuity. This concept sees "value" as (future) benefits, limited to those which are economic in nature, which accrue to the enterprise as a result of its given activity and possession of certain resources. Financial Position is thus the economic potential of the enterprise as expressed by the productive resources under its control.

The Adaptability Assumption

Professor Chambers, through his deductive approach of relating an individual to his environment to establish his financial relationships with that environment, maintains

. . . an individual in a market society *adapts* himself to prevailing circumstances through indirect exchanges. He will, therefore require to know his stock of severable means expressed in terms of the unit medium of exchange . . . *Financial Position* may be defined as the *capacity* of an entity at a point of time *for engaging in exchanges*.[3] (emphasis added)

and

. . . trading firms are no less adaptive entities than are persons as such.[4]
"The notion of adaptive behaviour applies as well to firms as to individuals. The postulated objective of optimal adaptation avoids the fallacy of a "single" goal such as profit maximization."[5]

This, of course, is no place to discover the thought processes behind the Professor's conclusions but to emphasize his assumption of Financial Position—the expression of the given means available at a particular point of time to a given entity for adaptability into the various ends as defined by the entity's objectives.

---

[2] W. T. Baxter and Sidney Davidson, *Studies in Accounting Theory* (Sweet and Maxwell, Ltd., 1962), p. viii.

[3] Raymond J. Chambers, *Accounting, Evaluation and Economic Behaviour* (Prentice-Hall, Inc., 1966), p. 81.

[4] *Ibid.*, p. 190.

[5] *Ibid.*, footnote.

The Economic Power Assumption

Many writers in accounting theory have adopted a concept of Financial Position which is similar to that in 2 above.[6] However this concept of wealth is not related to the firm's going-concern value as an operating enterprise generating economic benefits (as in 2). Rather it is related to a notion of "economic power" in the market as a result of the resources under its control—the degree of exchange value as an expression of purchasing power wealth. Unlike Chambers' model this wealth is seen in terms of entry prices rather than exit prices, although Philips provides for an exit price as a lower limit.

The Nature and Definition of Assets

As has been indicated, the definition of assets depends very much on the postulated notion of Financial Position or Value and thus is obtained by a process of deductive logic from that assumption. It is obvious that varying assumptions will produce varying models of what an asset is, each model conflicting with each other but in perfect harmony within its own framework. It is but one step further in the deductive process to obtain the method of asset measurement (valuation) from the definition derived.

The Historical Cost Definition

The definition of an asset by traditional accountants follows on from their conception of the Balance Sheet as a sheet of remaining cost balances. Paton and Littleton promote the following definition:

> The factors acquired for production which have not yet reached the point of the business process where they may be appropriately treated as "cost of sales" or "expense" are called "assets" and are presented as such in the balance sheet. It should not be overlooked, however, that these "assets" are in fact "revenue charges in suspense" awaiting some future matching with revenue as costs or expenses.[7]

The corresponding measure of income is a matching of realized revenues with expired costs.

The Economic Wealth Definition

John B. Canning was one of the first writers to develop an asset definition

---

[6] A prominent exponent of this concept is G. Edward Philips, (see "The Revolution in Accounting Theory," *The Accounting Review*, xxxviii (October, 1963) pp. 696–708). Russel Matthews [*Accounting for Economists* (Australia: F. W. Cheshire Pty., Ltd., 1962), p. 155] while not drawing exactly the same conclusions as Philips, also looks upon Buying Market Value as Asset Value without reference to future cash flows.

[7] Paton and Littleton, *op. cit.*

which was comprehensive of all characteristics attaching to assets. In his 1929 classic he wrote:

> An asset is any future service in money or any future service convertible into money . . . the beneficial interest in which is legally or equitably secured to some person. . . . [8]

Paton and Littleton hinted at such a concept when they suggested that " 'Service' is the significant element behind the accounts, that is, service potentials"[9] while Vatter further developed on the "service-potential" notion by application of his definitional constraints of operational content and homogeneity of substance to derive an asset definition of "embodiments of future wants satisfaction in the form of service potentials."[10] A wider acceptance, however, of this definition of an asset in terms of economic notions and ability to satisfy human wants, came with the exposition by the Committee on Concepts and Standards of the American Accounting Association in 1957 who subscribed to the idea that:

> Assets are economic resources devoted to business purposes within a specific accounting entity; they are aggregates of service-potentials available for or beneficial to expected operations.[11]

Sprouse and Moonitz similarly defined assets in *Accounting Research Study No. 3* as "expected future economic benefits, rights to which have been acquired by the enterprise as a result of some current or past transaction."[12]

The emphasis on service potentials of this concept of an asset has the merit of providing an all-inclusive definition and also separates the measuring problem from the definition problem, a factor not associated with the historical cost or the economic power definitions.

It follows, then, that the "value of an asset is the money equivalent of its service-potentials."[13] This is, conceptually, the amount of the future net cash flows generated by the asset discounted to their present value by interest and

---

[8] John B. Canning, *The Economics of Accountancy.* (The Ronald Press Co., 1929), p. 22.

[9] Paton and Littleton, *op cit.*, p. 13. It is a pity that they do not perpetuate this observation. They conclude "accounting, is, therefore, strongly rooted in economics even though its objectives are different and its medium of expression, price aggregates, falls short of being a suitable medium for economic reasoning."

[10] William J. Vatter, *The Fund Theory of Accounting and Its Implications for Financial Reports,* (Uni. of Chicago Press, 1947), p. 17.

[11] American Accounting Association Committee on Concepts and Standards, *Accounting and Reporting Standards for Corporate Financial Statements and Preceding Statements and Supplements* (American Accounting Association, 1957), p. 3. They too, return to a cost measurement from this ideal (*op. cit.*, p. 4).

[12] Robert T. Sprouse and Maurice Moonitz, "A Tentative Set of Broad Accounting Principles for Business Enterprises," *Accounting Research Study No. 3.* (American Institute of Certified Public Accountants, 1962), p. 20.

[13] American Accounting Association Committee on Concepts and Standards, *op. cit.*, p. 4.

probability factors—commonly referred to as Net Present Value (N.P.V.). The corresponding measure of income is the increase in Net Present Value over a period.

Definition under the Adaptability Assumption

The adaptability assumption demands the definition of an asset as "any severable means in the possession of an entity."[14] This has two implications. First, the asset must have the quality of severability (otherwise it cannot be utilized for adaption into alternatives) and legal right must attach to the owner so that he has the exclusive right to sell the asset in order to fulfill his adaptive requirements. In a broad sense, assets are basically *means* to obtain *ends* with the necessary qualities attaching to provide adaptive movements to obtain ends.

It follows, then, that the value of an asset to an entity is the value of that asset in exchange, that is, the cash which the entity can obtain from sale of the asset in order to further an alternative goal. Chambers calls this the "current cash equivalent" of the asset, which is virtually its net realizable value in a current market to available buyers.

The Economic Power Definition

G. Edward Philips, in criticizing *A.R.S. No. 3* writes that, "In *PRINCIPLES* Moonitz and Sprouse define assets in terms of future economic benefits rather than simply in terms of values."[15] He continues:

> Assets exist in the present, not in the future. If we know the market price, we know the value of an asset. The value of an asset depends not only upon the future economic services they are capable of rendering but also upon the market's estimates of these services and the market interest rate.[16]

Thus, it would seem that Philips (and the others that take the same stand) recognizes the nature of assets as future benefits potential but sees first that assets are in the nature of values in a market—economic power (wealth) in a dynamic economy. Hence "economic power does not exist without market values,"[17] and thus assets are really market exchange values.[18] Philips, in criticizing *A.R.S. 1 and 3*, summarizes by saying:

> The theoretical difficulties in *POSTULATES* and *PRINCIPLES* stem pri-

---

[14] Chambers, *op. cit.*, p. 104.

[15] Philips, *op. cit.*, p. 701.

[16] *Ibid.*

[17] G. Edward Philips, "The Accretion Concept of Income," *The Accounting Review*, XXXVIII (January 1963), p. 17.

[18] This must not be confused with those who wish to adopt current market prices as approximation to the ideal of N.P.V.

marily from a failure to choose between two alternative ultimate measures of value: (a) exchange value as determined by the market or (b) present worth of future benefits.[19]

He makes this choice in favor of (a) to form a base to his "pure theory of accounting" which "rests on a definition of resources (the balance sheet) in terms of economic power of an entity."[20] In applying this notion of market wealth he adapts his "current exchange value" which lies somewhere between current market buying price (the upper limit) and salvage value (the lower limit) but in normal circumstances is geared strongly to the former. The corresponding concept of income—the "accretion concept of income" is the increase in this economic power over a period.

The Philosophical Notions of Relevance and Objectivity

There exist, common to all disciplines, several notions which are derived from the central core of philosophical thought-logic, mathematics and metaphysics and which provide constraints upon those disciplines which themselves take on the form of positive fields of knowledge developed by reference to a restricted environment. These notions do not form part of a theoretical structure of a field of knowledge (although they can be utilized in the formation of the structure) but rather act as constraints upon the application of the theory. Two[21] such notions are:

- a. relevance
- b. objectivity

Let it be reiterated that the above four models or structures of asset valuation theory are complete in logical necessity within themselves and thus acceptable for application to the accounting situation. However, how do they bear up when subject to these constraints?

Relevance

Relevance, of course, remains merely a philosophical standard until it is related to the specific environment. The question is, what is relevant? It is submitted here that accounting, as an information provider, must present figures upon which rational decision making can be made. The following decisions are pertinent to accounting data:

---

[19] G. Edward Philips, "The Revolution in Accounting Theory," *op. cit.*, p. 706.

[20] *Ibid.*, p. 708.

[21] Of course there are other such notions—consistency materiality etc.—but these are the two considered most "relevant" here.

  a. Decisions of shareholders
     (i) in their appraisal of management
     (ii) in respect of their shareholdings
  b. Decisions of potential investors
  c. Decisions of management in their function of manipulation of scarce resources to maximize business goals and of obtaining optimum resource allocation and combination.
  d. Decisions of creditors, governments and employees in their relationships with the entity.

This is no place for a detailed research into the functions of accounting, so the above cannot be viewed as complete or necessarily in correct order. Let us now apply relevance in terms of the above to the four models enumerated.

The Historical Cost Model

To submit a statement of financial position as a list of costs not yet charged to revenues, although consistent within the cost model, is, in the opinion of the writer, no basis for the formulation of the above decisions. Of what significance is an emphasis on increase in "wealth" (income determination) during a period if the figures at the beginning and end of the period themselves do not express wealth at those points of time? While historical cost methods may give some indication to the shareholders of the stewardship of management in the management of costs and money capital under their control, the records give no indication of the real worth of the enterprise as a going concern except to the extent that operating profit is a predictive device. In short, it is a static concept in a dynamic economy with its changing prices.

Hence, on the basis of relevance, the traditional accounting model is rejected.

The Net Present Value Model

John B. Canning, in his 1929 work, has stated, "Beyond doubt, the accountant would like to mean by 'financial position' a position declared by direct positive measures of funds to be provided by enterprise operations."[22] This would mean that asset values would be expressed as the capitalized earning power they possess, that is, in terms of discounted future fund flows.

It is the opinion of the writer that this model, and only this model, meets the requirements of relevance for decision making. Only by reference to the worth of the firm in its continuous activity can shareholders appraise management or make decisions to buy and sell their shares. Only by reference to discounted cash flow values can creditors recognize security and can governments make decisions of economic policy affecting business. Management, too, must know the expected returns and effects of past decisions in order to formulate new decisions, especially those concerning alternatives.

The Current Cash Equivalent

It is interesting to note that in one of his early papers, Professor Chambers, in demanding a deductive approach to accounting theory, maintained that although a theory should be developed without reference to practice, the final vindication of the theory is its utility (relevance) in practice.[23] It is believed that his model incorporating the C.C.E.'s of assets does not meet this requirement.

The criticism is directed along two lines. First, it is thought that adaptive behaviour, although perhaps a characteristic of individuals to some extent, is not evident in the case of a company "machine" in a highly inflexible environment and with large blocks of fixed long-life assets. Companies (less so, shareholders, except by selling shares!) just do not adapt.[24] Physical factors and other realities prevent such action. That is an environmental observation. Second, to record the disposition value of an asset when there is no thought of disposing of that asset seems to be illogical. It would seem reasonable to report liquidation values if liquidation was intended or even foreseen. Even if adaptation were a possibility, it would seem reasonable to report the N.P.V.'s of alternatives firstly to the constituents and then C.C.E.'s *after* (and if) an alternative with a higher N.P.V. than the present operation appeared and if adaptation was decided upon.[25] The valuation of assets at C.C.E. would then be the result of a decision to adapt (to give means for adaptation) not the cause of it and indeed it would be the N.P.V. under the changed circumstances. The Chamber's model confuses this cause-and-effect relationship in decision making.

It would seem a little harsh to dismiss such a well-developed thesis as Chamber's with one sentence but it seems to the writer that, while Chambers must be commended for his methodology, and in particular his demand in building a theoretical model, to analyze the environment, his perception of that environment must be questioned. It is submitted that the model is developed on part only of the environment, and not the whole.

Of course, the irrelevance of the Current Cash Equivalent model for the decision makers listed above needs hardly to be stated. As liquidation or second hand values give no indication of earning power of a going-concern in its specified operations, share prices could react in an erratic fashion without any relationship to earning potential, management could make no

---

[22] Canning, *op. cit.*, p. 191.

[23] Raymond J. Chambers, "Why Bother with Postulates?" *Journal of Accounting Research*, 1 (Spring 1963), p. 5.

[24] This does not mean to say they do not diversify. However, diversification is usually done gradually by use of principles of financial planning. Seldom, if ever, does a company adapt in "large chunks."

[25] Of course, N.P.V. may be relevant to management in decisions to sell or keep specific assets. This, however, is a matter of internal reporting not affecting statements of financial position.

decisions as to optimum asset combination without reference to a secondary analysis and creditors, shareholders (actual and potential), governments and employers make misguided decisions.

The C.C.E. model is thus rejected as a basis for sound decision making in the existing environment with the reservation that, if adaptation into alternative actually *does* becomes a reality, then the model is relevant, and then only for those sections of the firm to be "adapted."

The Economic Power Model

The measurement of assets at market exchange values as a measure of the entity's economic power or wealth in the market bears, the writer believes, the fallacy that the entity is a *holder* of assets rather than a *user* of assets. Enterprising concerns possess assets not to increase or maintain their economic power or market status but to apply them to operations in order to derive cash inflows. Therefore the value that is relevant is not market value as determined by supply and demand factors, but economic use value as determined by future cash flows.[26]

Thus this model must be rejected on the basis of its irrelevance for decision making concerning a going-concern involved in *operations*.

The Net Present Value Model: The Constraint of Objectivity

One model—the N.P.V. model—then survives the test of relevance. It remains, then to apply to this model the second constraint of objectivity.[27]

If the value of an asset to a particular enterprise is the discounted net present value of all future cash inflows derived from that asset, it follows that its measurement is obtained by discovering those future cash flows and discounting them back at the prescribed rate of interest to the present date. This is the conceptual ideal. If men were omniscient (in which case there would be no need for accountants), they could see the actual cash streams flowing from each asset and the problem would end here. However, this is not the case and so the following difficulties remain:

   a. The estimation of the *total* future revenue and cost streams for the *whole* firm with the existence of uncertainty.

   b. The assignment of these total cash streams to specific assets (including such "imponderables" as good management, brand name, efficiency of staff, etc.) in exact proportion to the measure of the assets' contribu-

---

[26] This does not prevent the recognition of "holding gains and losses" on *gross* values of fixed assets by recognition of market prices. However, market prices, it is argued, should never affect net asset values which are the expression of "financial position."

[27] Of course, some of the other models also could be subjected to this constraint and fail but these have already been rejected on the grounds of lack of relevance. Chambers' model would come into this category.

tion to the total stream. This is further complicated by the fact that cash flows are derived, not from specific assets, but rather from combination of assets. For example, no cash flows can be generated from a machine until it has a building around it. Similarly, one part missing from the production line can reduce the total cash flow from the production line to zero, but is it correct to attribute all of the cash flows from the process to that part? If so, which one of the many parts? This has been called the "homogeneity problem."

c. Cash flows are generated, in an economic sense, by the whole process of production. Hence the possession of certain productive assets in a given combination is not the sole cause of cash flows. Cash flows result also from the application upon those assets in future periods of other factors such as materials and labor.

Hence, cash flows can be seen to be derived from three sources:

(i) the individual assets (including "intangibles").
(ii) the combination of those individual assets in an economic way. The degree of management efficiency in this area (i.e., obtaining an optimum resource combination) will affect future revenue flows.
(iii) the combination of combined assets with other economic factors in the future.

It is of importance to recognize that there exists *one* asset only in the entity and that is the firm itself. As it is becoming increasingly possible to derive *total* future cash flows (especially with the current developments in probability theory and computerized simulation techniques) it remains then a problem of assigning those total flows to the three cash flow sources in order to provide data for decision making concerning the use, combination and disposal of the assets. For clarity these three sources are restated again together before each is discussed in turn:

(i) cash flows arising from *individual* assets,
(ii) cash flows arising from the *combination* of those assets, and
(iii) cash flows arising from the *combination* of those *combined* assets with other economic factors in the future.

(i) The N.P.V. of the Individual Assets

At once we are confronted with the problem of what is a separate asset in terms of physical existence. Is it the group of machines, the individual machine, or should we break the machine down into component parts (e.g., motors, rollers or even screws) and measure the cash flows from those parts rather from the whole machine? By applying the constraint of relevance once again the writer believes that the total firm asset should be broken down only into severable elements, if the separate valuation of each can be useful for decision making. For example, if a choice can only be made between one production line and another production line, and not between alternative machines within one production line, the asset is the production line and not a number of machines. Similarly, if two items of inventory can be sold separately both are distinct assets, whereas if they can only be disposed of together, then there is only one asset as there is only one way of affecting future cash flows. Future developments of N.P.V. will perhaps cause a change in the method of classifying individual assets. Instead of using the conventional classifications of "Buildings," "Land," "Plant and Machinery," "Furniture and Fittings," and so on, the cake may be cut the other way (across and not down) with classifications such as "Facilities for Product A," "Facilities in Division B," etc. can be used. This will provide information that is far more relevant for decision making and will also facilitate the isolating of cash flows.

It is useful, for purposes of analysis, to break assets up into two distinct types:

a. those which will be converted into cash in the ordinary course of business within one operating cycle of the business. These include debtors, cash, trading stock and short term investments.
b. those assets which will not be converted directly into cash in the ordinary course of business. These include land, buildings, plant and equipment, investments, and intangible items including goodwill.

The convenience here is apparent. Type (a) assets provide an *objective* measure of future cash flows, and type (b) assets present a definite practical problem.

Type (a) assets. Like all types of assets, these will be valued at the net expected cash flows to be derived from them, which in this case is their net expected future exchange price. Cash and bank balances will then be valued at stated money amount and debtors at stated amounts less an element of probability of non-collection. Debts that are likely to carry over into a second year will have a discount rate applied to them. Short-term investments held as an application of surplus cash will be valued along similar lines.

Inventories provide a more complicated situation. The writer believes that the ideal basis of inventory measurement is selling price less costs of sale and completion, less a factor for probability of non-sale, less profit attributable to remaining processes and selling activity, this principle being applicable to all stages of work-in-progress. This is consistent with the previously stated ideal of N.P.V.

However, this must be subject to our constraint of objectivity. Unfortunately not all inventories are as marketable as we would wish. It is proposed that in the cases where N.P.V. is not objectively obtainable (and, in many cases until stock is actually sold, cash inflows are a mere conjecture) recourse be made to current replacement costs. This is argued from the fact that the relationship of cash to inventory is twofold:

(i) The true benefit that stock on hand passes into the next period is measured by the net *inflow* of cash to that period by holding the stock now.

(ii) However, when this cash inflow is not objectively determinable, it is possible to measure the cash *outflow* avoided in the next period because the stock was possessed at the start.

It is suggested that a measure of cash outflow avoided to the next accounting period is an acceptable (although not so satisfactory) alternative to net present value. It must be emphasized, however, that this recourse to current replacement costs is for very different theoretical grounds than the current replacement cost proposed by Matthews, Edwards and Bell, Sprouse and Moonitz and the Committee on Concepts and Standards—Inventory Measurement. These writers recommend current input costs on three bases:

a. a means of meeting the price-level problem by restating the historical costs by specific indexes to maintain an operational capacity,[28]

b. a means of matching current costs with current revenues and the segregation of holding gains and losses from trading transactions,[29] and

c. as a substitute for net present value where this cannot be estimated with a reasonable degree of accuracy.[30] Current replacement costs are used here merely as the best alternative of value, rather than because of their relationship to cash outflows avoided to next period.

These arguments are invalid, it is contended, because of their reasoning

---

[28] For example, Sprouse and Moonitz, *op. cit.*, p. 29, say, "Measurement of inventories at current cost means that goods sold should also be measured at current cost, thereby accomplishing the avowed purpose of the last-in, first-out method."

[29] The Committee on Concepts and Standards—Inventory Measurement, *op. cit.*, p. 706, "believes that replacement cost is a superior conceptual measurement device; historical cost is practical substitute where price losses or gains are insignificant." Also they say, in discussing Replacement Costs, "When meaningful measurement can be made, it seems evident that the segregation of price or holding gains or losses and trading or transaction gains or losses will be more helpful than their usual combination in one gross margin measure."

Sprouse and Moonitz, *op. cit.*, declare "the use of current (replacement) costs has the further advantage of introducing a clean-cut distinction in the accounts between profit from holding . . . and profit from 'operating margins,'. . ." Of course, the Edwards and Bell stand is well known. See Edgar O. Edwards and Philip W. Bell, *The Theory and Measurement of Business Income* (The University of California Press, 1961), p. 705.

[30] See Sprouse and Moonitz, *op. cit.*, pp. 28–29.

from factors other than cash flows. The emphasis must be on future cash convertibility and not on cost or even current value for its own sake.[31] Where future cash inflows are uncertain, cash outflows avoided presenting a satisfactory alternative.

Type (b) assets. The inherent nature of these items, together with the factors mentioned in sections (ii) and (iii) later in this paper make objective measurements of future cash flows derived from them a practical impossibility.

Fixed Tangible Assets—Land, Buildings, Plant and Equipment

The constraint of objectivity demands that we find a practical approximation of N.P.V. for these assets. A number of such approximations have been suggested, and these are discussed below.[32]

1. Current Market Buying Prices (Current Replacement Cost)

The Committee on Concepts and Standards—Long-lived Assets came to the conclusion that:

> "Whenever sufficient objective evidence is not available, or when cash flow estimates cannot be identified with specific assets, a practical approximate measure of service potential may be attained by reference to the *current cost of securing the same or equivalent services.*"[33] (emphasis added).

The arguments put forward by the proponents of this approximation involve the acceptance of objective valuation by the market of the future cash benefits potential in the asset. This is supported by the fact that "the prices of all producers' goods are derivatives of the expected prices of consumers' goods, the demand for which give rise to their use,"[34] and it follows that their current market buying prices (netted for depreciation on the asset owned) reflect future cash flows.

However, doubt arises as to whether the estimate of future cash flows placed on the asset by buyers and sellers in the market represent the economic benefits in the asset *to the enterprise* in all or most cases both at the

---

[31] Of course this does not mean that one would not recognize holding gains and losses on Inventory items or changes in current costs in order to maintain operational capacity. This, however, is a different matter from inventory valuation to calculate financial position.

[32] It should be noted that we are dealing here with *net* asset values which are the only ones which reflect "financial position." Gross asset values can be calculated according to the capital maintenance concept held or the view held on "holding gains or losses."

[33] The Committee on Concepts and Standards—Long-Lived Assets, *Accounting for Land, Buildings and Equipment*, "Supplementary Statement No. 1, *Accounting Review*, XXXIX (July, 1964), p. 694.

[34] Raymond J. Chambers, *Accounting, Evaluation and Economic Behavior*, p. 199.

date of purchase or at all times afterward. Different buyers have different expected future cash flows due to different applications of the asset involving the production of a wide variety of consumer goods. Buyers face different markets for their products and also may be able to combine the asset in a more economical way with other resources to produce larger cash flows than the firm's asset. Also different buyers in the market will have widely varying discount rates (depending on the degree of risk and uncertainty) to apply to future cash flows even if all did have the same future cash flows from the asset.

These doubts are further supported by the fact that current market buying prices, as an approximation of N.P.V., assume first, that increases in replacement costs change as do service-potentials. If there has been no change in expected revenues or costs there can be no change in service potential, and thus historical cost represents the best measurement of service potential despite the fact that market prices may have soared. Second, this approximation assumes that historical cost equals N.P.V. at the date of the acquisition of the asset. If this is not so, an increase in current market price is merely an objective measurement of a gain which existed at the date of acquisition, not a current increase in service-potential. A third assumption is, of course, that of the perfect market—perfect knowledge and perfect mobility—which rarely exists in practice.

2. Historical Cost

We have seen that the use of current replacement costs gives the effect of declaring that the user of the asset would be willing to purchase the asset in the present for that current price. It is possible, in criticizing this assumption, to return to an historical cost basis of asset valuation on the following basis (not to be confused with a return to conventional accounting): historical cost equals, at the date of acquisition, the minimum valuation of expected cash benefits from the asset, otherwise it would not have been purchased. The objectivity of this basis cannot be disputed. If, perchance, the future cash flows were seen to be greater than acquisition cost, then a "buying" or "holding" gain would be recognized.

This basis, it is suggested, is perfectly sound so long as future revenue and cost streams expected at date of acquisition remain the same. Then depreciated historical cost remains the best measure of service potential. However, as this is seldom the case and future cash streams *do* change as a result of changes in the assets' environment, so acquisition cost as a basis of net asset valuation[35] is unsatisfactory.

[35] It should be noted that this discussion refers again only to *net* asset values. Historical cost as a gross value would be adjusted by a relevant index according to the capital maintenance concept held.

3. Current Cost of Equivalent Services—Value to Owner Concept

Some writers,[36] in recognizing the vast problem of obtaining the net present values of individual fixed assets due to the factors that cash flows are only derived when assets are *combined* and not from the specific assets *per se*, have turned to another concept of opportunity value to the owner. They argue that, while assets are indeed service potentials, this is true only of combined assets. Even then future cash flows are impossible to trace. Thus they see the real value of the asset to the owner as *the current cost of replacing the service benefits given* by the asset. For example, Solomons[37] considers the case of a railroad which has obvious future cash flows potential in its assets. However, if the wheels of the railway engines strangely disappeared, then the future cash flows would be reduced to zero. Is it correct, then, he argues to attribute all cash flows to the wheels and carry the engines, carriages and railroads at zero value? He insists not, but instead suggests that the real value to the owner of the wheels (and all other items) is the cost to him of replacing the services given by these items if they were lost or destroyed.[38]

Although this concept[39] has the advantage of overcoming the technology (obsolescence) problem which haunts so many models of depreciation accounting, the writer has two objections. First it produces an asset model with hybrid accounting concepts, because it is not merely an attempt to approximate N.P.V. but rather an introduction of another totally different concept. The valuation of current assets at N.P.V. and fixed assets by the "value to the owner" concept produces an asset valuation based on two different concepts and suggests that current assets and fixed assets are different in nature, and that assets are not capable of one broad, overall definition. Second the concept produces a "goodwill" valuation as merely a balancing item between the total N.P.V. of the firm and the replacement costs of other assets. Such a notion is not a definite asset with its own characteristics and service potentials; in short, it is a balancing hybrid.

This concept, therefore, is also rejected as not consistent with the N.P.V. model.

How then can we determine the net value of fixed assets in practice? The

---

[36] See David Solomons, "Economic and Accounting Concepts of Cost and Value" in *Modern Accounting Theory*, ed. by Morton Backer (Prentice-Hall, Inc., 1966), pp. 117–127., and F. K. Wright, "Capacity for Adaption and the Asset Measurement Problem." *Abacus* (August 1967), pp. 74–79. Wright calls the concept "opportunity value."

[37] Solomons, *op. cit.*, p. 123.

[38] Solomons recommends C.R.C. as an upper limit and N.R.V. as a lower limit for comparisons with N.P.V. for disposal decisions.

[39] This should be differentiated from the concept of current replacement cost developed by Edwards and Bell. They want a current replacement cost of historical inputs as a measure of management's efficiency in having those particular inputs, rather than a current cost of *equivalent* services.

writer is in a dilemma. Historical cost is invalid when future expected cash flows change after acquisition date. Current market buying prices do not approximate benefits *to the enterprise*, and "opportunity value" is, in concept, a departure from the N.P.V. ideal. Whether this amounts to the rejection of the whole N.P.V. model as a result of application of the constraint of objectivity is then a decision to be made. But what will replace it? Other models must be rejected on the basis of relevance. The dilemma is acute.

Investments

Again, long-term investments should be valued at the ideal of the amount of cash they are likely to earn over their life, discounted to the present. Thus, for investments which are held for dividends only, the N.P.V. will equal the present discounted value of future dividends. This may not, it is submitted, be equal to the market price of the security because market price not only expresses investment worth but also contains a speculative factor. It is an error for those who hold to the N.P.V. model to value such investments at market price (as most do) because of this speculative factor. Clearly, in this case, MacNeal's famous example does not apply. However, if there is a possibility of the security being sold and capital gains being reaped, then current market price is then applicable as it would represent the cash inflows which would result if the security were sold.

Intangibles, "Goodwill," Human Assets and the "Imponderables"

The writer believes that cash flows are derived not only from tangible assets but also from the "imponderables"–human assets, good management, product name, etc., and therefore that these should be valued in the accounts at their respective N.P.V.'s.

However, the constraint of objectivity makes this a practical impossibility. Their measurement can, however, be effected by a calculation of the total N.P.V. of the firm and deducting from this the sum of the N.P.V.'s of individual tangible assets (plus the N.P.V.'s of those "intangibles"–patents, licences, etc., which are separately identifiable). The extent to which the values of fixed assets are not attainable or must be approximated, affects, in a secondary way, the valuation of these items.

This idea of a Canning "master valuation account," adapted from a paper by Reg S. Gynther,[40] rejects the traditional notion of "goodwill" as the excess of future earnings over those normal to a firm in that industry, and attributes such earnings collectively to identifiable assets.

The problems associated with identifying cash flows from separate assets are many. We find, however, that these become multiplied when we recognize and analyze our second and third sources of cash flow.

---

[40] Reg S. Gynther, "Some 'Conceptualizing' on Goodwill," *The Accounting Review*, XLIV (April 1, 1969), pp. 247–255.

(ii) The Asset Combination: Another Asset?

The discussion in (i) above has been limited to the valuation of *specific* assets—whether tangible or intangible. As was suggested earlier, cash flows are derived, not only from specific assets but from the combination of those assets in an optimum way. Attempts have been made to attribute all cash flows to individual assets by use of marginal analysis[41] or averaging techniques. However, it is argued that these methods are basically wrong as they attribute all cash flows to the individual, severable assets which must lead to incorrect decisions as to disposal or replacements of those assets. It is thought, instead, that there exists another asset from which cash flows are derived—the asset combination asset.

The thought of omniscience aside, it is practically impossible to separate out this asset for valuation. It could, however, be included in the "master valuation account" along with the other "imponderables" as described above. But we are still left with the problem of separating out this asset from other assets for purposes of valuation of those other assets. To the writer, this remains an unsolved problem, a further contribution to the dilemma surrounding fixed asset valuation and another which, through the application of the objectivity criterion, may lead to the rejection of the N.P.V. model. One avenue of escape seems possible: ignore the "combination asset" and for expediency attribute all cash flows to the specific assets. This, of course, amounts to a deviation from the N.P.V. ideal with its resultant effect on decision making.

(iii) The Application of Other Resources on Combined Assets

Cash flows are derived from individual assets, from the combination of assets, and finally from application, in successive periods of other economic resources (labor, management, materials, etc.) to combined and specific assets. These latter cash flows, it is argued, should not be discounted back to the present in order to obtain financial position at the present because they result from a current resource allocation in the period they are derived. Hence they are not an asset and thus not a determinant of financial position. There is nothing inherent in assets held at the present that determines these cash flows—no cause and effect relationship. Rather they are a result of application *upon* assets held in the present of other resources to increase current operating profit. (These cash flows, it should be noted, are not to be confused with those which are inherent in the asset of management efficiency—this *is* a potential cash flow.) Further, the argument put forth here, is not that future resources should be included as assets now, as, at this moment they are not scarce and therefore not *economic* resources, but rather that recognition should be given to cash flows resulting from combination of those resources with present assets.

[41] A. L. Thomas, "Discounted Services Again: The Homogeneity Problem, *The Accounting Review*, XXXIX (January 1964), pp. 1–11.

There are those who would *see* these cash flows as inherent in assets held at the present. They would argue that the going-concern financial position is all future cash flows discounted. This, however, denies the definition of an asset upheld by them as a reservoir of economic benefits. Cash flows from future factor application are *not* inherent in assets currently held—not even management.

Of course, the separation of these cash flows is not of importance in determining the *total* N.P.V. of the firm but is a prevalent problem in the dividing up of those total flows upon individual assets. It remains, however, a practical problem to add to the rejections from the N.P.V. model by the application of the constraint of objectivity.

Conclusion

The paper here presented may seem, at first glance, a little destructive as an unfortunate conclusion of despair is sensed. However, examination will indicate that, while much has been knocked down, much also has been built up. Basically, an ideal has been attained. Competing ideals (at least to the satisfaction of the writer) have been rejected in order to establish one relevant model. Where despair is sensed, it is a result of the attempt to apply that ideal objectively in an environment of uncertainty. As has been suggested before, objectivity remains only a constraint on the application of theory, and is not part of the theory. The ideal still stands. At the worst, accountants can adopt a valuation of assets which is even only a very rough approximation to the ideal but which is intrinsically relevant. An approximated relevance is far better than an accurate irrelevance. Therefore, the task in hand is to discover a workable approximation to the ideal here presented.

Bibliography

W. T. Baxter, and S. Davidson, *Studies in Accounting Theory* (Sweet and Maxwell Ltd., 1962).

R. J. Chambers, *Accounting, Evaluation and Economic Behavior* (Prentice-Hall, Inc., 1966).

Committee on Concepts and Standards, American Accounting Association, *Accounting and Reporting Standards for Corporate Financial Statements and Preceding Statements and Supplements* (American Accounting Association, 1957).

Committee on Concepts and Standards—Inventory Measurement, American Accounting Association, "A Discussion of Various Approaches to Inventory Measurement," Supplementary Statement No. 2, *The Accounting Review*, Vol. XXXIX (July 1964) pp. 700–714.

Committee on Concepts and Standards—Long-Lived Assets, American Accounting Association, "Accounting for Land, Buildings and Equipment," Supplementary Statement No. 1, *The Accounting Review*, Vol. XXXIX (July 1964), pp. 693–699.

E. O. Edwards and P. W. Bell, *The Theory and Measurement of Business Income* (The University of California Press, 1961).

E. S. Hendriksen, *Accounting Theory* (Richard D. Irwin, Inc., 1965).

R. S. Gynther, "Accounting for Price Changes—Theory and Practice," *Society Bulletin No. 5* (Accountants Publishing Company, Ltd., 1968).

R. S. Gynther, "Some 'Conceptualising' on Goodwill," *The Accounting Review,* XLIV (April 1968), pp. 247–255.

W. A. Paton, and A. C. Littleton, *An Introduction to Corporate Accounting Standards* (American Accounting Association, 1967).

G. E. Philips, "The Revolution in Accounting Theory," *The Accounting Review,* Vol. XXXVIII (October 1963), pp. 696–708.

D. Solomons, "Economic and Accounting Concepts of Cost and Value," *Modern Accounting Theory.* Edited by Morton Backer (Prentice-Hall, Inc., 1966).

R. T. Sprouse, and M. Moonitz, "A Tentative Set of Broad Accounting Principles for Business Enterprises," *Accounting Research Study No. 3* (American Institute of Certified Public Accountants, 1962).

W. J. Vatter, *The Fund Theory of Accounting and Its Implications for Financial Reports* (University of Chicago Press, 1947).

F. K. Wright, "Depreciation and Obsolescence in Current Value Accounting," *Journal of Accounting Research*, Vol. 3, No. 2 (Autumn 1965), pp. 167–181.

Keith Shwayder is Vice President–Finance of Samsonite Corporation.

A Critique of Economic Income as an Accounting Concept

Keith Shwayder

Economic income as defined in Hicks's influential book, *Value and Capital*,[1] has achieved wide acceptance in accounting literature—especially since the publication of Alexander's monograph, *Income Measurement in a Dynamic Economy*.[2] Hansen, for example, enthusiastically endorses this concept: 'Profit as capital interest, . . . may be characterized as a theoretically complete concept, which is superior to other concepts of profit as a definition and as a guide point for an ideal practical procedure.'[3] Solomons is equally sanguine: '. . . growth in present value . . . alone appears to be significant; and since it seems to carry out the function generally attributed to income, growth in present value must be what we had better understand income to mean. The concept of income to which we have been led corresponds, of course, to Hicks's definition of income.'[4] Goldberg questions this acceptance: '. . . the definition of income as given by J. R. Hicks . . . has been widely adopted both implicitly and explicitly, and often without question, in

The writer wishes to thank Professors Yuji Ijiri and Charles Horngren of Stanford University for their many helpful comments and suggestions.

[1] J. R. Hicks, *Value and Capital*, Oxford University Press, 1939, p. 172.

[2] Sidney Alexander, 'Income Measurement in a Dynamic Economy,' *Five Monographs in Business Income*, New York, American Institute of Certified Public Accountants, 1948, as revised by David Solomons, in *Studies in Accounting Theory*, W. T. Baxter and Sidney Davidson (eds), Homewood, Illinois, Richard D. Irwin, Inc, 1962.

[3] Palle Hansen, *The Accounting Concept of Profit*, Amsterdam, North-Holland Publishing Company, 1962, p. 19.

[4] David Solomons, 'Economic and Accounting Concepts of Income,' *The Accounting Review*, July 1961, p. 375.

Reprinted by permission of the author and publisher from *Abacus*, Vol. III (August, 1967), pp. 23–35.

accounting and economic writing, even though Hicks himself pointed out it impracticability.'[5]

Economic income is generally defended as an ideal theoretical concep which is impractical to implement because of the difficulty in an uncertair world of measuring future cash flows. Not only is economic income ar impractical concept, but it is also, in my opinion, an unsound theoretica model for accounting income measurements. In defending this opinion, I will analyse five situations where the economic income method allocates income to accounting periods in a manner which violates our intuitive notions concerning periodic income:

1. A firm with a single venture.
2. A long lived firm.
3. A firm where the subjective rate of interest approaches zero.
4. A firm where the past is known with certainty and the future is highly uncertain.
5. A firm where some future events are known with certainty and others are uncertain.

Since the operational difficulties with economic income are recognized, the paper will deal only with theoretical problems.

'Economic Income'

'Economic income' usually denotes income as defined by economists. As accountants differ among themselves in measuring income, economists also have divergent income concepts and potentially there are as many definitions of economic income as there are economists. However, since the publication of Alexander's monograph, economic income has taken on a more restricted connotation in accounting literature—income as defined by Hicks and modified in Alexander's monograph. Hicks defined income as the amount a man can consume during a period, and still remain as well off at the period's end, as he was at the period's beginning.[6] Alexander adapted this concept to the corporation, describing income as the amount the firm could distribute to shareholders during a period and still remain as well off (have as much residual equity) at the end of the period as it was at the beginning of the period.[7] 'Well-offness' was defined entirely in terms of cash flows discounted at subjective rates of interest.[8] The timing and amounts of cash flows and the future subjective interest rates were assumed to be known with certainty. The subjective interest rate is the discount rate where the

---

[5] Louis Goldberg, *An Inquiry into the Nature of Accounting*, American Accounting Association, 1965, p. 247.

[6] Hicks, *loc. cit.*

[7] Alexander, *op. cit*, p. 139.

[8] *Ibid*, pp. 140–142.

entity is indifferent to future money and current money. Alexander argued that if management was maximizing the owners' 'well-offness,' this rate should be greater than or equal to the stockholders' time value of money.[9]

For example, suppose the firm knows with certainty the timing and amount of its future net cash flows from operations (the net cash flows from all sources except contributions from or distributions to residual equity shareholders). Let P_t be the present value at the beginning of period t of all of the future net cash flows of the firm, discounted at the appropriate future subjective interest rates. Economic income for period t then equals $P_{t+1} - P_t +$ the net cash flows occurring during period t.[10] Economic income is generally defended as a concept appropriate when the future is known with certainty, but difficult (though sometimes possible) to apply in an environment where the future is uncertain.[11] It is argued that, in a world of certainty, a firm can only become better off by moving forward in time. If the firm's internal rate of return exceeds its subjective rate of interest, as it moves forward in time the present value of the future net cash flow increases. This increase is a function of the subjective rate of interest.

Case One: Single Venture, ex ante Certainty

Let us now compute economic income in a concrete example, a firm with but one venture. Suppose I start a firm and invest no capital in it. I do nothing for two periods. Shortly after the start of the third period, I invest $1,000 in the firm and buy some land for $1,000. Shortly after the start of the fourth period I sell the land for $2,000 and immediately withdraw the money from the firm. At the end of the fourth period I liquidate the firm. My subjective interest rate during the four periods is 5 percent per annum.

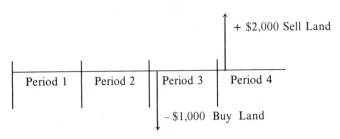

Case One: Cash Flow from Operations

At the end of the fourth period I wish to prepare a set of periodic income statements to describe the economic history of the firm. From this certain net cash flow I can compute the economic income for each period as follows:

---

[9] *Ibid*, p. 149.

[10] *Ibid*, p. 142.

[11] See for example, Solomons, *op. cit*, p. 378.

Period	Present value of the cash flow at the beginning of the period discounted at 5%	Net cash flow occurring during the period	Income for the period
(t)	(P_t)	(CF_t)	$P_{t+1} - P_t + CF_t$
Instantaneous profit recognized at the inception of the firm			$821
Period 1	$821		$41
Period 2	$862		$42
Period 3	$904	−$1,000	$96
Period 4	$2,000	+$2,000	$0
Total lifetime entity profit			$1,000

Table 1   Calculation of Periodic Income Using the Economic Income Method

Opinion in accounting literature is divided as to whether instantaneous gain (such as the $821 in the above example) is income or merely the discovery of capital.[12] In this paper we will use Alexander's approach and treat instantaneous gain as a part of lifetime entity income.[13] Under this formulation, lifetime entity income equals lifetime entity net cash flow. Lifetime entity income can be divided into capital gain (instantaneous gain) and capital interest components. In the example above, the firm had a capital gain of $821 at the beginning of the first period. The firm earned $41 capital interest in the first period, $42 capital interest in the second period, etc.

Let us now consider additional information concerning the land venture which, although not necessary to calculate economic income (in fact ignored under the economic income method), may give us insight into evaluating the validity of the economic income method. Suppose the land purchase in period 3 was from a seller who had imperfect information concerning the market. The land was purchased for $1,000 when its 'market value' was $1,500. Suppose that in period 4, when I sold the land, I again found someone with imperfect market information who purchased the land for $2,000 when its 'market value' was $1,500.

From this information we can conclude that 1. there was a strong causal relationship between the firm's net cash flow and the bargain purchase and sale of land, and 2. there was a very weak relationship between the firm's net

---

[12] Alexander (*op. cit*, p. 130) considers instantaneous gain to be part of the lifetime income of the firm. Robert K. Jaedicke and Robert T. Sprouse (*Accounting Flows: Income, Funds and Cash*, Prentice-Hall, Inc. 1966, p. 22) and Maurice Moonitz and L. H. Jordan (*Accounting: An Analysis of Its Problems*, vol. 1, revised ed, Holt, Rinehart and Winston, 1963, p. 134) on the other hand exclude such instantaneous gain from the lifetime income of the firm under their interpretation of the economic income method.

[13] Alexander, *loc. cit.*

:ash flow and the activities occurring in periods 1 and 2. With this data we :an impute 100 percent of the lifetime monetary profit to periods 3 and 4 'say 50 percent to period 3 and 50 percent to period 4). Such an imputed income reflects how much better off the firm is for having performed the activities which are temporally associated with the period.[14] Let us now compare the two periodic income allocations (economic income and 'imputed' income). (See Table 2.) The reader is asked to decide which allocation method gives the most reasonable economic history of the firm. If one is concerned with trends in profitability or with the relative performance of the firm in periods 3 and 4 as opposed to periods 1 and 2, imputed income seems to be the more valid measurement.

Why does the economic income method give such a distorted picture of the firm's activities?

1. All economic events relating to the firm are ignored except the timing and amount of net cash flow and the subjective interest rate. Thus, the income of the period does not reflect such important events as advantageous sales and purchases.

Period	Economic income	'Imputed' income
Captial gains recognized at the beginning of period 1	$821	0
Period 1	$41	0
Period 2	$42	0
Period 3	$96	$500
Period 4	0	$500
Total lifetime income	$1,000	$1,000

Table 2   **Comparison of Periodic Income Figures under Economic Income and 'Imputed' Income Calculations**

Such omissions result in patterns of periodic income allocations which distort the firm's economic history. Under the economic income method, over 85 percent of the lifetime profit of the firm is allocated to the first accounting period (capital gains of $821 and capital interest of the first period of $41). Yet, insignificant contribution to the lifetime profit of the firm occurred in this period. Only 10 percent of the total profit is allocated to period 3, and only 0 percent of the total profit is allocated to period 4. Yet, in these periods the most significant profit-producing events took place; in these periods the lifetime monetary income of $1,000 was actually earned by the firm.

---

[14] This definition of imputed income is similar to Alexander's definition of activity profit. Activity profit reflects 'how much better off is the corporation for having performed certain activities which are somehow associated with the period.' (Alexander, *op. cit*, p. 173)

2. A large portion of the lifetime income of the firm is allocated to th⬤ point in time when the firm obtained the information about the futu⬤ profitable operations (82 percent of the venture income is allocated to th⬤ inception of the firm when the knowledge concerning the future profitabl⬤ operations was assumed to occur). The timing of the income realized und⬤ the economic income method describes the timing of our knowledge con⬤ cerning future economic events; it does not describe the timing of the occur⬤ rence of the economic events.

3. The reported profitability of the firm is a function of the subjectiv⬤ interest rate rather than of the internal rate of return. Changes in the interna⬤ rate of return are suppressed.[15] In the land venture the internal rate of retur⬤ jumped from 0 percent to approximately 100 percent between period 2 an⬤ period 3. This change was not recognized under the economic incom⬤ method.

Case Two: A Firm With a Long Life, ex ante Certainty

Our previous example concerned a firm with a short life. Let us now conside⬤ a firm with a very long life. Only a limited class of such firms has a measur⬤ able economic income. More specifically, as the life of the firm approache⬤ infinity, only firms with a growth rate of capital lower than the subjectiv⬤ rate of interest have a measurable economic income.

Assume the subjective rate of interest, I, and the internal rate of return, R, are constant in all periods. That is, $I_i = I_{i+1} = I$ and $R_i = R_{i+1} = R$ for all i. P_t as before is the present value of the firm at the beginning of period t. The timing and amounts of future cash flows are known with certainty; CF_i is the net cash flow of period i (assumed to occur at the end of the period). C_i is the cost of the net assets invested in the firm at the beginning of period i. Suppose the firm grows or declines (in terms of capital investment) at a constant rate. That is,

$C_{i+1} = C_i(1 + G_i)$ and $G_i = G_{i+1} = G$ for all i.

1. Present value of CF_i evaluated

   at time $i + 1 = C_i(R + 1) - C_i(I + 1) = C_i(R - I)$

---

[15] Here the writer assumes that it is meaningful to talk about changes in the internal rate of return at different points in the firm's history, even when the firm's future is known with certainty. In particular, this assumption is justified when there is independence among the several accounting periods. In the example above, the first two periods are assumed to be independent of periods 3 and 4. The life of the firm could be meaningfully divided into two sections: a quiescent section (periods 1 and 2) where the internal rate of return was zero, and a trading section (periods 3 and 4) where the firm had a positive internal rate of return.

$$. \; P_t = \sum_{i=t}^{\infty} \frac{CF_i}{(1+I)^i} = \sum_{i=t}^{\infty} \frac{C_i(R-I)}{(1+I)^i}$$

$$\text{3. } P_t = (R-I)\left(\frac{C_t}{(1+I)} + \frac{C_{t+1}}{(1+I)^2} \cdots + \frac{C^{\infty}}{(1+I)^{\infty}} \right)$$

$$\text{4. } P_t = (R-I)\left(\frac{C_t}{(1+I)} + \frac{C_t(1+G)}{(1+I)^2} + \frac{C_t(1+G)^2}{(1+I)^3} \cdots + \frac{C_t(1+G)^{\infty}}{(1+I)^{\infty}(1+G)} \right)$$

$$\text{5. } P_t = (R-I)\left(\frac{C_t}{1+I} \right)\left(1 + \left(\frac{1+G}{1+I}\right) + \left(\frac{1+G}{1+I}\right)^2 \cdots + \left(\frac{1+G}{1+I}\right)^{\infty} \right)$$

$$\text{6. } P_t \approx (R-I)\left(\frac{C_t}{1+I} \right)\left(\frac{1}{1 - \frac{(1+G)}{(1+I)}} \right), \text{ if } \frac{(1+G)}{(1+I)} < 1$$

$$\text{no finite answer if } \frac{(1+G)}{(1+I)} > 1$$

Equation 6 converges to a finite answer if, and only if, the growth rate is strictly lower than the investor's subjective rate of interest. If the growth rate is higher than the subjective rate of interest, we cannot compute economic income. Economic income depends upon a comparison of beginning and ending present values. This comparison is impossible if these present values are not finite.

We rarely expect the subjective rate of interest greatly to exceed the market interest rate (M). If an entity's subjective interest rate exceeds the market rate, it should borrow until its time preference for cash approaches the market rate. (Some small difference, D, between the market rate and the entity's time preference for cash can be maintained by the firm's being a poor credit risk, being averse to risk, etc.) The entity's subjective rate of interest for riskless projects should probably not greatly exceed say 7 percent. Moreover, G must be at least zero for the firm to have a long life. Thus, there is a very restrictive set of going concerns which have measurable economic income. More specifically, only those long lived firms whose growth rate falls within the range:

$$0 \leq G \leq I = M + D$$

have a measurable economic income.

One of the difficulties in applying economic income to a going conceri results from the extremely liberal realization criteria. The present value o net cash flows resulting from projects started 25, 50 or 75 years in the future are capitalized (and are in this sense realized), even though the interdependence of these projects with the economic Gestalt of the current period is, a best, highly tenuous, and, more likely, is negligible.

Case Three: Zero Subjective Interest Rate, ex ante Certainty

Previously we assumed that the entity had a strictly positive subjective interest rate. However, it is possible for the entity to have a zero subjective interest rate. Consider an economy where the price level is falling and the real level of interest rates (adjusted for general price level changes) exactly offsets the price fall. The aggregate interest rate for the investors in the economy would, under these conditions, be zero. Suppose the opportunities available to the entity for investing capital were either to invest in the firm at an incremental rate of return of 0 percent, or to lend the money at a zero interest rate. Moreover, suppose the time preference for consumer goods by the owners of the entity was equal to the real level of interest rates. It is apparent that the appropriate subjective rate of interest for the entity is zero.

If the firm has an indefinite life, it has a measurable economic income only if it maintains approximately a constant level of capital investment. Consistent with the reasoning of the last section ($0 \leq G \leq I = 0$), the growth rate must be zero.

If the firm has a limited life and a zero subjective rate of interest, the economic income for all accounting periods, except the first period, is zero. All income is recognized as instantaneous gain at the firm's inception. That is, the present value of the total cash flow over the life of the entity does not change as the firm moves forward in time. Suppose, however, that this firm was profitable as determined by conventional accounting measurement rules (the internal rate of return was positive).[16] Clearly the continued operation of the firm is improving the shareholder's 'well-offness'—the internal rate of return is higher than the shareholder's subjective interest rate. Yet none of this increase in 'well-offness' is recognized as the firm moves forward in time.

The above example vividly illustrates the peculiar way in which those who employ economic income attribute income to accounting periods. As indicated earlier, economic income is recognized when cash flows are discovered rather than when they are created. Thus if I know with certainty that in ten years I will write a best-selling novel, receiving in the tenth year $50,000 in

---

[16] The firm could have a positive internal rate of return and a zero time preference for cash if, say, the average internal rate of return was positive, and the marginal internal rate of return was zero.

royalties, and if I have a very low subjective rate of interest (say 0 percent), under the economic income method I would assign all income to the year in which I became aware I would write the novel, assigning no income to the year in which I actually did the work. That is, I impute greater importance to my knowledge that I will write the novel than to my actual labour in creating the book. Economic income describes the timing of our information about future events, rather than the timing of the economic events themselves, as we have already said.

Case Four: ex post Certainty

In our previous discussion we considered certainty in an ex ante sense—the timing and amounts of the firm's lifetime cash flow was known with certainty before the cash flow occurred. It is interesting to look at certainty in an ex post sense—the timing and amount of the firm's lifetime cash flow are known with certainty, but after the cash flow occurs. Ex post certainty of cash flow is approximated in some accounting measurements. For example, the lifetime cash flow from operations of a firm with complete records is known with certainty at the time of the firm's liquidation.

Under ex ante certainty there is some balance sheet justification for capitalizing the present value of cash flows known with certainty to occur in the future. Having complete confidence that the cash flows will occur increases the investor's psychological satisfaction. This information also has economic benefits. The firm could be sold to another investor with an equal or lower time preference for cash for at least the discounted present value. We have merely attempted to argue that realizing income on this basis leads to unreasonable results in the income statement.

Under retrospective certainty of cash flows, however, even the balance sheet argument fails. Consider the land venture discussed in Case 1, dropping the assumption of ex ante certainty. Suppose the accountant at the end of period 4, after the liquidation of the firm, wished to reconstruct the firm's economic history. He knows the cash flow from operations and the subjective rate of interest with certainty. Under what justification can he capitalize the present value (as of the beginning of period 1) of the cash flows from periods 1 to 4? Even the 'well-offness' definition of Hicks will not support this balance sheet valuation. The investor derived no economic or psychological benefit from the firm until the land was purchased. He could not hypothecate the future earnings of the firm, since neither he nor the prospective purchaser could know at the beginning of period 1 whether the timing and amount of cash flow from operations would be favourable.

But what is the relevant difference between ex ante and ex post certainty? It is not the accountant's measurement problem; the accountant can assign magnitudes to ex ante and ex post cash flows with equal reliability if they are both known with certainty. The difference occurs in the value of the cash flow to the investor. Because the investor cannot, in general, know future cash flows with certainty, he cannot derive economic benefits from the knowledge of these cash flows until they occur (or until their occurrence can be predicted with a sufficiently high a priori probability). However, many accountants only cite the measurement problem when discussing the difficulties of economic income.[17]

Case Five: Partial ex ante Certainty

We have assumed so far that the future timing and amount of cash flow are either known with complete certainty or with complete uncertainty. Now we will examine economic income when the firm's ex ante knowledge concerning future cash flows is between these two extremes.

In the typical situation, the firm has high prior probabilities concerning some cash flows, and low prior probabilities concerning other future cash flows. For example, the firm has a high a priori confidence that the cash inflow from interest on United States Government Bonds will be of a certain amount at a certain time. There is comparatively higher uncertainty concerning the timing and amount of cash realized from a more speculative project such as the introduction of a new product. At least two factors influence the firm's ability to predict the future: 1. the mix of projects in the firm's investment portfolio (for example, the comparative amount of speculative projects and projects whose outcomes can be easily predicted), and 2. the amount of effort the firm invests in gathering information for predicting the future. One would expect that these factors would change over time, and that such changes would materially affect the firm's ability to predict the future.

We will approximate the above situation by assuming that a firm knows some future events (the cash flows of periods $t, t+1, t+2, \ldots, t+x$) with certainty, and is completely uncertain about other future events (the cash flows of periods $t+x+1, t+x+2, \ldots, N$). We will further assume that x, the number of future periods into which the firm can forecast with certainty the timing and amounts of net cash flow, changes over time. This approximates the typical situation of the firm; there is a mix of certainty and uncertainty about the future, and this mix changes over time. Assume that the firm has a constant net cash flow from operations every year of $1,000, which it promptly distributes to its shareholders. The firm maintains a constant monetary level of owner's equity. Suppose x took on the following values for the first five periods of the firm's life:

---

[17] See for example, Jaedicke and Sprouse, *op. cit*, p. 26, and Edward G. Philips, "The Accretion Concept of Income," *The Accounting Review*, January 1963, p. 17.

At beginning of period	x (Number of periods in the future where net cash flows can be predicted with certainty) equals
1	1
2	2
3	3
4	3
5	2
6	3

Table 3   Ability of the Firm to Forecast Future Cash Flows

At a 5 percent subjective interest rate, the capitalization under the economic income method at the beginning of each period would be as follows:

Period	x	Present value at Beginning of Period
1	1	$1000(105)^{-1}$ $= \$\ 952$
2	2	$1000(105)^{-1} + 1000(105)^{-2}$ $= \$1,859$
3	3	$1000(105)^{-1} + 1000(105)^{-2} + 1000(105)^{-3} = \$2,723$
4	3	$1000(105)^{-1} + 1000(105)^{-2} + 1000(105)^{-3} = \$2,723$
5	2	$1000(105)^{-1} + 1000(105)^{-2}$ $= \$1,859$
6	3	$1000(105)^{-1} + 1000(105)^{-2} + 1000(105)^{-3} = \$2,723$

Table 4 Calculation of Present Values

The economic income of the firm could then be easily calculated:

Period (i)	Present value at the beginning of the period (P_i)	Present value at the end of the period (P_{i+1})	Net cash flow during the period (CF_i)	Economic Income $(P_{i+1} - P_i + CF_i)$
Beginning of period 1	$\ \ \ 0	$\ \ 952	$\ \ \ 0	$\ \ 952
1	$\ \ 952	$1,859	$1,000	$1,907
2	$1,859	$2,723	$1,000	$1,864
3	$2,723	$2,723	$1,000	$1,000
4	$2,723	$1,859	$1,000	$\ \ 136
5	$1,859	$2,723	$1,000	$1,864

Table 5   Calculation of Economic Income

Notice the wide fluctuations in economic income. Such volatility does not seem consistent with the firm's constant annual net cash flow and constant internal rate of return.

This example illustrates an earlier point. Economic income describes the timing of changes in the firm's information (and therefore expectations) concerning the future. It does not describe the timing of changes in the firm's profitability (i.e. changes in the firm's internal rate of return). Fluctuations in reported periodic income were entirely due to the firm's varying ability to predict the future.

Although Solomons recognized this problem, he felt Alexander's concept of variable income could explain the effect of changes in expectations on economic income measurements.[18] Variable income was defined as 'equal to the net receipts from the security plus or minus any change in its value which was, *at the beginning of the period*, expected to take place during the period.'[19] Thus:

$$\text{economic income} = \text{variable income} = \text{unexpected gains.}[20]$$

Some of the spurious variability in economic income created by changing expectations in an uncertain world would be explained by dividing economic income into variable income and unexpected gains. This dichotomy, however, does not completely solve the problem:

1. All variability in income caused by changing expectations is not factored out of variable income into unexpected gain. For example, Solomons states, 'We must include in variable income any change in the value of the enterprise which is the result of managerial activity during the year.'[21] In the above example, x could well be a function of managerial activity (the selection of the asset portfolio or the determination of the extent of market research undertaken by the firm). If x is entirely determined by managerial policy, variable income equals economic income.

2. Although this paper is a critique of economic income as a theoretical concept, it is appropriate to note that variable income is even less operational than economic income. With economic income you merely have to predict future cash flows. With variable income you have to segregate cash flows into cash resulting from good luck and cash resulting from good judgment.[22]

Although ex ante certainty is never realized in actual measurement situations, some accountants have suggested that we try to estimate economic income as closely as possible with the information we have available. It is often pointed out that some cash flows (i.e. interest from United States Bonds) can be estimated with such confidence that, for all practical theoretical purposes, we can consider them to be known with certainty. Yet, note that in the above example we did know some events with certainty. To avoid having economic income confounded by changes in expectations we must

---

[18] Solomons, *op. cit*, p. 379. The interpretation of variable income used in this paper is Alexander's concept as modified by Solomons in Alexander, *op. cit*, and Solomons, *op. cit*.

[19] Solomons, *op. cit*, p. 380.

[20] *Ibid*, p. 381.

[21] *Loc. cit.*

[22] This point was made in *ibid*, pp. 382–383.

know all future events with certainty. We cannot relax even slightly the assumption of certainty and still have a meaningful economic income calculation.

Conclusions

The five cases have brought out some of the weaknesses of economic income:

1. All of the firm's important economic events except cash flows and rates of subjective interest are ignored in the income allocation process.[23] Economic income ignores, for example, changes in the input values of assets, changes in the liquidity composition of assets (unless a liquidity change affects the cash account) and changes in the state of production or distribution of the firm's inventories. In Case 1 we observed that the two most significant events in the firm's economic history, the bargain purchase and resale of land, were completely ignored when allocating lifetime income to accounting periods. In effect, economic income is a glorified form of cash accounting. True, economic income recognizes expected cash flows where cash accounting recognizes only past cash flows. Economic income discounts expected cash flows by the subjective interest rate, a refinement absent from (and not needed in) cash accounting. However, both cash accounting and economic income are similar in their use of cash flows as the income realization mechanism.

2. There is too much emphasis on the future. Periodic income measurements should reflect the results of economic activities which are temporally related to accounting periods. To evaluate these results, some estimates of the future are necessary, since the economic events of the firm's several accounting periods are interdependent. It should be sufficient to estimate only as far in the future, as is needed to trace all material interdependencies between the past and the future. For example, in estimating the depreciation expense relating to an asset, one need only look far enough into the future to estimate the pattern of service value decay of the asset. However, under the economic income method, theoretically one attempts to estimate, and recognize as income, cash flows far in the future, which may or may not have any interdependence with events which occurred in the current or past periods. In the "extreme" case of the going concern, cash flows indefinitely far into the future are capitalized. Such a realization rule is of doubtful validity.

3. Economic income describes the firm's predictions of its future. It does not describe the firm's past and current success in dealing with its economic environment. In the extreme example of Case 3, all the income from writing a book was allocated to the period when the author first learned that he was going to write the book. None of the income from the book was assigned to the period where the book was actually written. Trends in income should

---

[23] A similar point in another context has been made by William Vatter, "Income Models, Bond Yield and the Rate of Return," *The Accounting Review*, October 1966, pp. 684–5.

reflect trends in the firm's profitability. Under the economic income method, trends in periodic income may well be caused by changes in the firm's predictive ability. This weakness is illustrated in Case 5 where the firm had a constant return on investment yet had a highly volatile periodic income. All of this volatility was caused by the varying ability of the firm to predict the future.

4. Profit trends are distorted, because the capital interest segment of economic income is tied to the subjective interest rate, rather than the internal rate of return. In Case 1 the internal rate of return of the firm jumped from 0 percent to approximately 100 percent between period 2 and period 3. This dramatic jump in profitability was not shown in the reported periodic income figures developed under the economic income method.

5. The certainty assumption is both a practical and theoretical limitation of the economic income method. Our discussion of Case 4 (retrospective certainty) showed that capitalizing the present values of the highly uncertain future cash flows is not only a practical measurement problem, but is also a distortion of the economic reality faced by the relevant decision maker. In Case 5 (variable expectations concerning the future) a slight relaxation of the certainty assumption resulted in changes in the firm's ability to predict the future and introduced a spurious volatility into the trend of periodic income figures.

The above-mentioned problems are not specific to the five cases; they occur in virtually all environments where accounting measurements take place.

It is this paper's hypothesis that economic income is not a useful model of the accounting income measurement process. The limitations described above lend support to this hypothesis. This is not to say that accountants know more about 'income' than economists, but rather that accountants and economists analyse economic phenomena from different viewpoints. Economists wish to describe how scarce resources are allocated, and, since expectations concerning the future determine this, economists are directly concerned with such expectations. Financial accountants are concerned with describing the firm's past economic history. Hence, they report the current effects of past decisions rather than describing the current expectations of decision makers.[24] The past, then, which is irrelevant to the economist (except as past experience changes expectations concerning the future), is relevant to the financial accountant. The future, which is irrelevant to the financial accountant (except as the past and future are interdependent . . . for example, a long lived asset whose service life straddles the past and future) is relevant to the economist. The accountant in drawing upon the methodology and wisdom of the economist must ensure that the subtle differences between economics and accounting are not obscured by superficial similarities between the two disciplines.

---

[24] This point was cogently made in Goldberg, *op. cit*, pp. 251–252.

*Matthews J. Stephens is Associate Professor of
Accounting and Vice Dean of Wharton
Undergraduate Division at the Wharton
School, University of Pennsylvania.*

Opening Pandora's Box
of Current Cost

Matthews J. Stephens

In 1929, H. C. Daines commented that: "Within the past few years, considerable discussion has arisen among accountants concerning such questions as the proper basis or bases for valuing balance sheet items, what constitutes income, what are proper elements to be included in costs. . . . "[1]

Daines provided a rationale and methodology for current costing similar to that advanced by Edwards and Bell,[2] even including a measurement of holding gains and losses.[3] Since Daines wrote some thirty-five years ago, something other than a pedantic stand on realization and objectivity seems to lie behind the unwillingness of accountants to abandon historical cost. Perhaps it is the fear of opening a Pandora's box. According to legend, once the original Pandora's box was opened, either all the blessings of the gods, except for hope, escaped, or all the evils of man were set loose to plague him. If the accounting box of current cost is opened, hope for better things may still remain, but the evils of confusion and misinterpretation now existent will, in many cases, be increased. The purpose of this article is to highlight some shortcomings of current cost measurements.

Unwise dilution and modification of certain generally accepted concepts

---

[1] H.C. Daines, "The Changing Objectives of Accounting," *The Accounting Review* (June, 1929), p. 94.

[2] Edgar O. Edwards and Philip W. Bell, *The Theory and Measurement of Business Income* (Berkeley: University of California Press, 1961). This book discusses possible valuations to be employed in accounting statements and concludes in favor of current cost measurements.

[3] While Daines did not specifically name these items, his discussion on page 100 leaves no doubt that he had the concept in mind. See also, Fritz Schmidt, "Is Appreciation Profit," *The Accounting Review* (December, 1931), p. 291.

Reprinted by permission of the author and publisher from *Financial Executive*, Vol. XXXV (May, 1967), pp. 56–66.

such as going concern, realization, and objectivity, which would be required to support current costing, might serve as a defense against its adoption. Such a defense, however, would raise the question of how necessary such concepts are when compared with the supposed utility of current cost to statement readers. It is the *utility* of current cost which will be examined here. Furthermore, arguments to be made will pertain to general-purpose external financial statements since it is doubtful if anyone denies that current cost estimates along with many other cost measurements are both useful and used for internal management purposes.

A primary aim of published financial statements is to report on steward-ship; i.e., income earned through the use of available resources. In addition, however, these statements are used as aids in estimating the future course of the firm. The Accounting Principles Board of the American Institute of Certified Public Accountants, in its pronouncements on such diverse items as income statement format and deferred taxes, clearly indicates its awareness that statement readers use the financial statements as a basis for prediction. The Board feels that accountants should avoid presentations that might foster incorrect inferences about future events.[4] Any proposal for accounting reform, such as current cost reporting, should meet this standard.

This writer contends that external financial statements should be directed primarily toward the needs of present and potential investors. Other parties interested in published statements (government, large customers or credi-tors, labor unions) usually need to rely on them only for initial approxima-tions since these parties can secure more detailed information as required. If this view is correct, it is pertinent to ask wherein lies the increased utility to investors of current cost over historical cost information? Edwards and Bell spell out three broad advantages of current cost information: (1) recognition of gains from holding assets as these gains accrue, (2) separation of operat-ing and holding gains, and (3) improved balance-sheet valuations. All of these advantages will supposedly lead to a better measurement of managerial efficiency.[5]

Gains from Holding Assets

Recognition on financial statements of unrealized gains as they accrue ap-parently cannot be a major argument for the replacement of historical with current costing. Until recently, the reporting of appraisal data was consistent with generally accepted accounting principles, even though asset increments

---

[4] See *Accounting Research and Terminology Bulletins* (New York: American Institute of Certi-fied Public Accountants, Final Edition, 1961), *Accounting Research Bulletin No. 43*, p. 62.

[5] Edwards and Bell, *op. cit.*, pp. 222–227. The terms "holding gains and losses" seems to have been adopted by most writers in this area, although Edwards and Bell use the terms "cost savings and dissavings" (p. 93). Holding gains will be used in this paper even though the savings term seems better. If the assets are sold, these gains may not be realizable when the markets in which the firm buys and sells differ or removal costs are significant.

had to be treated as unrealized.[6] Tables 1 and 2, however, show how rarely appraisals are recorded. The fact that appraisals are time consuming and costly might be advanced as the reason for this, but if the information were vital, the appraisals could be made less frequently than annually.[7] Further, it might be mentioned that some companies in the tables which have reported appraised or revised values did so, not because of advancing prices, but because it was necessary to establish an initial valuation ("cost") basis.

Separation of Operating and Holding Elements

Financial statements in current use already include a partial report on holding operations. Gains and losses on the sale of marketable securities are reported separately from operating profit. Market value, noted parenthetically on the balance sheet, can be compared readily to cost in order to determine unrealized gains and losses. Such assets are bought for holding, and gains or losses on them are not entered as elements of operating income. This partial reporting is not satisfactory to advocates of current costing. Apparently they feel that if sales revenue is matched with the current cost of the assets used in obtaining the revenue, the production plan as well as the managerial efficiency demonstrated in the operation of this plan can be evaluated. Moreover, the reflection of the difference between the historical and current measurements of the costs of assets and between the current and

Table 1   Valuation Bases of Fixed Assets for 600 Companies

Basis of Valuation	1965	1960	1955	1950
Cost (historical)	545	515	457	396
Cost plus appraised values	3	10	11	22
Appraised values with subsequent additions at cost	1	5	13	24
Revised values with subsequent additions at cost	0	2	2	5
Reproduction values with subsequent additions at cost	0	1	4	2
Other catagories not indicating appraisal data	29	29	60	86
Total number of companies starting a valuation basis	578	562	547	535
Total number not starting a valuation basis	22	38	53	65
Total number of companies	600	600	600	600

Source: Adapted from "Table 17: Property, Plant and Equipment" on page 74 of *Accounting Trends and Techniques*, 1966 edition, American Institute of Certified Public Accountants.

---

[6] *Opinion No. 6* of the Accounting Principles Board of the AICPA indicates that upward appraisals may no longer be generally accepted, but this should not affect the arguments presented here.

[7] While periodic appraisals would not provide information for the strict reporting of gains as they accrue, they would overcome the major objection that these gains are never reported as long as the assets are held.

historical yield to creditors will indicate managerial efficiency demonstrated in holding operations.[8] The total of operating and holding incomes will be equal to presently reported accounting income provided realization of holding elements is postponed until assets are sold or used.[9] The breakdown of net income into operating and holding components, however, depends upon the definition of current cost and how it is measured. The current cost of an asset may be defined as the outlay necessary to acquire the asset presently. The current cost of a creditor equity may be defined in terms of the yield that investors are presently demanding on these instruments in the market. These definitions appear to be straightforward, but many questions arise concerning them. Questions associated with the definition and selection of the appropriate current cost probably account for the reluctance of accountants to adopt current costing. Certain of these questions will be examined, not for the purpose of giving definitive answers, but rather for the purpose of demonstrating that an evaluation of management based upon current cost statements is as dubious as one based upon historical cost statements.

Table 2	Number of Companies from a Total of 600 which Reflect Property Reserves Related to Revaluations of Property				
Category of Reserve		1965	1960	1955	1950
Within stockholders' equity for—					
1. Revaluation of property		1	2	2	4
2. Higher replacement costs		0	4	6	13
Above stockholders' equity section for higher plant replacement costs		0	1	3	9
With related fixed assets for revaluation of property		4	6	2	7

Source: Adapted from "Table 37: Property Reserves" on page 135 of *Accounting Trends and Techniques*, 1966 edition, American Institute of Certified Public Accountants.

Valuation of Service Potential

In order to illustrate the idea of service potential, consider the difficulties involved in the definition of the current cost of a productive asset such as a machine. A machine has value because it provides services to the entity. The services which the machine renders, however, might be provided by more labor and less or no machine services. Alternatively, the services might be

---

[8] Edwards and Bell, *loc. cit.*, pp. 222–227.

[9] If current cost measurement is accurate, there does not appear to be any pressing reason for not abandoning realization altogether. Holding gains or losses to be realized in later periods could be reported separately, however, for purposes of tying in supplementary current cost statements with statements based on historical cost. See opinions of Sidney Davidson and Jack Gray as cited in "AAA Committee Report: The Realization Concept," *The Accounting Review* (April, 1965), p. 322. Also Henry Sweeney, "Income," *The Accounting Review* (December, 1933), p. 535.

provided by another type of machine and more or less labor. The various combinations of agents which can provide service equivalent to that rendered by the machine are probably numerous. What, then, should the financial statement measure, the machine itself, the services represented by the machine,[10] or the cheapest source of equivalent service potential? Professor Canning advocated the latter.[11] Moreover, he felt that the valuation of service potential should be limited to that necessary to meet the prospective requirements of the firm, not necessarily the maximum which the machine can render.[12] Regardless of the current cost of the machine, it is worth no more than the cost of the cheapest source of equivalent service or net realizable value, whichever is greater. Canning's assessment has logical appeal, and conceptually would appear to be the ideal value of the machine for statement purposes.

The valuation of service potential thus requires forecasts of—

1. the output required to meet future demand,
2. the costs of agents used jointly with the machine to produce the prospective output, and
3. the costs of various combinations of other agents which can produce a given output.

The streams of costs would have to be discounted to present worth, and the difference between the stream from (3) having the least present worth and the present worth of stream (2) would be the present worth of the service provided by the machine.[13] A continuous appraisal of equivalent sources of service must be made by internal management in order to maintain efficient productive processes. Investors would also like this information in order to appraise managerial efficiency. However, in the judgment of the author, the subjective estimations required for the forecasts of costs and the determination of appropriate discount rates preclude the adoption of such a valuation scheme for published financial statements. Canning dismissed the idea because of the difficulties associated with the substitution of one process for another. He concluded that the actual cost of services embodied in a given asset is usually more appropriate than any other value.[14]

---

[10] This seems to be the position of the Committee on Accounting Theory of the American Accounting Association, but for purposes of implementing current cost data, the current replacement cost of specific assets is recommended. See *A Statement of Basic Accounting Theory* (Chicago: American Accounting Association, 1966), p. 31, and Charles T. Zlatkovich, "A New Accounting Theory Statement," *The Journal of Accountancy* (August, 1966), p. 34.

[11] John B. Canning, *The Economics of Accountancy* (New York: The Ronald Press Company, 1929), p. 188.

[12] *Ibid.*, p. 243.

[13] I am ignoring the joint cost (valuation) problem which results when more than one fixed factor is used in the production of any given output. I am also assuming that revenue is sufficient to cover cost.

[14] Canning, *op. cit.*, p. 244.

Specific Assets and Equities

Most expositions on current cost do not focus on the cost of equivalent service potential, but rather on the cost of specific assets held by the firm. This may be because the current cost of specific assets is more easily measured than equivalent service. Measurement problems associated with the current cost of specific assets will be discussed below; but, even if measurement problems are solved, definitional problems will still remain. For example, is the current cost of work-in-process or finished goods the current cost of inputs used to make these goods, or is it the cost for which these goods could be purchased elsewhere? In order for management to appraise its productive processes and for the investor to appraise managerial operations, both valuations would be required. The reporting problems for a firm employing a multi-stage productive process which yields intermediate goods that could be sold but which the firm uses in further production would be complicated in the extreme.

Even if one agrees with Edwards and Bell that the current cost of inputs used in production is the proper measure of the present productive process,[15] the current cost of many inputs is open to argument. Practical, as well as theoretical, difficulties arise in the determination of the current cost of services for which the firm has contracted. As an example, consider a company operating in the second year of a three-year labor contract. The current cost of labor inputs would be the cost of labor if a new contract were signed today. Management, however, might be loath to estimate this cost, not only because of the difficulties involved in estimation, but also because of a possible sacrifice of future bargaining position.

Operating and Holding Profits

A similar problem can be examined on the equity side. Is the current rate of cost of a bond outstanding the current yield to maturity, the estimated yield to maturity of a new obligation with the same total life as the original life of the bond outstanding, or the yield of the shortest term obligation that could be issued? Edwards and Bell appear to favor the first, but the second would seem to be appropriate if the corporation normally issues bonds with the same total life and contract features. As will be seen below, a case can be made for the third alternative if the definitions of operating and holding profits are appropriately modified.

Customary Definitions

Current operating profit may be defined in the customary sense as revenue less related expenses measured at current cost at the point of sale. Realized

---
[15] Edwards and Bell, *op. cit.*, p. 91.

holding gains or losses are the difference between the current and historical measurement of the expense.

Total income delineated in this way might be useful as a tentative guide to a new company planning to enter the field or to managements of existing companies when they plan to invest in assets similar to those already held and to finance them in a similar manner.[16] As a basis for evaluating the current performance of management, however, it is largely irrelevant. This is so for a number of reasons.

First, current operating profit is a net figure and thus its use in judging performance is limited. Enough revenue may be produced through excellent marketing ability to more than offset other operating inefficiencies. At the same time, revenue may be increased or decreased in the short run through a price policy that draws down or enhances the intangible asset, goodwill.[17] Examination of operating expenses would not be particularly helpful in spotting inefficiencies because these are net figures in themselves, particularly when the firm is multi-divisional and produces a variety of products.

Second, the current costs of production of a firm using old assets may actually be materially overstated relative to firms with newer assets because methods of estimating the current cost of old assets do not compensate fully for the disadvantage at which such assets stand in relation to newer and more efficient assets. More will be said about this when methods of measuring cost are discussed.

Third, holding gains and losses are often by-products of operating decisions rather than direct results of purposeful acts of management. For example, in the over-all operation of any production process, management certainly tries to anticipate price movements with an eye to advantageous purchase. However, assets such as plant and equipment and raw material often must be bought today even though better prices are foreseen in the future. Business planning cannot simultaneously maximize both operating gains and holding gains because the "stop and go" procedures beneficial for the holding function would be detrimental to the operating function. In any case, without careful explanation, such holding gains and losses looked at by themselves might materially misrepresent management's performance.

Finally, it should be noted that depreciation based on either current or historical cost does not measure the cost that management must recover in order to justify using the asset or holding it for future use or sale. User cost is pertinent in these instances. The calculation of user cost depends upon the subjective capital value of the asset and/or upon the net amount realizable from the sale of the asset. These values should be estimated both currently

---

[16] When one considers the numerous combinations of inputs that can be used to obtain any given output, it should be noted that this measure of operating profit must be used with caution.

[17] See Myron H. Ross, "Depreciation and User Cost," *The Accounting Review* (July, 1960), pp. 426–427.

and one period ahead, assuming the asset will be used and unused.[18] More generally, efficient management will hold an asset whenever the capital value of the asset determined by discounting to the present the expected net cash receipts from use and/or sale at some future date exceeds the greater of—

1. net realizable value from immediate sale of the asset, or
2. the capital value of the best alternative use of the proceeds from immediate sale of the asset.[19]

Subjective capital values will exceed the current cost of a new asset except at the margin. On the other hand, estimates of current cost to replace an owned asset may be less *or more* than the subjective capital value. Current cost may be more because the net realizable value of the owned asset may be so low that the present value of expected cost savings or increased revenues associated with a replacement asset may not exceed the net cost of abandonment and replacement. The net realizable value of an asset may be materially less than the current replacement cost because of market imperfection or large installation and removal costs. Further, methods advocated for the determination of current cost do not fully compensate for technological change.

In summary, current cost implies replacement of assets, services, or processes when in fact replacement may not be intended. The values upon which decisions to hold assets are based almost always will differ from current cost estimates. It is difficult to see, therefore, how holding gains and losses measured by the difference between current and historical cost would indicate the efficacy of management's retention of assets. Indeed, a management that appears to be inefficient based upon current cost statements may actually be operating in a sound manner.[20]

The foregoing considerations are not all-inclusive, but they serve to indicate why an evaluation of management based upon current cost statements may be misleading. In order to demonstrate this in a different way, an alternative definition of operating and holding profit will be presented.

Alternative Definition

Conventional expositions of current cost first define what is meant by current cost and then the holding items are given as the difference between the

---

[18] For a full discussion of user cost, see W. Arthur Lewis, "Depreciation and Obsolescence as Factors in Costing," contained in J. L. Meij (ed.), *Depreciation and Replacement Policy* (Chicago, Quadrangle Books, Inc., 1961), pp. 35–45.

[19] The inter-relationship of cost of capital and investment and dividend decisions is beyond the scope of this paper, but it should be noted that the discount rate used to determine the capital value of the owned asset may differ from the one used to determine the capital value of the alternative investment because of differences in uncertainty and timing of the two receipt streams. Further, if net realizable value from immediate sale of the asset is greater than either of the capital values, a distribution to shareholders seems to be warranted.

[20] A fuller discussion of these and other considerations may be seen in David F. Drake and Nicholas Dopuch, "On the Case for Dichotomizing Income," *Journal of Accounting Research* (Autumn, 1965), pp. 192–205.

current and historical measurement. If one turns the process around and views the holding function first, alternative but nevertheless logical measures can be presented. It is suggested that the pure holding function is often a long-run phenomenon that begins at the end of the planning stage when long-lived assets are acquired and long-term, fixed-return equities are issued. The success of the plan (holding policy) could be assessed by (1) the difference between the actual cost of the assets and the short-term cost of the services provided by the assets, and (2) the difference between the actual yield on long-term equities and the short-term yield. Operating profit, on the other hand, would be measured by matching revenues with the short-term cost of services used.[21]

Operating and holding profits measured in this way may be useful, but they are in a sense arbitrary. Management acquires long-lived assets and issues long-term equities because they are considered preferable to short-lived ones for any number of reasons, not all of which can be evaluated strictly in dollar terms.[22] It would seem to follow, therefore, that operating profit should be measured by matching revenues with the actual planned costs; *but this concept of operating profit is now employed in historical cost income statements.* Operating and holding often is a combined function rather than two distinct functions. Measures which attempt to evaluate them separately must be arbitrary and dependent upon the viewpoint of the person making the evaluation.

In summary, a singular notion of current cost does not exist nor is there a preferable distinction between the operating and holding functions. Even when the results of these functions are measured along the lines suggested by Edwards and Bell, they are still more combined than separate. The operating profit is a one-period estimation of the profit which would have occurred if management had purchased its assets and issued its equities at some date other than when it did. Holding items are the positive or negative differentials which result from the timing of asset acquisition or equity issuance. Such hypothetical figures might be useful in a world of what might have been, but their use as measurements of the results of a particular entity's operation is severely limited.

Measurement of Current Cost of Specific Tangible Assets

If perfect markets existed for all or most of the assets held by firms, a

---

[21] There are many combinations of assets and equities which a firm can employ. Measurement of operating profit should be based upon the least cost method of producing and financing, and the result of the holding policy should be measured by the difference between the least cost alternative and the historical cost of methods employed. Such a scheme would involve the concept of equivalent service potential which was dismissed earlier. For purposes of positing a meaningful holding measure alternative to that set forth by Edwards and Bell, the short- and long-term dichotomy seems reasonable.

[22] The analysis of risk and uncertainty along utility lines as is often suggested in expositions on capital budgeting would seem to be pertinent here.

determination of current cost might be feasible. That markets for fixed assets—the category of assets which causes the most concern when prices are changing—are not perfect is generally known. The difference between the net realizable value and the current cost to replace is likely to be significant. A determination of market values in such a situation would be almost impossible to verify in any meaningful sense since the accountant would be at a loss to certify that any price quotation was authentic, firm, and the best obtainable. It is small wonder, therefore, that current cost advocates rarely rely on market price quotations, but rather emphasize appraisals or specific index number adjustments of historical cost.

Appraisals fell into disrepute in the 20's and 30's because of the infinite variety of opinions, techniques, and results which depended upon the appraiser and the purposes of the appraisal. Nothing has been noted which has changed basically the nature of appraisals, and the problem of verification of appraisal facts remains.[23]

Index-number adjustment of historical costs presents many problems, but a determination of current costs by this method seems to be suggested more frequently than either of the other methods. Ease, less expense, and the supposed objectivity of an index number probably account for this preference.[24] However, the question of which index to use becomes important. Generally speaking, a specific index would be appropriate, but just how "specific" is debatable. Yet, the current cost of an asset can vary substantially depending upon the choice of the index. For example, the machinery and automotive products section of the wholesale price index stood at 153.1 (1947–49=100) in December, 1961, but the sub-sections of this index ranged from 182.3 for metal working machinery to 140.7 for motor vehicles.[25]

The most pertinent objection to index number adjustment of accounting statements arises from the fact that there is no general agreement on how to handle implicit quality improvements that stem from technological change. If improved design and methods of manufacture, as examples, do not involve cost increases, they are generally overlooked in the price index. These improvements, however, can lead to greatly reduced costs to users of the assets. A recent study by Deere and Company shows that tractor prices advanced 29

[23] See George O. May, *Financial Accounting* (New York: The Macmillan Co., 1943), pp. 92–95; Homer Kripke, "Accountant's Financial Statements and Fact-Finding in the Law of Corporations," *The Journal of Accountancy* (September, 1941), pp. 206–207; "Dispraise of Appreciation," *The Accounting Review* (December, 1931), pp. 305–306; comments by Carman G. Blough and William W. Werntz in Robert T. Sprouse and Maurice Moonitz, *A Tentative Set of Broad Accounting Principles for Business Enterprise* (New York: American Institute of Certified Public Accountants), 1962, pp. 62 and 80–81 respectively.

[24] Edwards and Bell, *op. cit.*, p. 284; Fred J. Sengstacke, "The Depreciation Dilemma Has More Than Two Horns," *N.A.A. Bulletin* (February, 1959—Section 1), p. 19.

[25] *Federal Reserve Bulletin* (February, 1962), pp. 225–227. The index for 1961 is used to emphasize the range of difference. This range is disguised in recent indices because of the shift in base from 1947–49 = 100 to 1957–59 = 100.

percent, but various measures of cost/output relationships of tractor use (such as cost per pound of shipping weight and cost per maximum drawbar horsepower) declined 31 to 59 percent.[26] Another study by the National Bureau of Economic Research reported that about three fourths of the rise in automobile prices reflected in the Consumers' Price Index since 1937 might be attributable to quality improvements.[27] Objections may be raised that these are specific examples and specific conclusions of certain individuals rather than general observations. Such objections merely beg the question, however, since the quality differentials cited are equally pertinent to other goods.[28]

Some authorities on index numbers seem to be against attempting to measure implicit quality changes because recognition of such changes would imply that the price rise of the past is overstated and output measures understated. Such an implication would inhibit attempts to correct inflation. For example, one authority, Mr. Milton Gilbert of the Bank for International Settlement, is concerned particularly with economic welfare as a measurable idea. He seems to feel that the measurable quantum is goods, not the character of or the satisfaction yielded by goods.[29] He says, for example:

"Simultaneously, the car may be improved in quality in ways that do not involve the producer in higher costs. The motor or moving parts may be better designed, the body made more comfortable, or technical improvements in steel making may have provided a more durable basic material. Such cost-free changes must be left out of account for the measurement of both the change in output and the change in prices."[30]

No attempt is made here to argue that inflation has not taken place, or that steps should not be taken to correct inflation, or even that index numbers may not be useful as general approximations of price changes. Possibly Mr. Gilbert's contentions are correct when price indices are used to measure changes in output. What is being argued, however, is that unless implicit quality changes are built into index numbers, adjustments of historical cost are unsuitable for accounting statements and can only lead to confusing and misleading results.

Current cost estimates are to be used for the measurement of operating

---

[26] *Facts About John Deere Tractor Wholesale Prices in the United States 1935-1961* (Moline, Illinois: Deere and Co., 1961).

[27] See a report by Zvi Griliches in *The 41st Annual Report of the National Bureau of Economic Research, Inc.* (New York: May, 1961), p. 50. Along the same lines see *The Price Statistics of the Federal Government*, General Series No. 73, National Bureau of Economic Research, Inc. (New York: May, 1961), pp. 31-49.

[28] Fred Weber quotes a survey of the McGraw-Hill Department of Economics that latest models of machine tools are 44 percent more productive than predecessor models of ten years before. G. Fred Weber, "Price Level Accounting," *The Accounting Review* (October, 1960), p. 648.

[29] Milton Gilbert, "The Problem of Quality Changes and Index Numbers," *The Monthly Labor Review* (September, 1961), pp. 992-993.

[30] *Ibid.*

costs and profits that are influenced significantly by quality improvements in productive assets. Changes in design and improvements in material and make-up of operating assets lead to lower factor and maintenance costs directly, not to mention possible indirect benefits from employee comfort, corporate prestige, and the like. Determination of the current cost of old assets through the multiplication of historical cost and an index number relative which ignores implicit quality changes distorts asset costs directly; as these asset costs are amortized, production costs and operating profits are likewise distorted. Companies with old equipment will be forced to reflect depreciation based on the current cost estimate, but there will be no offset for the higher material, labor and maintenance costs often associated with older assets. Assuming rising prices, rate of return computations suffer in two ways: income is too low and asset valuations are too high relative to companies with newer assets. The end result of index number adjustments might be more meaningful than strict use of historical cost in any particular case, but it would be extremely difficult to identify the case or quantify the meaning. The public accountant could not certify the adjustment in any sense other than arithmetically.

Improved Balance Sheet Values

If one is interested in balance sheet value for management decisions such as pricing or plant replacement, the net realizable value of owned assets and discounted expected future costs are equally, if not more, important than current cost. Only net realizable value reflects what can be obtained if an asset is replaced. Where markets are imperfect and installation costs are significant, net realizable value may be more closely represented by historical cost than by current cost. In planning for future replacement, discounted expected future cost would seem to be relevant. Little can be said for the sole use of either yesterday's or today's current cost as a measure of expected future costs. Very few, however, argue for resale value of assets[31] or discounted future costs as a basis for accounting statements. Lack of objectivity, short- versus long-run considerations, and forecasting difficulties probably account for most of the resistance to these measurements.

As a measure of the value of the firm, the total of current costs of individual assets is often so far removed that it is meaningless. Table 3 illustrates this for selected companies and years. Figures in this table clearly show that a more than generous adjustment for estimated current costs still leaves 80 to 90 percent of per share market price unexplained. The persistence of the differential suggests that accounting statements made up on any cost basis

---

[31] A notable exception is Professor Chambers, whose concept of "current cash equivalent" is equivalent to net realizable value. R.J. Chambers, "Measurement in Accounting," *Journal of Accounting Research* (Spring, 1965), p. 42.

may omit a great deal of asset value even when one allows for market irrationality.

The growth companies illustrated in the table dramatize the difference between cost and value, but value is not always in excess of cost, even in these days of rising prices. Contrasting results can be seen in an article in *Forbes* which listed sixty-six companies that sold for less than book value and in some cases less than current asset value per share.[32] The point is that investors do not buy individual assets; rather they buy a part of entity value which

Table 3	Stock Values for Selected Companies and Years[1]		
	Book Value Per Common Share	Adjusted Book Value Per Common Share[2]	Market Price Range Per Common Share
IBM			
1955	69	174	450–349
1957	54	116	376–270
1959	46	90	488–385
1961	43	75	607–447
1963	57	94	509–384
1965	73	143	549–404
Minnesota Mining			
1955	18	34	115– 80
1957	12	23	101– 58
1959	16	29	182–111
1961	7	13	87– 66
1963	9	17	73– 52
1965	12	21	71– 54
Honeywell			
1955	14	32	70– 50
1957	23	46	131– 73
1959	27	52	150–111
1961	30	67	170–123
1963	35	75	150– 84
1965	21	50	79– 58

Source: Underlying data taken from *Moody's Manual of Industrial Securities*—1962 and 1966.

[1]No adjustment was made for splits. Values are based on the number of shares outstanding in the given year in order to compare the book value measures with the market price existing in each year. IBM has had several stock splits over this time span; Minnesota Mining split 3 for 1 in 1959; and Honeywell split 2 for 1 in 1964.

[2]Based on residual equity plus an amount equal to 100% of net plant and equipment and inventory.

[32]"Loaded Laggards: 1966," *Forbes* (May 1, 1966), p. 20.

is based upon future cash flows. If aiding investors is the primary aim of financial statements, accountants would do better to present cash flow forecasts[33] than current cost estimates of assets that may or may not be replaced in productive processes that may or may not be continued.

Aiding Investor in Search for Value

In this article, the author has attempted to point out that current cost statements do not overcome deficiencies that exist in historical cost statements, but instead add other dimensions of confusion. The appropriate definition of holding items is ambiguous, and under any definition the separation of the result of holding and operating functions is more artificial than real. Also, there is the question of whether to measure the current cost of equivalent service potential or the current cost of specific assets and equities. The former is at once both subjective and complex; as a result it would be virtually impossible to measure. The latter suffers from lack of definitional clarity and from imperfect measurement devices that make the results highly questionable. Finally, current cost does little to improve balance sheet values. It does not measure the incurred cost of assets and equities, the opportunity cost of holding assets or equities, or the value of the firm. As is true of any cost measure, it fails to include the intangible value of the going concern. This value, however, is often the most important value to present and potential investors.

If accountants truly are interested in aiding the investor in his search for value, they would do better to present factors relevant to value determination. One such factor, measurement of past results, is already provided. The past, however, is only concerned with valuation indirectly as a reference point and guide to future expectations. Another factor which is directly relevant to value and which is probably compiled internally is a cash flow forecast. Accountants might do well to investigate the possibilities of such forecasts as supplemental financial statements, rather than to pursue another imperfect measure of past decisions and actions.

---

[33] See John W. Coughlan, "Industrial Accounting," *The Accounting Review* (July, 1959), pp. 415–428; Diran Bodendorn, "An Economist Looks at Industrial Accounting and Depreciation," *The Accounting Review* (October, 1961), pp. 583–588. This writer does not feel that formal statements embodying the capitalized value of expected future net cash receipts can be prepared today because of the imperfection in longer term forecasts, the deficiencies of internal rate of return measures (suggested by Coughlan), and present difficulties associated with cost of capital estimates (suggested by Bodenhorn). Budgeted cash forecasts for a short, but relevant period—say five years—might be a very useful type of supplementary statement.

George J. Staubus is Professor and Chairman
of the Accounting Committee at the University
of California, Berkeley.

Current Cash Equivalent for Assets: A Dissent

George J. Staubus

Accounting, *Evaluation and Economic Behavior*,[1] by R. J. Chambers, appears destined to grace the reading list of many a graduate course in accounting theory and can be expected to exert a good deal of influence on future publications in this field. By almost any standard it is a valuable contribution to the literature and deserves the critical attention of all who are interested in the development of this subject. The stimulating effect of the book is of particular significance.

One prominent feature of the Chambers' theory is the emphasis it places on "current cash equivalent," opportunity costs, net realizable values of assets, and the like. While this emphasis may seem to have considerable merit because of the relevance of exit prices to several types of decisions for which the amounts of assets are of interest, further thought along this line is likely to lead one to question the general relevance of such prices. This question will be given detailed attention later in this paper, but first let us attempt to locate the source of the emphasis on direct exit prices.

A key point in Chambers' argument is the recognition of the role of exchanges in reconciling specialization in production with the satisfaction of individual wants (pp. 64–5 and argument 3.51). Exchanges involve markets and prices as well as the decision to execute an exchange or not, i.e., the

---

[1] Prentice-Hall, 1966. Other writings by Chambers that embody closely related ideas are "Edwards and Bell on Business Income," *The Accounting Review*, October 1965; "The Price Level Problem and Some Intellectual Grooves," *Journal of Accounting Research*, Autumn 1965; and "Measurement in Accounting" *Journal of Accounting Research*, Spring 1965.

Reprinted by permission of the author and publisher from *Accounting Review*, Vol. XLII (October, 1967), pp. 650–61.

decision to hold or exchange an existing asset. This decision clearly requires knowledge of the asset's current market price, or ratio of exchange. An obvious conclusion is that current market price less any costs necessary to obtain the market price (net realizable value) is always relevant to the choice of holding or selling an existing asset. What is not so obvious is the relative importance of the sell-or-hold decision in the entire population of decisions to which the amount of an asset is relevant. Is this such a dominant class of decisions that the measurement needed for it should be accepted as the basic measurement of assets? Or, is net realizable value the measure of assets that is most relevant to the other types of decisions as well? The ensuing discussion will attempt to answer these questions.

Asset Measurement Methods

A brief survey of the generally recognized measurement methods (types of evidence of asset amount) used in accounting may help to place the discussion in proper perspective. *Historical cost* is probably the most widely used basis of asset measurement. The most popular version of historical cost does not include any consideration of changes in the purchasing power of the measuring unit since asset acquisition date. It does, however, attempt to take into account the expiration of service potential by eliminating portions of the total historical cost from the asset amount. If the accountant feels that something must be done to recognize the change in the size of the measuring unit over time, a conversion factor may be applied to historical cost as traditionally measured to yield a *converted historical cost* (or adjusted historical cost) that more nearly states the real (economic) cost of the asset.

Converted historical cost represents a measure of the economic significance of the asset at the date of acquisition, but it tends to lose this significance as time goes by. As between market prices at alternative dates, the more recent price is typically more relevant to today's, and tomorrow's, problems than an older price. This leads to the concept of *replacement cost*, or what it would cost to acquire the asset at the reporting date.

Readers of financial statements are interested in information that will help them choose among alternative courses of action. To the extent that asset amounts are relevant to such decisions they must be measures of what could, is likely to, or will happen in the future. *Net realizable values* of assets in their most likely (currently planned) use or method of disposition is a measure of asset amount that could be more useful than any measure related to the source of the asset.

Net realizable value represents the net cash inflow that could be realized at the reporting date by disposing of the assets. An alternative measure that is even more closely related to likely future events is *discounted value of future cash flows* that have been contractually determined with respect to time and amount.

The brief survey of asset measurement methods provides a basis for an evaluation of the relative usefulness of asset amounts calculated in alternative ways in making common types of decisions.

Decisions Involving Monetary Asset

Receivables and temporary investments are to be discussed under the monetary assets headings. Cash, the premier monetary asset, will be ignored because its measurement does not provoke controversy.

The Planning and Control of Liquidity

The dates and amounts of cash inflows from debtors are crucial to the planning and control of liquidity. A treasurer who is drawing up a cash budget, or comparing actual receipts with budgeted receipts, is interested in the actual cash flows emanating from receivables. Bad debts must be taken into consideration, but discount for waiting is less likely to be of concern in liquidity planning. Times and amounts of future cash flows are here the major considerations. Net realizable values that may result from sale or assignment of the claims may be of great interest in a minority of cases; replacement cost or historical cost surely would be irrelevant.

Temporary investments acquired and held for the purpose of providing secondary cash reserves or to meet a substantial near-term cash need have a much different status. Whereas accounts receivable typically represent a normal stage in the conversion of goods or services to cash, temporary investments are acquired with the expectation that they will be converted to cash in response to a need for cash rather than in accordance with the general terms arranged with the debtor and at the specific date chosen by the debtor. While some temporary investments may be acquired with the expectation that they will be held to a specific maturity date, in which case the discounted value or undiscounted maturity value may be of greatest interest, the more typical case terminates with a "premature" sale to another investor at a date selected by the holder after acquisition. Under these circumstances net realizable value is likely to be of greatest interest to the treasurer.

Decisions by External Investors

Short-term lenders are particularly interested in the firm's prospective liquidity. They must predict the firm's ability to pay at a near future date, an interest very closely allied to that of the corporate treasurer. We shall assume that the remarks made above with respect to planning and control of liquidity are generally applicable to the short-term lender as well as the corporate financial officer.

Rather than deal with each common type of investment arrangement separately, we shall discuss the decision of the common stock investor or other owner as a good example of long-term investment decision-making. To the owner, the asset amount to be associated with a receivable is not entirely determined by the face value of the claim and the probability of collecting it when it will be collected is also relevant. The owner of a business cannot help but recognize the time value of money. If the anticipated waiting period is material, the expected receipts should be discounted. The logic of discounting could be clearly demonstrated if he were required to choose between 10% interests in two finance companies which are identical in every respect except that company A has $1,000,000 (maturity value) of receivables with an average maturity of thirty days while Company B has receivables with a maturity value of $1,010,000 and an average maturity date six months hence. If the face values of these receivables were reported as the asset amounts in both cases and if the investor were to choose between interests in the two companies solely on the basis of those face values, he presumably would make the wrong decision. If the accountant measured the assets at discounted value, even assuming the rate he chose was one or two percent off the mark, the balance sheets would provide more reliable bases for the investment decision. Net realizable values of the receivables obtainable by selling or assigning them to someone else prior to their maturity would not be the proper basis for an external investment decision, unless that method of disposition were actually expected to be utilized by the firm.

The owner's interest in temporary investments is very similar to that of management. If holding to maturity is assumed, discounting is just as appropriate as in the receivables case discussed in the preceding paragraph. But if premature disposition is likely, net realizable value would appear to be more relevant to the owner's problem.

Inventories of Goods Held for Sale

In this section we shall concern ourselves with selecting the most useful methods of measuring the asset amounts pertaining to inventories of goods held for sale (whether manufactured by the firm or purchased in existing form). Three possible uses of this information will be considered.

Appraisal of Management Performance

Two cases will be dealt with separately. (a) the situation in which production is critical and sale is a simple matter, and (b) the stock of goods which requires considerable sales effort for its disposition in the normal course of business. The former category is exemplified by the relatively raw products of the mine, smelter, mill, farm, or forest which can be graded and sold at a price that is largely dependent on the grade and location rather than on the reputation of the producer, advertising, and style factors. The measurement of management's accomplishment with respect to an inventory of a commodity requires a measurement of the ending inventory that associates ac-

omplishment with time periods in a reasonable manner. Our ideas of rea-
,onable association may be clarified if we assume a turnover of management
.t the balance sheet date. Under these conditions measurement of the ending
nventory at net realizable value, if it can be determined with acceptable
)bjectivity, appears to assign credit for production to the deserving manage-
nent team. The new management then has the choice of selling the goods
.mmediately or "speculating" on the commodity market.

The answer to the above-stated problem is readily apparent; if profit is to
)e used as a measure of managerial performance, replacement cost and
nistorical cost are distinctly inferior to net realizable value if there is objective evidence of net realizable value. But let us consider another highly
relevant possible measure of the asset. Suppose the management has made a
contract for the sale of the goods on hand at a fixed price but title has not yet
passed. Now we have a choice between current market price less selling costs
and contractual evidence of the future cash flow. The making of the contract
is a part of management's overall performance so we surely must take its
effect, for better or for worse, into account as soon as possible. The anticipated future cash receipt, perhaps reduced by discount, would have to be
accepted as the measure of the asset amount of the goods on hand if we are to
make the best appraisal of managerial performance.

The next case to consider involves goods that are "difficult to sell." Cloth-
ing, furniture, appliances, automobiles, and most durable producer's goods
fall into this category. Production is not the only difficult part of the operating cycle; sale is here a "critical event"[2] which must occur before the management is entitled to receive credit for increasing the net worth of the
owners. Without either a contract to sell or an active quoted market for the
goods the accountant has little evidence of managerial accomplishment; he is
forced to assume that the goods will eventually be sold for at least a break-
even price vis-à-vis production costs at the time of sale. (The tendency of
selling prices and costs to move together is so marked that the accountant
must have specific evidence to the contrary in order to justify a contrary
assumption). Replacement cost seems to be the best measure of accomplishment under such circumstances.

Decisions by External Investors

The investor who is trying to assess the value of a fractional interest in the
business surely wants to know as much as he can about future cash flows. He
would like to know what the existing stock of goods will contribute to the
firm's cash balance. If direct (for example, contractual) evidence of future
cash flows is available it will be of maximum interest to the investor. Otherwise, what the goods could be sold for today would be of interest if objec-

---

[2] John H. Myers, "Critical Event and Recognition of Net Profit," *The Accounting Review*,
October 1954, pp. 528–32.

tively ascertainable. Replacement cost would be distinctly inferior evidenc of future cash flows; it should be utilized only in the absence of acceptab evidence of actual or available future cash flows. The conclusions reached i the discussion of appraisal of management performance are also applicab to investment decisions.

Pricing Existing Stocks of Goods

Product pricing is not a very good example of a decision to which aggregat money amounts of assets are likely to be relevant, so we shall not devot much time to it. The present discussion involves short-run or single orde pricing of goods that are presently on hand: long-run pricing and pricing o orders for future production are not included because asset amounts of good: on hand are even less relevant to such problems.

The key information necessary for making the decision to accept or rejec a bid for existing goods or what price to accept is the value of the bes alternative use of the goods. As of any given balance sheet date the account ant should provide the best evidence he can of the most valuable use of th goods, i.e. the maximum net proceeds indicated by the objective evidence a hand. This typically could be called net realizable value. How useful such information can be in determining an acceptable selling price is doubtful.

Inventories of Goods Held for Use

Commodities held for use are commonly labeled raw materials or supplies. Recognition of a distinction between goods held for sale and goods held for use implies that those in the latter category are expected to be blended with other materials and service before making a contribution to revenues. We shall examine the relevance of alternative bases for measuring the asset amounts of such goods for the purposes of (a) making a decision about the worth of an interest in the business and (b) planning, control, and perform-ance appraisal.

Decisions by External Investors

Investors want to predict their own cash inflows from the firm. The depen-dence of these cash returns upon the firm's cash inflows and outflows attracts investors' attention to the latter. The most interesting property of an asset is its capacity to contribute to future cash receipts of the firm (and its owners). If good evidence of that capacity is available to the accountant, he should pass it on to the investor. Unfortunately, in the case of goods held for use, direct evidence of their contribution to future cash flows is extremely rare. Net realizable value, in the sense of the price for which the materials or supplies could be sold in their existing condition (less specific costs of dispo-sition), is not relevant if this is extremely unlikely to happen. The investor wants to learn as much as he can about what will happen or could happen under existing conditions (usually including continuity of enterprise activities), not what could happen under quite different conditions. Net realizable value would be of interest if the goods, purchased for use, are now viewed as obsolete. In this case they really fall under the heading of goods held for sale.

Another possible meaning of net realizable value of goods held for use is current selling price of the finished product less costs still to be incurred, including cost of capital. This form of net realizable value is relevant, but its computation typically involves too many estimates and assumptions to meet the standard of objectivity required by most accountants.

Rejection of net realizable value leaves us with entry prices as alternatives. While it may not be necessary, at this stage of our discussion, to provide further justification for selecting replacement cost as the most useful way of measuring goods held for use—the likelihood of a dissenting opinion by the reader seems small—nevertheless, it might be helpful to summarize the arguments for replacement cost before proceeding.

1. The obviation argument.[3] An asset is valuable because its ownership by the firm obviates the necessity of buying it in the future. Present acquisition price is an estimate of the future price we would have had to pay in its absence; so it is a measure of the benefit the asset will yield to the firm.

2. In the absence of direct evidence of future cash inflows we must rely upon the relationship of current prices of cost factors to the selling price of the product by way of a normal profit margin.

3. If no direct evidence of future cash flows is available and net realizable value of raw materials in their existing form is discarded for lack of relevance to future events and net realizable value by way of the production process in the ordinary course of business is rejected for lack of objectivity, entry prices are left as our only reasonable choice. Recent entry prices are preferable to older entry prices if we assume that future selling prices of final products will reflect cost levels no more than one conversion period old. (This reasoning is based on 2 above.)

4. Some accountants may emphasize 1 above as the proper justification for use of an entry price; others may prefer 2. A third choice is to accept the second justification for replacement cost measurement of stocks of materials that need to be carried to meet the demands of an efficient purchasing program, uncertainty of receipts, and uneven usage, and to accept the first explanation for replacement cost measurement of "excess" or speculative inventories. It makes a good deal of sense to say that the only benefit contributed by excess inventories is avoidance of future purchases while the benefits to be derived from basic buffer stocks are related to their contributions to

---

[3] Professor David Green, Jr. emphasized cost obviation in his "A Moral to the Direct-Costing Controversy," *The Journal of Business,* July 1960, pp. 218–26; reprinted in Davidson, Green, Horngren, and Sorter (eds.), *An Income Approach To Accounting Theory* (Prentice-Hall, 1964), pp. 183–93.

efficient production and sale of the products of the firm—benefits which affect future cash receipts from sale of the goods rather than reductions in future cash outlays.

The relationship between entry price and net realizable value in the case of a manufacturing firm is illustrated in Exhibit I. It shows that working backwards from selling price and working forward from material cost might be expected to yield roughly similar results. In the typical case, with the manufacturer earning a normal return on investment, the residual profit would be small. Under equilibrium conditions in an industry with a high degree of freedom of entry one might expect the residual income to be zero. The use of

Exhibit I
Relationship between entry price and exit price

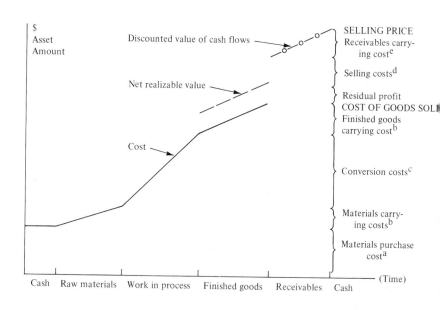

[a] Including fringe acquisition costs such as transportation.
[b] Interest, insurance, storage space, etc.
[c] Including carrying charges during conversion.
[d] All costs are assumed to be allocable to one or more of the categories shown.
[e] Interest, collection costs, uncollectibles etc. Uncollectibles could be deducted from selling price at the collection date so as to make the final amount represent the "expected value" of the collection from the customer.

n interest rate not representing the economic cost of capital (such as a zero ate) in discounting the selling price or in accumulating carrying charges on ie production costs would affect the reported residual profit. Absence of quilibrium conditions would also contribute to such a profit (or loss). Nevrtheless, it is fair to say that replacement cost is related to net realizable alue and to present values of future cash flows even though the relationship s likely to be sufficiently loose to lead us to prefer one of the latter measureient methods if it can be applied with acceptable objectivity.

Planning, Control, and Performance Appraisal

Ve shall now concern ourselves strictly with the cost of using materials to ccomplish some objective such as production of a product. We shall refer to iis accounting problem as "costing" the product or other object of accomlishment. The object of costing may be called y and the material to be used, . Thus, the issue is the cost of using x for y. We assume for the present iscussion that proper accounting in this area is facilitated by carrying the sset x at a unit price equal to the cost of using it rather than at the cost of cquiring it. Otherwise costing would not be directly dependent upon asset neasurements.

The cost of using x *for* y *is the value of* x *in its best alternative use.* If type-x naterial is to be purchased again in the future, the use of x adds to future urchase requirements which require cash. Therefore, one alternative to sing x is a reduction in future purchases and cash disbursements for type-x naterial. This is undoubtedly the most common alternative to using x for y, o replacement cost is the indicated solution to the problem.

An alternative situation is the case in which type-x material is not to be urchased again and the use of x for y eliminates the opportunity of using it or z. This implies that z is less valuable than either y or the replacement cost of x; if use of x for z is more valuable than replacement cost, additional quantities of material x should be purchased. The value of using x for z, vhere z is an internal use, is likely to be so difficult to ascertain as to be inavailable for use in accounting; but if z is sale of the material in its existing orm, net realizable value may be ascertainable.

The cost of carrying on various activities is information that is often useful o management. The control of costs requires knowledge of costs. The seriousness of unfavorable variances depends upon the actual cost involved; the nanager must be more concerned about the wastage of a ton of copper if it osts $1,000 rather than $200. Yet differences of this magnitude could be nvolved in the choice between current replacement cost and Lifo acquisition ost (when an old layer of stock is "dipped into"). If a foreman has a choice etween a low-labor, high-materials-cost method of performing an operaion and a high-labor, low-materials-cost method, he can not make a proper lecision unless he knows the current costs of using materials and labor. If the lecision at hand (for example, pricing) requires the projection of future production costs and past production costs are used as evidence of futu costs, the most up-to-date past costs typically will be the best guide.

The appraisal of overall management performance depends upon measu ing the accomplishments of management and the sacrifices made to achie them. The measurement of accomplishment requires measurement of the r assets of the enterprise at the end of the appraisal period; the appraisal costs requires similar measurements at the beginning of the period. To t extent that the desired performance is the earnings of profit on the residu equity, these measurements must be consistent with the residual equityhol ers' point of view. As discussed earlier, it was concluded that replaceme cost would most frequently be the appropriate choice of measurement met ods for goods held for use.

Depreciable Plant Assets

We shall next consider the use of information about the amounts of pla assets in investment decisions by owners, asset replacement decisions l managers, and in costing services yielded by such assets.

Investment Decisions by Owners

The investor is interested in judging the future cash flows of the firm. Th contribution of an individual depreciable asset to those flows—especially if is a "complementary"[4] asset—can not be measured, but until we are pr pared to accept the omission of such properties from the asset category w shall find ourselves struggling with the problem of quantifying them i monetary terms. One thing is clear: to the extent that amounts of depreciab assets are relevant to the investment decision, they must be the greate amounts available to the firm. The investor has no interest in second or thir greatest values of assets because he has a right to assume that managemer will not elect to accept second or third best alternatives. Value in use presun ably is the greatest value of an asset which the management chooses t continue using. Net realizable value of an asset held for use typically is poc evidence of what it will contribute to the firm and its owners, especially if th asset is technically and/or geographically specialized.

Unfortunately, we have no direct approach to the calculation of value i use. We are forced to fall back on the assumption inherent in any use of entr prices, viz., that management's judgement when it decided to acquire th asset was a good one. This judgement is followed by an estimate of th pattern of decline in the remaining stock of services which the asset repre sents. If we believe that these services are sufficiently useful to justify acquisi tion of a similar stock if the existing one were not on hand, replacement cos may be apportioned in accordance with the pattern of "expiration" of serv ice stocks that is foreseen. We believe that such a basis will result in reportin

---

[4] Chambers distinguished complementary assets from solitary assets on p. 202.

set amounts that are more relevant to the investor's problem than any ternative procedure in the typical, but not every, case.[5]

Asset Replacement Decisions

wo different types of assets may be considered: the solitary asset and the mplementary asset. A solitary asset is one not closely related to or depen- ent upon other assets in operation. One may be able to formulate a judge- ent of the value of such an asset by considering the net revenues that it is xpected to produce. An apartment house is an example. One needs to know ree values of such an asset in order to make decisions about its possible sale nd replacement: value in use, net realizable value, and replacement cost. he asset should be held if its net realizable value is less than both value in se and replacement cost; it should be sold if either of the latter is less than et realizable value. If it is sold, it should be replaced if value in use exceeds eplacement cost. All three values—net realizable value, replacement cost and alue in use—are relevant to these decisions, but value in use is not likely to e available for stating the amount of the asset. Thus, either net realizable alue or replacement cost may be used depending upon the accessibility of bjective evidence.

Now let us turn to the case of the complementary asset, one which can ake no independent contribution to revenues but works as a member of a :am. Sale of this asset without replacing it is not a likely course of action. he common decision situation requires a choice between retention or an lternative source of the service provided by the asset. In this context value in se is not in question. A continuing flow of service is taken for granted; only s source is in doubt. It is entirely a matter of costs; revenues are not involved ecause of their constancy. The information needed is the costs of obtaining he services under the alternatives being considered, viz., the future outlays ɔ be made plus receipts foregone (i.e., opportunity costs) (a) if the services re obtained through the existing asset and (b) if the services are obtained ia a replacement.[6] The net realizable value of the existing asset is included s an opportunity cost in (a). Value in use need never be calculated in a ardinal sense, but if (a) is less than (b) we know that the value of the xisting stock of services is greater than the assets' net realizable value, and he asset should be retained to yield its stock of services. If (a) is greater than b) sale is in order and the alternative source of services should be called pon. Hence, net realizable value appears to be the measurement most rele- ʾant to replacement decisions regarding complementary depreciable assets.

---

[5]See David Green, Jr. and George H. Sorter, "Accounting for Obsolescence—A Proposal," *he Accounting Review*, July 1959, pp. 433–41, for an interesting version of replacement cost of :maining services of depreciable assets.

[6]This does not seem to be the appropriate occasion to consider the interest (time) problems nvolved in making (1) and (2) comparable.

Costing for Planning, Control, and Performance Appraisal

The use of information on the cost of doing something was discussed briefl in the subsection on planning, control, and performance appraisal in th section dealing with goods held for use. Here we shall concern ourselves wit another case of the cost of using x for y. The x in this case is machine service rather than materials. We must, of course, rely upon the opportunity cos concept: the cost of using x for y is the value of the best alternative use of x.

Solitary and complementary assets may be grouped for this discussion. W should, however, recognize the distinction between time-expiring assets an use-expiring assets because the services of use-expiring assets may be store until a valuable use comes along whereas the services of time expiring asset are like the products of a fruit tree; if they are not picked as they ripen the are lost forever. Storability opens up more opportunities for valuable alter native uses of the asset services and therefore increases the likelihood tha there is an opportunity cost of using x for y.

Adaptability is the most important attribute of a depreciable asset i determining whether there is a cost of using it. Location, physical mobility technical specifications, and the variety of products and services produced b the asset's owner affect the prospects for alternative uses. Building spac frequently is quite adaptable as are general purpose machines such as auto mobiles, road and in-plant trucks, common machine tools, etc., whereas blast furnace located in the middle of a California steel mill is limited to on use by one owner. An asset may be adapted to another internal use in th owning firm, or it may be switched to another firm by lease or by sale. Th opportunities for internal adaptation are likely to be greater in a larg multiproduct firm than in a small single product firm. Adaptability is als improved by increases in the scope of y. If we are costing a large project suc as the production of 1968 model automobiles, the length of time involve increases the possibility that a given asset usable in the production of 196 autos could be switched to some valuable internal or external alternative. I we are costing one 1968 model auto, alternative uses of an asset may b much more difficult to find. Short-run production costs are frequently lowe than long-run costs, although a backlog of work could be thought of as short run alternatives that make the use of the asset on one small task costly.

The value of the best external alternative may be thought of as the ne realizable value of the asset. Many specialized, immobile assets have ver low net realizable values. Flexible, mobile assets in large multi-product firms typically have alternative uses (second best uses) that are nearly as valuable as the best use and frequently more valuable than replacement cost. In orde to reach a general conclusion about the opportunity cost of using depreciable assets one would have to consider the relative frequency of internal and external second best uses and the extent to which second best internal uses o greater value than replacement cost offset second best internal and externa ses worth less than replacement cost. It does seem safe to say that if there is a queue for an asset's services, the cost of using it is not likely to be adequately represented by referring to net realizable value. But if there is a great deal of idle capacity in a plant, the short-run cost of using the assets may, on the average, be very low. It is absolutely essential that we recognize the difference between the cost of using facilities that would otherwise be idle and the cost of using scarce facilities. Only scarce resources are costly. On the whole, accountants would probably prefer to assume that internal alternative uses typically are superior to external alternative uses and typically are worth something closer to amortization of replacement cost than to amortization of net realizable value. A genuinely relevant type of costing, however, must provide for flexibility in this area.

Summary

We have made brief analyses of selected decision situations in an attempt to determine which method of asset measurement can be expected to provide the most relevant information. This survey has not been complete in any sense, but was intended to be representative. Even if it fails this test it can be instructive; a count of the frequency with which net realizable value is relevant is not so important as an assessment of the reasons for its relevance. A summary of our findings appears in Exhibit II.

The most general conclusion suggested by the above is that decision makers are interested in knowing as much as possible about what will happen. For the purpose of making investment decisions, in liquidity planning and control, and in measuring the accomplishments of company or divisional management, "actors" would like to know the present value of the asset's contribution to future cash flows. "Goods are acquired and held . . . because of the belief that they will be serviceable directly or indirectly in generating cash."[7] On the assumption that both the managers and the investors are economically motivated, we must assume that the latter are interested in and the former will attempt to obtain the *maximum time-adjusted cash potential.* We conclude, then, that the choice of a measurement method to apply to a particular asset for financial reporting purposes should be made on the basis of two criteria: (1) proximity of the measurement method to the ideal of maximum time-adjusted cash potential (MATACAP), and (2) availability of a reliable reading of the particular type of evidence (measurement method) chosen. The latter, in turn, is dependent upon objectivity, freedom from bias, accuracy of computations, intertemporal consistency and interfirm comparability.

Our disagreement with Professor Chambers is this: he believes that current cash equivalent (CCE) is the property of assets that accountants should

---

[7] Chambers, p. 198.

**Exhibit II   Summary of Analyses of Relevance
of Measurement Methods to Decisions**

Asset Category	Decision Situation	Most Relevant Measurement
Receivables	Liquidity planning and control	Future cash flows
	External investors	Future cash flows
Temporary investments	Liquidity planning and control	Net realizable value[a]
	External investors	Net realizable value[a]
Goods held for sale:	Performance appraisal	
Sale not critical		Net realizable value[a]
Sale critical		Replacement cost
	External investors	
Sale not critical		Net realizable value[a]
Sale critical		Replacement cost
	Pricing extant stocks[b]	Net realizable value
Goods held for use	External investors	Replacement cost
	Costing for planning, control, and performance appraisal	Replacement cost
Depreciable plant assets	External investors	Replacement cost
	Asset replacement decisions	Net realizable value
	Costing for planning, control, and performance appraisal	Replacement cost and net realizable value

[a]In these cases net realizable value is relevant because it is the best availiable evidence of what will happen. The discussion about the goods held under a contract to sell showed that if superior evidence of what will happen is availiable it should be used. Net realizable value, then, is not the ideal measurement in these cases.

[b]There is some doubt as to whether information from the accounting records can be of much value in this very limited pricing situation.

seek to measure. We believe that MATACAP is the most appropriate focus of attention. While these two terms sound similar, they have very different meanings in the context of our respective analyses. CCE is most commonly associated with "What we could sell our assets for if we did not go ahead and use them in the ordinary course of business." MATACAP characteristically means "the net contribution our assets will make to cash flows in their most likely future course." For many assets which are held because of management's belief that they will contribute more through use than through immediate sale, CCE represents a second best value.

Costing, however, calls for different information, viz., second best values. This seems to result in a wide gulf between costing and other accounting. But the best of the measurable alternative uses of an asset frequently is substitution for a future purchase of a similar asset so that replacement cost is frequently the best for costing out materials or services of depreciable assets. Since replacement cost typically is the least irrelevant evidence of future contributions to company cash flows that is objectively ascertainable, costing and financial reporting may not be as far apart as they appeared to be.

The basic meaning of cost is what economists call opportunity cost. Cost without an adjective should be taken to mean opportunity cost. Costing of a product or service means determining the values of the best alternative uses of the commodities and services that are used in producing the object of costing. The value of cost accounting is a function of the accuracy with which the accountant can approximate opportunity cost. Historical cost in the usual sense has no inherent relevance to the problems for which cost information is useful except to the extent that it approximates true opportunity cost. We must keep this point in mind when choosing among alternative imperfect accounting methods.

Chambers places a great deal of emphasis on adaption through markets. This leads to heavy emphasis on the sell-or-hold decision pertaining to assets. Our analysis indicated that net realizable value was indeed the most relevant measure of an asset for this decision. But need we be so concerned about the sell-or-hold decision? It frequently is not a difficult one. For some time after acquisition of depreciable assets sufficient technological advances to make the asset obsolete are unlikely. The immediate discrepancy between cost and net realizable value due to installation costs of machinery, immobility of structures, purchasing costs, the disadvantages to a prospective buyer of acquiring a second-hand asset (uncertainty of condition, lack of a warranty, less pride and prestige of ownership) make sale extremely unlikely and rarely a serious consideration. If management has recently decided that the asset is worth at least full installed cost it is not likely that it will soon question whether it is worth less than a net realizable value that is much below cost.

The pervasive influence of Chambers' concern with actions in markets is apparent from the following quotations: "What men wish to know, for the purpose of adaption, is the numerosity of the money tokens which could be substituted for particular objects and or collections of objects if money is required beyond the amount which one already holds."[8] "Financial position may be defined as the capacity of an entity at a point of time for engaging in exchanges."[9] "Accounting is a systematic method of retrospective and contemporary monetary calculation the purpose of which is to provide continuous sources of financial information as a guide to future action in markets."[10] Here we see the abandonment of the traditional continuity assumption. It is not-however-giving way to a liquidation assumption but rather to a switching assumption. The purpose of accounting is seen as providing information for switching decisions. We believe that a broader view of the uses of accounting information is more appropriate and that it leads accountants to direct their attention to maximum time-adjusted cash potential as the most useful asset property to measure.

---

[8] *Ibid.*, p. 92.

[9] *Ibid.*, p. 81.

[10] *Ibid.*, p. 102.

*Raymond J. Chambers is Professor of
Accounting at the University of Sydney,
Australia.*

Measures and Values: A Reply to Professor Staubus[1]

R. J. Chambers

I am not at all sure that Professor Staubus reads me. I have been at some pains to point out that more than one kind of information is necessary to every choice; and that monetary magnitudes of quite different types are necessary. At the risk of being tedious they may be mentioned. First, there are the monetary magnitudes (measures) of the assets and equities a firm has at any time. Second, there are the monetary magnitudes (valuations, as distinct from measures) obtained by discounting the expected cash inflows and outflows from proceeding in the same way as up to the point of choice, and from every alternative course which seems to be feasible at the point of choice. There is no problem of dealing in money and goods in a deliberate and informed manner for which both types of magnitudes are not necessary.

A Managerial Problem

Consider first a managerial problem—the switching of the holding of one asset (A) for the holding of another (B). The requirements for a solution of this problem are as follows:

---

[1] George J. Staubus, "Current Cash Equivalent for Assets: A Dissent," *The Accounting Review* (October 1967).

Reprinted by permission of the author and publisher from *Accounting Review*, Vol. XLIII (April, 1968), pp. 239–47.

Let $CCE(A)$ be the current cash equivalent of A.
$P(B)$ be the purchase price of B.
$V(A)$ be the net present value of continuing to use A up to some specified time, exclusive of $CCE(A)$.
$V(B)$ be the net present value of using B, assuming for convenience the same time horizon, but exclusive of $P(B)$.

Assume, in the first instance, that $CCE(A) = P(B)$, so that no other change in the use of funds occurs.

Then, all other things being equal, the firm will choose

$$A \text{ if } V(A) - CCE(A) > V(B) - P(B) \tag{1}$$

and

$$B \text{ if } V(A) - CCE(A) < V(B) - P(B) \tag{2}$$

which under the assumption abovementioned makes the resolution of the problem depend on whether $V(A)$ is greater than or less than $V(B)$). But notice particularly that it is first necessary to discover that $CCE(A) = P(B)$.

Assume in the second instance that $CCE(A) < P(B)$, and that the deficit must be made up by borrowing, at a cost, the present value of which is I for the stipulated time of the project; and let $V(B)$ be exclusive of I.

Then, all other things being equal, the firm will choose (A) if

$$V(A) - CCE(A) > V(B) - P(B) - I. \tag{3}$$

Notice in this case that it is first necessary to discover $CCE(A)$ in order to discover the amount to be borrowed, for on this depends the value of I.

The demonstration applies to all combinations of the elements, including cases where the time horizons differ, for the discounting entailed in $V(A)$, $V(B)$ and I allows for this. In all cases knowledge of $CCE(A)$ is necessary to choice; I have not claimed that it is both necessary and sufficient. It should be clear from the above expressions that no single magnitude ever can be both necessary and sufficient.

Staubus contends that decision makers want to know the present value of an "asset's contribution to future cash flows" (p. 659), or as they are maximizers, the "maximum time-adjusted cash potential." Presumably in both cases the terms are to be understood as net of costs of continuing to use an asset, for maximizers would not be interested in gross inflows. Before going further it should be pointed out that no decision makers can ever *know* the present value of an asset's contribution to future cash flows. All they can know is what some specific person *thinks may be* the contribution to future cash flows. Now, there is no way in which "what any person thinks may be the contribution" may be challenged (for no two persons have equal degrees of optimism, pessimism, pugnacity, and so on). It must follow that any statement purporting to say something about what someone thinks may say more about the person than about the firm and its assets. And as one of the objects of reading the accounts is to assess "the accomplishments of the company" (p. 659), it seems, at least to me, patently improper to judge past accomplishments on the basis of what some person (a manager, in particular) may think about the future. This is mixing two quite distinct things. One cannot assess how far he has travelled in the last hour by taking account of where he expects to be an hour hence. He may take account of both in making the whole of a journey, but progress to date and what lies ahead are in no sense the same; neither is part of the other.

But to return to the substance of the argument: what is the meaning of maximum time-adjusted cash potential? This surely is the same as $V(A)$ in the example instanced above, on the assumption that managers are maximizers. At the very least, Staubus' proposal comes no closer to giving all the monetary magnitudes necessary for choice than does current cash equivalent; it supplies no more than one of the four (at least) necessary magnitudes. But notice the defects of $V(A)$. Its magnitude depends on someone's assessment or stipulation of the particular receipts and particular outlays, period by period, which are expected to ensue from the continued use of A; on someone's stipulation of the discount rate; on the assumption that A will be used to the stipulated future date—all of which are speculative and in no sense factual as at the date of any balance sheet or choice. Further $V(A)$ or MATACAP, to use Staubus' acronym, will never tell what is available as asset-backing for a loan management may seek, and never help in obtaining an indication of the financial capacity of a firm at a point of time to switch from one asset to another, with or without upsetting the investment in other assets. Only current cash equivalent will help; and even it will give no more than an approximation for it takes no account of hard bargaining or bargaining from weakness.

An Investor's Problem

Consider, now, an investor's problem—the switching of the holding of one security (E) for a holding of another security (F). We could consider the case of switching a holding of cash for securities or securities for cash; but the case we choose to consider is inclusive of more of the variables than these simpler cases. The requirements for the solution of this problem are substantially similar to those for a switching of business assets. But we have to take account of the particular part the financial statements of the two companies may play in the decision.

At the moment of choice, $CCE(E)$ and $P(F)$ are given; they are prices of the securities. For the investor at the time, the contents of the companies' financial statements do not affect these. The contents of financial statements can only affect $V(E)$ and $V(F)$. In very few cases can an investor know the specific consequences of the choices which managers have in fact made; this would be possible, for example, where the specific security investments of the firm and the dividend or interest income received from these were matters of public knowledge; but the circumstance is rare. All that investors can know is the *general* effect of all the choices or decisions of management taken together. If we were to expect them to be able to judge whether or not the specific choices of management were good, bad, or indifferent, for every one of the firms in which a given investor may invest, we would be expecting the impossible. We would be expecting that investors could know and would know more about more firms than any manager could know—which, at least to me, seems absurd.

Among the things an investor might expect to know are the rates of return earned by the two companies, their liquidities or degrees of solvency, and their leverages. The general significance of these was argued in *Accounting, Evaluation and Economic Behavior*. In forming expectations, every investor and every manager may place different weights on these characteristics of the firms, in the light of his more general knowledge of their markets and expectations of the future of those markets.

Consider the firm issuing securities E; call it the E Company. Let the characteristics of the state of the company at a given time be represented by S; S includes all aspects of financial position at the time, including degree of solvency and leverage which are entailed in its statement of financial position. Let there be a certain amount of public knowledge, K, about the industry of the E Company. Let Q_m, Q_n be the expectational quotients of the manager and of an investor in E Company respectively; by analogy with the concept of intelligence quotient, we posit a complex of attitudes which affect the way in which a person views prospects, personal factors which affect expectations. Let R be the rate of return of the E Company as obtained from its financial statements, and D the dividend paid by the company.

Using current cash equivalents, S will be a close approximation to the factual state of the company at any time and R will be a close approximation to the rate of change in the factual state in the immediately past period. There will be two values of the company's enterprise:

the managerial valuation

$$MV(E) = f(S, R, K, Q_m) \qquad (4)$$

and

the investor's valuation

$$NV(E) = f(S, R, D, K, Q_n).$$ (5)

The valuation will be different not only because Q_m and Q_n will differ, but also because the manager may have some influence on future values of D which investors cannot anticipate; investors will tend therefore to be influenced by past values of D.

The values S, R, D and K will form the basis on which investors may estimate the future cash flows they can expect. It is common to represent the expected proceeds of an investment, exclusive of the initial amount of the investment as above, by

$$NV(E) = \sum_{t=1}^{n} PVD' + CCE(E)_n'$$ (6)

where the first term is the sum of the present values of the expected dividends through to time n, and the second term is the expected resale price at n, the primes signifying *expected* values in each case. But this expression does not indicate the foundations of the dividend and price expectations. A little reflection will show that S, R, D and K or various components of these are necessary for the formation of dividend and price expectations. To lay these bare has been the object of the expression in the previous paragraph.

Using the MATACAP concept will entail different concepts of S and R; let them be denoted by S' and R'. S' and R' will not be close approximations to S and R, for their values will have been obtained by the operation of Q_m on some data, which, in the nature of the case, are not available to the investor. The Q of any individual cannot be known to any other. We may try to assess it, but we can only do so if we have factual expressions of its consequences from time to time. But as the factual results of business operations are the consequences of many other causes, besides the Qs of the managers, we cannot assess the Qs even if we have factual expressions of business results.

Now S and R will not be known to investors in the present case; they will have S' and R' which are based on some data or estimates, which we may designate as U (unknown to investors); S' and R' are functions of (U, K, Q_m); we will write them as $s(U, K, Q_m)$ and $r(U, K, Q_m)$. Making the appropriate substitutions in the expression for the investor's valuation, (5) above, we have:

$$NV(E) \quad = f(S', R', D, K, Q_n)$$ (7)

$$= f[s(U, K, Q_m), r(U, K, Q_m), D, K, Q_n]$$ (8)

Notice that S' and R' are not independent values. Both depend on the use made by the manager of the knowledge K; they are the result of the operation of Q_m on K and other data or estimates. Suppose K is suggestive of some growth to any member of the public, although the expectations of different persons differ in degree. Instead of K operating once only on an investor's valuation, it will have operated in some sense exponentially; first, through the determination of the values reported to investors by the manager, and second, through the response of the investor to what is reported. It is hard to say what the consequences could be of the operation of Q_n on values which have already been affected by the operation of Q_m; but the exponential effect suggests serious overvaluation by investors in the growth case, and serious undervaluation in the opposite case. (The demonstration seems to suggest a hypothesis explanatory of at least some of the marked swings in market prices: for even under traditional accounting there is an element of some Q or Qs in the magnitudes assigned to the constituents of S' and R'.)

In rebuttal of the above, it may be contended that investors should accept the operation of Q_m and make no attempt to interpose their own expectational quotients; but I know of no serious contention in this direction. It may also be contended that an investor should ignore S' and R' and apply his Q_n only to (D, K); but this would entail that financial statements serve or should serve no function, and I know of no serious contention in this direction.

So far we have dealt with the investor as though there were no alternative investment; we now take up again the securities F. We work through the case using current cash equivalent first. Putting together the expressions developed for the managerial problem (1, 2 above) and the investor in E, the choice of holding E or switching to F will turn on whether

$$NV(E) - CCE(E) \gtrless NV(F) - P(F). \qquad (9)$$

In the simple case in which a straight switch can be made without cash deficit or surplus, this reduces to

$$NV(E) \gtrless NV(F).$$

Using current cash equivalents for the derivation of the S and R for both E and F Companies we obtain sets of magnitudes which are themselves comparable, for they are all in principle prices from the interdependent set of all prices ruling in the community at any time. Q_n is therefore being applied to two sets of facts, one for E and one for F, which are in principle the same in kind. The same applies however great the number and variety of alternative opportunities to E, provided all firms derive S and R in the same way.

Using the MATACAP concept the problem is much more, if not completely, confused. Suppose, for simplicity that K is some public knowledge which has implications for the future of both E and F. As before (8 above)

$$NV(E) = f[s(U_e, K, Q_{m1}), r(U_e, K, Q_{m1}), D_e, K, Q_n], \qquad (10)$$

and

$$NV(F) = f[s(U_f, K, Q_{m2}), r(U_f, K, Q_{m2}), D_f, K, Q_n].   (11)$$

The two sets of facts U_e and U_f on which the managers $m1$ and $m2$ base their financial statements, are unknown to the investor; Q_{m1} and Q_{m2}, the expectational quotients of the two managers, are different but unknown to the investor; S_e', R_e', S_f' and R_f' are sets of magnitudes which are not factual and the investor does not know the extent to which Q_{m1} and Q_{m2} have entered into the determination of them. D_e, D_f and K are all known to the investor but the application of Q_n to the collections of non-factual and factual statements in respect of each company cannot possibly provide comparable values for $NV(E)$ and $NV(F)$. The investor is unable to make an informed choice—informed about the facts of the companies—in such circumstances. And as an investor may have many opportunities alternative to investing in E, for each of which there is an unknown but unique Q_m, the possibilities of him being mistaken or misled are legion.

That the operation of Q_m on the opportunities, and with the resources, of a company contributes to its profits or losses, its growth or failure, is not questioned. But we will not learn of its profits or losses if we allow Q_m to influence the measures of these. It is widely acknowledged that managers seek personal aims in the management of companies—power, prestige, continuity of tenure and so on. We may consider Q_m, in its actual effect in any instance, to be a composite of pure expectations and consciously or unconsciously self-protective predilections. Even if we could absolutely trust that in some cases Q_m is pure expectation, we cannot so trust in all cases. Where we have any doubt we would like to have evidence on which trust could be based. But Q_m, being entirely subjective, is not open to inspection; we can never have any such evidence. If wishes were horses, beggars would ride, they say; it seems a poor service to give investors a wish when they want a horse.

Some Conclusions

The conclusions from the above demonstrations are two:

(a) For any choice between holding an asset and acquiring another, whether by managers or investors, current cash equivalents of the assets held enter into the statement of conditions for informed choice.
(b) For any valuation of a future project, aggregative statements based on current cash equivalents (i.e. indicative of factual states at specific times) provide certain of the materials.

None of the argument denies the necessity of valuations, however varied and tenuous the grounds for making those valuations may be. In a certain world valuations would be less tenuous, for there would be no use for expectations in making valuations; but we live in an uncertain world which necessitates the forming of expectations as a first step in setting up valuations; and there are personal, and therefore unique elements in both, elements which are matters of private knowledge only.

As was argued, both in *Accounting, Evaluation and Economic Behavior* and above, choice requires both factual information about the firm's holdings and valuations of its prospects on the basis of those holdings. To provide the former is the function of accounting as we see it; we leave the valuing to be done by whomsoever wishes, for we accept the impossibility of knowing the personal components of valuations. The MATACAP proposal, on the other hand, provides only valuations. It implies the existence of some facts, but denies these to the users of financial statements; or it implies that valuations can be made without facts, a proposition it is impossible to swallow; it certainly entails, if accounting is to give the valuations Staubus requires, that some function other than accounting must supply the facts—some accountant to fill the gap left by some quasi-accountant, no doubt.

Some Difficulties

I have refrained, to this point, from any criticism of particular points in the Staubus text. But it bristles with difficulties lightly brushed aside by convenient phrases. A sample is given.

"Readers of financial statements are interested in information that will help them choose among alternative future courses of action" (p. 651). But what is help? help in what way? We have tried to show specifically the way in which information helps; and it seems that current cash equivalents or aggregations of these invariably help. Staubus sets up no demonstration to the contrary.

"The dates and amounts of cash inflows from debtors are crucial to the planning and control of liquidity" (p. 651). Doubtless. But so also is knowledge from time to time of actual holdings of cash and receivables—both current cash equivalents; and the actual amounts are the only basis on which steps can be taken, and the only indication whether or not steps should be taken, to tighten or relax the rules which influence liquidity.

"Short-term lenders . . . must predict the firm's ability to pay at a near future date" (p. 652). Why must they? and what does predict mean? Lenders have contractual rights against borrowers; this is some protection even if they never predicted, and most short-term lenders rely on their legal rights. But they would, of course, want to have "some idea" that the debtor will pay. Predict in any very definite sense they cannot.

"The making of the contract is a part of management's overall performance so we must surely take its effect, for better or for worse, into account as soon as possible" (p. 653). There's many a slip 'twixt cup and lip. If we are to take the making of contracts into account (before their execution), must we not also take account of all the possible variations, revocations, novations and so on in respect of every contract—for the right to these also arises out of the contract.

Where goods are "difficult to sell," the accountant "is forced to assume that the goods will eventually be sold for at least a break-even price vis-à-vis production costs at the time of sale" (p. 653). Why is he forced so to assume? If the assumption were valid, surely no firm would ever find the production of any good unprofitable.

"As of any given balance sheet date the accountant should provide the . . . maximum net proceeds (of existing stocks of goods) indicated by the objective evidence at hand" (p. 654). How can he do this? Maximum net proceeds he cannot know; it is a future sum, and he is not an operator in the market himself—on both scores he can only have subjective evidence.

"The investor wants to learn as much as he can about what will happen or at least what could happen under existing conditions . . . , not what could happen under quite different conditions" (p. 654). This is an odd investor; surely he wants to know what might happen under future, not existing, conditions. But however much he *wants*, he also wants to know what the company has now, so that he can form an opinion about the company's present capacity to face those conditions.

One of the most common provisos through Staubus' article has reference to objectivity—"acceptable objectivity" (p. 653), "objective evidence" (p. 653), "if objectively ascertainable" (p. 653), "objective evidence" (p. 654), "standard of objectivity" (p. 654), "lack of objectivity" (p. 655), "acceptable objectivity" (p. 655), "objective evidence" (p. 658), "objectivity" (p. 660), "evidence of future contributions to company cash flows that is objectively ascertainable" (p. 661). The frequency of use of the term in the course of an argument supporting statements colored by expectations of the future raises some doubt as to Staubus' understanding of objectivity. He does not say what he understands. But it is incontrovertible that no statement embodying beliefs or expectations about the future can be objective; beliefs and expectations are always personal, not open to inspection by others, and therefore subjective.

In contrasting the uses of CCE and MATACAP, Staubus asserts "CCE is most commonly associated with 'What we could sell our assets for if we did not go ahead and use them in the ordinary course of business'" (p. 660). What he fails to see is that this description does not entail that the firm shall or shall not go ahead and use them. It is not a notion that has sale in contemplation at all. It is a concept which yields an indication of the resources presently under control so that managers and others can choose one way or the other. MATACAP entails that the choosing has been done; there is no factual foundation of choice; and there is no possibility of change up to the horizon of expectations on which MATACAP values are based, for MATACAP gives the "net contribution our assets *will make* to cash flows in their *most likely future course*" (p. 660); note the finality of the italicized words.

Points of View

Much of the debate about the magnitudes accounting should deal in is due to failure to apprehend the necessity, in all choice situations, of having knowledge of the immediate facts. This failure is never complete; but the adoption of some specific point of view tends to push the significance of the immediate facts aside. And it is so in the course of Staubus' argument. "The appraisal of overall management performance depends on measuring the accomplishments of management and the sacrifice made to achieve them . . . measurement of the net assets . . . at the end of the appraisal period . . . and similar measurements at the beginning of the period" (p. 657). We agree. But we disagree with the concept of measurement adopted by Staubus, and others. The word is very loosely used. No one would think of measuring a man's weight at age 30 with reference to what he expects to weigh at age 40. We would measure his weight at age 30, simply. No one has yet demonstrated that the measurements relating to business from time to time must be based on any other rule than the best possible observations of things *as they are* at a given time. To measure the performance of management on the basis of what has been done plus what is still *undone* (i.e. what is expected) entails a curious meaning of performance.

It is the lack of a conception of the importance of the state of a firm in any immediate present, both for assessing performance and as a basis of expectations, which causes much foot-shuffling. Dealing with depreciable assets Staubus asserts: "We are forced to fall back on the assumption inherent in any use of entry prices, viz. that management's judgment when it decided to acquire the asset was a good one." Why we are *forced* to accept such an assumption is not clear. One of the objects of accounting surely is to show up whether management's judgments have been good or bad. We cannot do this if in the very process we are forced to assume that management's judgments have been good. In a similar way every "futuristic" statement, and all MATACAP statements are of this class, presumes that we can rely on management's judgments. But a very large slice of human experience shows that this is foolish—otherwise there would be no loss companies, no liquidations, many fewer decisions than there now are. The whole argument for reporting other than what is rests on some vague deterministic notions which ill consort with the experience we have of business. The sooner we give up being believers in or apologists for managerial omniscience, and concentrate on showing what has occurred, the better for managers, investors and the rest c us.

One of the traps in campaigning for a particular form of accounting is th tendency to feel that one has the best solution to problems which cannot b resolved without the aid of things beyond accounting. Thus Staubus say "CCE represents a second best value" (p. 660). As I have expounded its use of course, CCE is not a method of valuation but a concept used in measuring In the places cited by Staubus, I have readily admitted the necessity both c measures and valuations. The preceding demonstration is perhaps a mor succinct way of expressing the necessity. It does not imply that some such notion as MATACAP is unnecessary. I have simply rejected it as part o accounting because the values it yields and the beliefs on which they ar based are matters beyond the competence and judgment of accountants.

Staubus derides our emphasis on the sell-or-hold decision. "Need we be se concerned with the sell-or-hold decision? It frequently is not a difficult one" (p. 661). To sell-or-hold is simply the most common form of all choices; al choices are in contemplation of some switch in holdings or uses. Choice and decision mean nothing other than switching. What "broader view of the use of accounting information is more appropriate" (p. 661) than a view which concentrates on choices I cannot conceive. Apparently Professor Staubus can And perhaps he will tell us what it is.

I do not dissent from Professor Staubus; one cannot dissent from what i beside the point.

Mr. Iselin's Observations[2]

Mr. Iselin's article came to my notice some months after the above wa written. The Editor was agreeable to my commenting briefly on its content.

Iselin's main points are the determination of the "short-run period" and my exclusion of anticipatory calculation from the ordinary accounting process.

The "short-run period" is not a phrase used by me in the development of the argument. I did use "in the short run," meaning now or very soon. Much more frequently I have used "at a point of time." Any moving phenomenon may be said to have a position at some point of time; over a "short-run period" it must occupy many positions, so that the notion of position, when associated with "short-run period," is itself extraordinarily vague. If we stipulate a point of time we eliminate one kind of vagueness. But we are faced with all the difficulties of determining position at that time. My approach to this is simply to state, as well as is possible, what is knowable; and, in principle, the prices of things at that point of time are knowable. No calculation indicating where a firm may be at some future time can contribute to a statement of where it is now. If I say that I expect to be in New York

---

[2] See *Chambers on Accounting Theory*, pp. 231–238.

ı eight hours' time, no person receiving that statement can tell where I am ow. I may be in Honolulu or London or Rio de Janeiro or Atlantic City. It is he same with the financial positions of firms.

Some of Iselin's objections arise from the juxtaposition of passages taken ut of order and without reference to intervening arguments in the text; ome from the disregard of words deliberately used to draw distinctions; ome from the interpolation of words in passages quoted or the interpolation ·f ideas foreign to the sense of the text. But I lay no claim to perfection of rgument or exposition. I strove to minimize laxity in thought and to pro->ose a scheme which would minimize looseness in practice. I tried to offer rgument rather than assertion or mere belief. I also tried to construct a tight et of basic notions, and then to relax some of them just sufficiently to make he system workable. That, of course, is what any engineer, chemist or other ›ractical specialist does. Perhaps I did not make this double-edged intention lear enough; for it is precisely at such points that Iselin and others have ound what they describe as "inconsistencies." But "inconsistencies" of this ind are no different from the incompatibility of the straight line in geome-ry and the nonexistence of any such straight line in practical affairs which ıre based on geometry.

Perhaps the attempt to produce something theoretically tighter than alter-ıatives, and at the same time to propose something which approached the deal but was workable, was over-ambitious. But I believe so strongly that a heory should aid in the resolution of practical problems that I cannot regret rying to meet practical difficulties without too great a sacrifice of principle. There is no principle known to men which is not relaxed somewhat in ıpplication.

George J. Staubus is Professor of Accounting and Chairman of the Accounting Committee at the University of California, Berkeley.

Alternative Asset Flow Concepts

George J. Staubus

The purposes of this paper are to clarify the relationships between several asset flow concepts and to explore their potential uses. The concepts discussed are earnings, the working capital concept of funds flow from operations, the net quick asset version of funds flow from operations, and a literal cash flow from operations. We shall commence with an elementary exposition of the four concepts and illustrations of the related financial statements. This presentation also serves to explain the conceptual advantages of each step in the conversion of a cash statement to an earnings statement in an attempt to satisfy the fundamental curiosity of owners about their enterprise. A more technical explanation of the four concepts and their differences, with emphasis on the balance sheet items that need not be measured as the concept is narrowed from earnings back to cash flow, follows. Next, we turn our attention to selected decision situations in which one or more of the four types of flow data may be helpful. Finally, we focus attention on the problems of measurement and lack of comparability that affect the more refined flow concepts.

The Development of Flow Statements

The relationships between several asset flow concepts may be visualized by thinking of the development of an accounting system by a businessman who

Reprinted by permission of the author and publisher from *Accounting Review,* Vol. XLI (July, 1966), pp. 397–412.

has had no training in accounting. The necessity for remaining solvent and his acquaintance with the value of money are likely to lead such an individual to maintain some kind of records of cash receipts and disbursements. The separation of receipts and disbursements and some breakdowns of both follow from the above considerations; a statement similar to Exhibit I could be the culmination of the businessman's first efforts at accounting.

Exhibit I
Hypothetical Company
Cash Receipts and Disbursements
1966

Receipts:	
Cash sales and collections from customers	$11,600
Collections of interest, etc.	450
Investments by creditors and owners	2,000
Sales of unneeded plant and other facilities	500
Total cash receipts	$14,550
Disbursements:	
For merchandise	$8,400
For selling and administrative costs	1,400
Interest	400
Income taxes	500
Capital expenditures for new plant facilities	2,300
Repayments to creditors	600
Dividends	350
Total cash disbursements	$13,950
Net change in cash balance	$ 600
Cash balance, January 1	500
Cash balance, December 31	$ 1,100

After some experience with the cash receipts and disbursements statements, the fledgling businessman may begin to see some relationships between cash movements other than their direction. As he, and perhaps his banker, attempt to foresee the results of operations, he may feel the need to distinguish between those cash transactions that tend to follow patterns, even though somewhat roughly, and those that show little tendency to recur. He may see that some categories of transactions keep happening over and over in sufficiently regular patterns that they can be used as indications of what is going to happen in the future. Such events may be distinguished, in the summary cash statement, from the non-recurring cash transactions. Also, inflows and outflows of cash in financing transactions could be paired on the statement as could receipts and disbursements in the sales and purchases of property other than the stock-in-trade of the business, especially long-lived items used in conducting the major activities of the organization. Such pairings would help the reader to comprehend the impact of financing activities and capital expenditures on the firm. Consideration of these points could easily lead to a report similar to Exhibit II.

Exhibit II
Hypothetical Company
Cash Flow Statement
1966

Routine operations:
Inflows:

Cash sales and collections from customers	$11,600	
Collections of interest, etc.	450	$12,050

Outflows:

Cash disbursements for merchandise	8,400	
Selling and administrative costs	1,400	
Interest paid	400	
Income taxes paid	500	10,700
Net recurring cash flow		$ 1,350
Dividends paid		350
Net recurring cash flow retained		$ 1,000

Financing transactions:

Cash invested by creditors and owners	$ 2,000	
Repayments to creditors	600	1,400

Capital expenditures, net of cash receipts from dispositions of unneeded facilities ($500) .... (1,800)

Net change in cash balance	$	600
Balance January 1		500
Balance December 31	$	1,100

Working with cash flow statements may give the businessman ideas for further improvements. If, for example, someone asks him how business was last month he may find himself answering, "Not bad, according to our cash flow statement, but I'm not happy with the month's operations." "Why not?" "Well, I'm afraid our sales took a beating. Traffic in the store was light and goods piled up in the reserve stocks. This month's cash collections on account may be way down, but we won't know until we make up the cash flow statement at the end of the month." A few situations like this could give our potential accountant the idea that he could record both the inflows relating to sales and the outflows needed to produce the sales more promptly if he did not wait for the cash movements to occur.

The advantages of knowing more about what his customers owe him and what he owes suppliers could provide additional incentive to convert to an accrual basis of accounting. Sales, whether the sale price has been collected or not, would replace cash receipts; purchases of goods and services would be recognized as the major offsetting group of transactions. The budding accountant may not think of it this way, but he would be recognizing increases in net quick assets as favorable flows and decreases in net quick assets as unfavorable flows. Exhibit III reflects this approach to the reporting of asset flows.

Further experience with asset flow statements as representations of the rm's operations may disclose deficiencies in the quick flow statement. A few ases of substantial changes in inventories, which reflect poor matching of eceipts of purchased goods with shipments of goods sold, may suggest the eed for a change in the procedure for accounting for the cost of merchandise. Despite steady sales and steady prices, heavy purchasing could result in negative net recurring quick flow in a short period, or slow purchasing ould result in a bulge in the net recurring flow.

The alert manager-accountant might see that his flow statement would ive a better indication of operating success if it included deductions from ales for the cost of those goods sold rather than those purchased. He might lso recognize a similar, although less significant, improvement from spreadng the cost of such things as insurance coverage evenly over the periods ather than deducting them when purchased. If his business operations involved frequent cases of collections from customers prior to the provisions of oods or services to those customers, he may feel that he is not entitled to eport the favorable flow until the related unfavorable flows can be matched vith it; the deferral of credits to revenue may be appropriate. The merits of natching costs with revenues in these ways might have sufficient appeal to ntice the recordkeeper to adopt the deferral technique of accounting for nventories of merchandise, short-term prepayments of routine operating osts, and precollections from customers.

Exhibit III
Hypothetical Company
Quick Asset Flow Statement
1966

Routine operations:		
Inflows:		
Sales of merchandise and related services	$12,000	
Interest accrued on investments, etc.	400	$12,400
Outflows:		
Purchases of merchandise	$ 8,700	
Routine purchases of supplies and services	1,600	
Interest cost accrued	400	
Income taxes for the year	600	11,300
Net recurring quick asset flow		$ 1,100
Dividends declared		300
Net recurring quick asset flow retained		$ 800
Financing transactions:		
Long-term investments by creditors and owners	$ 2,000	
Current maturities and premature retirements of debts	600	1,400
Capital expenditures, net of receipts from sales of unneeded facilities ($500)		(1,800)
Net change in net quick assets		$ 400
Net quick asset balance January 1 (credit)		(100)
Net quick asset balance December 31		$ 300

Exhibit IV
Hypothetical Company
Working Capital Flow Statement
1966

Routine operations:
Inflows:

Sales of merchandise and related services	$12,000	
Interest accrued on investments, etc.	400	$12,400
Outflows:		
Cost of goods sold	$ 8,000	
Selling and administrative costs	1,600	
Interest cost accrued	400	
Income taxes for the year	600	10,600
Net recurring working capital flow		$ 1,800
Dividends declared		300
Net recurring working capital flow retained		$ 1,500
Financing transactions:		
Long-term investment by creditors and owners	$ 2,000	
Current maturities and premature retirements of debt	600	1,400
Capital expenditures, net of receipts from sale of unneeded facilities ($500)		(1,800)
Net change in working capital		$ 1,100
Working capital balance January 1		2,400
Working capital balance December 31		$ 3,500

To defer the reporting of such transactions until some time after the cash movement permits a more logical cause-and-effect matching on the working flow statement than on the previous flow statements. This is shown in Exhibit IV above.

The adoption of the accrual and deferral techniques of accounting for short-lived assets has resulted in an asset flow statement that appears to have important advantages over the cash statements of Exhibits I and II, but the stockholders and other readers of these statements may feel that the net recurring working capital flow could be converted to a figure that would provide a better indication of the management's success in serving the owners' objectives if it took into account the consumption of long-lived assets. While the working flow statement shows the application of working capital to acquire plant assets, it does not include those transactions in the computation of net recurring working capital flow and it does not give any indication of whether the acquisitions were greater or less than the consumption of such properties by use or wastage during the reporting period. A measure of the consumption and loss of service potential embodied in long-lived assets would seem to be an appropriate deduction from revenues in the computation of a net recurring flow to be used as an indicator of the effects of routine operations on the owners' interests.

While this may seem to be a more difficult accounting task than the previous refinements (we assume have been adopted), the accountant may feel

Exhibit V
Hypothetical Company
Earnings and Net Worth Statement
1966

Revenues:		
Sales of merchandise and related services	$12,000	
Interest and miscellaneous earnings	400	
Total revenues		$12,400
Expenses:		
Cost of goods sold	$ 8,000	
Selling expenses	1,000	
Administrative expenses	1,400	
Income taxes	700	
Interest expenses	500	
Total expenses		11,600
NET EARNINGS		$ 800
Extraordinary charges and credits:		
Loss on sale of real property	$ (400)	
Gain on premature retirement of debt	300	(100)
Dividends declared		(300)
Proceeds of stock issue		2,000
Net change in stockholders' equity		$ 2,400
Stockholders' equity January 1		10,000
Stockholders' equity December 31		$12,400

that he can improve the statement if he simply deducts from the revenues of
each period during which a long-lived asset is expected to be used a systematically computed portion of the acquisition cost of that asset. The accountant who has worked out such a refined system may also see the need for
recognizing some costs that have not yet been paid for and do not require
payment in the near future. Some types of pension plans and gimmicks
permitting postponement of income for taxing purposes are relevant examples. When such factors have been taken into consideration a net asset flow
statement, or earnings statement, reflecting greater use of the accrual and
deferral techniques, may be prepared as in Exhibit V immediately above.

Four Recurring Asset Flow Concepts

Exhibits II through V are organized so as to distinguish between recurring
and nonrecurring flows. The reflection of such a distinction on the statement
implies that the accountant believes that some categories of transactions can
be projected more reliably than others. The analyst who is interested in
predicting these transactions is likely to start with historical data on the
amounts of such transactions and make such adjustments as he sees fit in
order to estimate the future amounts. Nonrecurring transactions, on the
other hand, are not so accurately predicted by this approach. Instead of
projecting from historical data, the analyst is more likely to make an inde-

pendent estimate based upon evidence relating specifically to the future, such as contractual debt maturities and capital expenditure budgets, rather than start with last year's amounts and adjust them for anticipated changes. This is not a black and white distinction, of course, but it may well be a usefully realistic distinction.

Recurring events exclude financing transactions involving principal amounts as well as purchases and sales of noncurrent assets and marketable securities. Recurring flows typically should include charges for income taxes and for interest on debt as well as dividends on preferred stock. Financial credits, such as interest and dividends on investment securities, are also included in the recurring operations category. This leaves the analyst with figures that are relevant to the common stockholder: earnings to the common equity and other asset flow figures that are comparable in this respect. The concept of income as a return on owners' investment is not emphasized in this approach, although it would be the same as earnings if there were no preferred shares outstanding. Nor is the broader concept of income as a return on all long-term capital featured.

This may be a good stage in our discussion at which to pause to define the four concepts we have been developing.

1. *Earnings* is the term for the net change in net assets (assets less liabilities) produced by recurring operations.
2. *Working flow*, or current flow, is the net change in net current assets, or working capital, in recurring operations.
3. *Quick flow* is the net change in net short-term monetary assets, or net quick assets, from recurring operations.
4. *Cash flow*, or literal cash flow, is the net change in cash from recurring operations.

Now let us examine the technical features of these concepts.

Earnings is the broadest of the group. If one were to condense all of the double-entry system into two accounts, one for net-asset items (assets and liabilities) and one for net worth, earnings would be the net change in either of these accounts from recurring operations. Transactions such as dividends on common stock, issue and acquisition by the corporation of its own stock, catastrophic losses, windfall gains, and so on would change these two accounts but would not be included in the earnings concept because they do not tend to recur in a reliable pattern. We could say that earnings occur in transactions that change net assets, or we could say earnings involve transactions that change the net worth. However, for comparison with the alternative asset flow concepts, we can define earnings as the changes in net assets from recurring operations.

Working flow (or perhaps current flow) deals with a portion of the balance sheet that is narrower than net assets. Current assets or current liabilities must be involved in working flows, and, as in the case of earnings, the transaction must affect the net of the category. Offsetting debits and credits within the category, such as collections of accounts receivable, are not working flows; nor are transactions recorded by offsetting debits and credits entirely outside the working capital area, such as depreciation expense. Neither the debit to depreciation expense, which will end up in retained earnings, nor the offsetting credit to the contra fixed asset account affects working capital. This also holds for expenses credited to accounts such as allowance for depletion, unamortized bond discount, deferred income tax liability, and estimated long-term pension liability.

To state this point more concisely, no expense credited to a noncurrent account affects the working flow, and no revenue debited to a noncurrent account affects the working flow.[1] As a corollary of the preceding statement, we may say that the degree of accuracy or error involved in entries recording expenses credited to noncurrent balance sheet accounts does not affect the working flow figure. Stated in terms of balance sheet accounts, the measurement of noncurrent assets and liabilities does not affect the working flow.

Quick flow is the term suggested for the net change in net short-term monetary assets (net quick assets) from recurring operations. Monetary assets include cash and claims to cash such as various types of receivables and bonds owned. Monetary liabilities are obligations to pay cash at some future time. The amount of net short-term monetary assets is the excess of current monetary assets over current monetary liabilities, sometimes called net quick assets; this amount is frequently negative. The most common items included in working capital but excluded from net quick assets are inventories of commodities, short-term prepayments and, among the liabilities, deferred credits to revenue, such as unearned rentals received in advance. Looking at related transactions, we can see that purchases of merchandise do not affect net current assets (working capital), so they are not a component of working flows; but they do affect net quick assets (by credits to accounts payable or cash), so they are negative quick flows.

The shipment of goods to customers, on the other hand, affects working capital and working flows, as well as earnings; but since it does not affect net quick assets, it is not a quick flow. Likewise, prepaying insurance is a quick-flow transaction but not a working-flow transaction; the expiration of prepaid insurance is a working-flow transaction but not a quick-flow transac-

---

[1] Similarly, any portion of a recurring credit to a current account that is offset by a charge to a noncurrent asset or liability account is a negative working flow item just like most expenses and any portion of a recurring charge to a current account that is offset by a credit to a noncurrent asset or liability is a positive working flow item, although this is a rare type of transaction. A good example of the former is the accrual of income tax payable in the later years of the life of an asset depreciated on a straight-line basis on the books but on a diminishing charge basis for tax returns by a firm practicing inter-period tax allocation. The journal entry follows:

Dr. Federal income tax expense $2,500
Dr. Deferred Federal income tax liability 500
      Cr. Federal income tax payable $3,000

The entire $3,000 is a negative fund flow, not merely the amount of the expense.

tion. Also, collecting rent in advance affects net quick assets but not working capital; earning the precollected rent affects working flow but not quick flow. All of this means that the measurement of the balance-sheet quantities of inventories, prepayments, and deferred credits to revenue affect working flow and earnings but not quick flow. To the extent that we are dissatisfied with inventory measurements in accounting we may lean towards the quick-flow concept rather than working flow. (Measurements of prepayments and short-term deferred credits to revenue are rarely cause for concern.)

Cash flow should be used to refer to changes in cash from recurring operations. It is a recurring asset flow concept comparable to quick flow, working flow, and earnings. Cash flow differs from quick flow in that collections of receivables that were created in revenue transactions are cash flows, while

Exhibit VI
Hypothetical Company
Asset Flow Statements
1966

	Earnings	Working Flow	Quick Flow	Cash Flow
Inflows:				
From customers				
Sales	$12,000	$12,000	$12,000	
Collections				$11,600
On investments				
Accrued	400	400	400	
Collected				450
Total inflows	$12,400	$12,400	$12,400	$12,050
Outflows:				
Merchandise:				
Cost of merchandise sold	$ 8,000	$ 8,000		
Purchases			$ 8,700	
Paid to suppliers				$ 8,400
Depreciation	600			
Pensions				
Funded	600	600	600	600
Additional	200			
Other operating costs	1,000	1,000	1,000	800
Interest				
Nominal	400	400	400	400
Amortization of discount and issue expense	100			
Income taxes				
Per returns	600	600	600	
Deferred	100			
Paid				500
Total outflows	$11,600	$10,600	$11,300	$10,700
Net inflows	$ 800	$ 1,800	$ 1,100	$ 1,350

the creation of those receivables were quick flows. Likewise, payments of payables are negative cash flows, while the creation of payables through purchases and many expense transactions are negative quick flows. The most difficult common measurement that affects quick flows that is bypassed by switching to the cash-flow concept is the estimation of uncollectible accounts receivable. The normal adjusting entry to provide for uncollectibles records a quick-asset transaction but not a cash transaction.

Further elucidation of the four concepts may result from the juxtaposition of the flow statements of Exhibits II through V as shown in Exhibit VI.

Inherent in these four definitions and the accompanying analysis of them are the reasons why earnings may not be the one and only useful asset flow concept. The measurement of the revenues and expenses that are offset in the calculation of earnings requires measurement of net assets (net worth), i.e. all assets and liabilities. Of all the measurement problems encountered by the accountant who is attempting to calculate earnings, those pertaining to non-current nonmonetary assets and noncurrent liabilities resulting from deferred payment of such expenses as pensions and income taxes are the most difficult.

Rather than undertake a digression to support this assertion, we will proceed on the assumption that the reader agrees that depreciation, depletion, amortization of leaseholds and intangible assets, income-tax allocation, and pension expenses constitute a package of problems that accountants would be very happy to avoid. Many users of the income statement would be just as pleased to be free of the uncertainties injected into the earnings figure by this group of measurement problems. Their yearning for an earnings concept that is free of the measurement errors and intercompany inconsistencies relating to noncurrent assets and liabilities may be so strong as to attract analysts to a working flow concept that is free of such defects. Unfortunately, the price of freedom from serious errors of measurement is loss of relevance to stockholders' interests. To accountants, this appears to be a classic case of throwing out the baby with the bath water; but to some readers of our statements it is a case of ranking reliability of calculation over conceptual relevance—a priority system with which adherents to historical cost ought to be sympathetic.

Just as the basic technical argument for relying upon working flow as opposed to earnings is that working flow is free of the worst measurement errors and inconsistencies that affect earnings, one could also argue that quick flow is based on more reliable measurements than is working flow. Working flow is the net change in net current assets from recurring operations, while quick flow is the net change in net short-term monetary assets from recurring operations. Since the major items included in net current assets that are excluded in the computation of net quick assets are inventories, prepayments, and deferred credits to revenue, the switch from working flow to quick flow avoids the measurement problems pertaining to these specified items. If we feel that inventory valuation (or, less likely, the measurement of prepayments or deferred credits to revenue) is such a weak component of working flow accounting that it seriously limits the usefulness of the net recurring working flow, we might be just as happy to substitute the quick-flow concept.

Having side-stepped the problems of depreciation, depletion, amortization, and provisions for deferred tax and pension liabilities, etc., as well as the inventory valuation problem (by substituting quick flow for working flow), we have made the problems of calculating a net recurring flow a great deal more manageable. The most serious ones that remain are the estimation of such contra receivable items as uncollectibles, collection costs, and cash discounts to be taken by customers. While these may not be cause for much concern in the typical case, firms that do a great deal of installment-sales business may find that there is a considerable difference in the reliability of quick flows as compared with cash flows. Under such circumstances, the analyst may seriously consider switching from quick flow to cash flow (in the literal sense) as the starting point for his analysis.

The technical advantages and disadvantages of the several flow concepts may be summarized in a series of comparative statements.

1. If we substitute working flow for earnings we may gain by omitting our crude measurements of depreciation, depletion, amortization, and provisions for deferred liabilities; but we must recognize the disadvantage of completely ignoring capital consumption costs and the portions of pensions, income taxes, etc. that are not paid currently.

2. If we substitute quick flow for working flow, we may gain by eliminating dependence upon the valuation of inventories, prepayments, and deferred credits to revenue, but we expose the resulting net flow figure to the problems of mismatching of costs with revenues by failure to defer them when appropriate.

3. If we substitute cash flow for quick flow we may gain by avoiding the problems of valuation of receivables, but we lose the contribution to matching resulting from the use of the accrual method of recognizing revenues and costs.

4. To reverse the substitution, if we switch from cash flow to quick flow we gain better matching of costs and revenues through the use of the accrual technique, but must accept the problems of valuation of receivables.

5. If we substitute the more refined concept of working flow for quick flow, we gain the better matching contributed by short-term deferrals of merchandise costs, prepayments of services, and revenue received in advance, but we take on the measurement difficulties relating to these deferrals, especially inventory valuation.

6. If we switch to earnings from working flow, we improve the relevance of the flow concept to investor's interests by providing for consumption of long-lived assets and for long-term delays in payment of some costs, but we must face up to the related measurement problems, especially depreciation.

From the point of view of the accountant who is considering the development of an accounting system by making improvements on a cash receipts and disbursements system, which refinements are worthwhile depend upon (1) the availability of the information needed to make the refinements, such as bases for estimating bad debts, collection costs and discounts to be taken by customers, and the service flow lives and patterns of depreciable assets; (2) the time (cost) required to make the refinements; and (3) the materiality of the differences between the refined flow concept (and related balance sheet data) and the cruder concept.

Uses of Asset Flow Data

In this section we turn our attention to the uses of asset flow data. We shall relate the alternative asset flow concepts to several types of decisions frequently encountered by investors and managers. The discussion will focus on *conceptual relevance* of the data to the decision, or prediction, that has to be made without regard to the measurement problems associated with the calculation of the flows.

One broad category of decisions that are made partly on the basis of financial statement data is external investment decisions. Those deciding to invest or to refrain from investing, to sell or to hold their investment positions—any of these investors or prospective investors may be interested in the asset flows of the firm that is the object of their attention. One explanation of their interest utilizes the residual-equity point of view. The residual equity in a corporation is normally held by the common stockholders. It is the residual interest in assets remaining after deducting all prior claims, including those of preferred stockholders. Common stockholders, it may be argued, are vitally interested in their equity in the firm and in recent changes in that equity.

A measure of the recurring changes in the residual equity in the recent past is useful in predicting changes in the future. Earnings is such a measure. Further, the amount of the residual equity and the rate and direction of change in it are of great interest to other investors because the residual equity represents a buffer of assets available as a margin of safety protecting the senior investor. Preferred stockholders and creditors, also, are concerned about the amount and fluctuations in this buffer equity.

From this residual equity point of view, changes in all net asset items are significant. The most significant distinction, aside from direction of change, is between recurring and non-recurring changes. The form of an asset and the anticipated timing of its contributions to the cash balance are of lesser importance. Thus, the monetary-nonmonetary dichotomy and the current-noncurrent distinction need not be emphasized. Even the difference between assets and liabilities may be played down once we recognize the difference in mathematical sign applicable to them when they are merged into the net asset concept. A reduction in the service potential of patents or buildings owned is just as undesirable to the residual equityholders (in the long run) as a relinquishment of inventory or the incurrence of an obligation to pay cash. The net change in net assets produced by recurring operations, i.e. earnings, is the most relevant concept of recurring asset flows.

A quite different view emphasizes the investor's interest in his own cash receipts from the firm. If the investor expects cash transfers from the firm, he must predict the firm's cash balance (a useful measure of capacity to pay) at the future date or dates in which he is interested. Since a future cash balance at any particular date is determined by the present cash balance and cash receipts and disbursements between now and the future date, investors are interested in predicting the firm's future cash flows. Past recurring cash flows provide a starting point for predicting future recurring cash flows. (A capital expenditures plan and a balance sheet disclosing the due dates of major monetary assets and liabilities, particularly those involving nonrecurring cash movements, are additional indications of future cash flows.) We may conclude that a cash flow statement can be of help to investors.

Which of these views is more useful? One simple answer is that the residual equity point of view is more relevant to long-term investment decisions and that the cash view is more suitable for short-term analyses. In the long run all costs have to be covered, including depreciation; profitability is vital. The short-term investor, on the other hand, may do very well despite losses by the company if it can maintain its liquidity.

The Common Stockholder

Let us turn to the specific problem of the common-stock investor and his decision. Despite his interest in predicting cash dividends from the company, he may have relatively little interest in recent cash flows. The value of common stock typically depends upon a long view of the future. While the investor will not be able to enjoy the long-run benefits of holding the stock if the corporation does not survive the short run, the firm's inability to pay one quarterly dividend or even a bond interest payment, because of a liquidity deficiency, is not likely to threaten its survival if its earnings hold up.

The common-stock investor is almost certain to be more interested in predicting profitability than liquidity, and an accurate earnings statement is likely to be far more important to him than a cash flow statement or even a working flow or quick flow statement.

Investors in Fixed Income Securities

The purchaser of fixed income securities must give more attention to corporate liquidity than the common stock investor, because he presumably is more dependent upon steady income. The fixed income security analyst must

ve a great deal of attention to predicting the probability of the issuer's
ailing to make the regular income payments or the maturity payment (in
the case of a security with a maturity date). Anticipated improvements in
ther profitability or liquidity are of much less interest than are potential
everses, particularly in liquidity. But it is also true that a temporary lack of
quidity is not likely to precipitate the ultimate financial disaster (business
ailure) as long as earnings are respectable. Both profitability and liquidity
re of concern to the fixed income security analyst.

A popular test of the safety of a fixed income security is the times-interest-
arned test. This measure gives the analyst an idea of the extent to which
arnings could decline and still cover the periodic interest payments to the
ond holder. A good case can be made for calculating the relationship be-
ween the net recurring working flow before interest, preferred dividends,
nd income taxes, and the bond interest cost—the number of times bond
nterest is covered by working flow. The major consideration in bond analy-
s is to judge the firm's ability to meet its fixed obligations under the *worst*
onditions that the firm is likely to face during the life of the bonds or as far
head as the analyst cares to look. Since poor operating results usually in-
olve a reduction in the volume of business, replacement of fixed assets can
robably be drastically cut back temporarily under such conditions; very
ttle or no provision for consumption of fixed assets need be made in calcu-
ating the flow of assets available to meet the fixed charges. The analyst is not
o concerned about the firm's ability to replace its plant assets as he is about
eeting the current operating costs requiring working capital. Under these
ircumstances, depreciation is a distinctly lower-ranking cost.

The Preferred Stockholder

A similar approach may be taken to preferred stock dividend coverage. The
umber of times that the dividend is covered by working flow is perhaps as
elevant a test as the number of times that the dividend is earned. Both of
hese tests may be used because both liquidity and profitability are required
f the preferred dividend is to be safe. Of course, the preferred dividend may
e paid even if not earned, but the fixed income investor can not count on
uch an attitude on the part of the board of directors. We conclude that both
working flow and earnings are relevant to the fixed income security investment decision.

The Short-Term Creditor

The short-term creditor is much more interested in forecasting the liquidity
of the firm than its profitability. He must attempt to predict the firm's
capacity to pay at a specific time in the near future. Such a prediction may be
based on short-term balance sheet items and the rate of net recurring flow of
net short-term assets. Working flow, quick flow or cash flow is almost certain

to be more relevant than earnings. For example, the analyst may compute the firm's quick ratio and its net quick assets. If the latter is negative, it might be related to the monthly net recurring quick flow to determine the number of months required to pay off the net quick liabilities if the rate of quick flow were to continue (and if no nonrecurring quick flows occur). Or the analyst may prefer to relate the net quick liabilities to the rate of working flow in order to allow for the "normalization" of purchases. If there is, or is likely to be, an unusually wide discrepancy between quick flows and cash flows, the latter may be of considerable interest instead of, or in addition to, working flow or quick flow. Earnings is unlikely to be the flow concept most relevant to the short-term credit decision, although it should not be ignored.

The Corporate Point of View

These discussions of the relevance of alternative flow concepts to investment decisions suggest that no one of the concepts is always the most relevant; any one of them may be the first choice of the investment analyst, depending upon the circumstances surrounding the decision. While the discussion emphasized the point of view of the external analyst, we should recognize that the corporate treasurer must make a very similar analysis. What is bad for the investor is likely to be bad for the corporation. For example, the corporate management is no more eager to issue bonds that it cannot service than an investor is to buy them. A satisfactory financing arrangement must be satisfactory to both parties. However, we should keep in mind the nature of the financial position that requires the issuance of securities.

Boards of directors do not decide to borrow money or issue securities to provide retained earnings; they do so to raise cash that is needed to supplement the flow from operations. A working flow projection may indicate a probable deficiency in working capital that should be met by intermediate or long-term financing. (Short-term borrowing does not increase net working capital.) A cash flow projection may show the need for a short-term loan. Earnings projections, on the other hand, cannot shed much light on the need for financing, although they may give a good indication of the reception the firm's securities will get in the money market—especially the long-term market.

We now turn to internal decisions about the uses of corporate funds. Since the various possible uses of funds compete with each other, decisions in this area have some tendency to merge into one grand determination of the distribution of the available funds among the several uses. Nevertheless, we must recognize that each use has its own peculiar factors that are relevant to the decision. For example, the declaration of cash dividends is usually based on consideration of both liquidity and profitability. Boards of directors usually give weight to both earnings and the availability of cash. If they foresee a cash stringency in the near future, it may affect their decision. For this

urpose, a cash flow, quick flow, or working flow analysis is likely to be
seful in addition to an earnings statement.

Capital expenditures is another common use of liquid funds. One major
rpe of information that is relevant to capital expenditure decisions is dif-
:rential cash flows—projected increases and decreases in cash operating
osts or increases in both revenues and cash costs that are expected to result
rom the initial outlay. In addition, some consideration must be given to the
vailability of the funds needed for the initial outlay and the effect of the
roposed outlay on the firm's ability to meet all of its obligations as they
ome due. This requires an analysis of future liquid flows; past and/or
rojected statements of cash flows, quick flows, or working flows are likely to
e more valuable than earnings statements.

The retirement of debt or stock is another possible use of funds. A decision
n this question, aside from the incremental analysis needed to establish its
esirability, requires consideration of liquidity. The management must de-
ide whether it can spare the cash required, and in order to make this
ecision it needs to analyze future sources and uses of cash. Projected profits
re not enough to justify retirement of securities if the profits will have to be
einvested, and lack of profits need not deter the management from contract-
ng its capital structure if the cash needed to accomplish it will not be
equired for other purposes. A contracting firm may not need to provide for
eplacement of plant assets.

To summarize this discussion of the relevance of several asset flow con-
epts to selected decisions, we may say that some decisions require heavy
mphasis on predictions of profitability, some require that major weight be
;iven to predictions of liquidity, while others require predictions of both. Of
he four asset flow concepts we have presented for consideration in this
aper, earnings is the only one that purports to measure profitability while
he other three relate more closely to liquidity. Accordingly, we conclude that
ll four of our asset flow measures are conceptually relevant to the decisions
acing users of financial statements. Next, we shall consider the practical
roblems of applying the concepts.

Asset Flows—Measurement, Consistency, and Uniformity

Conceptual relevance is an important attribute of a financial datum which is
o be used in making a decision. Accuracy is an equally important attribute.
A beautiful concept cannot justify the trust of the decision maker if the
ccountant cannot obtain accurate perceptions that will permit him to exe-
:ute the concept. Theory without measurement is no better than measure-
nent without theory.

Of the four flow concepts we have discussed in preceding pages, cash flow
s the most easily measured. While one may encounter problems in the

measurement of cash receipts and disbursements, surely the reader will accept the above conclusion without requiring consideration of those problems. We may, of course, find it difficult to distinguish between recurring and nonrecurring movements, but this same problem arises in the application of any of the flow concepts.

The timing of cash transactions may result in poorer comparability than would be obtained by recognition of events on an accrual basis. For example, the month of July may have five weekly payroll dates while August has only four, while next year July may have four and August five. This makes it difficult to visualize trends from month to month and year to year. Also, a cash basis of accounting for the results of routine operations provides the opportunity for control over the reported results by juggling the timing of cash payments of accounts payable.

The opportunities for manipulation of the reported results may not be quite so great when the other flow concepts are used, although we must recognize that the timing of purchases permits this type of control over reported quick flow. Working flow and earnings may be manipulated in some firms by the use of specific identification of inventory units, by the timing of end-of-year purchases on Lifo, and by the range of judgment that may be applied in writing down obsolete, slow-moving, damaged goods, etc. On the inflow side, quick flow, working flow, and earnings may be influenced by liberal or conservative provisions for bad debts and, in many firms, by some degree of control over billing dates. However, we should recognize that cash flow is typically the most susceptible to manipulation of any of the asset flow concepts.

Quick flow reporting introduces one group of substantial measurement issues—those pertaining to the valuation of receivables. Since the amount of the inflow in a sale is the amount of the asset that came into the firm, the measurement of the amount of that asset is a prerequisite to the preparation of a quick flow statement. While we are accustomed to conditions under which we can measure accounts receivable to within one percent of the amounts to be collected, the recent experience of Brunswick Corporation, involving a $111 million additional provision for the uncollectibility of receivables, most of which were on the books at the previous statement date, indicates that serious errors can be made in the measurement of trade receivables. Payables generally are easier to value.

Alternative generally accepted accounting principles play a modest role in reducing the intercompany comparability of net recurring quick flows. Grady lists five areas in which alternatives are available that affect quick flows.[2] Two relate to the timing of the recognition of the basic revenue flows, two relate to sales and purchase discounts, and the fifth involves accounting

---

[2] Paul Grady, *Inventory of Generally Accepted Accounting Principles for Business Enterprises*, Accounting Research Study No. 7 (American Institute of Certified Public Accountants, 1965), pp. 373–7.

or property taxes. The last three are unlikely to result in a material lack of comparability, but the alternative methods of revenue recognition could make a great deal of difference in times of rapid change in the volume of business.

The working flow concept involves the accountant in inventory valuation. Other measurement problems related to working flow in addition to all of those connected with quick flow, include some relatively immaterial ones pertaining to short-term prepayments, such as prepaid advertising, and those related to nonmonetary liabilities such as deferred credits to revenue and estimated liabilities on warranties. While these other nonmonetary working capital components sometimes involve some interesting and serious problems of measurement, the inventory area is sufficient to indicate the defects, from the point of view of the user of financial statements, that are picked up by broadening the funds concept to include nonmonetary working capital items.

At this point in our deliberations, we should note that as we substitute a more relevant flow concept we find accountants applying less relevant measurement techniques. The cash flow concept requires use of only the most impeccable of measurement methods—counting the face value of money. This method can be applied with great accuracy and it measures a quality—present purchasing power—that is highly relevant to the managers and investors who may be using the data to make a decision.

The quick flow concept requires the determination of the future cash flows that will be involved in existing contractual obligations of, or to, the firm. These amounts must then be discounted at an appropriate discount rate to obtain their present values. These procedures provide opportunities for error, a common one being failure to discount for the waiting period. These errors usually are not serious, although they certainly can be, but they definitely result in less accurate measurements than are made of cash and, if timing is ignored by substituting estimated future cash flows for their present values, the evidence being utilized can be said to be less relevant to the needs of decision makers.[3]

The working flow concept requires major concessions in the realm of measurements. The nonmonetary items are not subject to measurement by the highly relevant techniques applicable to monetary assets and liabilities. Net realizable value and replacement cost are sometimes used for inventories, but most goods are valued at some version of historical cost. Net realizable value is both current and forward looking, replacement cost is current and backward looking, and historical cost is both noncurrent and backward looking—the least relevant of all the accepted measurement methods from the point of view of decision makers. The measurements of cost of goods sold

---

[3] We believe that the valuation of receivables and payables by discounting is a part of generally accepted accounting theory.

made in current accounting practice may be characterized as irrelevant measurements of a relevant flow, whereas the purchases figures that go into the quick flow computation are based on relevant measures of an irrelevant concept.

Grady lists seven cases of alternative generally accepted accounting principles that affect working flow; five of these also affect quick flow and have been previously mentioned. One of the others is a relatively minor one—the choice between carrying spare machinery parts as inventory items or depreciating them as fixed assets. The seventh—really a whole group of alternative situations—is the big one: the whole field of inventory valuation. Included in this group are (1) the choice of assumption as to the flow of costs (Fifo, Lifo, etc.); (2) the choice of standard cost or "actual" cost; (3) the choice of the portion of fixed overhead that may be included in inventory values; (4) the choice of applying the lower of cost or market rule on an item-by-item class, or total basis; and (5) the choice of carrying inventories at sale price or cost in some industries, such as mining and meat packing.

In addition to accepted alternatives, managements choosing the Lifo cost flow assumption have an opportunity to control cost of goods sold to some extent by shifting the timing of purchases from period to period. "Dipping into" Lifo inventories also results in lack of comparability between periods and between firms. Fifo contributes its share of problems too. If the carrying costs of an aging inventory are not capitalized and/or if prices change substantially over the years it takes to develop the desired flavor, in some industries the cost of goods sold on a Fifo basis may be a poor measure of the outflow of service potential related to the shipment of goods to customers.

The measurement of earnings opens Pandora's box to accountants. In Grady's list of situations in which alternative methods of accounting are generally accepted, there are five that affect quick flow but not cash flow, two (including the group of inventory alternatives) that affect working flow but not quick flow, and twenty-one that affect earnings but not working flow. Among these were situations relating to accounting for pensions, income-tax allocation, the investment credit, depreciation and depletion methods and rates, intangibles, research, exploration and development costs, investments in unconsolidated affiliates, and business combinations. When we add to this list of alternatives the uniform practice of adhering to historical cost[4] in accounting for noncurrent assets—a uniform practice with varying undesirable effects upon the earnings of different firms and years—we can see that the concept of earnings is not measured as precisely and uniformly as the other flow concepts. Whether or not these practical limitations offset its superior conceptual relevance to many decision situations requires a balancing that we must leave to the reader.

---

[4] We believe that it is generally accepted among accounting theorists that historical cost is often a poor basis of valuation.

Conclusion

The value of an asset flow concept depends upon its relevance to the problems facing decision makers and on the accuracy and uniformity with which it is applied. Accounting practices include many examples of rejection of a relevant concept in favor of a less relevant one for the sake of accuracy and objectivity in the necessary measurements. The "cost principle" is the most prominent example of this priority arrangement. Accountants cannot argue that the cost of an asset is forever relevant to the problems facing readers of financial statements but they do argue that cost can be measured with greater accuracy and objectivity than a more relevant concept such as net realizable value or replacement cost.

Similarly, when choosing an asset flow concept for reporting to investors, or for reporting to management, the accountant may not choose the most relevant concept if it is too difficult to apply. We found that no one asset flow concept is most relevant to all decisions commonly made by readers of financial statements. Furthermore, the measurement difficulties and lack of comparability of earnings and, to a lesser extent, working flow calculations indicate that users of financial statements should ask accountants to give careful consideration to their choice of flow concepts to emphasize in financial statements. The proper choice is not obvious and is not always the same.

3. MEASUREMENT AND ALLOCATION OF ASSETS

The primary function of the traditional accounting model has been either measurement of assets and liabilities or the allocation of costs and revenues to different time periods. Emphasis on either function accomplishes the necessary allocation. If measurement of assets and liabilities is completed, the change from the beginning of the period to the end of the period becomes the income of the period. If income is determined by allocating revenues and expenses to different periods, the unallocated amounts represent the measurement of assets and liabilities. It is important to note that abandonment of the historical cost principle would have little if any impact on the allocation problem. It may be no easier, for instance, to allocate current market values than historical costs. Also, if existing assets are to be measured, the future benefits approach does not escape allocation problems. The future benefit stream will have to be allocated between the existing assets and assets to be added in the future. No theory of measurement has yet been developed that avoids the problem of allocation.

It is charged that any allocation the accountant makes will necessarily be arbitrary in the sense that his particular allocation cannot be justified to the exclusion of all other possible allocations. Carried to its logical conclusion, this argument demonstrates that asset measurement and income determination methods must also be arbitrary.

The readings in this section were chosen to show both the arbitrary nature and the general assumption of usefulness of accounting allocations. The first reading is from a monograph by Arthur L. Thomas. Only parts of Thomas's monograph are included here; he has been kind enough to provide a summary of the excluded portion of his monograph. The excluded parts contain discussions of the present approaches to depreciation, the net revenue contribution (both simultaneous allocation and capital budgeting) approaches, depreciation allocations over time, and some responses to the problem. The result is a convincing argument concerning the arbitrary nature of accounting allocations. He relies heavily on depreciable assets for his illustrations, but he effectively demonstrates the application of his points to all asset allocations. Students are encouraged to study the entire monograph in order to obtain a better understanding of the logic of his arguments.

Thomas concludes with some interesting comments on how accountants might avoid making allocations.

The allocation problem associated with inventories is discussed in the second article, by Kenneth S. Most. He notes that items in inventory may or may not be part of the normal inventory level. According to his argument, if items have not been acquired to replace items sold or used, they should not be valued on a replacement basis.

Some items in inventory are passed forward from the current period to the next because they are not necessary to continue the operating cycle. Since they must or should be disposed of, they ought to be valued on the basis of the proceeds they will produce upon disposal. This sort of valuation requires attention to the quantity considerations of inventories, in addition to the traditional price considerations.

The impact of allocations on the balance sheet is amplified in the third reading, by Robert T. Sprouse. He supports the proposition that the balance sheet embodies the most fundamental elements of accounting theory, from which the essential elements contained in the income statement are necessarily derived.

Sprouse sets out three balance sheet views: 1.) the sheet of balances, 2.) the static funds statement, and 3.) the financial position. The sheet of balances view maintains that through matching, the income statement can be made superior to the balance sheet. The static funds statement view holds the balance sheet to be a statement of the sources and general composition of the firm's capital. This view is essentially a stewardship view of the balance sheet. The financial position view requires that all transactions be analyzed in terms of their effect on assets, liabilities and owner's equity. The income accounts are simply measures or explanations of these changes.

Sprouse suggests that if there is to be a theory of accounting among these three views, the financial position view offers the only hope.

The fourth article is a discussion of Sprouse's article by Alfred Rappaport. Rappaport challenges the primacy of the balance sheet, leaning toward a user approach to accounting as opposed to Sprouse's more structural approach. He suggests that the articulation between the balance sheet and the income statement should not be treated as axiomatic. In his view, the greatest hope for progress in accounting theory rests with the user approach.

The fifth article, by Reg S. Gynther, deals with allocation of intangible assets. He discusses the conceptual measurement of goodwill and asserts that the nature of goodwill is often confused with the method of calculating goodwill, i.e., capitalization of excess earnings. He asserts that intangible assets are, in an economic sense, no different from tangible assets as regards their valuation, and people making financial decisions outside the firm need to know the value of intangibles.

The final reading in this section is the summary from AICPA Accounting Research Study No. 10, "Accounting for Goodwill." The study recommends an immediate or periodic write-off of purchased goodwill directly to capital surplus. Contrary to Gynther's position, the authors of "Accounting for Goodwill" suggest that the valuation of the firm (which would presumably require the valuation of goodwill) must be done by the investor. Such a valuation is, according to them, simply not an accounting function. The study recommends that purchased goodwill be accounted for as a reduction of stockholders' equity, demonstrating the degree of controversy surrounding this particular asset.

*Arthur L. Thomas is Professor of Accounting
at McMasters University. Professor Thomas
has provided here a summary of the deleted
material from his monograph. The reader is
encouraged to read the entire monograph for
further support of his position.*

The Allocation Problem in Financial Accounting Theory: The Nature of the Problem

AAA Studies in Accounting Research No. 3

Arthur L. Thomas

The Roots of the Problem

The allocation problem in financial accounting has many of its roots in the concepts that underlie our notions of assets, expenses, and the like—and in the ways in which we associate numbers with these notions. The first part of this chapter is an elementary description of what the profession presently is doing in its reports. I will not be concerned until later with the alternative practices being proposed by accounting theorists. But . . . the conclusions reached in this chapter apply equally well to most of these proposed alternatives.

A word of caution is important. Various authorities are cited for the

Reprinted by permission of the author and publisher from "The Allocation Problem in Financial Accounting Theory," *American Accounting Association Studies in Accounting Research No. 3*, 1969, pp. 1–14 and 104–05.

observations made in this chapter.[1] But the matters at issue are not ones that can be settled simply by reference to authority. Instead, it is important that the reader *satisfy himself* from his own experience of financial accounting and its literature that a fair (though somewhat simplified) description of present practices has been given.

Economic Goods

The accountant's notion of an asset is closely related to the economist's concept of an economic good. A *good* is *anything* wanted or desired by some entity, or capable of satisfying some entity's wants, whether it be a physical thing (like a building), a service, or whatever. The economist narrows this notion by restricting his attention to *economic goods*, which are goods that can be bought and sold in a market—goods that command a price. To command a price they must be scarce—any good that is readily available, free, is not an economic good.[2]

Some economic goods are either cash itself or a legally enforceable claim to receive cash. These may be called *monetary* goods. All other economic goods may be called *nonmonetary*. Nonmonetary economic goods include buildings, advertising campaigns, services of skilled mechanics, merchandise inventories, fire insurance policies, results of research and development efforts . . . *any* economic goods that are neither cash nor legally enforceable claims to receive cash.[3] Although there are allocation problems associated

---

[1] Primary reliance is placed on the following standard references, though other sources are cited in the body of the discussion: Rufus Wixon and Walter G. Kell, editors, *Accountants' Handbook* (New York: the Ronald Press Company, 1960), Chapters 1, 11, 12, 16, 17; Robert T. Sprouse and Maurice Moonitz, *A Tentative Set of Broad Accounting Principles for Business Enterprises*, Accounting Research Study No.3 (New York: American Institute of Certified Public Accountants, 1962), Chapters 1, 3, 4, 6; Eric L. Kohler, *A Dictionary for Accountants*, Third Edition (Englewood Cliffs, New Jersey: Prentice-Hall, Inc., 1963), various entries; Paul Grady, *Inventory of Generally Accepted Accounting Principles for Business Enterprises*, Accounting Research Study No.7 (New York: American Institute of Certified Public Accountants, 1965), Chapters 2, 4, 6, 11; Eldon S. Hendriksen, *Accounting Theory* (Homewood, Illinois: Richard D. Irwin, Inc., 1965), Chapters 6 and 8; and the following reports of committees of the American Accounting Association: "Accounting and Reporting Standards for Corporate Financial Statements—1957 Revision," *Accounting Review*, XXXII (October, 1957), 536–46; "Accounting for Land, Buildings, and Equipment," *Accounting Review*, XXXIX (July, 1964), 693–99; "A Discussion of Various Approaches to Inventory Measurement," *Accounting Review*, XXXIX (July, 1964), 700–14; "The Realization Concept," *Accounting Review*, XL (April, 1965), 312–22; and "The Matching Concept," *Accounting Review*, XL (April, 1965), 368–72.

[2] Technically, for a good *not* to be an economic good it must be readily available, free, *in the location where it is desired, and without effort*. As an example, wild rice is readily available, free, but it commands a high price because of the difficulties of gathering it.

[3] For a non-cash asset to be a monetary asset, it must satisfy both the requirement of being a claim to receive cash *and* of being a legally enforceable claim. For example, the holder of a fire insurance policy has at most a *contingent* claim to receive cash, until a fire occurs; therefore, a fire insurance policy is classified as nonmonetary. (If a fire does occur, there then will be a receivable from the insurance company—a monetary asset—but this is a different asset from the policy itself.)

with monetary goods,[4] we will see that some especially difficult allocation problems in financial accounting relate to nonmonetary goods. The remainder of this study concentrates on these problems of *non*monetary goods allocation.

The accountant's notion of a nonmonetary *asset* takes the theoretical concept of a nonmonetary economic good and narrows it down, attempting to give it operational content in the process. First, financial statements report economic data about individual economic entities. An accounting asset is not just an economic good, but a good that is of economic significance *to the particular entity* preparing the financial statements upon which the asset is reflected.[5] The significance of the asset consists of its promise of offering future economic benefits or services to the entity.[6] The entity must have a legally enforceable claim to receive these benefits or services.[7] If a good does *not* offer such services to the entity, it is not an asset of that entity. (The reverse is not always true: for example advertising services contracted for in one year, but to be received and paid for in the next year, ordinarily would not be reported as an asset.)

Present accounting practice imposes some additional restrictions. Accountants wish to represent economic phenomena by numbers.[8] With minor exceptions (such as gift assets), accountants wish initially to record nonmonetary goods at their acquisition prices to the entity.[9] Under present accounting rules, the allocation problem arises when a nonmonetary economic good's estimated services to the entity are of limited duration, but of a duration greater than a single accounting period; the problem is to determine how much of the acquisition price should be associated with each period.

---

[4] These include amortization of bond discount and premium, the timing of profit recognition on installment sales, and the like. There are also less widely acknowledged problems of allocating costs of holding monetary items, extending credit, and so forth.

[5] It also, of course, is a good *owned* by the entity (with occasional exceptions for such things as mortgaged assets).

[6] "Assets are economic resources devoted to business purposes within a specific accounting entity; they are aggregates of service-potentials available for or beneficial to expected operations."—AAA (1957), p. 538; see also AAA (Land), p. 694; AAA (Matching), p. 368; Sprouse and Moonitz (1962), pp. 19–23, 32–33; Grady (1965), pp. 99–102, 148–49; and Hendriksen (1965), pp. 194–95.

[7] Hendriksen (1965), pp. 194–95. Note that, cash excepted, both monetary and nonmonetary assets involve legally enforceable claims—in the one case to receive cash, in the other to receive services.

[8] See Hendriksen (1965), p. 195.

[9] Wixon and Kell (1960), pp. (1–16), (1–17), (16–2)-(16–5); Kohler (1963), pp. 14–17; Grady (1965), pp. 27, 229; Hendriksen (1965), pp. 196–97. As we will see later in this chapter, this "acquisition price" is the sum of: a) any cash paid or liability assumed to acquire the good; and, b) all, or parts of, the acquisition prices of any *other* goods given up or allocated to the particular economic good under consideration.

Three Kinds of Economic Goods

For simplicity, the following discussion will assume calendar-year accounting periods. (If need be, the conclusions reached can easily enough be modified to handle cases of quarterly and other non-annual reporting.) The *service life* of a nonmonetary economic good is the number of years during which it is assumed that the good will provide economic services to the entity.[10] In effect, accountants divide all nonmonetary economic goods into three classes.

1. Unlimited-life Goods. Some nonmonetary economic goods, most notably industrial site land, are regarded as having unlimited service lives. Under present accounting rules, if an entity has purchased such a good, and services are expected from it for an unlimited period, the accountant will report this good as an asset, and will (in current and subsequent years) associate with it a number that equals its original acquisition price.

2. Single-year Goods. At the other extreme, the services of some nonmonetary economic goods are considered to be expended between the date of their acquisition and the date at which financial statements are prepared. Newspaper advertising paid for on December 12th and run on December 17th would be an example of a single-year good.[11] Similar advertising paid for on December 12th to be run next January 4th would be an example of a good that was *not* regarded as single-year. Under present accounting rules, a single-year good is handled in one of two possible ways:

a) If the expenditure of its services is perceived as relating to the acquisition of some other nonmonetary economic good (which will provide services to the entity), then the acquisition price of the single-year good will be included in the acquisition price of the other economic good. An example of this is the inclusion of the costs of raw materials in the costs of a manufactured inventory.[12]

b) If no other nonmonetary economic good is perceived to result from expenditure of the single-year good's services, then the acquisition price of the single-year good is treated as an expense or a loss on the current year's income statement.

---

[10] The next chapter will develop a more precise definition of the nature of economic services in accounting. However, it might be mentioned here that if a good has a scrap value at the end of its service life, receipt of that scrap value is of course one final economic service that it provides to the entity.

[11] Notice that single-year goods are defined here in terms of the *treatment* they receive under present accounting rules, not in terms of their actual economic services. The *benefits* of advertising may extend beyond the year in which the advertisement is run, but the accountant usually chooses to ignore this and to *treat* the advertising as a single-year good. The terminology used in this chapter is descriptive, not normative; it is concerned with what accountants *are* doing, not with what they possibly should be doing.

[12] Wixon and Kell (1960), p. (1–17); Sprouse and Moonitz (1962), p. 49.

In neither event is the single-year good *per se* reported as an asset on the entity's financial statements—though similar goods may be reported *per se* as assets if, like the January 4th advertising, their services to the entity happen to be expended in a year other than the year of acquisition. [13]

3. Multi-year Goods. In contrast, a multi-year good is any nonmonetary economic good of limited service life which the accountant treats as yielding services to the entity during at least one year subsequent to its year of acquisition. (A multi-year good may also be defined negatively as any recognized good which is *not* treated as single-year or unlimited-life.) In the previous example, the January 4th advertising was a multi-year good. So is a building.

Under present "generally accepted" accounting rules, the acquisition price of a multi-year good is handled in much the same way *over its entire service life* as is the acquisition price of a single-year good during its single year: it either is incorporated in the acquisition prices of one or more other economic goods, or is expensed (or treated as a loss). *During* the service life of a multi-year good, the accountant assigns portions of its acquisition price to the income statements or to other economic goods acquired at least one year subsequent to the year of the good's acquisition.

At the end of the year of the good's acquisition (and perhaps at the ends of one or more subsequent years) this allocation will be incomplete; the good is then reported as an *asset*, at an amount equal to the unallocated portion of its acquisition price.

> Expired costs (expenses) to be charged against the current period's revenue . . . must be distinguished from unexpired costs (inventories, prepaid and deferred costs, and fixed assets) to be charged against the revenue of future periods in order to present net income fairly. [14]

Why are the acquisition prices of these goods allocated to years other than the year of acquisition? In part because, were they not, the entity's net income could fluctuate widely from year to year, even though other economic activity remained constant both in intensity and profitability; in part, for reasons discussed in the next chapter: costs are allocated to those revenues which the goods are perceived as having *caused*, or to the periods that the goods are

---

[13] Wixon and Kell (1960), pp. (12–3), (12–23). Notice, finally, that the definition of single-year goods relates to the way in which goods are reported (or not reported) on the entity's *financial statements*. The single-year good never appears on the financial statements as an asset. But nothing is said here about the ways in which these goods may be recorded on the entity's *books*. For example, merchandise inventories acquired and sold within the same year often are initially *recorded* as assets, then expensed when sold. But from the vantage point of the published financial statements, such inventories are not reported as assets, so they are single-year goods.

[14] Grady (1965), p. 100; see also pp. 102, 228; and Wixon and Kell (1960), pp. (1–18), (11–59), (16–2), (16–7).

deemed to have benefitted.[15] Such goods include the following (the sense in which inventories are included is discussed below):

Buildings	Inventories of merchandise, finished
Equipment	goods and supplies
Leases and patents	Prepaid insurance, and many other
Mineral deposits	kinds of prepayments

An even more interesting question is: why are many similar-seeming goods usually allocated only to the year of acquisition? These goods include:

Our previous example of advertising campaigns (since the indirect benefits probably extend beyond one year). Research and development expenditures. Improved efficiency expected from providing special training to employees.

Reasons usually given are that the future benefits are uncertain and that the necessary estimates are too subjective, or arbitrary, for allocation to be meaningful.[16] The treatment given such a good may depend on the accountant as well as upon the nature of the good itself. This is particularly evident with certain expenditures for research and development, where present "generally accepted" rules allow either capitalizing the expenditure or expensing it in the current year.

Summary of Nonmonetary Economic Good Allocations[17]

Here, then, is a summary of how the financial accountant allocates the acquisition prices of nonmonetary economic goods:

1. Unlimited-life Goods. So long as these are owned by the entity, the acquisition prices are not allocated. If eventually sold, the acquisition prices are allocated to the year of sale.

---

[15] Wixon and Kell (1960), p. (16-6).

[16] Wixon and Kell (1960), pp. (12-3), (12-4), (12-7); Grady (1965), p. 101; Hendriksen (1965), pp. 152-53.

[17] Grady provides a convenient, if simplified, summary of the accountant's treatment of limited-life nonmonetary economic goods:

"Expenses are costs which have expired in the process of producing revenue or with the passage of time. The term 'cost' here means the sum of applicable expenditures and charges, directly or indirectly incurred, in acquiring a good or service in the condition and location in which it is used or sold. Initially, cost incurrence produces an asset or provides a service, the benefits of which are expected to produce present or future revenues. As the benefits are used up or expire, the portion of the cost applicable to the revenues realized is charged against revenue." —Grady (1965), pp. 99-100. For further background, see Wixon and Kell (1960), pp. (1-15)-(1-18), (11-59)-(11-61), (12-2)-(12-4); Sprouse and Moonitz (1962), pp. 8-9; Kohler (1963), pp. 144-46, 162-63, 208; Grady (1965), pp. 74, 99-102, 228, 409, 433-44; Hendriksen (1965), pp. 142, 151-54, 192-97; AAA (1957), pp. 539-41; AAA (Matching), pp. 368-70;

2. Single-year Goods. The entire acquisition price is allocated to the year of acquisition (either to the expenses or losses of that year, or to the acquisition prices of other economic goods acquired during that year).

3. Multi-year Goods. The acquisition price is allocated to at least one year other than the year of acquisition, and often to many such years. Part of the acquisition price may be allocated to the year of acquisition. (Once again, allocations may be either to expenses or losses, or to the acquisition prices of other economic goods.)

Finally, the acquisition price of a nonmonetary asset will be the sum of any cash paid or liability assumed to acquire the good, plus any allocations of the acquisition prices of other nonmonetary economic goods that were made in the manner indicated above.

Inventories

A bit more needs to be said about inventories. Usually supplies, merchandise, raw materials, and finished goods are acquired in batches, or *lots*, rather than by the individual item.[18] In this sense, the acquisition price of, say, a particular raw material may be allocated to more than one year, or to several other economic goods. An advantage to perceiving things this way is that it becomes evident that the accountant's problems with differing inventory and depreciation methods are really forms of the same allocation problem— though, as it were, at different points along a continuum. (In both cases the

William A. Paton and A.C. Littleton, *An Introduction to Corporate Accounting Standards* (Columbus, Ohio: American Accounting Association, 1940), pp. 10–18, 24–27, 33, 65–74, 77, 81–85, 88–93; William J. Vatter, *The Fund Theory of Accounting and Its Implications for Financial Reports* (Chicago: University of Chicago Press, 1947), pp. 14–19; Oscar S. Gellein, "The Decreasing-Charge Concept," *Journal of Accountancy*, C (August, 1955), pp. 56–57; Carl Thomas Devine, *Essays in Accounting Theory* (privately printed, 1962), II, 258–70, 338–41; Earl A. Spiller, Jr., "Theory and Practice in the Development of Accounting," *Accounting Review*, XXXIX (October, 1964), 850–59; Glenn L. Johnson, "The Monetary and Nonmonetary Distinction," *Accounting Review*, XL (October, 1965), 821–23; Delmer P. Hylton, "On Matching Revenue With Expense," *Accounting Review*, XL (October, 1965), 824–28; Willard J. Graham, "Some Observations on the Nature of Income, Generally Accepted Accounting Principles, and Financial Reporting," *Law and Contemporary Problems*, XXX (Autumn, 1965), 660–64; Morton Backer, "The Measurement of Business Income, Part I—The Matching Concept," in Morton Backer, editor, *Modern Accounting Theory* (Englewood Cliffs, New Jersey: Prentice-Hall, Inc., 1966), pp. 68–69, 76–78, 81–83, 90; Carl Thomas Devine, "Asset Cost and Expiration," *ibid.*, pp. 141–57; Raymond C. Dein, "Inventory Costs," *ibid.*, pp. 158–89; Norton Bedford, "Research, Selling, and Administrative Costs," *ibid.*, pp. 213–31; Michael Schiff, "Accounting Tactics and the Theory of the Firm," *Journal of Accounting Research*, IV (Spring, 1966), 62–63; and Robert R. Sterling, "Elements of Pure Accounting Theory," *Accounting Review*, XLII (January, 1967), 62–73.

[18] I argue this point in "The Amortization Problem: A Simplified Model and Some Unanswered Questions," *Journal of Accounting Research*, III (Spring, 1965), 104; compare A.C. Littleton, *Structure of Accounting Theory* (Madison, Wisconsin: American Accounting Association, 1953); p. 9; and Robert R. Sterling, "An Operational Analysis of Traditional Accounting," *Abacus*, II (December, 1966), 124. Other reasons for regarding inventories as similar to prepaid expenses and depreciable assets are given in Hendriksen (1965), pp. 246–47.

problem is to determine what portion of an acquisition price should be associated with each of two or more periods.) Our previous discussion has concluded that *all* nonmonetary economic goods are part of the same continuum and subject to the same allocation problem, no matter how short the period from their acquisition to the point at which the accountant treats their services as exhausted.

The Allocation Problem

Except for unsold unlimited-life goods, all nonmonetary economic goods are allocated to the expenses or losses of one or more years—or to the acquisition prices of other nonmonetary goods acquired in one or more years. The allocation problem in financial accounting—and it is sufficiently pervasive and important to be called *the* allocation problem[19]—is to select and justify the particular allocation methods employed. This problem overlaps those which accountants traditionally have designated as problems of "cost accumulation" and of "matching costs with revenues."[20] These latter problems are among the most widespread and crucial in financial accounting.

As the Introduction asserts, given the present state of allocation theory it often will be impossible to give theoretical justification of the accountant's allocation methods, no matter which method he chooses. For simplicity, this will be demonstrated in detail for only one kind of nonmonetary economic good: depreciable assets. But (as we will see later) the arguments developed for depreciable assets are pertinent to *all* nonmonetary economic goods. Therefore, it will be argued that at present the accountant cannot justify his cost accumulation and matching efforts, no matter what methods he uses.

---

[19] This study is *not* directly concerned with such problems as the interperiod allocation of taxes, or the assignment of tax charges to individual projects (see Howard J. McBride, "Assigning Tax Loads to Prospective Projects," *Accounting Review*, XXXVIII [April, 1963], 363–70.) Nor is it concerned with cost accounting allocations, and the like. The author anticipates that many of the same considerations would apply to these problems as to the ones discussed here, but further research needs to be done. The allocation problem is also related to the general problem of assigning joint or common costs to different activities within an entity. Bows describes this problem well:

"Every diversified business of any size has joint costs for facilities, common personnel and overall financial resources which it uses in the various activities of its business as it sees fit. The most common joint costs are:

1. Financing costs, such as interest and preferred dividends
2. General and administrative expenses
3. Research and product development
4. Institutional advertising
5. Federal and other income taxes."

(Albert J. Bows, Jr., "Problems in Disclosure of Segments of Conglomerate Companies," *Journal of Accountancy*, CXXII [December, 1966], 35.) The conglomerate company problem discussed by Bows is a new and interesting one in financial accounting allocations. A similar problem may arise if federal regulatory agencies actively seek entity profit data by product lines.

[20] Grady (1965), pp. 74, 99–100; AAA(Matching), pp. 368–69. The term "allocation" is used rather than "cost accumulation" or "matching" because it has greater precision and corresponds better to language employed in economic theory.

Theoretical Justification of Allocations[21]

"Theoretical justification" could mean various things. The issue of theoretical justification arises when the accountant wishes to prepare financial statements.[22] For any individual nonmonetary input, various different allocation methods may be available. If the accountant is to prepare a report, he must choose one, and only one, of these possible methods for each input. The problem of theoretical justification is one of defending his choice. . . . But there are several possible alternate criteria of what would *constitute* defense of an allocation method. It is essential for subsequent arguments to be as precise as possible here. In the remainder of this chapter, I try to discuss all of the different possibilities. It is demonstrated that most of the alternate criteria either are not germane to accounting, or are not germane to the particular accounting problems being examined in this book. But three of the possible criteria *are* pertinent. The following are minimum requirements for theoretical justification of an allocation method; these, and the various rejected alternate criteria, are discussed in detail below:

1. The method should be unambiguous.
2. It should be possible to defend the method. (Different possible ways of conducting such a defense are discussed below.)
3. The method should divide up what is available to be allocated, no more and no less. The allocation should be *additive*.

Later, the first and second requirements will be combined into:

It should be possible to specify, unambiguously and in advance, the method to be used, and defend that choice against all competing alternatives. But this latter version must itself be defended. The discussion that follows is closely related to matters that are discussed in subsequent chapters. For this discussion to be efficient, it must at points summarize matters that later will

---

[21] The section from here to the end of this chapter is crucial to the rest of this study. If the choice of requirements for theoretical justification of allocations has overlooked something, or otherwise erred, many subsequent conclusions collapse. Comments are invited. All that can be claimed is that I have tried to defend the requirements chosen, and to discuss as many alternative approaches as possible.

[22] Of course, the issue may also arise as an *abstract* question. For example, a philosopher might argue that anything that exists is justified—by the very fact that it exists:

Margaret Fuller: "I accept the Universe!"

Thomas Carlyle: "Gad! she'd better."—See *Oxford Dictionary of Quotations*, 2nd Edition (Oxford: The Oxford University Press, 1955), s.v. "Carlyle." But this leads to deeper waters than we need to plumb. The existence of abstract problems does not negate the existence of a concrete problem; the concrete problem of defending the accountant's choice must be faced regardless of whatever *other*, more abstract, problems may also exist. And it is this concrete problem with which this book is concerned.

be considered in more detail.[23] But it still will be possible to outline the main difficulties in justifying allocation methods.

Requirement 1: The Method Should Be Unambiguous

The first of these requirements is easily discussed. An allocation method should be unambiguous. It should yield an unique allocation. This is to say that the accountant should have made a clear-cut unequivocal choice of method. One should not be left undecided among a set of possible alternatives, each consistent with the accountant's decision, yet each leading to different allocation patterns. An allocation method should not leave one at a loss for how to allocate. Instead, it should provide clear instructions as to how the allocation should be conducted, and provide them *in advance* (theorists are seeking methods consistent with *general* justification—a method which had to be altered with the facts of each case would not be very satisfactory).

Requirement 2: It Should Be Possible to Defend the Method

The second requirement, that the method be defensible, leads into deep waters. It will be demonstrated in the next chapter (using depreciation as an example) that accounting's allocations cannot be defended by the kinds of physical proofs that are possible in some of the sciences—that, for example, knowledge of the engineering characteristics of a machine is not sufficient to settle how that machine should be depreciated. Therefore, we must ask: how does one give theoretical justification to something that is not subject to physical demonstration?

It is generally accepted (and some believe it has been proved by Gödel[24]) that any theoretical structure must ultimately depend upon *some* assumptions or axioms which have not been given theoretical justification within that structure. And it has long been recognized that financial accounting requires such axioms:

> The fundamental concepts or propositions of accounting, like those of other fields, are in themselves assumptions in considerable measure or are predicated upon assumptions which are not subject to conclusive demonstration or proof.[25]

---

[23] The problem faced here is that most of the concepts developed in this book are interrelated, yet one must begin discussing them one at a time. This means that it also is necessary in places (during the earlier chapters) to assert conclusions that will not be proven until later. I am intensely aware of the potential danger of circular argument that this creates, but believe that by the time the reader has completed Chapter Four it will be apparent that circularity has been avoided.

[24] For an unusually clear discussion of Gödel's conclusions, in layman's language, see Ernest Nagel and James R. Newman, "Gödel's Proof," *Scientific American*, CXCIV (June, 1956), 71–86.

[25] Paton and Littleton (1940), p. 21.

It would of course be ridiculous to claim that no theoretical structure can be given theoretical justification! Instead, the way in which a theoretical structure ordinarily is justified *despite* its need for axioms that cannot be justified within that structure is to appeal to some more general framework of thought—to look to a broader context in which there is a rule to which all parties agree, then demonstrate that the matter in question is a consequence of that general rule. (As an example, in discussing possible traffic controls for a residential area, one might argue that the framework in which traffic controls should be evaluated is merely one aspect of a broader framework in which decisions are evaluated in terms of their effects on general human welfare. Within this broader context, there is a general rule that preservation of children's lives takes priority over most other considerations. This rule could be cast in specific terms, then taken as an axiom of the traffic control discussion.)

This study is concerned with whether financial accounting's allocations can be theoretically justified, or whether they must inevitably be arbitrary. In discussing this, the broader appeal cannot be to what other *accountants* would agree to or believe.[26] That would be circular: "what other accountants believe" includes the very matters at issue.[27] So, the broader appeal must be to what *non*accountants believe.[28] (Of course, should an allocation method *violate* what accountants believe, it could not be considered part of any "generally accepted" system of accounting.) This appeal could be in either of two directions:

1. One might appeal to rules upon which intelligent laymen would agree,

[26] Even were such an appeal legitimate, it would not suffice. A strong case can be made that the choice of particular allocation methods cannot be defended against alternative methods even from *within* the financial accounting system, except by arbitrary fiat. But this argument need not be presented in this study.

[27] This is not to say that the accountant's customary appeal to generally accepted accounting principles is *usually* circular, only that it would be circular *in this case*. Usually when this appeal is made the matter at issue is some particular accounting *practice*. But here the matter at issue is of fundamental importance to the generally accepted accounting principles *themselves*.

. . . The way in which accountants perceive allocations, and their beliefs about allocations, are basic to much of the rest of their thinking about accounting—the effects of these beliefs are pervasive. . . . If accountants' allocation methods *cannot* be given theoretical justification, then neither can the bulk of conventional accounting practice, nor most of the alternatives to conventional practice that have been proposed by theorists. But this conventional practice and these alternatives have conditioned and dominated what accountants would agree to and believe. Therefore, it is circular to appeal to what other accountants would agree to or believe *when one is questioning their basic approaches to allocation*.

[28] In more technical language, the problem is to insure that financial accounting's allocation theory is "bounded," i.e. that its primitive terms extend at least as far as other contexts, and are acceptable primitive terms in these contexts (or derivable from other primitive terms in those contexts).

One cannot eliminate *all* arbitrariness from a theoretical structure, because of the necessity of such primitive terms; attempts to do so lead to the dilemma of philosophical doubt reached by Descartes: nothing is known without *some* arbitrariness, except the bare experience of cognition. But for one's theoretical structure to be theoretically justified, its arbitrariness should be no greater than that found in adjacent contexts.

arguing that accounting rules should be consequences of propositions which readers of accounting reports would concede. In the traffic example, the appeal to the priority of preserving children's lives might end the discussion.

2. One might appeal to some other discipline in which allocation theory has been studied. For accounting, the relevant outside discipline is economics,[29] and economists *have* studied allocation carefully and at length.

Difficulties with These Appeals

Unfortunately (to anticipate the conclusions of this study) both appeals lead to difficulties. When one tries to defend allocation methods, each appeal to a rule or a principle usually leads to another issue. Each answer usually leads to another question that, to the layman, is as sensible as the one before. . . .

The allocation theories developed by *economists* have been created for quite different kinds of problems than those that confront the accountant. Not only are there reasons to doubt that the economists' theories are adaptable to the accountants' problems, but it will be argued that typically the economists' theories are simply irrelevant to financial accounting's allocations.

The Appeal to Purpose

Several readers of earlier versions of this study have made what amounts to a reply to the previous comments. "The difficulties mentioned," they might say, "are consequences of discussing allocations *in the abstract*. The justification of any allocation method will depend on the purpose to be served. Once objectives, alternatives, and payoffs have been identified, there really should be no further difficulties with allocations." There are two main weaknesses to this position:

1. Presently, there is no unanimity about the purposes to be served by accounting, much less the purposes to be served by allocations. Nor, despite much effort by theorists, is there any sign that such agreement is near. To extent that the different goals give any guidance for allocation at all, they seem to lead to differing allocation methods that conflict with the accomplishment of other purposes.[30]

---

[29] This comment is applicable only to *present* financial accounting theory. . . . Much promising research is being done in relating financial accounting to such things as measurement science and the behavioral sciences. But none of this effort has yet reached the point where it allows a fully convincing appeal to be made.

[30] This can be seen readily enough for certain goals, such as obtaining the social or financial benefits of suppressing fluctuations in reported profits. But it is true in more subtle cases, too. The following is offered tentatively, and only as a possible example of the difficulties one can experience using this approach.

Suppose that we perceive company profit maximization by management as the purpose to be served by accounting. Allocation in terms of a good's marginal net-revenue contributions seems a natural consequence of using marginal contributions analysis for management's decisions. Costs determined in this way are highly relevant for managerial profit-maximizing purposes. But there is no reason to believe that these figures also are relevant to the decision processes of

What is needed is general agreement on a priority of financial accounting goals. Should such agreement eventually be reached, it *might* lead to conclusive ways to justify allocation methods in accounting. But there is no such general agreement yet, and it must be realized that whatever may happen eventually is no help in justifying allocation methods *now*.

2. Even were agreement reached on the purpose of accounting, it does not follow that our first requirement for justifying allocation methods (that the method be unambiguous) would be met. Most of the purposes proposed for accounting in recent years seem consistent with a great *variety* of possible allocation methods. The truth of this observation is obvious when the proposed purpose is broad and unspecific (for example, for such broad criteria as *fairness* or *relevance*). But it is equally true of more detailed statements of purpose, such as those in the recent AAA "Basic Theory" statement, or Grady's Inventory.[31]

Accounting is an artifact. The purpose of any artifact depends on the purposes of its users. Whatever the purpose of financial accounting may eventually be agreed on to be, presumably that purpose will be a *derived* one that depends on the purposes of some or all of the readers of financial statements. Much of the allocation problem in financial accounting results from the present dearth of a rigorous theory of relating allocation methods to reader purposes (and a lack of rigorous theory about such things as appropriate reader decision models).

All of these are negative conclusions, and therefore hard to support in detail except by a very inefficient process of elimination. Instead, the reader is invited to provide counter-examples. Specifically, the reader is challenged to read the rest of this study, then specify a serious purpose for financial accounting that stands a reasonable chance of gaining general acceptance, and provides unambiguous guidance in, say, the choice of depreciation and inventory allocation methods.

Certain highly specialized purposes, such as those of tax or regulatory accounting, may provide such unambiguous guidance. But these are not appropriate for general financial accounting. . . . Two approaches to accounting that *avoid* the allocation problem by *refusing to make* allocations of nonmonetary goods,[32] but that is another matter entirely.

---

readers of financial statements. The figures are relevant to decisions concerning resource allocation within the firm. They are at best only tangentially relevant to, say, the stockholder's decision of whether to buy, hold, or sell shares of common stock—indeed, . . . arguments are advanced that they are *irr*elevant to such decisions.

[31] Committee to Prepare a Statement of Basic Accounting Theory, *A Statement of Basic Accounting Theory* (Evanston, Illinois: American Accounting Association, 1966), *passim*; Grady (1965), pp. 56–67, 73; see also Kohler (1963), pp. 10–11, 212; and Hendriksen (1965), pp. 81–83.

[32] Somewhat simplified forms of the current-price approaches recommended by Chambers and Sterling, and a net-quick-assets version of the cash-flow approaches recommended by some financial analysts.

Paralleling my earlier remarks, future research may lead to development of a generally accepted purpose for financial accounting that provides unambiguous guidance in the choice of allocation methods. But there does not seem to be any such purpose available *now*, and once again the appeal to purpose is irrelevant.

"Satisficing" Justifications

The present failure of the appeal to purpose results in the failure of another possible approach to theoretical justification of allocation methods. One might argue that it is unnecessary to demonstrate that a particular allocation method is better than all possible alternatives—that it is enough that the method be a satisfactory one. But satisfactory for *what*? Presumably for whatever purposes are to be served by the allocation.

One always can assert that for one's *own* purposes a particular allocation method is satisfactory. This is a psychological statement—at least in part. Therefore, it may be impossible to challenge its truth. However, at most it gives only a personal, private, theoretical justification to the allocation method—one which does not necessarily pertain to anyone else.[33] But theorists have been seeking to give *general* theoretical justifications to allocation methods. Lacking any general agreement about purpose, the satisficer is left in the awkward position of having to demonstrate that his method is satisfactory for all purposes. The literature of accounting controversy (of which a number of examples are cited in this study) suggests that such demonstrations are impossible. Usually, only trivial rules satisfy all goals.

Besides, there is another problem. Once one is willing to assert that various conflicting methods all are satisfactory, one also is willing (by implication) to ignore whatever differences in the reported figures result from choosing one method rather than another.[34] In effect one is satisfied with bias in one's allocations, so long as the bias does not exceed the difference between the results of those satisfactory allocation methods whose results conflict the most. . . . Except under fairly rigid conditions, the amount of bias involved will often be more than is satisfactory to many readers of financial statements. When this is true, the "satisficing" method once again fails of general theoretical justification.

Surrogates and Materiality

It is not unusual for theory to indicate that a particular approach to a problem is desirable, yet for that approach to be barred by practical consid-

---

[33] A case could be made that, instead of being a psychological statement, this is an assertion that the method satisfies certain subjectively defined ends. The result would still be personal, rather than general, theoretical justification.

[34] As an example, suppose that someone has two exterior thermometers on his house, and that they give readings as much as five degrees apart. If he is indifferent to which thermometer he looks at, then he is indifferent to a five degree difference in reported temperature.

erations. (For example, in the next chapter we will see that several theorists believe this is true of discounted-contributions, or "economic" valuation of assets.) Under such circumstances it can be quite justifiable to employ some surrogate approach that *is* practical.

But the use of surrogates does not allow one to avoid the underlying problem of justifying the allocation method that was chosen as being theoretically correct. Much the same can be said of approximations made for convenience and other matters falling under the heading of materiality—such as assertions that various different methods are satisfactory because they all differ insignificantly from the theoretically correct method. If one could determine that a complex monotonic decreasing function was appropriate for depreciating an asset, it might be appropriate to approximate it with a simple linear function. But if one wishes to give theoretical justification to depreciation allocations, the appropriateness of the original complex function must be defended.[35] And if such a defense cannot be provided, that failure is not merely a matter of *employing an approximation.* (Similarly, the use of accelerated depreciation to compensate for inflation implies that otherwise some depreciation pattern closer to straight-line would have been appropriate; rules of thumb imply defensibility as adequate replacements to theoretically justified solutions that we did not have the time to calculate; and so forth.)

Surrogates are an appropriate response to lack of data, but *not* to a lack of theory: for convenience, this study will assume throughout most of its arguments that there *are* no data problems. This is not because data problems are not serious, but because we are going to examine more fundamental difficulties. So the question of surrogates will not arise.[36] Similarly, since the points discussed in this study are mainly theoretical ones, the issue of materiality is not vital.

Summary

We may now combine the first two requirements. If an allocation method is to be theoretically justified, it should be possible to specify unambiguously and in advance the method to be used, and to defend that choice against all competing alternatives. At present, whatever approach one adopts to finan-

[35] The reader is invited to compare this discussion with that in Wixon and Kell (1960), p. (12–4); and Raymond J. Chambers, *Accounting, Evaluation and Economic Behavior* (Englewood Cliffs, New Jersey: Prentice-Hall, Inc., 1966), pp. 229–31, 260–61.

[36] Otherwise, we would make extensive use of the discussion of attributes of a satisfactory surrogate in Yuji Ijiri, Robert K. Jaedicke, and Kenneth E. Knight, "The Effects of Accounting Alternatives on Management Decisions," in Robert K. Jaedicke, Yuji Ijiri, and Oswald Nielsen, editors, *Research in Accounting Measurement* (Evanston, Illinois: American Accounting Association, 1966), pp. 188–92. The discussion on page 189 is particularly relevant to some of the remarks made previously in this chapter. A "satisfactory" surrogate is satisfactory with respect to a particular decision, a particular purpose. But we have seen that in financial accounting the purposes are varied and conflicting, with no way at present to set priorities.

cial accounting, there usually will be a variety of conflicting methods, all of which seem consistent with what one is trying to accomplish: the allocation problem often is one of an embarrassment of riches. Further research may provide better answers. But, as subsequent chapters will demonstrate, at present there seems no way to defend our choices conclusively.

Partial Defenses

All of this relates to a point that will become quite important in the next chapter. Often an accountant who wishes to employ a particular allocation method will give a *partial* defense of it. Anticipating an example that will be used later, an accountant might try to justify straight-line depreciation of a machine by arguing that he expects the machine to be run an equal number of hours each year. But if he stops here his defense of straight-line depreciation is incomplete. For one could ask: why should an equal portion of the machine's acquisition price be allocated to each hour?

Perhaps the machine produces more in the early years than it will later. Or perhaps its output will command a higher price in the early years. In either case some declining-charge method might be more appropriate. In the next chapter we will examine this kind of problem in more detail. For the present, the point to be emphasized is that if one is going to give theoretical justification to what one does, *all* implicit decisions must be justified (in the sense of "justification" given earlier in this section), not just some of them. Otherwise there always will be *some* conflicting alternative against which one has no defense, holes in one's reasoning allowing mutually inconsistent methods to be equally acceptable, with no conclusive way of *settling* the conflict. Some method or other *will* be chosen, of course. But the choice will be arbitrary.

It should be repeated that there are limits to how far an allocation method need be defended. If the method chosen can be defended by an appeal to rules upon which intelligent laymen would agree, or by an appeal to economists' theories of allocation, the justification may suffice. It also should be observed that there is nothing necessarily wrong with arbitrary methods. Most of us chose our wives by methods that at various crucial points were indifferent to theory. Many successful business decisions are made without full theoretical defense; sometimes this is what is involved when we say that a decision has been influenced by considerations that cannot be quantified, or that a decision required expert judgment. But if an allocation method is to be theoretically justified, it must be defended completely, in the sense indicated above. Lacking a complete defense, the choice of method inevitably is arbitrary.

Decisions Under Ignorance

Certain other disciplines have tried to develop ways to deal with situations similar to those to which accountants respond with partial defenses—ways to give theoretical justification to decisions when no explicit way to defend one's choices is known. An example is Bernoulli's principle of attaching equal probabilities to future events when one has no idea of which events might materialize.[37] It can be argued that such rules for behavior in the face of ignorance are justified (in a theory of uncertainty) when decisions must be made despite incomplete knowledge. However, such rules do not seem pertinent to this discussion.

1. Whether accountants *must* make allocation decisions is a major question under examination in this study. . . . [There are] reasons why accountants should *not* make allocations, thereby eliminating a large part of the justification for rules of behavior under ignorance.

2. Much of the theory of appropriate behavior under ignorance pertains to cases in which the ignorance arises from lack of data—data which, if available, would support a decision. Here, the problem turns out to be much more serious: lack of a theory to justify one's allocation methods, *no matter what data are available.* . . .

3. In any case, accountants do not at present have any systematic theory of appropriate behavior under ignorance. Similarly, they lack any theoretically justified way of ranking arbitrariness—of saying "this kind of arbitrariness is preferable to that kind"—except as a psychological (or subjective) statement with which others may agree, but just as well may not agree. Once again future research may provide what is presently lacking, but no such theory exists *now* to justify our allocation methods.

Requirement 3: The Method Should Divide Up What is Availiable to Be Allocated

The first two minimum criteria for theoretical justification of an allocation method—unambiguity and defensibility—have now been discussed. The third requirement for theoretical justification of an allocation method is that it should *allocate*: should divide up what there is to be divided, no more and no less. There is nothing subtle about this requirement. There are various ways to divide a pie among three people. But it is clear from the outset that an allocation method that requires each person to receive half the pie cannot be justified. If one is trying to dispose of the entire pie, a method that requires each person to receive one quarter of the pie cannot be justified, either.[38]

Consider an artificial example from elementary cost accounting.[39] Sup-

---

[37] Or any of the alternative strategies that have been recommended—for example, see Robert Schlaifer, *Probability and Statistics for Business Decisions* (New York: McGraw-Hill Book Company, Inc., 1959), pp. 445–46.

[38] Devine argues that there are cases in accounting where it is unnecessary that the amounts allocated add up to the total amount to be allocated. But he is speaking of situations in which different measurement conventions are applied to the whole and to the parts, something which we will take care to avoid in what follows. See Devine (1962), pp. 205–206.

[39] No departure from the emphasis on financial accounting should be inferred from this use of a cost accounting example; it is employed merely because it is simple, familiar, and clear-cut. Examples from financial accounting will be discussed later in this study.

Exhibit 1-1
A simple allocation involving interaction

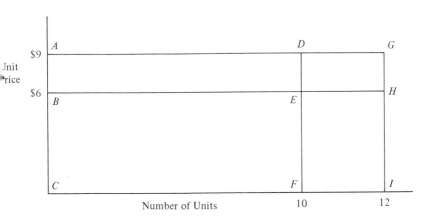

pose that product standards specify that 10 units of raw material costing $6 per unit shall be used in manufacturing one unit of product. Instead, 12 units are used at a cost of $9 per unit. Exhibit I-1 is the usual diagram provided for such cases.

The total cost of raw material used was $12 \times \$9 = \$108$. In an elementary discussion of variance accounting, this $108 would be allocated as follows:

Number of units used

	Rectangle	Amount
To the acquisition price	*BEFC*	$ 60
To a price variance	*AGHB*	36
To a quantity variance	*EHIF*	12
Total	*AGIC*	$108

Consider the price variance, *AGHB*. This is made up of two components: a "pure" price variance (*ADEB = $30*) *and an interaction* variance (*DGHE = $6*). *This interaction variance is a joint* result of too much usage at too high a price. In elementary cost accounting this interaction variance is added to the "pure" price variance, for reasons that need not concern us here. The point to recognize is that cost accounting theory does not ignore the interaction variance.

Interactions will be present in accounting whenever the effects of different factors are not independent. Ordinarily, we would expect the firm's nonmonetary goods to interact. If these inputs *are* independent (if, for example, the total receipts earned by the firm are not greater than what the individual

inputs would have earned alone) the company should consider liquidating
It will be argued in Chapter Three that these interaction effects are substantial. To be theoretically justified, an allocation method cannot just pretend
that interaction effects do not exist. In a similar context (later extended to
include the kinds of cases discussed in this study) Gould points out the
logical fallacy in allocations that "attempt to treat B as independent of A
when the conditions of the problem state that A and B are interdependent."[40]

Summary

The minimum requirements for giving theoretical justification to an allocation method are that it should be possible to specify, unambiguously and in
advance, the method to be used, and to defend that choice against all competing alternatives—and that the method should divide up what there is to
allocate, no more and no less. We have seen that appropriate defenses for
allocation methods may be found in what laymen would agree to, or in
allocation theories developed by economists. Several other possible appeals
have been examined, but found to be of no present help. During this study
several more possible ways of justifying allocation methods will be examined.

The discussion indicated that there are several areas in which further
research might help in justifying allocation methods. It would be very valuable were general agreement reached on the priority of accounting goals,
and were goals selected that had unambiguous implications for the choice of
allocation methods; it also would be valuable were a theory of appropriate
behavior under ignorance developed for accounting. During this study several more areas in which valuable research might be performed will be
mentioned.

Finally, theoretical justification of an allocation method requires defense
of *all* its implicit assumptions, up to the limits set by an appeal to economic
theory or the rules followed by intelligent laymen. However, there is nothing
necessarily wrong with arbitrary allocations—so long as one does not treat
them as being theoretically justified.

[*Professor Thomas has written the following summary of this study's conclusions. For brevity, technical arguments that support these conclusions are necessarily omitted:*]

Many accounting measurements are theoretically justified. For instance,
quantities of cash or other assets may be counted without arbitrariness.
Unfortunately, though, almost all accounting allocations are arbitrary.

[40] J. R. Gould, "The Economist's Cost Concept and Business Problems," in W. T. Baxter and
Sidney Davidson, editors, *Studies in Accounting Theory* (Homewood, Illinois: Richard D. Irwin,
Inc., 1962), p. 231.

Depreciation allocations exemplify this. All efforts to justify depreciation practices boil down to a single approach. Firms buy depreciable assets because they expect that these assets will provide services. The accountant estimates the pattern by which these services will be received, then selects a depreciation method that will be consistent with this pattern.

For example, if the asset is expected to provide the same level of service during all years, the accountant may use straight-line depreciation to allocate its purchase price to the years of its life. If he expects greater services in earlier years than in later ones, he may use an accelerated depreciation method, instead.

The same rationale governs accounting for all other nonmonetary inputs. For instance, the accountant allocates costs of single-year goods entirely to their years of acquisition because he perceives them to provide discernable services only during those years. Finally, it can be demonstrated that these "services" must be interpretable as the effects of the input on income or cash (its *contributions to net income*, or just *contributions*, for short).

From this, it is evident that financial accounting's allocation theory depends upon an implicit assumption that each input's individual contributions to income can be measured. Such measurements require determining the firm's total income for each period, then making a *second* allocation whereby each input is credited with what it contributed. Let us designate this as the *income-to-inputs* allocation.

Surprisingly, this approach to justifying allocations just won't wash. The income-to-inputs allocation must almost always be arbitrary. This renders the amounts calculated for individual contributions equally arbitrary, which in turn makes the input's pattern of services arbitrary. But the theoretical justification of the input's depreciation (or other form of amortization) depends on this pattern of services; if the latter is arbitrary, theoretical justification of amortization has failed. The arbitrariness of the income-to-inputs allocation makes the whole justification effort collapse like a row of dominoes.

Why are allocations of total income to individual inputs arbitrary? The reasons are complex, but ultimately depend upon a simple fact: most inputs *interact*. The output generated by two or more inputs working in combination differs from (and usually exceeds) the total output that would be generated by two or more inputs working in combination differs from (and usually exceeds) the total output that would be generated by these inputs operating in isolation. Almost any input offers examples of interaction: men and equipment working together generate more output (and income) than the total that hand labor and untended equipment could generate. Often, these inputs are even more productive if combined with a third input, electricity. Yet, in isolation, electricity produces nothing.

Let us designate the output (if any) that each input would produce in isolation as that input's *separate effect*, and the difference between total output and the total of all separate effects as an *interaction effect*. It is easily demonstrated that most of any firm's income is an interaction effect.

More laboriously, it can be proved that there is no theoretically justifiable way to allocate interaction effects to individual inputs (at least as far as general-purpose financial reporting goes). This means that most of the firm's income cannot be allocated to individual inputs, except arbitrarily. The income-to-inputs allocation collapses, and with it collapses theoretical justification for depreciation and other amortizations of nonmonetary inputs.

Here is a highly simplified example of the difficulties of allocating output to interacting inputs. Brown and Jones work as a team in manufacturing a product. Brown is paid $4.00 per hour; Jones is paid $6.00 per hour. Were Brown to work alone, he could make 250 units of this product per day; working alone, Jones could make 450. Working as a team (and specializing) they produce 1,050 units per day. The separate and interaction effects (in units of product) are:

Total output		1,050
Separate effect of Brown	250	
Separate effect of Jones	450	700
Interaction effect		350

Let us suppose that the firm wishes to calculate how much of the total 1,050 output each employee produced (perhaps for bonus purposes). There are at least eight ways this could be done (in what follows, $B = 600$ will signify that Brown's contribution is calculated to be 600 units per day, and so forth).

1. Were Brown to work elsewhere, total output would decline to Jones' separate effect of 450 units per day, a decline of $1,050 - 450 = 600$ units; $B = 600, J = 450$.

2. Similarly, were Jones to work elsewhere, output would decline by 800 units; $B = 250, J = 800$.

3. Total output could be split 50/50; $B = 525, J = 525$.

4. Each worker could be credited with his separate effect, then the interaction effect split 50/50; $B = 425, J = 625$.

5. Same as 4, except that the interaction effect is split 250/450, in proportion to the relative separate effects; $B = 375, J = 675$.

6. Same as 4, except that the interaction effect is split $600/800$, in proportion to the decline in total output caused by either worker working elsewhere; $B = 400, J = 650$.

7. Same as 4, except that the interaction effect is split $4.00/6.00$, in proportion to the salaries of the two workers; $B = 390, J = 660$.

8. The *total* output could be split $4.00/6.00$, in proportion to the salaries of the two workers; $B = 420, J = 630$.

Of course, this example was greatly simplified. Contributions made by other inputs were ignored, and the total interaction effect is much smaller than it would have been had all inputs been considered. In real firms, thousands of inputs interact in a tangle of reciprocal influences; there simply is no way to allocate total output to individual inputs then defend the results against conflicting calculations. Therefore, the second requirement for theoretical justification of an allocation (defensibility) is not met. Because allocations of outputs to inputs cannot be justified, income-to-inputs allocations will be arbitrary—and so will all consequent allocations, such as depreciation allocations. This conclusion has disturbing consequences:

1. Since all depreciation calculations are arbitrary, so are the related depreciation expense and accumulated depreciation figures in financial statements.[41]

2. The same is true of all other nonmonetary inputs, since all interact with each other. Because one cannot identify any input's contributions, one cannot distinguish contributions received to date from those to be received in the future. Therefore, the traditional distinction between an asset and an expense cannot be made, except arbitrarily.

3. Therefore, customary goals of "matching" revenues and expenses cannot be accomplished, except arbitrarily.

4. Therefore, accounting's conventional notions of a firm's net income are also revealed to be arbitrary.[42]

An expanded version of the final conclusion was phrased as follows in the monograph:

---

[41] Subsequent research has shown that this arbitrariness cannot be dismissed as trivial, or dismissed on the grounds that depreciation is, after all, "only an estimate." The arbitrariness in any year's depreciation charge for any one asset is at least as great as the total purchase price of that asset! See "Useful Arbitrary Allocations (With a Comment on the Neutrality of Financial Accounting Reports)," *The Accounting Review* (July 1971), pp. 472–79. As its title suggests, this article also discusses some special purposes for which arbitrary allocations may be useful, despite their inappropriateness for general-purpose financial reporting.

[42] These four conclusions seem to have withstood criticism to date (September 1972). However, their implications may not be quite as bleak as the final passage quoted from the monograph suggests. I am currently writing a second allocation study designed both to answer criticisms and

. . . my own guess is that, so far as the history of accounting is concerned, the next twenty-five years may subsequently be seen to have been the twilight of income measurement.[43]

In the present state of accounting theory and allocation theory, there us ally will be only a few ways to escape the problems discussed in this boo Accountants might stop reporting economic information about nonmon tary goods (in the sense discussed immediately above). Or accountan might stop allocating.

The possible ways to stop allocating have been discussed: the current-pri valuation approaches recommended by Chambers and Sterling, and th substitution of net-quick-assets funds statements for income statements. C course these two approaches are not mutually exclusive. The funds statemer approach could employ a current-price balance sheet (though doing s would destroy the present agreement between changes in magnitudes r ported on the balance sheet, and the magnitudes reported on the incon statement). Both of these ways to stop allocating lead to other difficultie Both lead to abandoning the effort to measure income—either to abandonin it explicitly, or to doing so *de facto* by following rules that violate the usu conceptions of the nature of income measurement.

The final alternative is to ignore the problem. Accountants may be conter to perform arbitrary allocations—that is, to continue doing what they a doing now. The main drawback to arbitrary allocations is that the signif cance of reported magnitudes becomes impossible to specify. Accordingl accountants seem to be faced with three main alternatives. They must either

1. Stop reporting economic information about nonmonetary goods an their amortization (except insofar as the beliefs of intelligent laymen a consistent with economics); or,

2. Abandon the effort to measure income; or,

3. Allow a large part (probably the *major* part) of their financial state ments to be nearly void of meaningful content.

The first of these alternatives will be theoretically justified only if th opinions of intelligent laymen about accounting are consistent and unambig uous—which seems unlikely. The second alternative suffers from all th weaknesses that characterize the related substitute measures. Unfortunatel the third alternative is always possible.

Financial accounting theory began to take its present form around th turn of the century. It crystalized into what are now the various orthodo

to suggest non-allocated measures that could be employed in financial statements. Convention. financial statements, with their ceaseless attempts to allocate the unallocable, are a deceit. Bu conventional statements might evolve into defensible reports satisfying a broad range of reade needs.

[43] David Solomons, "Economic and Accounting Concepts of Income," *Accounting Review* XXXVI (July, 1961), 383.

les and ways of perceiving things by the 1930's. Recently, signs of major
nange have become visible. Perhaps the majority of academic theorists now
ject the historical cost rule. And many theorists are attempting far more
veeping changes than this. Many writers, especially the younger theorists,
re trying to reconstruct financial accounting on entirely new foundations.

This book has ended with some very gloomy conclusions. But they pertain
nly to the ways in which we *now* perceive accounting. A long winter of
rthodoxy seems to be nearing its end. It is impossible to say what the new
ccounting will be like. But most of the problems discussed in this book are
nlikely to survive the thaw.

Kenneth S. Most is Professor and Head of the
Department of Accounting at Texas A & M
University.

The Value of Inventories

Kenneth S. Most

Inventory valuation is usually considered as a problem of pricing.[1] All accounting data represent quantities multiplied by prices, and pricing is thus only a part of the inventory valuation problem. In this paper, attention will be directed to some less frequently considered difficulties of quantification and their effects on the pricing problem. It will be argued that valuation can only be approached from a study of the nonmonetary characteristics of inventory, i.e., the physical or time quantities of materials, labour and overheads and the position of these quantities in relation to the business operating cycle.

Inventory valuation serves period accounting: the old period hands over its "values in suspense" to the new one. In this way, the old period is purged of matters which do not affect its results, and the new period is made to account for the values transferred to it. Considering the problem in this light may show how some conventions of accounting practice arise out of business conditions, and must therefore be applied differently in different firms.

Importance of Inventory

Inventory valuation is of major importance in accountancy, for three main reasons. First, of all the values which may be in suspense at the beginning and end of an accounting period, inventory is the largest single item for firms

---

[1] E.g., Gerhard G. Mueller, "Valuing Inventories at Other than Historical Costs—Some International Differences," *Journal of Accounting Research*, Autumn, 1964, pp. 148-57. See also, *Accounting Research and Terminology Bulletins*, Chapter 4, "Inventory Pricing" (New York: AICPA, 1961).

Reprinted by permission of the author and publisher from *Journal of Accounting Research*, Vol. V (Spring, 1967), pp. 39-50.

ther than manufacturers and public utilities, and the second largest after xed assets, for manufacturing firms.[2]

On a national basis, values of inventories ranged from 43% to 48% of the J.K. gross national product, and it has been demonstrated that the percentge hardly changed between 1947 and 1962 over the decade ended 1961.[3]

It is accepted that an over- or under-valuation of inventories can produce a naterial effect on calculation of profit, in the case of firms, and gross national roduct in the case of nations. For example, a firm reporting a net profit of 0 and a closing inventory of 50 would have doubled its profits if it had overtated its inventory value by 20%. Where inventories amount to almost 50% f gross national product, an error in valuation of ±10% may easily be esponsible for the entire variation between successive years.

The effect of inaccurate measurement is greater for inventories than for ixed assets, which present the other significant valuation problem. Both lasses of assets are turned over by firms in the course of their profit-making ctivities, but at widely different rates. In most cases, inventories are completely replaced within a period of one year; where this is not the case, as in building construction, special problems occur similar to those encountered vith fixed assets. Fixed assets are completely replaced in accordance with nvestment cycles ranging from about three years as with industries subject o rapid technological change, to centuries as with cities and their ports. Thus, whereas the effect of wrongly valuing inventories has an immediate nfluence on the viability of the firm, errors in estimating depreciation may ake many years to work themselves out. The maintenance of "circulating apital" is a necessary condition of short-term survival; the evidence of our lecaying residential, commercial and industrial centres in cities demon-,trates how long it can take before the effects of failure to maintain "fixed apital" become apparent. This was brought out in a celebrated but often criticised judgment in one of the earlier British cases on auditing.[4]

Finally, the possibility of accurate measurement seems to be relatively high for inventories. Goods which have been acquired within the accounting period will generally have been purchased at prices not too far removed from their current replacement prices; where prices have changed materially, real-.stic replacement prices can be ascertained from suppliers ready and able to

[2] Internal Revenue Service, U.S. Treasury Department, *Statistics of Income 1957-58: Corpora-ion Income Tax Returns* (Washington, D.C.: U.S. Government Printing Office) and *Estimated Balance Sheet, All U.S. Manufacturing Companies*, Federal Trade Commission and Securities and Exchange Commission, Quarterly Financial Reports for Manufacturing Corporations Washington, D.C.: U.S. Government Printing Office).

[3] C. H. Feinstein, "Stocks, Sales and Stockbuilding," *London and Cambridge Economic Bulle-*in, No. 45, March, 1963.

[4] *Verner* v. *General and Commercial Investment Trust* (1894) "... fixed capital may be sunk and lost and yet ... the excess of current receipts over current payments may be divided but ... floating or circulating capital must be kept up."

supply at them. In addition; the method whereby inventories are counted is
of superior accuracy to the depreciation calculations which provide the key
to valuing fixed assets. These facts present accountants with a professional
challenge which fixed asset valuation does not.

Inventory as Values in Suspense

In analysing the nature of inventories to determine a basis for valuation we
should first isolate the elements of which they are composed. These are
materials, labour, and expense; any factors of production may be "values in
suspense" at the end of an accounting period and therefore carried forward
to the next period. Values which are not "in suspense" have been either
consumed or wasted during the period and are chargeable to the period.[5]

Use of this costing terminology permits postponement of the problems
which arise when inventories are classified into raw materials, work in progress, and finished products. The inputs which may be in suspense at the end
of the accounting period are common to each of these classes and therefore
represent a primary classification.

There seems to be a majority view that the following are proper charges to
inventory for financial accounts:[6]

The elements making up the cost of stock are:
- (a) Direct expenditure on the purchase of goods bought for resale, and of
  materials and components used in the manufacture of finished goods.
- (b) Other direct expenditure which can be identified specifically as having
  been incurred in acquiring the stock or bringing it to its existing condition and location; examples are direct labour, transport, processing and
  packaging.
- (c) Such part, if any, of the overhead expenditure as is properly carried
  forward in the circumstances of the business instead of being charged
  against the revenue of the period in which it was incurred.[7]

Accountants have not taken the lead in drawing attention to the waste
problem implicit in valuing inventories.[8] Where goods bought for resale or

---

[5] This statement differs from the conventional "matching costs against revenues" approach.
Waste is not a cost, and it cannot be a value in suspense. It must therefore be offset against
revenues or charged to expense even if no revenues have been earned or production achieved.
See Appendix: "Problem in Inventory Valuation."

[6] Recommendations on Accounting Principles of the Institute of Chartered Accountants in
England and Wales, No. 22, "Treatment of Stock-in-Trade and Work in Progress in Financial
Accounts," 1960 (S. 4). See also, *Accounting Research and Terminology Bulletins*, Chapter 4,
"Inventory Pricing" (New York: AICPA, 1961), pp. 28–9.

[7] This point is usually avoided in financial accounting textbooks by diverting attention to the
"cost or lower market" rules.

[8] This has been done by production engineers who have devoted much attention in recent years
to economic batch quantity, exponential smoothing and other calculations designed to quantify
required inventory levels as distinct from discretionary ones. A leading authority in the U.K. has
estimated that modern methods of stock control could reduce material holding in British indus-

materials and components bought for production are lost or destroyed, they do not appear in the inventory and are therefore not valued. It frequently occurs, however, that goods are bought for resale in excess of market requirements, and that materials and components are bought for production which cannot take place. These items are physically present when inventory is taken, but they cannot be valued on the same basis as regular inventories of good and materials.

E. Schmalenbach[9] brings this out clearly:

> Some of them [i.e., inventories] are ready to be released on to the market but require immediate replacement (retail stocks, manufacturers' and wholesalers' catalogues); in this case, they are tied up not *in specie* but *in genere*, the effect on the profit and loss account being the same. The prior period hands over its stocks to the subsequent one, without reference to the attainable price, without any element of speculation but solely in order to keep the business going. The prior period could no more have ended without stocks than the subsequent period could have continued without them.

Schmalenbach goes on to say that these conditions exist in respect of the greater part of the contents of business inventories, but recent discoveries resulting from operations research and the work of management consultants indicate that this statement does not apply at the present time.[10] The origins of nonregular inventories may be traceable to changes in markets (e.g., mature females wishing to imitate teenage shapes) or in technology (use of ½″ mild steel bars in place of ⅝″ for a certain product). They may arise out of weaknesses in the structure of markets[11] or errors of business policy, such as the creation of over-capacity. Whatever the cause, that part of "direct expenditure on the purchase of goods bought for resale and of materials and components used in the manufacture of finished goods" and of "other direct expenditure which can be identified specifically" with them, which relates to such items of inventory, ceases to be relevant to the valuation of inventory.

In other words, if inventories are not replacement articles, they should not be valued on a replacement basis (whether at historical or replacement

---

try by twenty percent. See A. Battersby, *Guide to Stock Control* (New York: Pitman Pub., 1962). See also, John F. Magee, "Guides to Inventory Policy," *Harvard Business Review*, Jan./Feb., Mar./Apr., May/June, 1956. The problem is stated, but not satisfactorily dealt with, in *Accounting Research and Terminology Bulletins, op. cit.*, pp. 30-1, and C. G. Blough, *Practical Applications of Accounting Standards* (New York: AICPA, 1957), p. 314ff, esp. p. 319 under "Is LIFO Proper in Valuing Excess over Normal Stock?"

[9] Schmalenbach, Eugen, *Dynamic Accounting*, translated from German by G. W. Murphy and K. S. Most (London: Gee and Company, Ltd., 1959), p. 182.

[10] A. Battersby, *op. cit.*

[11] See J. W. Forrester, "Industrial Dynamics," *Harvard Business Review*, July/August, 1958. The author shows how a change in demand is amplified through the supply chain by successive over-ordering. This is an aspect of concentration of demand which has tended to be overlooked.

prices). The alternatives are the proceeds basis where the articles are to be exteriorised, and the substitution cost basis where they are to be used within the business for purposes for which they were not acquired.

As an example of this we may take the case of a manufacturer in the metal-working industry whose inventory at a certain date includes a quantity of steel rod of a dimension which is no longer required for current production. This steel rod is nonregular inventory and therefore cannot be valued on that basis. Two possibilities exist; either the rod will be sold (as scrap or perhaps to another firm at a price lower than cost) or it will be used as a substitute for rod of another dimension which is preferred on the grounds of price or better utilisation. In the former case, it will be included at proceeds value, in the latter, at substitution value, i.e., the cost of whatever it is used in substitution for. It can happen that both of these values are negative, e.g., the manufacturer may have to pay to take the stuff away or decide to substitute at a loss.

If we now consider the expense factor, we can see the application of the same principle. Part (c) of the Recommendation quoted begins "such part, *if any*, of the overhead expenditure. . . . " This statement implies the possibility that overhead expenditure may be associated neither with goods sold nor with finished goods or work in progress on hand at the end of a period, that is, neither consumed by use nor in suspense. Expense of this kind would be charged to the old accounting period as a loss. It should be pointed out that this need not be expense incurred during the old accounting period. Values in suspense at the beginning of this period, and properly carried forward in inventory at that time, may include expense of the prior period which becomes valueless as a result of events occurring during the subsequent one. Where such goods are in the inventory at the end of the period, they will be valued on a different basis from regular inventories. This may result in a loss properly chargeable to the accounting period of expense incurred during the prior one.

Looking again at (c) we find the statement ". . . such part . . . of the overhead expenditure as is properly carried forward in the circumstances of the business. . . ." The following sections of the Recommendation (5-10) list the prevailing practices in the treatment of overhead expenditure. These are divided into three groups:

(i) No overhead expenditure included.
(ii) Only the differential overhead expenditure included.
(iii) The full overhead expenditure applicable to production is included on the basis of a normal level of activity (the capacity cost).

The practice of dividing overhead expenditure by actual production is rejected as being incorrect.

It is interesting that this Recommendation then looks to the actual conditions of the firm as the indicator of which practice is correct (nature of the business, levels of production and sales, continuity or discontinuity, risks of realisation, and the special cases of maturing stocks and long-term contracts). It is interesting because the Recommendation specifically deals with financial accounts, yet proceeds from relevant costing considerations. AICPA Statements reveal the same approach. So much for the "financial v. management accounting" controversy and the argument for "different figures for different purposes." Accountancy is concerned with facts.

The Case of Retail Inventories

At this point we may consider prevailing practices in the valuation of wholesale and retail stocks and their origins. Purchase price (acquisition cost) has been the basis of such valuations for centuries, and the practice of reducing the value of inventory for lost and damaged goods is of equal antiquity. This accords with the idea of inventory as a deferred charge to cash[12] and belongs to the era of the primacy of the balance sheet.

It also accords with business conditions in a mercantile society. Such businesses are not organised to provide a constant stream of goods to a known market. They do not carry stocks as a permanent feature of their asset structure.

The trader traveling from fair to fair bought in accordance with his day-to-day requirements; where he carried an inventory he did so because of the necessity to be supplied, arising out of the infrequency of arrival of ships from the East, or the difficulty of bringing goods overland from Antwerp or Genoa. The artisan carried inventory only where it was necessary to guard against interruption of supplies or where it consisted of materials to be matured before use, such as timber. Usually the customer supplied his own materials. In such cases, the inventory was only significant as an "index of funds to be produced."[13]

Why then, if such inventories were treated as a deferred charge to cash, were they not valued at selling prices? Perhaps the fact that selling prices were not fixed by the supplier but negotiated with the customer may have had some influence on this. Quite apart from the pricing difficulty, however, there is an important conceptual reason. The businessman must distinguish between acquisition values and proceeds values. In calculating period profits, he must take out of inventory goods unsold at the same prices at which they were put in, i.e., at acquisition prices. The old period is selling to the new one, at not more than the new period would have been willing to pay to another supplier, which leads directly to acquisition cost.

---

[12] See Stephen Gilman, *Accounting Concepts of Profit* (New York: Ronald Press, 1939), p. 303 and *Accounting Research and Terminology Bulletins*, Chapter 4, "Inventory Pricing" (New York: AICPA, 1961), p. 28, "Statement 2."

[13] Gilman, *op. cit.*, p. 304.

With the change over from a mercantile to an industrial society, a new kind of wholesaler and retailer emerges. He undertakes to assure the supply of goods produced by manufacturers on a regular replacement cycle to a known market. This undertaking creates a necessity to carry inventories in accordance with lead times and rates of turnover varying from one branch to another. The necessity to carry inventories results in certain overhead expenses which are costs of bringing the goods to the point at which sales are made. Why, then, do many businesses of this kind continue to disregard overhead expenses in valuing inventories?

In fact, wholesale and retail firms treat their costs as period costs for reasons of convenience and materiality. It is difficult to separate procurement and storage costs from selling costs. It is not likely that they will be a material addition to inventory value when prorated over the entire turnover of goods during the accounting period. In the case of department stores, supermarket chains and discount houses, however, neither of these arguments holds good at the present time, but here an additional factor must be considered. In such businesses, the prevailing method of inventory valuation is to price the goods at retail prices and reduce by a known departmental margin. This procedure is known to be inaccurate, but if the result is within the required tolerances established by the firm, it is preferred because of the important reduction in clerical costs which it allows. In other words, the additional cost of greater accuracy is believed to exceed its value. If the value of inventory is known to be subject to a 10% margin of error, then the significance of acquisition costs amounting to 4% of the total is not great.[14] In certain cases, such as furniture stores, acquisition costs may be substantial, rate of turnover low, and the retail inventory method unnecessary. In such cases, to omit overhead expenditure of this kind is wrong.

Principles of Inventory Valuation

We thus arrive at the following propositions:[15]

(1) The inventories of a business are divisible into a part which is necessary for the continuity of its operating cycle, and another part which is redundant to that continuity.
(2) The part which is necessary for continuity should be valued at cost on a replacement basis, i.e., on the fiction that the new period buys from the old one at a price which is acceptable to both.

---

[14] It has been suggested that omission of storage costs is compensated for by pricing inventories at invoice prices and ignoring the effects of cash discounts.

[15] See a similar set of propositions, framed in more general terms, by F. K. Wright, "Towards a Theory of Inventory Measurement," *Calculator Annual*, Singapore Polytechnic Society of Commerce, third issue, 1964/65.

(3) The part which is redundant should be valued on a proceeds basis ("net realisable value") if it is to be placed on the market, or on a substitution basis ("substitute replacement price") if it is to be used for normal operations in place of some other commodity.

In financial accounting, these propositions are concealed behind the "lowest value" rule. This rule states that inventories should be valued at cost, or replacement price, or net realisable value, whichever is the lowest.[16] It is erroneous to conclude from this that *every* item in the inventory should be tested for its lowest value, and that used. "Cost" is relevant for regular inventories only and no other value is applicable. "Replacement price" is relevant only for items to be used as substitutes. "Net realisable value" is relevant only for items destined to be realised outside the regular operations of the business.

It will be seen that two of these cases depend upon the definition of "cost" for their pricing, i.e., upon a valuation which proceeds from factors of production. The third, "net realisable value," depends upon the determination of prices outside the firm, i.e., upon a valuation which proceeds from market factors. The ascertainment of "cost" is therefore fundamental to inventory valuation except for those items which are capable of being disposed of outside the business with no effect on the continuity of operations.

We now return to the ascertainment of cost. The problem of ascertaining cost is complicated by the terms "direct" and "indirect" which suggest that some materials, labour, and expense can be identified with a product, whereas other materials, labour, and expense cannot. In theory (and frequently in fact) all factors of production are required to produce and sell a product (or service); this conceptual point of departure is not affected by the methodological problems involved in identifying them with the product.

To juxtapose "product costs" and "period costs" is therefore an error of logic. All costs are product costs, in the same way that all costs are period costs. To argue, for example, that materials purchased in 1965 and processed in 1966 are not period costs (of 1966) but that factory rent of December, 1965, is a period cost of 1965, although all materials processed in the factory in that month were finished in January, 1966, is not defensible simply by reference to the physical presence of the materials in 1966.

The distinction which is relevant here is that between cost and waste. All factors of production which were required to bring the inventory to that state of completion and place for which it was required at the date of the balance sheet are proper components of its value. It may be that the expense component, in a given case, is nil; it may equally be the case that the materials component is nil and the expense component substantial.

---

[16] The "base stock" method is a variation on "cost."

Valuation at Selling Prices

In some industries it is a trade custom to value inventories at selling prices because it is impossible to determine costs, or the production of the accounting period is sold forward for delivery after the end of the period, or wide fluctuations in market prices are so prevalent that net realisation is preferred for reasons of financial prudence. It will be seen, however, that there is a sound conceptual argument for the valuation of inventories at selling prices (net realisable value) in certain other cases besides those already mentioned.[17] This is where any part of the inventory may be treated as sold at the end of an accounting period, but has not been included in sales because there has been no invoiced delivery.

In law, a sale of specific goods not in a deliverable state transfers property from the seller to the buyer when they are brought to a deliverable state and the buyer has notice of it. A sale of unascertained goods takes place when the goods described in the contract and in a deliverable state are appropriated to the contract either by the seller with the assent of the buyer or by the buyer with the consent of the seller. The buyer's assent may be either expressed or implied.[18]

In the normal course of events, these conditions are satisfied by the delivery of the goods to the buyer or his order, and the invoice which is made out is evidence of this fact and of the realisation of the sale. From the viewpoint of economic value, however, the sale may be deemed to have taken place even though there has been no delivery, providing that the risk of failure through nondelivery is negligible or fully covered by insurance.

Suppose, for example, that a gown manufacturer has a contract to deliver 3,000 garments weekly to a large department store. Deliveries are made on a Monday; the year ends on a Saturday. The year-end inventory includes 3,000 garments appropriated to the contract and these are in fact delivered to the customer and invoiced to him two days later. It is submitted that the proper value for inventory purposes of these 3,000 garments is their sales value, less only the relevant delivery expense.

Limitations of Accuracy

We shall now turn to the physical problem of taking inventories. We have said that the count lends itself to a high degree of accuracy but this does not imply that the accuracy is total, and reference has already been made to the problems of retail stocktaking. To the layman, these difficulties may have

---

[17] See also, G. L. Battista and G. R. Crowningshield, "Inventories at Realizable Values," *NAA Bulletin*, May, 1965, where the argument is considered in relation to the totality of the inventory of a firm.

[18] U.K. Sales of Goods Act, 1893 (S. 18).

become apparent only recently, as a result of the Billie Sol Estes and De Angelos cases.[19]

In some industries, however, the difficulties are equally clear. Counting a large herd of steers on a ranch in Arizona, or the timber contents of a vast forest in Canada, or the mountains of coal which pile up at pit-heads anywhere, for example, can only be approximate.[20]

Even in manufacturing industries of more modest dimensions there is room for approximation, particularly in view of the fact that for reasons of cost, a physical inventory may have to be taken during one or two days at the end of the accounting period.

A major source of inaccuracy occurs in the physical identification of work in progress. As far as the material content is concerned the matter is fairly straight-forward, but the labour and expense contents are an approximation at two removes. In the first place, we have the methodological problem of allocating and apportioning labour and expense costs to cost centres. In the second, we have the physical problem of identifying the stage of completion of the semi-finished products on hand in those cost centres. Some of them may have been put into production to employ surplus capacity, whereas others are part of the normal loading of a cost centre; it is not always easy to distinguish them at the count. Rule-of-thumb assumptions are often made to facilitate the task.

Many manufacturers make some or all of the components they require for the assembly of their finished products. In the electrical industries, electric motors are made by firms which install them in washing machines. Although these motors are finished products from one manufacturing viewpoint, they are work in progress from another. Components of this kind are usually made in batches, following an economic batch quantity calculation, and at a given date an entire batch may be held in some intermediate store. The assessment of their labour and expense contents, or even their material content, in the light of whether, or in how far, they are needed for the continuity of operations, may be difficult.

Some firms engage in continuous inventory counting so that all items are physically counted at least once annually, but not necessarily at the end of the accounting period. Such firms accept the probability that, for a substantial part of the inventory, the quantities on hand shown by the perpetual inventory records, and which are priced for valuation, will be incorrect.[21] And, to add to the general insecurity, we have the problems associated with fraud—at

---

[19] Reported in *Fortune*, July, 1962, pp. 166–70, and January, 1964, pp. 74–8, esp. p. 76.

[20] See, e.g., R. M. Trueblood and R. M. Cyert, "Test of Physical Inventory Quantities of Bulk Materials," Chapter 11 in *Sampling Techniques in Auditing* (Englewood Cliffs: Prentice-Hall, 1957).

[21] For a discussion of this problem from the auditor's point of view, see C. G. Blough, *Practical Applications of Accounting Standards* (New York: AICPA, 1957), pp. 23–7.

any time there are ships sailing the seas with cases in their holds containing stones instead of crockery or toys, and bags in warehouses full of newspaper instead of wool.

Although the valuation of inventory is an accountant's responsibility, taking inventory is a management function. In order to discharge his responsibility the accountant would need to be supplied with an inventory classified into regular and nonregular items, items produced as a part of the normal load of the various cost centres and those produced with spare capacity, and items still on hand but sold in all but a strictly legal sense. Further, in respect of nonregular items, he would need to know which of them would be used as substitutes, and for what, and which were free to be exteriorised by sale as excess stocks, and in what markets. He would then have to ascertain the cost prices which were appropriate for the regular stocks of raw materials, the materials, labour and expense components of the regular inventories produced as part of the normal load of the various cost centres, the marginal cost prices of items produced with spare capacity, the net realisable values of products already sold, and of nonregular items due to be sold, and the substitution cost prices of items to be used as substitutes.

Needless to say, this information is rarely available to him, nor even to the management of the firm. The inventory sheets will show damaged and obsolete items, but the counters are not in a position to know the effects of business conditions and business policy on the seemingly good and usable contents of the stores and the work in progress on the shop floor.

An interesting case in point concerns stocks of spare parts held by automobile dealers and other wholesalers and retailers responsible for supplying replacement parts for consumer durables. The manufacturers of these durables give no advance warning of their intention to replace a particular model since surprise is an essential ingredient of competitiveness. The dealer knows from experience, however, that one or more models will be replaced next year and that when this happens, the parts he holds for the old models will be drastically reduced in value. In short, he knows that the value of his inventory is less than the calculated total based on cost, but he cannot know how much less without knowing which model is shortly to become obsolete.

In view of all this, and of the recognised inaccuracy of physical inventory data, within limits, the manager and the accountant bring to bear their knowledge, judgement, and skill on the valuation problem as best they can. In one case they may use prime cost for all work in progress and finished products, assuming that the elimination of overheads will compensate for the overvaluation of unsaleable items and excessive raw materials. In other cases, an "arbitrary" percentage reduction is applied to all or part of a valuation made at cost to achieve a similar result. The application of the "lowest value" rule to all items of inventory may also be regarded in this light, and adherence to historical prices in preference to current replacement values during a period of rising prices acts as a reduction of the total value of inventory. LIFO, it may be noted, has an even more marked effect in the same direction.

The use of replacement value by Dutch firms is not correctly described by calling it "replacement cost."[22] This would imply that quantities on hand are multiplied by replacement prices whereas replacement quantities are multiplied by current replacement prices to obtain replacement value. Hence, the use of the term "replacement values" in Note 5 of the Algemene Kunstzidje Unie N.V. 1960 annual report.[23] It is perhaps not generally appreciated that the management of major Dutch firms, such as AKU, Philips, and the Dutch state corporations, has been greatly influenced by the schools of managerial economics in Amsterdam, Gronnigen, Rotterdam and other universities, and by managerial economists such as Limperg, Tinbergen and the brothers Mey.[24]

It does not follow, therefore, that Dutch inventory valuations at replacement values are necessarily higher than the inventory valuations which would be made in similar circumstances by U.S. or U.K. managers and accountants during periods of rising prices. If Dutch firms are working with scientific management concepts of budgeting, purchasing, production planning and control, and marketing, they are limiting their inventories to levels necessary to ensure the continuity of operations and disposing of surplus quantities as and when they are ascertained. In addition, they are revising the material, labour, and expense quantities of the regular inventories in accordance with market and technological developments and their pricing as changes in price levels make it necessary. All this must be kept in view when using the term "replacement cost."

Conclusion

It appears from this that the rules of inventory valuation based on "lower of cost or market" are inadequate and that the statements published by professional accountancy bodies on this subject require amplification and clarification if they are to serve as guides for students and practitioners. The objective should be to develop a theoretically sound basis for inventory valuation which accommodates both the quantity and the price factors, while at the same time allowing those concerned with it to apply the basic principles in the light of actual business conditions. The use of flat-rate inventory write-downs, even of the order of 90%, may then become acceptable to auditors, tax departments and statisticians, in circumstances where their appropriateness is demonstrable, e.g., where unsold Xmas trees are bundled away on December 26 to await the revival of demand ten months later.

---

[22] G. G. Mueller, *op. cit.*, p. 153.

[23] *Ibid.*, p. 153.

[24] Directors of these firms include former students of these professors.

Appendix

Problem in Inventory Valuation

A fully automated plant is set up to manufacture a unique product from one raw material. The material is the waste product of another industry, and delivered cost is nil since the other industry pays the cost of transporting the material from its premises to the place of utilization.

The cycle time of the plant is 32 days from receipt of material to finished product. It can produce 1,000 units of product at the end of each 32 day period. Fixed costs, including depreciation, total $365,000 p.a. and accrue evenly from day to day.

(1) If the plant is put into operation on January 1 at full capacity to supply the February market, what is the value of inventory at January 31?

(2) If the plant is put into operation on January 1 at 50% of capacity to supply the February market with 500 units of product, what is the value of inventory at January 31?

(3) Suppose that the finished product must be held in store for 365 days in order to mature, and that the plant operates at full capacity during January. What is the value of January production included in inventory at December 31?

Robert T. Sprouse is a Member of the
Financial Accounting Standards Board,
formerly Professor of Accounting at Stanford
University.

The Balance Sheet—Embodiment of the Most Fundamental Elements of Accounting Theory

Robert T. Sprouse

The assertion is frequently made that in accounting's house the income statement is our most important product. To the extent that this is intended to mean that the attention of most users of financial statements tends to focus on the income statement, the assertion is acceptable. To the extent that the assertion refers to the most important elements of accounting theory, the assertion is delusory. This paper is written in support of an alternative proposition: the balance sheet embodies the most fundamental elements of accounting theory, from which the essential elements contained in the income statement are necessarily derived. Indeed, the income statement can properly be described as merely a summary of one class of transactions resulting in changes in one balance-sheet account.

I offer two forms of support for this proposition: (1) An analysis of two contending views of the components and function of the balance sheet that have emerged over time. The purpose is to demonstrate the fallacies and futilities of such opposing views. For convenience, let me designate these the sheet of balances view and the static funds statement view. (2) A positive case for reviewing the balance sheet as a statement of financial position which provides a basis for the measurement of a meaningful concept of income and which, at the same time, provides useful information in its own

---

Reprinted by permission of the author and publisher from *Foundations of Accounting Theory*, University of Florida Press, 1971, pp. 90–104.

right. Each of these three distinguishable views has strikingly different im plications for the construction of accounting theory—implications that a readily discernible in their application to the analysis of transactions an financial reporting.

The Sheet of Balances View

The sheet of balances approach views the statement as a summary of deb and credit account balances that remain after the determinants of incom have been decided upon and the retained earnings account has been adjuste for the amount of income that results. This is a "balance sheet" in the mo literal sense of the term. Increasingly, this view has been adopted in accoun ing practice, as manifested by many of the pronouncements of the AICP and by most of the financial statements published by corporations.

Accounting Terminology Bulletin no. 1 defines the balance sheet as " tabular statement or summary of balances (debit and credit) carried forwar after an actual or constructive closing of books of account kept according principles of accounting."[1] An asset is "something represented by a deb balance that is or would be properly carried forward upon a closing of book of account according to the rules or principles of accounting."[2] Similarly, liability is "something represented by a credit balance that is or would b properly carried forward upon a closing of books of account according to th rules or principles of accounting."[3]

Exaggerating only slightly, then, one might say that, according to thi view, a balance sheet is a summary of debit and credit balances and that th primary difference between an asset and liability is the side of the account o which the balance happens to appear.

The sheet of balances view of the balance sheet stems from the notion tha a valid and viable framework for accounting analysis—that is, an accounting theory—can be constructed on the basis of the pre-eminence of the income statement and the application of the "matching" concept. Which of these two—the pre-eminence of the income statement and the matching concept— is the chicken and which is the egg is difficult to determine. One migh hypothesize that because both are sterile—at least as foundations for account ing theory—they were necessarily created simultaneously.[4]

Pre-eminence of the income statement is the offspring of confusion be tween the derivative information that decision-makers may find most useful

---

[1] AICPA, Committee on Terminology, *Review and Resume*, Accounting Terminology Bulletin no. 1 (New York, 1953), p. 12.

[2] Accounting Terminology Bulletin no. 1, p. 13.

[3] Accounting Terminology Bulletin no. 1, pp. 13–14.

[4] Delmer P. Hylton comments on the concurrent ascendancy of the income statement and "the accounting convention known as 'matching revenue with expense'" in "On Matching Revenue with Expense," *The Accounting Review* (Oct. 1965), pp. 824–28.

and the fundamental elements of a framework for accounting analysis from which that useful information is derived. More about that later. First let me elaborate on the sterility of the matching concept as an element of accounting theory.

Without pretending to have traced its historical origin, it seems safe to say that the matching concept first began to receive widespread attention with the publication of *An Introduction to Corporate Accounting Standards*[5] by Paton and Littleton. There, as one of the basic concepts that constitute a suitable foundation for accounting standards, the authors cited the matching of effort and accomplishment. The economic concept of income as a change in wealth during a period of time was explicitly rejected, even as an ideal, and the notion of an income associated with each item of goods sold or service rendered was expounded. The authors stated that "if this conception could be effectively realized in practice, the net accomplishment of the enterprise could be measured in terms of units of output rather than of intervals of time. . . . Time periods are a convenience, a substitute, but the fundamental concept is unchanged. The ideal is to match costs incurred with the effects attributable to or significantly related to such costs."[6]

The implications of this approach become particularly vivid with the following statements: "Accrual and deferment are closely related phases of the process of matching. The full accrual of labor cost, under the terms of the various contracts in effect, needs to be recognized; otherwise the amount of labor-service received is incorrectly expressed. It is perhaps of secondary importance that wages earned but unpaid are recorded as part of the process. Deferred charges, broadly defined to include most assets, need to be recognized; otherwise the goods furnished or services rendered currently will be loaded with charges not significantly applicable. The flow of cost factors, in other words, needs to be appropriately divided between the pool of charges to be held back, deferred, and those representing elements from which the utility has been fully exhausted. Assets accrued but as yet uncollected should be recognized because, if they are ignored, services rendered will be incorrectly expressed."[7]

Note the relegation of the balance sheet to a sheet of balances created as a by-product of the matching process so that costs will not be incorrectly

[5] W. A. Paton and A. C. Littleton, *An Introduction to Corporate Accounting Standards* (Evanston, Ill.: AAA, 1940).

[6] Paton and Littleton, p. 15. The AAA's 1964 Concepts and Standards Research Study Committee—The Matching Concept adopted some of the same language (e.g., "costs constitute a measure of business effort, and revenues represent accomplishments coming from those efforts") and concluded "that it is desirable to emphasize the matching concept in financial reporting." The committee meticulously avoided any reference to assets and liabilities although at times it appears to have been a strain (e.g., losses are viewed as "product or service factors given up in return for a zero quantity of revenue"). "The Matching Concept," *The Accounting Review* (Apr. 1965), pp. 368–372.

[7] Paton and Littleton, p. 16.

expressed. Although the deferred charges may include most assets, the objective is to avoid matching revenues with charges that are not significantly applicable and allow costs to be appropriately divided between deferred charges and expenses. This approach places a premium on judgment as to whether a cost is significantly applicable or inapplicable to a revenue and whether a division of a cost into amounts to be deferred and amounts to be expended is appropriate or inappropriate. Presumably, the matching process does not even require a concept of income to serve as a basis for making those judgments. Instead, as suggested by some: "Time is what we measure with a watch. Income is what we measure with a profit and loss statement."[8]

Inevitably, of course, it is recognized that, even if it were conceptually desirable, in most cases the matching of costs and revenues is a practical impossibility. In practice, most costs are identified with a period of time in much the same way that even proponents of the matching concept identify revenues with a period of time. Nevertheless, the matching concept, based as it is on the pre-eminence of the income statement and relying heavily on subjective notions of correctness, applicability, and propriety, is responsible for those unique accounting products that one so frequently finds in today's sheet of balances: deferred charges that are not assets and deferred credits that are not liabilities.

In its Opinion 11, "Accounting for Income Taxes," the APB cited certain general concepts and assumptions as relevant in considering that problem. Among them, matching was recognized as one of the basic processes of income determination. The inherent sterility of the matching concept as a basis for resolving accounting issues is especially glaring, however, in the board's tautologous explanation that "expenses of the current period consist of those costs which are identified with the revenues of the current period and those costs which are identified with the current period on some basis other than revenue."[9]

Nevertheless, in rejecting the liability method, in rejecting the net of tax method, and in adopting the deferral method of interperiod tax allocation, the board stated explicitly that the "measurement of income tax expense becomes thereby a consistent and integral part of the *process of matching revenues and expenses* in the determination of results of operations."[10] In so doing, the board acknowledged that "deferred charges and deferred credits relating to timing differences represent the cumulative recognition given to their tax effects and as such do not represent receivables or payables in the usual sense."[11]

---

[8] John C. Burton, ed., *Corporate Financial Reporting: Conflicts and Challenges* (New York: AICPA, 1969), pp. 49–50, 225.

[9] "Accounting for Income Taxes," APB Opinion 11 (New York: AICPA, Dec. 1967), p. 160.

[10] APB Opinion 11, p. 169.

[11] APB Opinion 11, p. 178.

Elevated to "one of the most important principles in income determina-ion"[12] and uninhibited by any meaningful concepts of assets, liabilities, and ncome, the matching concept may be deemed to supply adequate support or virtually any accounting procedure. As one author puts it: "In the minds of many accountants, this single convention outweighs all others; in other words, if a given procedure can be asserted to conform to the matching concept, nothing else need be said; the matter is settled and the procedure is justified."[13]

Obviously, the sheet of balances approach is operational; its everyday use is very much in evidence. At opposite extremes, however, this approach either permits maximum latitude in deciding which balances to carry for-ward, or it requires an ever increasing list of detailed rules and procedures to be promulgated designating which balances may properly be carried for-ward.

When new accounting problems arise—like the investment credit—this approach either allows a variety of individual decisions to be made or re-quires that some recognized authority such as the APB designate by vote what is the best rule or procedure. The process is much like that of judges in a beauty contest where a winner is designated by vote based primarily on personal preference, there being no established concepts in determining beauty and in determining proper matching.

In keeping with democratic principles, the majority of such a group might "conclude that the allowable investment credit should be reflected in net income over the productive life of acquired property and not in the year in which it is placed in service,"[14] while the majority of another equally intelli-gent and experienced group might well conclude exactly the opposite.

One might ordinarily expect that an explicit concept of net income would be prerequisite to deciding what should be included in its measurement and what should not be included in its measurement. But, to my knowledge, no one has ever successfully managed to formulate a concept of income that is not directly or indirectly dependent upon the concept of assets and the concept of liabilities. It follows that the concepts of assets and liabilities are more fundamental than the concept of income. If this is the case, equal acceptability of three different methods of carrying forward deferred invest-ment tax credit balances cannot be rationalized.[15]

In addition to the deferral method of accounting for the tax allocation and the deferral method of accounting for the investment credit, the matching concept and the sheet of balances view are responsible for a variety of other

---

[12] Paul Grady, *Inventory of Generally Accepted Accounting Principles for Business Enterprises,* ARS 7 (New York: AICPA, 1965), p. 74.

[13] Hylton, p. 824.

[14] "Accounting for the 'Investment Credit,'" APB Opinion 2 (New York: AICPA, Dec. 1962), par. 13, p. 7.

[15] APB Opinion 2, par. 14, p. 7.

balance-sheet anomalies. Unamortized bond discount, unamortized discount, issue cost, redemption premium on bonds refunded, and the LIFO method of inventory valuation are a few that are sometimes found among assets. Deferred gain on sale and leaseback, equity in net assets of subsidiary over cost, provision for replacement of LIFO inventories, and reserve for decline in conversion value of Canadian assets are examples of reported liabilities.

In summary, the sheet of balances approach, stemming from the preeminence of the income statement and the matching concept, necessarily relies on ad hoc decisions rather than on accounting theory—on independent value judgments rather than on consistent analysis.

The Static Funds Statement View

A second approach to the balance sheet has emerged in recent years in which it is viewed primarily as a kind of static funds statement. A number of accounting textbooks describe the balance sheet in this way.[16] This development seems to have paralleled the increased attention given to reporting a summary of the transactions resulting in changes in working capital during periods of time—that is, to so-called statements of sources and applications of funds.

Raymond P. Marple has suggested in an article in *The Journal of Accountancy* that, to describe the balance sheet "as a statement of financial position, tells little about the balance sheet. It would be much more appropriate to refer to it as 'a statement of the sources and composition of company capital.'" According to Marple, "If this were done, and the form of the statement revised to better display the sources from which the capital was obtained and the forms in which it is held, the function of the balance sheet would be much clearer."[17]

In *An Inquiry Into the Nature of Accounting* Louis Goldberg contrasts the nature of the balance sheet according to the "commander" theory with the balance sheets of other theories. "If we allow ourselves to become imbued with the notion of ownership as the basis of accounting, the balance sheet becomes a statement of 'values' owned and owed; and the question of who owns and who owes is controversially but inconclusively raised. If, however, we adopt the position that the balance sheet is prepared by or on behalf of and from the point of view of a commander—the chief executive officer, be he

---

[16] For example, Leonard E. Morrissey, *Contemporary Accounting Problems* (Englewood Cliffs, N.J.: Prentice-Hall, 1963), pp. 4, 44; Myron J. Gordon and Gordon Shillinglaw, *Accounting—A Management Approach*, 4th ed. (Homewood, Ill.: Richard D. Irwin, 1969), pp. 23, 497: Robert N. Anthony, *Management Accounting—Test and Cases*, 4th ed. (Homewood, Ill.: Richard D. Irwin, 1970), pp. 45, 325; Harold Bierman, Jr., and Allan R. Drebin, *Financial Accounting: An Introduction* (New York: Macmillan Co., 1968), p. 21.

[17] Raymond P. Marple, "The Balance Sheet—Capital Sources and Composition," *The Journal of Accountancy* (Nov. 1962), p. 58.

the proprietor himself or the small group of partners or the president or managing director—it can be seen as a statement of the sources from which he has (or they have) derived resources and the directions in which those resources have been applied, and it is therefore more directly a statement of stewardship than of ownership."[18]

Another proponent of the static funds statement approach to the balance sheet has attempted to analyze a specific accounting issue from that point of view. In a recent article in the *Financial Executive* David F. Hawkins has argued that considerable progress could be made in resolving the controversy surrounding income tax allocation if:

> financial accounting is regarded as being concerned with maintaining a continuing record of a company's flow of financial resources;
>
> the balance sheet is viewed as presenting a two-sided look at a company's capital (the left-hand side reflecting where the company's capital is lodged, the right-hand side showing the current status of capital obtained from creditors, owners, and other sources);
>
> net income is seen as measuring principally the funds available for dividends and reinvestment obtained through the use of capital in the operations of the company; and
>
> it is agreed accounting for deferred taxes should reflect (1) the way businessmen handle tax considerations in capital investment decisions. (2) the way they incorporate the deferral in their financial planning, and (3) the nature of income taxes.[19]

Earlier, in a similar article in the *Harvard Business Review*, Hawkins had hailed APB Opinion 11, "Accounting for Income Taxes," as one which seems to "Encourage, in its implicit move toward the sources and uses of funds approach, the aim of corporate executives and CPAs to find ways to make more understandable a number of items on the balance sheet which cannot be explained satisfactorily to stockholders by the more traditional accounting concepts."[20]

He criticized the opinion, not because of the board's conclusion in favor of comprehensive allocation—he supports that conclusion—but because the deferred tax account is not adequately rationalized. His analysis: "In the past the deferred tax issue has revolved around the question of whether the deferral should be treated as a liability, in the traditional accounting sense. But if the right-hand side of the balance sheet is regarded as presenting the current status of a company's source of funds obtained externally, then this

[18] Louis Goldberg, *An Inquiry Into the Nature of Accounting* (Evanston, Ill.: AAA, 1965), pp. 170–71.

[19] David F. Hawkins, "Deferred Taxes: Source of Non-Operating Funds," *Financial Executive* (Feb. 1969), p. 35.

[20] David F. Hawkins, "Controversial Accounting Changes," *Harvard Business Review* (Mar.–Apr. 1968), p. 20.

argument becomes irrelevant. The question should be: Is the deferral a significant enough source of funds to be disclosed on the right-hand side of the balance sheet? By its support of comprehensive allocation, the Board has indicated that this is a meaningful source of capital and that it is misleading to include it in earnings."[21]

Of course, the amount of income taxes in question inevitably shows up on the right-hand side of the balance sheet either as deferred income taxes or as retained earnings.[22] But, using a "standard of meaningful and fair disclosure of invested capital," Hawkins argues that "the capital *retained* in the business through *postponement* of income tax payments" should be separately identified as a "source of invested capital."[23] His argument, however, is self-contradictory. Capital *retained* in the business through postponement of income tax payments must necessarily have had some other source; otherwise, the capital would not have been there to be retained.

The *nonuse* of funds is not the same thing as a *source* of funds. If sources were viewed as all those things for which funds were not used, rejected capital expenditure proposals and rejected union demands would qualify. Indeed, the possibilities boggle the mind. Furthermore, it seems unlikely that Hawkins' standard of meaningful and fair disclosure of invested capital has sufficient rigor to determine which transactions can be reflected in retained earnings and which require separate identification as a source of invested capital. For example, he states that the funds approach can be extended to include "profits on sale-and-leaseback arrangements."[24] Then, how about the gain on an outright sale? And, is it only the gain that is a source of funds, or is it the entire proceeds?

The observation has been made that, although the initial balance sheet of a newly formed concern may be a good statement of funds, "at some relatively early point along the way after operations have begun, the balance sheet, standing alone, begins to lose its function as a funds statement."[25]

Although for some purposes it may be useful to equate "funds" with assets, it is unfortunate that a term so commonly used as a synonym for cash and net working capital should be given this much broader meaning as well. And, even if funds and assets may properly be used synonymously, any attempt to describe the nature of liabilities as sources is at best diversionary and at worst fallacious.

Balance sheets do not report the sources of the assets on hand, except perhaps coincidentally, and describing balance sheets as though they do is

---

[21] "Controversial Accounting Changes," p. 30.

[22] This observation was also made by Lawrence Revsine in "Some Controversy Concerning 'Controversial Accounting Changes,'" *The Accounting Review* (Apr. 1969), pp. 354–58, where he examines Hawkins' analysis of accounting for income taxes in some detail.

[23] "Controversial Accounting Changes," p. 32.

[24] "Controversial Accounting Changes," p. 30.

[25] Maurice Moonitz, "Reporting on the Flow of Funds," *The Accounting Review* (July 1956), p. 376.

likely to be misleading. Frequently, liabilities arise as a result of transactions that are not even remotely related to sources of funds. For example, none of the accrued liabilities such as accrued wages, accrued interest, and accrued taxes can properly be characterized as sources of funds. The declaration of cash dividends is properly reported in a statement of sources and applications of working capital as an application; the declaration of cash dividends is not a source of funds simply because it creates a liability. If a source of additional assets is being sought, the declaration of dividends with a concomitant increase in the amount of dividends payable is not likely to be fruitful. And one can be sure that liabilities resulting from legal actions, such as the antitrust actions against certain electrical equipment manufacturers a few years ago, are not viewed by the defendants as sources of funds.

Finally, the question of relevance must be raised. Even if it were possible to prepare a balance sheet reporting at a given point of time the funds on hand and where those funds came from, for what purpose might such information be used? The potential uses of measures of "flows of funds"—sources and uses of funds during periods of time—are widely proclaimed. For example, the board of directors of the Financial Analysts Federation has endorsed the publication of statements of sources and applications of funds in corporate reports to shareholders, stating that "the analysis of a company's past and projected flow of funds can provide valuable insight into such matters as: (1) future dividend policy, (2) the financing of capital expenditures and the extent to which additional debt and/or equities may be issued to finance same, and (3) the ability to meet debt service requirements. . . . "[26] Note the concern with flow of funds. Those purposes could not be fulfilled by measurements of the sources of the particular assets on hand at any given time. The relevance of the balance sheet as a static funds statement is not at all clear.

The Financial Position View

Viewed as a statement of financial position, the balance sheet represents the embodiment of the most fundamental elements of accounting theory and, at the same time, provides useful information in its own right. But the structure begins with the notion of an entity.

The concept of an entity is among the most primitive elements of accounting theory. In accounting, the entity may be defined as "an area of economic interest to a particular individual or group."[27] Neither a statement of income nor a statement of financial position is feasible without first circumscribing the entity for which an accounting is to be made.

At the first level of derivation are the concepts of assets (expected future

---

[26]"News Report," *The Journal of Accountancy* (June 1964), pp. 9–10.

[27] An entity is fundamental to the sheet of balances and the static funds statement, as well. For a discussion of the fundamental nature of the entity concept and the development of this definition, see 1964 Concepts and Standards Research Study Committee—The Business Entity Concept, "The Entity Concept," *The Accounting Review* (Apr. 1965), pp. 358–67.

economic benefits, rights to which have been acquired by the entity as a result of some past transaction) and liabilities (the entity's obligations to convey assets or perform services, obligations resulting from past transactions and requiring settlement in the future). Once the entity is identified, one can contemplate accounting for its assets and its liabilities.

At the next level of derivation are the concepts of owners' equity or net assets (the residual interest in the assets of the entity) and income (the amount of any change in net assets during a period of time, assuming no additional investments or distributions to owners).[28] Of course, a variety of potential bases for measuring these concepts exist: invested cost in terms of numbers of dollars, invested cost in terms of purchasing power, current cost of replacing equivalent service potential, current cost of replacement in kind, current cash equivalent, etc. But, whatever the basis, it must be acknowledged that the measurement of income is dependent upon the measurement of net assets, which, in turn, is directly dependent upon the measurement of assets and liabilities.

According to this view, all transactions are analyzed in terms of their effect on assets, liabilities, and owners' equity. The measurement of income does not even require revenue and expense accounts; such accounts merely provide subsidiary information about changes in owners' equity in the same way that customers' accounts provide subsidiary information about the total amount of accounts receivable. This does not detract from the informational content of revenue and expense accounts. The information such accounts supply about the nature and extent of various operating transactions that give rise to changes in assets and liabilities and hence owners' equity can be extremely useful in making predictions about the results of the entity's future operations.

The financial position view does not eliminate all the problems and resolve all the controversies surrounding the analysis of accounting issues, but it does sharply limit the number of eligible alternatives and, most important, it focuses the resolution of accounting issues on fundamental concepts. As a result, it permits attention to be devoted to the refinement of those fundamental concepts rather than to the invention of new rationalizations for individual preferences.

As a statement of financial position that summarizes the assets, liabilities, and residual equity of the entity, the balance sheet is also an economic document providing useful information in its own right. The financial position of a business enterprise is the relationship of the resources available to the enterprise and the obligations of the enterprise that require the future utilization of resources. The resources reported in statements of financial

---

[28] These concepts of assets, liabilities, owners' equity, and income are adapted from Robert T. Sprouse and Maurice Moonitz, *A Tentative Set of Broad Accounting Principles for Business Enterprises*, ARS 3 (New York: AICPA, 1962).

position are necessarily limited to those assets that have been acquired as a result of past transactions, but the essence of reported assets is their ability to provide future economic benefits. Similarly, the liabilities reported in statements of financial position are necessarily limited to obligations that have been incurred as a result of past transactions, but the significance of reported liabilities lies in the future utilization of resources that their settlement will require.

Presumably, the financial statements supplied to current and prospective stockholders and creditors are intended to provide information about two matters of critical importance: profitability and risk. Traditionally, the income statement has been the major source of information about the former and the balance sheet the primary source of information about the latter. These two statements, however, are inextricably related. Profitability cannot really be evaluated without reference to the resources employed in creating profits, and risk cannot really be evaluated without reference to the expected results of the firm's operations. Two firms with identical income streams are not necessarily equally profitable; two firms with identical financial positions do not necessarily involve equal risk.

Balance-sheet classifications—especially the current versus noncurrent classification—and the use of financial ratios in the analysis of financial statements frequently manifest concern with financial position.[29] For example, the current ratio is a measure of the relationship of the liquid resources available to an enterprise and its most pressing future obligations—obligations that will require the use of liquid resources. We are all aware of the widespread significance attached to the current ratio, the acid test ratio, the debt/equity ratio, the average cost of capital, and other ratios, each of which depends upon meaningful content and classification in the accounts reported in the balance sheet.[30]

The task of the analyst in evaluating financial position is bound to be complicated by the sheet of balances approach, where the balance sheet serves as a dumping ground for balances that someone has decided should not be included in the income statement. The analyst's necessary reclassification of such items in attempting to determine a firm's assets and liabilities

---

[29] Roy A. Foulke, vice-president of Dun and Bradstreet and author of a well-known book on financial statement analysis, advocates the use of a set of fourteen financial ratios. The numerators or denominators for thirteen of the fourteen are taken from the balance sheet; for half of the fourteen ratios, both the numerators and denominators are taken from the balance sheet. *Practical Financial Statement Analysis* (New York: McGraw-Hill Book Co., 1961).

[30] In an empirical study, William H. Beaver tested the efficacy of thirty popular ratios in predicting the inability of a firm to pay its financial obligations as they mature. Of these, the best predictor—the cash-flow to total-debt ratio—proved to have excellent discriminatory power. Either the numerator or denominator was taken from the balance sheet for each of the top six predictors; for three of those six, both the numerators and denominators were taken from the balance sheet. "Financial Ratios as Predictors of Failure," *Empirical Research in Accounting: Selected Studies 1966* (Chicago: Institute of Professional Accounting, Graduate School of Business, University of Chicago, 1967), pp. 71–111.

is almost certain to be based on less information than was available to the accountant.

Summary and Conclusions

In summary, let me attempt to delineate the three alternative views of the balance sheet in terms of their consequences.

The sheet of balances view of the balance sheet is an outgrowth of the notion that, by employing the matching concept, the income statement can be made superior to the balance sheet—superior in content and superior as a basis for accounting analyses. The ultimate result of a continuing extension of this view is highly predictable; a precedent exists—the *Internal Revenue Code* and the *Regulations* which interpret the code. The similarities are most striking. Because no concept of taxable income exists and individuals obviously have very different opinions about appropriate components and measurements, detailed rules for its computation must be promulgated. Amendments and revocations are commonplace, as judgments about the propriety of inclusions, exclusions, and measurements change. The role of the practitioner increasingly becomes one of checking the code to determine whether clients' treatments of transactions are acceptable according to the letter of the law.

This approach to financial reporting will work. Indeed, it may be the only feasible practical solution. But the costs are extraordinarily high—costs in terms of the time and talent that must be devoted to the promulgation of detailed rules and procedures and costs in terms of the sacrifice of intellectual stimulation and personal gratification that one normally associates with the professions.

The static funds statement view leads to a drastic departure from the balance sheet as we know it. This, in itself, is not necessarily fatal, but much work needs to be done in analyzing and explaining the consequences of such a departure. For example, in what way would the income statement be related to the balance sheet if this view were fully implemented? How shall guidelines be established to distinguish between transactions that may properly be reflected in funds from operations and transactions that should be separately identified in the balance sheet as a source of invested capital? And probably most important, who is interested in a static funds statement and for what purpose?

If there is to be a theory of accounting, among these three views the financial position view of the balance sheet provides the only hope. The theory calls for the identification of an entity and an accounting for the resources and obligations of that entity. The entity's income during any period of time is based on the changes in its resources and obligations during that period, and the basic distinction is between those transactions taking place between the entity and its owners and all other transactions. Obviously, this is oversimplified; the mere adoption of a particular view of the balance sheet will not solve all the problems of measuring financial position and income. It is, however, a necessary first step.

A few years ago one of the leading practitioners in the United States expressed his opinion that there is "a much bigger gap between the academic researchers and the practicing members of the accounting profession than in any other profession . . . including law, medicine and engineering."[31]

This gap has most likely widened still further since that statement was made. The academic emphasis is necessarily on theory, analysis, and logic—not on the memorization and unquestioning acceptance of rules that have been promulgated. The objective is to develop systematic, orderly thought processes that one can rely upon in striving to arrive at sound decisions about accounting issues as they arise and to insure that the solutions to such problems are consistent with the whole body of accounting thought. In other words, the objective of the academician is the development and application of accounting theory. To the extent that the primary intellectual ingredient in accounting is merely the experienced personal judgment of its senior practitioners, if there is no body of concepts and theories that can be utilized in the analysis of accounting problems, the study of accounting in the universities is rightfully in jeopardy.

---

[31] Herman W. Bevis, "Progress and Poverty in Accounting Thought," *The Journal of Accountancy* (July 1966), p. 39.

*Alfred Rappaport is Professor of Accounting
and Information Systems, Graduate School of
Management, Northwestern University.*

Discussion of "The Balance Sheet—Embodiment of the Most Fundamental Elements of Accounting Theory"

Alfred Rappaport

Whenever Bob Sprouse, one of our most respected and articulate spokesmen, comments on the current scene in accounting, there is great interest in his observations. When I learned that Bob would be discussing the balance sheet, a statement relegated to obscurity by recent generations of accounting theorists, I awaited his manuscript with more than ordinary interest. I speculated at the time that, in the noblest tradition of good sportsmanship, Bob had decided to champion the cause of an underdog. The accuracy of this speculation was quickly confirmed when I read his manuscript. As a result, I find myself in the doubly unenviable position of being cast as a critic of Bob Sprouse defending an accounting underdog.

Sprouse's paper aims at providing support for the proposition that "the balance sheet embodies the most fundamental elements of accounting theory from which the essential elements contained in the income statement are necessarily derived." In support of this proposition, three views of the balance sheet (the sheet of balances view, the static funds statement view, and the financial position view) are examined. From this analysis, Sprouse concludes that one view, the financial position view, is superior to the other two. My purpose here is to examine briefly the claimed primacy for the balance

Reprinted by permission of the author and publisher from *Foundations of Accounting Theory*, University of Florida Press, 1971, pp. 105–113.

sheet in accounting theory development and Sprouse's assessment of various balance-sheet approaches or views. In addition, I propose to offer for your consideration a fourth balance-sheet view.

Consider, first, Sprouse's initial proposition. It is important to recognize that this proposition is based on a structural or designer's view of the accounting system, not on the user's or consumer's view. Sprouse appropriately makes this distinction at the very beginning of his paper by accepting the primacy of the income statement in terms of user interest; on the structural or logical form level, he suggests that "concepts of assets and liabilities are more fundamental than the concept of income" since the latter depends upon the former. The relative merits of the structural-versus-user view of the accounting system will be discussed subsequently. First, let us turn our attention to Sprouse's structurally based argument on the primacy of the balance sheet.

The structural view offers no explicit user decision models or behavioral theory to provide guidelines for choice among alternative configurations of information. Instead, such a view in accounting is characterized by the implicit assumption that the duality framework per se, including the necessary articulation between the balance sheet and income statements, is in some general sense useful and hence should be accepted a priori. Sprouse, using a structurally based argument, contends that the balance sheet embodies more fundamental elements of accounting theory than the income statement. The purported rationale for this contention would presumably include the following statements: (a) "the income statement can properly be described as merely a summary of one class of transactions resulting in changes in one balance sheet account"; (b) "the measurement of income is dependent upon the measurement of net assets which, in turn, is dependent upon the measurement of assets and liabilities"; and (c) "no one has ever successfully managed to formulate a concept of income that is not directly or indirectly dependent upon the concept of assets and the concept of liabilities."

For purposes of direct contrast, consider the following three alternative propositions:

a) The balance sheet can properly be described as a summary of stocks or residuals that results from income statement transactions.

b) The measurement of net assets is dependent upon the measurement of income, which, in turn, is dependent upon the measurement of revenue and expenses.

c) No one has ever successfully managed to formulate a concept of assets that is not directly or indirectly dependent upon a concept of income.

Is this set of three propositions more accurate than the Sprouse set enumerated earlier? Or is the Sprouse set perhaps more accurate? Adhering once again to the structural or logical form approach to accounting systems, we are necessarily indifferent about these two sets of propositions. Within the context of an explicitly defined analytical system such as the accounting double-entry system, one can define a given systems variable in terms of other systems variables. For example, a system with only two variables, a and i, can be described in terms of a = f(i) or i = f(a). If we were to adopt a somewhat oversimplified view of the accounting system, we would perhaps designate i to represent income and a, net assets. The two propositions a = f(i) and i = f(a) are analytic rather than synthetic propositions, since their validity depends solely on the definitions of the symbols they contain rather than on empirical observation.[1]

Returning for a moment to Sprouse's set of three propositions, note that the first two propositions are essentially two ways of asserting i = f(a), while the third proposition is simply a logical consequence of the first two. As you would expect, the first two of my three alternative propositions assert that a = f(i), and the third proposition is once again a logical consequence of the first two.

The important point to emphasize here is that the structural approach to accounting systems does not admit exogenously derived postulated systems objectives, and hence there is no logical basis for choosing one systems representation over another. For our specific purposes, the structural approach allows us no basis for choice between the Sprouse propositions and the alternative propositions. Fortunately, we are not at an impasse, since Sprouse implicitly rejects the structural view as he begins his discussion of the three balance-sheet views.

Unlike the structural approach, the user approach to accounting theory is based upon some user decision model or models. While Sprouse does not explicitly present a user model, it is reasonable to assume that some underlying user model was employed to rank one approach to balance-sheet measures—the financial position view—above two alternative approaches—the sheet of balances view and the static funds statement view. In the absence of an explicit designation of user models, there is no logical basis for either acknowledging or denying the validity of Sprouse's balance-sheet preferences. In light of this, I propose to offer a number of general observations about the three balance-sheet views and then briefly discuss a fourth view based on a postulated user decision model.

Let us begin with the sheet of balances approach, which views the balance sheet "as a summary of debit and credit account balances that remain after the determinants of income have been decided upon and the retained earnings account has been adjusted for the amount of income that results." Surely the contention that this approach is not likely to result in a particularly useful statement is a foregone conclusion, assuming even a relatively

---

[1] Alfred Jules Ayer, *Language, Truth and Logic* (New York: Dover Publications, 1952), pp. 78–79.

wide spectrum of different user models. Is the basic problem simply the treatment of the balance sheet as a secondary or residual statement, or is there perhaps a more fundamental problem? I submit that the real answer lies in the futility of implementing the matching concept. As Sprouse forcefully states, "the matching concept necessarily relies on ad hoc decisions rather than on accounting theory—on independent value judgments rather than on consistent analysis." This observation is not only central to the Sprouse paper, but in large measure helps explain the difficulty facing accountants today. In light of its significance, I would like to elaborate on the measurement problems associated with the matching concept.

If we were to develop present-value financial statements under conditions of perfect certainty, the results would be identical whether we treated the balance sheet or the income statement as the residual statement. Residual approaches such as the sheet of balances approach affect results only when means of dealing with uncertainty are required.

What has been the accountant's response to uncertainty? Conservatism, consistency, increasing disclosure, and demands for objectivity as manifested by adherence to historical cost conventions represent key mechanisms for dealing with uncertainty. Consider the serious income-determination problems found in the cost-matching area. The cost-matching decision, that is the decision concerning the assignment of costs as deductions from revenue in specific accounting periods, reflects the accountant's broad perception of the relative risks associated with cost outlays. Accountants appear to be concerned with two types of risk—economic and measurement.[2] An economic risk may be viewed as the probability that an outlay will result in no net benefit to the firm. Where the economic risk is judged to be high, the outlay is treated as an expense in the same period as the commitment for the outlay is incurred. Costs associated with pure research serve as an outstanding example of a high-risk outlay generally treated as an expense.

Measurement risks are best characterized as the uncertainties of implementing the matching principle. High measurement risks occur when either it is difficult to identify the tangible benefits or revenues arising from certain costs (e.g., executive salaries paid largely for planning activities, campaigns to promote company name and products, executive and employee educational programs, administrative facilities such as buildings and information systems, philanthropic contributions) or when estimates of the magnitude and timing of benefits are subject to a significant degree of error (e.g., product improvement programs, patents, copyrights, new productive facilities). The accountant's reaction to the basic forms of measurement risk can be summarized as follows:

---

[2] The term "measurement" is used here only in the general sense of assigning numbers to real world phenomena according to rules.

Measurement risk	*Measurement procedure*
1. Difficult to identify revenues arising from a given cost.	1. Expense in current period.
2. Estimated time duration of expected benefit or revenue flow subject to significant measurement error.	2. Expense in current period.
3. Estimated time duration of expected benefits subject to relatively small margins of error, but magnitude and timing of benefit or revenue flows subject to significant measurement error.	3. Choice of a systematic write-o basis over the estimated time du ation of expected benefits.

It should be clearly recognized that, while the three measurement-ris categories enumerated above may broadly indicate the basis for the accoun ant's choice of a measurement procedure, there is ample evidence to sugge that accountants evaluating a given cost outlay may in many cases not agre upon the appropriate measurement-risk category for the outlay. The ac countant's subjective assessment of management's expectations for, say, re search and development outlays will influence the choice between measure ment risk no. 2 (expense in current period) and measurement risk no. (systematic write-off). Furthermore, the choice of measurement risk no. leads to a wide range of possibilities of systematic write-off patterns. Indee it is useful to view the basic income-determination alternatives as constitu ing the intersection between management-risk categories no. 2 and no. 3 plu the discretionary measurement alternatives available within measurement risk category no. 3. Indeed, one can reluctantly view many of the controver sies in accounting today as essentially a debate between uniform arbitrari ness and flexible arbitrariness.[3] In summing up the sheet of balance view, submit that its failings derive from, in Sprouse's words, "the matchin; concept (which) necessarily relies on ad hoc decisions rather than on ac counting theory—on independent value judgments rather than on consisten analysis."

The static funds statement view, so named because it purports to show th sources and composition of company capital at a prescribed point in time, i rejected by Sprouse on grounds that it is not feasible, and, secondly, even if i were feasible, the relevance or usefulness of such disclosure is questioned. A is the case with the sheet of balances view, the lack of feasibility of the stati funds statement view is clearly attributable to the accountant's difficulty ir coping with uncertainty. The question of relevance is best deferred in th absence of an explicit user model.

---

[3] For a comprehensive demonstration of the arbitrariness of accounting allocations, see Arthur L. Thomas, *The Allocation Problem in Financial Accounting Theory* (Evanston, Ill.: AAA, 1969)

Of the three balance-sheet views, Sprouse clearly prefers the financial position view. Indeed, he suggests that, "if there is to be a theory of accounting, the financial position view of the balance sheet provides the only hope." The evidence to support such a far-reaching assertion is far from apparent. Indeed, it is difficult to reconcile Sprouse's forceful presentation on the futility of the matching concept with his advocacy of the financial position view which depends directly on matching.

The distinctions between the financial position view and the other views proposed are not sharply delineated. For example, the description of the financial position view as "the relationship of the resources available to the enterprise and the obligations of the enterprise that require the future utilization of resources" is uncomfortably close to the static funds statement view of the balance sheet as "a statement of the sources and composition of company capital." Nor is it clear whether the financial position and the sheet of balances views are antithetical.

Sprouse suggests that stockholders and investors should be provided information about a firm's earning power and solvency. If we impose the constraints of current practice, that balance sheets and income statements must articulate with one another and that historical cost be employed, then it is quite possible to find important situations in which the goals of providing information about earning power and solvency may be in conflict. Consider, for example, the question of alternative inventory cost methods. Because LIFO, in most circumstances, generates a better matching of current costs with current revenues, it may result in a better indication of a firm's earning power than other methods such as FIFO or average cost. In a growing firm and under inflationary conditions, LIFO inventory cost appearing on the balance sheet may, however, be significantly less than current cost. The adoption of FIFO is likely to lead to the reverse situation. The advocate of the sheet of balances view would presumably choose the LIFO method since he is more willing to tolerate shortcomings in the balance sheet than in the income statement. Would the financial position advocate suggest FIFO under these conditions? Perhaps he would, but Sprouse has not set forth how he would logically assess information trade-offs between the balance sheet and the income statement.

One final observation concerning the financial position view warrants comment. Sprouse's preference for the financial position view appears to be based largely on the usefulness of balance-sheet outputs for assessing probable failure or insolvency. While this focus is particularly useful for creditors in extremely risky firms, there should be equal concern for the informational needs of investors in the vast majority of going concerns. Whether this broader notion of the accountant's audience would change Sprouse's preference ordering is once again dependent upon postulated user models.

At this point I would like to note a fourth possible view of the balance sheet recently presented by the AAA 1966–1968 Committee on External

Reporting. In its attempt to develop information useful to equity investors and creditors, the committee outlined the following steps:

1. Select normative investors' and creditors' valuation models. The committee selected a dividend model for equity investors.
2. Select a model for the prediction of dividends and other distributions to stockholders and creditors.
3. List object and activity inputs (potentially relevant identifications of items and events) and their related attributes and measurement concepts.
4. Evaluate each of the attributes of each object or activity input for relevancy (its ability to permit a prediction of a variable or relationship in the models).
5. List potentially acceptable measurement procedures.
6. Assess each procedure for each attribute in light of the standards of quantifiability, verifiability, and freedom from bias.
7. Select the attributes and measurement procedures that should be included in financial reports.[4]

Using the foregoing approach, some of the committee's broad recommendations are as follows:

1. External financial reports should include at least a statement of resources and commitments and a statement showing current monetary flows such as those suggested in exhibits A and B. These two statements should complement one another in analyses for forecasting future cash flows. The statement of resources should include information regarding objects likely to contribute to future cash flows and the report of commitments should represent probable future outflows. The current monetary flow statement should represent an enumeration of changes in resources and commitments.

2. External financial reports should not be expected to "balance" or articulate with each other. In fact, we find that forced balancing and articulation have frequently restricted the presentation of relevant information.

3. Reported information should not be restricted to that which can be expressed in dollar terms. Wherever they meet the standards adequately, physical measures, classifications, and nonquantifiable descriptions should be included in reports in addition to monetary measurements.[5]

Perhaps at this juncture the committee's methodology is more interesting and useful than its recommendations. In my view, however, employing the user's approach to accounting theory, not the structural or designer's approach, holds the greatest hope for progress in accounting theory. The structural approach to accounting theory, which treats balance-sheet income

---

[4]"An Evaluation of External Reporting Practices: A Report of the 1966–68 Committee on External Reporting," *The Accounting Review*, Supplement to vol. 44 (1969), p. 80.

[5]"An Evaluation of External Reporting Practices," pp. 117–18.

statement articulation as axiomatic, seriously limits the search for more useful information constructs. The fourth view of the balance sheet presented as exhibit A, which some may wish to refer to as the nonbalancing balance-sheet view, must, as any other proposed disclosure, meet certain empirical standards of usefulness. On the other hand, it should be noted that this, as well as other innovative departures from current practice, can be logically derived from the user's approach, but not the structural approach to accounting theory. Therefore, I submit that the question of whether or not the balance sheet as we know it today embodies the most fundamental elements of accounting theory is not as crucial as the question of what recommendations would result from rigorously developed accounting theory based on user needs. It is at least open to debate whether any of the conventional balance-sheet views would survive such inquiry.

In closing, let me emphasize that while Bob Sprouse and I may have some differences over research methodology, I am in absolute agreement with his fundamental observation that "if there is no body of concepts and theories that can be utilized in the analysis of accounting problems, the study of accounting in the universities is rightfully in jeopardy."

Reg S. Gynther is Professor of Accountancy at the University of Queensland.

Some "Conceptualizing" on Goodwill

Reg S. Gynther

"Goodwill" has been a thorny problem in the discipline of accounting for many years, and even as long ago as 1929 Canning was able to write:

> Accountants, writers on accounting, economists, engineers, and the courts, have all tried their hands at defining goodwill, at discussing its nature, and at proposing means of valuing it. The most striking characteristic of this immense amount of writing is the number and variety of disagreements reached.[1]

Since then many more authors have written a great deal in this area, and the subject is probably just as thorny now as it ever was. The purpose of this paper is to endeavor to throw some light on what is believed to be the basic cause of many of the "disagreements," and to examine the accounting treatment of Goodwill.

Some "Conceptualizing"

The main cause of the arguments seems to be that the real nature of Goodwill has been submerged in the literature by the methods that we have been forced to use in practice when calculating the total values of entities, e.g., for sale purposes. Goodwill is *not*:

---

[1] J. B. Canning, *The Economics of Accountancy* (The Ronald Press Company, 1929), p. 38.

Reprinted by permission of the author and publisher from *Accounting Review*, Vol. XLIV (April, 1969), pp. 247–55.

the discounted value of the estimated excess earning power—the amount of the net income anticipated in excess of income sufficient to clothe the tangible resources involved with a normal rate of return.[2]

This is not what Goodwill is. This is merely a rationalization of the method commonly used to calculate the value of Goodwill, and it is this rationalization that has come to be accepted by many as being the nature of Goodwill. If we are to get to the nature of Goodwill, we must ask the question, "Why does excess earning power on tangible assets exist?"

Goodwill exists because assets are present, even though they are not listed with the tangible assets. For example, "special skill and knowledge," "high managerial ability," "monopolistic situation," "social and business connections," "good name and reputation," "favorable situation," "excellent staff," "trade names" and "established clientele" are assets in this category. The sum of the value of these assets (commonly referred to as intangible assets) is the value of Goodwill.

Assets are things of value; and economic assets are economic assets because they have economic value to the entity[3] that acquired their services. Economic assets have economic value because they contain future, beneficial service potentials (or rights to future, beneficial service potentials, or rights to future economic benefits[4]), and the "future" includes this afternoon, tomorrow, next year, or twenty years hence. Beneficial service potentials can exist in various forms, and if the form *does* have physical substance, it merely provides greater evidence that service potentials may exist.

Conceptually, the economic value of each asset is the net present value of its service potentials (or rights to future economic benefits, etc.), and this:

> . . . is the sum of the future market prices of all streams of service to be derived, discounted by probability and interest factors to their present worths.[5]

---

[2] W. A. Paton and A. C. Littleton, *An Introduction to Corporate Accounting Standards* (American Accounting Association, 1940), p. 92.

[3] "Entity," herein includes any private person, sole proprietor, or partnership—as well as company, division of a company, government department, club, association, etc.

[4] Several similar terms have been used; for example see: W. J. Vatter, *The Fund Theory of Accounting and Its Implications for Financial Reports* (The University of Chicago Press, 1947), pp. 17–19; American Accounting Association Committee on Concepts and Standards, *Accounting and Reporting Standards for Corporate Financial Statements* (American Accounting Association, 1957), p. 3; R. T. Sprouse and M. Moonitz, *A Tentative Set of Broad Accounting Principles for Business Enterprises* (American Institute of Certified Public Accountants, 1962), pp. 20–21; E. S. Hendriksen, *Accounting Theory* (Richard D. Irwin, Inc., 1965), p. 194; R. H. Hermanson, *Accounting for Human Assets* (Bureau of Business and Economic Research, Michigan State University, 1964), p. 4.

[5] American Accounting Association Committee on Concepts and Standards, *op. cit.*, p. 4. For similar assertions by accountants see: Hendriksen, *op. cit.*, pp. 202–203; R. T. Sprouse, in R. K. Jaedicke, Y. Ijiri, O. Nielsen (Eds.), *Research in Accounting Measurement* (American Accounting Association, 1966), p. 111; D. Solomons, in M. Backer (Ed.), *Modern Accounting Theory* (Prentice-Hall, Inc., 1966), p. 123.

And, conceptually, the value of each entity is the total net present value of all of the service potentials of all of its assets (both tangible and intangible)—less the net present value of its obligations. *If we were omniscient* it would be possible to name all of the intangible assets (as well as the tangible assets) *and* to calculate for each its net present value. This would mean that we would also have values for all assets such as "special skill and knowledge," "high managerial ability," etc.,—i.e., if they existed. *There would be no Goodwill item as such.*

In the valuing process, each asset would be valued by discounting *all* of the net future cash flows that it was expected to create, *irrespective* of whether or not these indicated excess profits, or normal profits, or low profits, or losses. For example, there would be no "skimming off" of any expected *excess* profits in the valuation of any asset (tangible or intangible), because to do so would result in the *under*-valuation of the asset concerned.

> Because the value of assets, indeed their existence, depends upon the future economic services they are capable of rendering to the business enterprise, the dollar amounts identified with assets should be related to those [and all of those] anticipated benefits.[6]

And as George O. May once said:

> Intangible values rest on earning power—which is, of course, true also of tangible capital assets.[7]
>
> However, we are not omniscient; and even if we *could* value the whole entity and at least all of its *tangible* assets by isolating and discounting their expected future net cash flows, it would still not be possible to calculate the net present value of the more subjective assets such as an entity's "good name and reputation," its "excellent staff," its "social and business connections," and so on (i.e., most intangibles). In these circumstances, the difference between (a) the total net present value of the whole entity, and (b) the sum of the net present values of those of its net assets that could be valued directly, is "Goodwill." Conceptually therefore, in this case, Goodwill would be the net present value of those assets that it has not been possible to list and value separately; but notice that the only "excess profits" included in this Goodwill figure would be those relating to the assets we could not value directly.
>
> But in practice we cannot calculate the net present values of most assets, because, at present anyway, their individual future cash flows cannot be isolated.[8] This is the "homogeneity" problem that Thomas has discussed

---

[6] Sprouse, and Moonitz, *op. cit.*, p. 23.

[7] G. O. May, *Financial Accounting* (The Macmillan Company, 1943), p. 155.

[8] The development of probability theory, sensitivity analysis, subjective probability and simulation techniques will, in the future, make possible the direct valuation of many assets, with a much higher degree of precision than at present.

and demonstrated at some length.[9] This means that the net present values of most assets can only be approximated; and any errors in the approximating process will cause compensating errors in the Goodwill figure (assuming that it is still possible to obtain the net present value of the whole entity). In such a case, the Goodwill figure is made up of:

(i) the value of intangible assets (with the possible exception of a few like "patents" and "trade names" whose present values might have been approximated individually), and

(ii) the errors (both "plus" and "minus") in approximating the individual net present values of those assets (mainly tangible assets) for which direct net present values could not be calculated.

However, here again there has been no deliberate attempt to "skim off" any expected *excess* profits (or losses) when valuing individual assets and to have these put in with the Goodwill figure.

There is nothing new in what has been stated here. This is an exposition of the Canning concept of Goodwill as a "master valuation account," in which account he included not only those intangible factors which "may be practically incapable of valuation as individual items," but also the sum of the under and over valuations of "those future items of future income that are shown in the asset schedule."[10]

This is the "residuum concept" of Goodwill—as opposed to the "future excess profits concept," which looks on Goodwill as being the present value of the excess of expected future profits over that considered to be a normal return on the total tangible assets. In the "residuum concept" of Goodwill:

The intangibles are the residuum, the balance of the legitimate values attaching to an enterprise as a totality, over the sum of the legitimate values of the various tangible properties taken individually. . . . The amount by which the total of the values of the various physical properties within the enterprise, inventoried unit by unit, falls short of the legitimate asset total for the entire business, expresses the intangible value.[11]

The "excess profits concept" of Goodwill does not *attempt* to give "legiti-

---

[9] A. L. Thomas, "Precision and Discounted Services," *The Accounting Review* (January 1962), pp. 67–72; "Discounted Services Again: The Homogeneity Problem," *The Accounting Review* (January 1964), pp. 1–11; *The Allocation Problem in Financial Accounting Theory* (An unpublished monograph), pp. 33–52. However, there need not be any "assumption of certainty" as he claims, and it *is* often possible to isolate cash flows as between divisions of an entity, and even between some individual assets of a division. Further, although this author is mainly in agreement with Thomas' main thesis, it is thought that his use of marginal analysis does not prove that the direct valuation of assets is not possible. It merely seems to prove that this cannot be carried out using the marginal approach.

[10] Canning, *op. cit.*, pp. 41 and 42.

[11] W. A. Paton, *Accounting Theory* (The Ronald Press Company, 1922), p. 310.

mate" values to individual assets when they are more (less) profitable than normal; and therefore, as mentioned previously, this concept often results in the deliberate under-valuations (over-valuations) of many listed assets, and hence in the resultant over-valuation (under-valuation) of Goodwill.[12] Further, most advocates of the "excess profits concept" do not insist on valuing *tangible* assets by any one consistent valuation method, and it seems that all that is necessary is to calculate (capitalize) the total value of the entity (using the normal rate of return), and to treat any difference between that figure and the sum of the book values of the assets (however valued) as Goodwill.

Even though an entire 10% return on the sum of recorded assets had been due to an intangible asset, e.g., the entity's "excellent staff," no attempt would be made under the "excess profits concept" to create such an intangible asset (or Goodwill) *if* the normal rate were 10%. Instead, some (or all) of the recorded assets would be left in their over-valued state; incorrect profit determinations then occur when, and as, the various incorrectly-valued assets are depreciated.

Hermanson[13] might argue, that in many or most cases, *all* of the above-normal (and below-normal) future cash flows are due to human factors, and that none are related to tangible assets. He might point to two empty identical factories and claim that once they are occupied, any differences in performances would be due to human factors, and not to the attributes of the tangible assets. In such a case, any difference between the values of the two entities would be due to human intangible asset items of some kind; *the values of the tangible assets would be identical.* Therefore, in those cases where all intangible assets *are* due to human factors, identical Goodwill figures could be calculated under either the "residuum" or the "excess profits" concepts of Goodwill.

Further, seeing it is *not* possible to calculate, with objectivity, the net present values of entities and of most assets (both tangible and intangible), the holders of the "residuum concept" of Goodwill are forced, in practice, to use a form of the excess profits *method* to *calculate* Goodwill; and depending on the way in which the other assets have been valued, they *could* arrive at Goodwill figures identical to those calculated by persons with an "excess profits concept" of Goodwill. For example, both could be making their calculations from a tangible asset base valued by using depreciated current market buying prices.[14]

If it is possible for the holders of both concepts to arrive at identical asset and Goodwill values in practice, what is the purpose of this "conceptual"

---

[12] As pointed out earlier, the Goodwill figure in this case is inflated (deflated) by the inclusion of the excess profits (subnormal profits or losses) "skimmed-off" the values of individual assets. The matter of valuation is considered more fully later. See footnote 28.

[13] Hermanson, *op. cit.*

[14] In *Society Bulletin No. 5* (Australian Society of Accountants, 1968) this author presents a case for using depreciated current market buying prices as a base from which to assess approximations of net present value.

discussion? The purpose concerns the treatment of Goodwill in practice. Advocacy in this area often suffers from a lack of understanding of the nature of Goodwill.

Some "Conceptualizing" Concerning Practice

The main thesis above has been that the "excess profits concept" of Goodwill is a rationalization of the method used in practice to calculate Goodwill (because of the subjectivity of more direct methods), and that the holders of this concept, instead of looking on the value of Goodwill as being the value of the sum of assets such as "special skill and knowledge," "high managerial ability," etc., have come to believe that Goodwill *is* the present value of future excess income. So when Goodwill is included in the accounts in practice (usually because the price paid for an entity exceeds the sum of the book values of the other assets), most holders of the "excess profits concept" insist on writing off such Goodwill against the revenues "during the period implicit in the computation on which the price was based"[15] (or on some other arbitrary basis), even in those cases where the overall profitability of the entity does not diminish.[16] Such a procedure results in an understating of profits during the years in which the Goodwill is amortized, and this can only result in incorrect decision making both inside and outside the entity.[17] When the nature of assets such as "high managerial ability," "good name and reputation," "excellent staff," etc., is examined, it is apparent that these are not likely to have depreciated in a flourishing entity. They are more likely to have appreciated.

Any changes from year to year in the net present value of an asset (tangible or intangible) are made up of the following factors in the mathematical discounting process:

(1) A decrease—caused by the reduction in expected future net cash flows by the amount which, last year, was estimated for the year now past (i.e., it is no longer included in the calculation).

(2) An increase—caused by the expected net cash flows for each other

---

[15] Paton and Littleton, *op. cit.*, p. 92. See also: J.M. Yang, *Goodwill and Other Intangibles* (The Ronald Press Company, 1927), p. 192; K.G. Emery, "Should Goodwill be Written Off?" *The Accounting Review*, (October 1951), p. 566; and G.T. Walker, "Why Purchased Goodwill Should be Amortized on a Systematic Basis," *The Journal of Accountancy* (February 1953), p. 212.

[16] And also in those cases where overall profitability actually increases—and substantially so!

[17] Further inaccuracies in the profit determination process will occur if no attempt has been made to give meaningful current values to the assets purchased (including Goodwill). As H.J. Barclay, said on p. 185 of *The Canadian Chartered Accountant* for September, 1963:

"When allocating the purchase price to the various net assets, the considered judgment of the new owner as to current price levels and the condition of the acquired properties should carry most weight, not the book values of the previous owners. The latter values are not significant for accounting purposes unless they happen to coincide with and represent the best evidence of the reasonable worth to the new owner."

future year coming nearer the present by one year (i.e., these will be discounted by one less year, and will therefore produce a larger present value).

(3) An increase—caused by the recognition of the expected net cash flows (if any) of the most distant year—now recognizable for the first time (e.g., if an amount is now included for year 10, and if in last year's calculation nothing was included for year 11).

(4) An increase or decrease caused by changes (if any) in the estimates of the yearly net cash flows being discounted.

(5) An increase or decrease caused by a change (if any) in the discount rate.

From the above it can be seen that there would be an increase in the overall net present value of an asset if factors "2" + "3" > "1" (and assuming no changes in "4" or "5").

Although such subjective calculations would not be possible for the valuing of Goodwill in practice, the above five factors are the ones which govern its value; and it can be seen that merely to amortize Goodwill over "the period implicit in the computation" of Goodwill ignores the "increase"—factors "2" and "3" above. Understatements of profits, therefore, must be the result in nearly all cases in which purchased Goodwill *is* amortized over such a period of time; and this is the procedure that is followed by most accountants in practice today even though the expenditures incurred on maintaining (and expanding) Goodwill items have *also* been expensed by them during the same period.

Over the years, several writers have been perturbed by this practice. As long ago as 1929, Canning was critical of accountants who amortize purchased Goodwill "despite the fact that the conditions that led to making the outlay may clearly be continuing conditions."[18]

George O. May was disturbed by the distortions caused by the indiscriminate writing off of intangibles:

> If the cost of all intangible values, even where earning capacity is unimpaired, is to be written off, if all permanent declines in earning capacity of any tangible fixed property are to be reflected in write-downs of property, *and if no appreciation from any cause whatever is to be allowed to be recorded*, the distortion will be increased.[19]

And more recently, Hendriksen has endeavored to prevent the incorrect financial reporting which follows the arbitrary amortization of intangibles:

> Amortization should occur only when there are indications of limited existence, and a write-off should be made only when there is evidence of loss of

---

[18] Canning, *op. cit.*, p. 43.

[19] May, *op. cit.*, p. 155 (emphasis supplied).

value. . . . A general license to amortize and write them off over arbitrary periods does not lead to responsible accounting. The result is an understatement of net income during the amortization period and a perpetual understatement of assets in subsequent periods.[20]

Spacek has also pointed out that the writing off of Goodwill over some arbitrary period results in the understatement of profits, and in order to avoid this, he has recommended that Goodwill be written off as soon as it is purchased, against reserves of some kind.[21] However, while this might help to solve the profit determination problem, it does not result in the balance sheet that some people want, i.e., one which endeavors to show the net present value of the entity.[22]

Chambers is another who has accepted the "rationalized" version of Goodwill,[23] and his recommendation to write-off purchased Goodwill immediately, against the "residual equity," is similar to that made by Spacek.[24] However, Chambers is not so much concerned with correct profit determination; his main purpose is to avoid the existence of an asset which does not meet his requirement of "severability," and which will "in no way increase the adaptability of the firm."[25] This is not the place to enter into a full-scale debate on his ideas concerning severability and adaptability, but when Goodwill is seen in its true light as comprising human and other intangible assets such as "high managerial ability," "special skill and knowledge," "favorable situation," etc., it is clear that it *can* have real value and that it *can* increase adaptability potential. These intangible assets can increase the current selling market price of a total firm (or a severable division of a firm), and it seems, therefore, that they should be included in the Chambers' statement of financial position, because a total firm (or a division) can be sold by the "constituents" in their "adaptive behavior process" in the same way that a single asset can be sold. (In his model a firm does not adapt; it is merely the "instrument" by which the "constituents" adapt.[26])

---

[20] Hendriksen, *op. cit.*, p. 344.

[21] L. Spacek, "The Treatment of Goodwill in the Corporate Balance Sheet," *The Journal of Accountancy* (February 1964), pp. 35-40.

[22] When Spacek says that he does not want to include as an asset in the balance sheet, "the present value of anticipated future earnings over the value of the assets to be used in producing the earnings" (*ibid.*, p. 37), he demonstrates that he has accepted the "rationalized" version of Goodwill, and that his "producing assets" (*ibid.*, p. 40) include tangible assets only.

[23] R. J. Chambers, *Accounting, Evaluation and Economic Behavior* (Prentice-Hall, Inc., 1966) p. 218: "The goodwill of a going concern subsists in the superiority of its expected rate of return by comparison with alternatives." (See also *ibid.*, p. 209).

[24] *Ibid.*, p. 211. This is also similar to the recommendation of J. E. Sands, in his *Wealth, Income and Intangibles* (University of Toronto Press, 1963), p. 83.

[25] Chambers, *ibid.*

[26] *Ibid.*, p. 187. Incidentally, this seems to be relevant to the "additivity" criticisms of the Chambers' model made by K. Larson and R. W. Schattke in "Current Cash Equivalent, Additivity, and Financial Position," *The Accounting Review* (October 1966), pp. 634-641.

Those people who would write-off Goodwill immediately on purchase—because not to do so would only result in the return-on-capital calculation giving the normal rate—also seem to have the "rationalized" concept of Goodwill, i.e., that which looks on Goodwill as being the present value of the excess earning power of the *tangible* assets. But if Goodwill is not amortized in this way, there is nothing to prevent the return-on-capital calculation being made on paid-up capital, on total shareholder funds less intangibles, on total net tangible assets, on total gross tangible assets, or on any other base desired.[27] In any case, there are limitations to the usefulness, to external people, of a return-on-capital calculation that includes a profit figure determined by a process which deliberately ignores the effects of changes in the value of the intangible items making up Goodwill, but which does not ignore all the expenses incurred in developing such items. And further, the most relevant financial-position information for external people in their decisions to buy, hold, or sell shares (for example) is the present value of the total expected net cash flows of an entity as assessed by skilled management—and comprising the values of all assets, including the human and other intangible assets.[28]

In view of the above, the purchase price of Goodwill (assuming that an attempt has been made to give present values to all assets purchased) must be treated for what it really is, and Goodwill must *at least* be left intact as long

---

[27] In any case, *ex-post* profit determinations, which take into consideration the movement of prices relevant to capital maintenance, when related to *ex-ante* asset valuations, would not produce a normal rate in many or most instances.

[28] It is difficult to avoid a full-scale discussion on value and asset valuation at this stage. What follows in this footnote is a brief summary of the author's position.

In arriving at this total net present value of an entity, only those assets that *are* to be sold (including fixed tangible assets) would be included at their net market selling price, which in such a case would also be their net present value. When a decision has been made by internal decision makers to continue to operate an asset (e.g., after looking at its current market selling price and at the economics of operating alternative assets), the relevant figure for external financial-position statements is the present value (to the internal decision makers) of the future expected net cash flows from operating the asset (or the best approximation of this figure). While current market selling prices are relevant for decisions regarding the disposition of assets, it is unrealistic to attempt to include external people in such decision-making by merely supplying them with such second-hand prices. Many other variables come into such decisions and these cannot be supplied to external people. Their decisions mainly concern the buying, selling and holding of shares, while management makes decisions concerning assets. Further, would-be buyers in second-hand markets could quite easily see different and/or fewer economic benefits in the operating assets of an entity; and many such markets are very imperfect, and their prices often take into account sizeable removal and dismantling charges. In any case there is some doubt as to what is meant by "net current market selling price." If we have one hundred lathes operating in our workshop, will the current market selling price of each be that for selling one at a time, or ten at a time, or fifty at a time, or what? (Considerable differences in the unit selling prices in each case are possible, and adaption could take place in several different ways.) And will the current market selling price be the one we could obtain in five minutes, or in five days, or in five weeks, or when?

Further, the current market *buying* price of an inventory item (say $100) is not relevant in the compilation of the total net present value of an entity, if the net market selling price (which is the net present value) of the item is $150. The value to the entity is $150.

as the earning power of the entity is unimpaired. Consideration must be given to amortizing Goodwill only when and if earning power diminishes.

But this does not do anything for the increasing value of purchased Goodwill where such an increase has occurred; and it does not make provision for the recognition of the value of Goodwill which exists in the many entities that have not been the subject of a sale. To have Goodwill in the financial-position statements of only those relatively few entities that change hands, is not the ideal solution.

Therefore, consideration must be given to the periodical recognition, re-valuation, appreciation, *and* amortization of Goodwill in order to present the most relevant financial-position information for external decision makers. In view of the present practical difficulties and the subjectivity involved in valuing the whole entity *and* all of its tangible and intangible assets by discounting their respective expected future net cash flows, the valuation and periodic revaluation of Goodwill would have to be carried out via a method involving the capitalization of the entity's profits, the net present values of some assets, approximations of the net present values of the other (most) assets,[29] management's knowledge of business conditions, advertizing and promotion programs, research and development activities, new patents, etc., and using sophisticated quantitative techniques.[30] Incidentally, the profit figures to be used in this capitalization process would be those determined in each period in accordance with the particular capital maintenance concept held.[31]

Details of the annual calculation could be set out in the annual financial statements, and these could be commented on by the auditors.[32] Ladd says:

> The essential fact is that management, because of the information it has, is in the best position to estimate the present worth and thereby the value of intangible resources of the corporation. Furthermore, it would be an important function of the public accountant to test the reasonableness of manage-

---

[29] Approximations of net present value of tangible assets would mainly be based on current market buying prices, and on current second-hand market prices in those instances where the current market buying prices were not suitable and where the second-hand market was a most active one. See *Society Bulletin No. 5* (*op. cit.*) for further treatment of this by this author.

[30] The capitalization of the market value of the entity's shares at the stock exchange would not be as suitable for this purpose because a variety of extraneous factors can affect share market prices, and because management is better informed concerning internal decisions and intentions of each entity than people operating on the stock exchange. Further, as share prices are often affected by certain announcements made by management concerning the future operations of the entity and on conjecture arising from these announcements, the capitalization of the market value of shares can be based on "second-hand" (or even circular) reasoning.

[31] *Ibid.* Various capital maintenance concepts are also dealt with in *Society Bulletin No. 5.*

[32] S. M. Grant, in his unpublished thesis, *An Examination of the Organizations of International Accounting Firms* (University of Queensland), reports that one of the "Big Eight" accounting firms interviewed by him in the U.S.A. had indicated that Goodwill existed in their accounts at a "large figure," probably in the millions. In this case, Goodwill was originally based on earnings and was recalculated each year. However, this figure was frozen some years ago at a "realistic figure."

ment estimates, utilizing his knowledge of the particular corporation, his ability to compare estimates with those made by other clients, and a knowledge of business conditions generally. The characteristic caution of most accountants should act as an antidote to either excessive optimism or excessive pessimism.[33]

A Goodwill figure calculated by a procedure similar to that described above, would be the value of the many human and other intangible assets of the entity, plus or minus the sum of the errors (if any) made in arriving at the net present values of (a) the entity, and (b) the tangible assets.

As all recognitions, revaluations, appreciations, and amortizations of Goodwill (and all other assets) would affect profit determinations in such a procedure,[34] all expenditures incurred in developing Goodwill items (e.g., expenditures on sales promotions, research and development, staff-training programs, management development, etc.) would have to be expensed as incurred.

As there is no market place for most intangibles, it is exceedingly unlikely that their cost would equal value. (There is a market place for most tangible assets and their cost often approximates value.) However, some intangibles (such as patents and trade names) do have a market, and when these are purchased they could be accounted for separately in the way that tangible assets are, because there is more chance here of cost approximating value.

In the profit statement, entries concerning the revaluation of Goodwill could be shown separately, and at the foot of the statement, so that they could

---

[33] D. R. Ladd, *Contemporary Corporate Accounting and the Public* (Richard D. Irwin, Inc., 1963), p. 155.

[34] Except to the extent that revaluations, appreciations, etc., were caused by changes in those prices relevant to the capital maintenance concept held.

In the following simplified example, assume that *all* (to avoid debate of another nature) prices rose by 50% in a certain period:

	Net Values at Beginning of the Period	Beginning Values Restated by +50%	Net Values at End of the Period
Tangible Assets	$ 8,000	$12,000	$11,000
Goodwill	6,000	9,000	11,000
Total	$14,000	$21,000	$22,000

Here, the increase in total values of $8,000 (i.e., $22,000 – $14,000) is made up as follows:

	Changes of a Capital Nature	Changes Affecting Profit	Total Changes
Tangible Assets	$ +4,000	$ −1,000	$ +3,000
Goodwill	+3,000	+2,000	+5,000
Total	$ +7,000	$ +1,000	$ +8,000

be added back (or deducted) easily by those who might want to do so. Similarly, in the Balance Sheet, the Goodwill item(s) could be included after a subtotal of other assets.

Conclusions

In this paper it has been asserted that the widespread "present value of excess profits" idea of Goodwill confuses the nature of Goodwill with a popular method of measuring it. The measurement method has been rationalized into a concept, but into a concept that is incorrect and misleading.

To find the true nature of Goodwill, we must seek the answer to the question, "Why does excess earning power on tangible assets exist?" If other assets are valued correctly, the answer will be found in some form of human or other kind of intangible asset, such as "high managerial ability," "excellent staff," "trade names," and so on. Although these assets might be characterized by a lack of physical substance, they often represent value in the form of future beneficial service potentials, and thus are no different, in an economic sense, from assets with physical substance. In fact, they can represent greater earning capacity than many tangible assets. The small quotation in the heading to this paper makes this clear.

If the total financial position that is relevant to those external people making decisions concerning the buying, selling, and holding of shares, is to be revealed to them, some attempt must be made to include the present value of these various intangible items in the financial-position statements of entities; and the "relevant financial position" is the one that gives the present value of all the future net cash flows that managements expect entities to earn.

This approach would eliminate the present incorrect treatment of purchased Goodwill that is brought about by the incorrect "excess profits concept" of Goodwill, and which results in Goodwill being amortized either over the period "implicit in its calculation," or immediately when it is purchased. It would also result in attempts to correctly recognize, revalue, appreciate, and amortize all assets, including those of an intangible nature.

Rapid advances are being made in probability theory, sensitivity analysis, subjective probability and simulation techniques, and it is believed that these, in the not too distant future, will make possible the direct valuation of many entities and assets, with a much higher degree of precision than at present. And it must be remembered that objectivity is not a part of theory—it is merely a constraint in the application of theory.

*George R. Catlett and Norman O. Olson are
partners, Arthur Andersen and Co.*

AICPA Accounting Research Study No. 10: Accounting for Goodwill

George R. Catlett and Norman O. Olson

Principal Recommendations

The principal recommendations of this study with respect to (a) accounting for goodwill and (b) the related broader problem of accounting for business combinations are:

1. Most business combinations, whether effected by payment in cash or other property or by the issuance of stock, are purchase transactions and should be accounted for the same as other purchases. Wyatt reached the same conclusion in *Accounting Research Study No. 5.*

2. The total value of the consideration given in a business combination should be accounted for in recording a purchase transaction. The value of the consideration is the amount of cash paid, the value of other assets or notes given, and/or the fair value of the stock distributed.

Reprinted by permission of the authors and publisher from ''Accounting for Goodwill,'' *AICPA Accounting Research Study No. 10*, 1968, pp. 105–15. Copyrighted 1968 by American Institute of CPAs.

3. The separable resources and property rights acquired in a business combination should be recorded at fair value at the date of the purchase. The difference between the value of the consideration given and the fair value of the net separable resources and property rights acquired should be assigned to purchased goodwill.

4. The amount assigned to purchased goodwill represents a disbursement of existing resources, or of proceeds of stock issued to effect the business combination, in anticipation of future earnings. The expenditure should be accounted for as a reduction of stockholders' equity. The accounting can be achieved by one of two methods: (a) an immediate direct write-off to capital surplus or retained earnings (the preferred method) or (b) showing a deduction from stockholders' equity in the balance sheet for several periods and a later write-off to capital surplus or retained earnings. The selection of method may involve significant legal and disclosure matters to be resolved by the board of directors but is not a question of accounting principle.

The recommended treatment of purchased goodwill results in balance sheet and income statement reporting for purchased goodwill which is consistent in principle with existing practices of accounting for internally developed or nonpurchased goodwill—practices which this study considers proper.

5. The conclusion that most business combinations are purchase transactions has the corollary conclusion that pooling of interests accounting is not valid. Hence, various related procedures which are based on the pooling of interests concept, such as carrying forward the retained earnings of the absorbed company to the retained earnings of the continuing entity, are not proper.

6. The relatively rare business combination in which no constituent clearly emerges as the continuing entity results, in effect, in the creation of a new business enterprise. The accounting should be that generally accorded the formation of new enterprises—that is, the separable resources and property rights should be recorded at fair value and no amounts should be recorded for goodwill.

Conclusions Supporting Recommendations

A summary of the principal conclusions supporting the recommendations of this study follows.

Nature and Valuation of Goodwill

1. The investor determines the value of a business enterprise, based on his appraisal of the earning power of a company. His appraisal is based in part on the information which financial statements provide as to the past performance of the business. The investor-determined value of a publicly held company is evidenced by the market price of the company's stock.

2. Investor opinion of values is influenced by innumerable factors including the investors' collective evaluation of and prejudices and reactions to political, economic, or social events; investor opinion is subject to the same types of factors and forces which mold public opinion generally. The role of accounting is to provide information which the investor can use in arriving at his opinion of the value of a business; accounting does not determine that value.

3. The difference between the value of an entire business and the value of its net separable resources and property rights committed to the production of earnings is called goodwill. Goodwill reflects the evaluation of the earning power of the business by investors and is generally not accounted for except when a business is a party to a business combination and is acquired by another.

4. Goodwill is not a resource or property right that is consumed or utilized in the production of earnings. Rather, it is a result of earnings, or of the expectations of them, as appraised by investors. Goodwill exists only as a part of the value of a business as a whole and has no existence or life separate from the business.

5. Goodwill value represents the aggregate opinion of investors and is subject to sudden and wide fluctuations. That value has no reliable or continuing relation to costs incurred in its creation, its purchase, or its maintenance.

These and other distinguishing characteristics of goodwill indicate that goodwill clearly differs from other elements of the value of a business.

Financial Statement Objectives

1. Financial statements provide information about business enterprises. The information is significant only if it is useful and meaningful to investors and other users of the financial statements. The principal test of the soundness of accounting principles and practices, therefore, lies in the usefulness of the resulting information.

2. The decisions of investors involve the process of choosing the securities of one business over those of others. Financial information is most useful for investor decisions if it is prepared on a comparable basis among businesses, so that the differences in the reported financial position and profitability of one company as compared with others represent differences in conditions and circumstances and not merely differences in accounting practices.

3. The quality of a business is judged principally by its success in achieving earnings, and earnings as reported in the statement of income are among the most important facts which financial statements provide about a business. The "earning power" of a business is also becoming increasingly significant. The record of past earnings is a significant factor in the investors' appraisal of a business enterprise's prospects for future earnings—an appraisal which, regardless of the myriad factors which influence investor opinion, primarily governs the market price of the enterprise's stock and the value of the business as a whole.

4. Information about the value of the separable resources and property rights committed to the production of earnings in a business is also of interest to investors and creditors. The balance sheet provides this information, subject to the limitations of the cost basis.

5. Accounting employs certain conventions to fulfill the financial statement objectives of providing information about the earnings and the value of the resources and property rights of a business. The conventions provide a practical framework to assure reasonable standards of objectivity and consistency in the information reported. Foremost among these conventions are the realization principle in recognizing revenue and, its corollary, the cost basis of carrying assets in the balance sheet. These conventions are necessary in accounting, even though they may restrict the usefulness of financial statements. For example, the cost basis is useful, but the balance sheet is more useful the closer the amounts ascribed to individual resources and property rights are to their current values determined objectively. Solutions to individual accounting problems must be sought with those conventions and effects in mind.

6. The realization principle for recognizing revenue gives rise to the central problem of accounting—the "matching" problem. Which expenditures should be deferred and matched against the benefits to future income resulting from the expenditures and which expenditures should be recognized as charges to income when incur-

red? A number of discernible conventions or accounting rules have evolved for matching. Only those expenditures attributable to specific resources or property rights which have values in and of themselves, apart from the business as a whole, have ordinarily been reported as assets. Thus, existing practices of accounting for purchased goodwill are inconsistent with accounting practices in other areas.

Effect of the Form of Business Combinations

1. Business acquisitions and combinations may be effected by stock or cash, but this is only a difference of substitute forms of consideration and is not a substantive difference. No logical basis exists for the two radically different approaches to accounting for business combinations: pooling of interests and purchase accounting.

2. One entity continues in most business combinations and it, in effect, buys the business and assets of the other entity or entities, regardless of (a) whether the purchase is effected by payment in cash or other property or by the issuance of stock, or (b) which company is merged into the other or which company becomes the parent. Thus, most business combinations are purchase transactions.

3. The amount paid for a business, including its goodwill, in a combination effected by issuing publicly traded stock must be related to the market price of the stock issued (with appropriate adjustments for fluctuations incident to the combination). The market price is the best representation of the consideration given, and the amount by which the market value exceeds par or stated value should be credited to capital surplus.

4. In a few business combinations, none of the constituents clearly emerges as a continuing entity. In effect, the business combination results in a new business enterprise.

Accounting Considerations

1. Except in a few business combinations in which the combination is not a purchase transaction but creates a new enterprise, the proper accounting for business combinations is found in the general concepts underlying purchase accounting. Pooling of interests accounting is not a valid method of accounting for business combinations.

2. The recognition, under existing practices of purchase accounting

for business combinations, of the fair value of the separable resources and property rights of the acquired company in the accounts of the continuing company is appropriate and consistent
with the cost basis of accounting. The fair values are more significant in the balance sheet and as bases for charges to income than
the older, historical costs in the books of the acquired company.
The carrying amounts of the acquired company are unrelated to
the accounts of the continuing company, except for their tax effects
where they are carried forward for income tax purposes.

3. The difference between the value of the consideration given (cash,
   other property, or stock) and the fair value of the net separable
   resources and property rights acquired represents the amount paid
   for goodwill and should be so allocated.

4. Current practices of accounting for goodwill purchased in a business combination and for nonpurchased (internally developed)
   goodwill are completely different. The difference in accounting is
   not supported by differences in the nature of the two types of
   goodwill, since the characteristics which distinguish goodwill from
   other assets apply to purchased goodwill as well as to nonpurchased goodwill.

5. Under existing practices of accounting, ordinarily neither the *cost*
   nor the *value* of nonpurchased goodwill is reported in the balance
   sheet to be amortized to future income. Current practices are appropriate and should not be changed because:

   > Expenditures which create goodwill cannot be identified with the
   > particular values which they may create, and any capitalization-amor-
   > tization of costs would be based on arbitrary or hypothetical assump-
   > tions and therefore could not form the basis for a meaningful measure
   > of assets or of charges to income.

   > Recognition of the value of nonpurchased goodwill in the financial
   > statements would suggest the untenable position that the continually
   > changing composite opinion of investors as related to the prospective
   > earning power of a business should be capitalized by the business and
   > amortized as a reduction of the earnings being evaluated. Such a
   > procedure would introduce investor opinions of values into the finan-
   > cial statements which are designed to furnish information which in-
   > vestors use in arriving at their opinions.

6. Purchased goodwill—the goodwill value of an absorbed company at
   the date of a business combination—has no continuing, separate
   measurable existence after the combination and becomes merged

with the total goodwill value of the continuing business entity. Thus, the existing capitalization-amortization procedures of accounting for purchased goodwill are not appropriate since the underlying concepts—that purchased goodwill may be measured in subsequent periods in terms of value and periods of existence—are not valid.

7. Purchased goodwill, as a value created by earnings or by expectations of them, does not belong as an asset in a balance sheet whose objective is to show the separable resources and property rights used in the production of earnings. That procedure introduces investor opinion as to the value at one point of one segment of the business of the combined company—a value which can have no continuing significance to investors and creditors who use the balance sheet.

8. The amortization of purchased goodwill in the determination of earnings does not represent the cost of a resource consumed to produce those earnings. Goodwill is a result of earnings or of the expectations of them; amortization of goodwill has an improper circular effect because the amortization may affect the values those earnings are designed to measure.

9. Amounts paid for goodwill in a business combination represent expenditures of a company's resources (a portion of the value of the stock issued in a combination effected by stock) for the opportunity to gain additional resources (earnings) in the future. The resources expended can be restored and additional ones added only if earnings are realized later.

10. Thus, amounts paid for purchased goodwill in a business combination represent reductions in stockholders' equity and should be accounted for accordingly. Accounting for purchased goodwill in this manner is also consistent with the accounting for the goodwill value of the continuing entity with which the purchased goodwill has in fact been merged.

11. Careful appraisal and allocation of the purchase prices should disclose few combinations in which the value of the net resources and property rights acquired exceed the value of the consideration given. "Negative goodwill" may arise occasionally, however, because sellers may encounter difficulties and delay in alternate dispositions of the assets of the absorbed company. In those rare

combinations, "negative goodwill" should be recorded as a liability for special expenditures which may be needed to improve profitability; if no special expenditures are contemplated, the amount should be added to capital surplus or retained earnings as determined by the board of directors after considering applicable legal requirements.

Legal and Income Tax Considerations

1. Business combinations must be carried out in accordance with the applicable state laws. Some business combinations are statutory mergers under certain state laws. The practices recommended in this study are not intended to violate any laws, since the effect of the recommendations is more restrictive than most laws. Statutory mergers, however, may require disclosures of significant information; for example, the amount of surplus available for dividends.

2. Some business combinations represent tax-free exchanges of stock, and no "step up" of the tax basis of the assets acquired is permitted. Tax-free exchanges do not prohibit the type of purchase accounting recommended in this study. The income tax treatment of the business combination must be considered in allocating the consideration paid to separable resources and property rights and to goodwill but does not affect determination of the value of the consideration given.

Recommended Procedures and Objectives of Financial Statements

This study concludes that all business combinations, whether effected by stock or by cash, are purchase transactions, except those relatively few combinations in which one constituent does not clearly emerge as the continuing entity and the newly created business enterprise is accounted for as such. This study recommends that the pooling of interests method be eliminated as acceptable accounting for business combinations.

Existing purchase accounting related to purchased goodwill, however, should be revised. For the reasons summarized in this chapter, this study recommends that amounts paid for goodwill in a business combination be accounted for as a reduction of stockholders' equity at the time of the combination.

The authors of this study believe that the recommended procedures satisfy the general criteria or guides established in the discussion of the objectives of financial statements in Chapter 3. The criterion of usefulness is discussed last, since the usefulness must be tested in the light of the other criteria.

Comparability. Elimination of pooling of interests accounting results in comparability in accounting for business combinations, a comparability that does not now exist under the two radically different accounting approaches considered to be optional for a large portion of today's business combinations.

Purchase accounting for business combinations, requiring an accounting for the fair value of the separable resources and property rights acquired, is comparable to the present accounting for the acquisition of such assets in other ways. Further, comparability in the future is achieved between the financial statements of businesses which have grown by business combinations and those which have grown by internal expansion, by deducting from stockholders' equity at the time of the combination the amounts paid for purchased goodwill.

Financial Statements Serve the Future. Earnings reported under the recommended procedure of accounting for purchased goodwill are a more useful guide in appraising earning power. The assignment of current values to separable resources and property rights acquired in a business combination produces more realistic charges for depreciation and other expenses than result from pooling of interests accounting which embodies the older historical costs of a predecessor company. Also, the recommended procedure eliminates charges to earnings for values not used or consumed in the production of earnings but which result from earnings or from expectations of them.

Current Values of Resources (Assets)—Important Information. Purchase accounting is clearly better than pooling of interests accounting in ascribing more current values to the resources of a business. A result of the cost basis is that purchase accounting adjusts to current values the assets of the absorbed company only. We noted in Chapter 3 that the cost basis places some limitations on the usefulness of the balance sheet in serving its objectives of disclosing information about the value of the resources and property rights of a business. However, this is a general limitation of the cost basis, and "mixed" costs or values exist in the financial statements of any business whose assets have been acquired at different dates under a variety of circumstances and is not a problem peculiar to business combinations.

Enterprise Value Determined by Investor—Not an Accounting Function. In recording purchased goodwill as an asset and in charging earnings for its amortization, present accounting practices for purchases introduce investor opinion of the value of a business into the information which accounting supplies the investor as a basis for that opinion. The procedures recommended by this study for accounting for purchased goodwill do not create the confusing results of this circular effect which impairs the usefulness of financial information.

Observance of Present Basic Accounting Conventions. Purchase accounting is consistent with the cost basis of valuing resources and property rights. Accounting for purchased goodwill as a reduction of stockholders' equity is consistent with the general rules adopted in accounting for deferring as assets only those costs which have reasonably clear periods of income benefit *and* which are directly associated with specific separable resources and property rights. Separable resources and property rights have values in themselves apart from the value of the business as a whole, which is not true for goodwill.

Usefulness. The principal conclusions of this study satisfy the criteria established in our discussion of financial statement objectives in Chapter 3 for judging the soundness of accounting practices for goodwill and business combinations. These conclusions lead to improvements in financial reporting by (a) recognizing the fair values of the separable resources and property rights acquired in business combination transactions, (b) providing for measurement and disclosure of any goodwill value acquired in a business combination, and (c) reporting as assets only those separable resources and property rights which have future value to the business and as revenue charges only those costs incurred which are identifiable with the revenue of the period or are assignable to a period on some other reasonable basis. Thus, adoption of the conclusions would make financial statements more useful in accounting for business combinations in a manner responsive to the objectives of financial statements.

4. OTHER ALLOCATIONS – FUTURE OBLIGATIONS AND DIVISIONAL REPORTING

This section demonstrates the pervasiveness of measurement and allocation problems. Future obligations are as subject to measurement and allocation controversy as are assets. Allocation is also a problem with respect to divisional reporting. It is impossible to provide examples of all of the varied areas of controversy such as research and development costs or leases, but the basic nature of the controversies is revealed through the four readings selected for this section.

In the first article, David F. Hawkins introduces a controversy between advocates of deferred income tax accounting and advocates of the flow-through method. The investment credit is discussed from both sides of the argument. He attempts to explain the investment credit as a liability, a source of capital, and a source of funds, which all justify the use of deferral accounting. APB Opinion No. 11 is considered in terms of its adequacy in settling the issue.

Lawrence Revsine's purpose in the second article is to critically examine Hawkins's attempt to explain the nature of the deferred tax credit. He argues against the liability notion and suggests that the funds flow justification is no more applicable to the deferred method than to the flow-through method. He suggests an accounting procedure that he sees as a solution to this particular issue, but recognizes that his solution would violate the recommendations of APB Opinion No. 9.

Turning to another controversy, G. Edward Philips attempts to outline an accounting theory approach to determining the appropriate allocation of the employer's expense under a pension plan. According to Philips, expense timing is a problem of asset and liability measurement. Asset valuation in connection with pensions presents the most significant problem, but he suggests that even this can be accomplished at two points, the beginning of employment and retirement. He considers the problem similar, therefore, to that of charging fixed assets to expense. Past service costs are also discussed and the article helps to demonstrate the relationship between theoretical constructs and financial reporting.

The final article, by David Solomons, deals with the contemporary controversy over divisional reporting by conglomerates. The article serves to point out the problems that confront accountants when trying to accomplish the task of divisional reporting. The problems include questions of allocation and the question of the equity of alternative allocations. It becomes clear that the task is enormous. Solomons does not reject segment reporting, and he even suggests some possible approaches to solutions.

David F. Hawkins is Professor of Business
Administration, Harvard University.

Controversial Accounting Changes

David F. Hawkins

When the Accounting Principles Board of the American Institute of Certified Public Accountants last fall tentatively endorsed deferral, rather than flow-through, treatment of investment tax credits, it was firmly opposed by many corporations as well as by the U.S. Treasury. So the APB delayed a final decision until this year. A less noticed part of the controversy was a stance which the Board did adopt, i.e., comprehensive allocation of deferred taxes. It is important, the author feels, because it is part of a trend toward relating corporate earnings more closely to operating efficiency. In the wake of expressions of great concern from corporate financial executives and the U.S. Treasury, the Accounting Principles Board in December 1967 issued perhaps its most important opinion.

Opinion No. 11 did not put into effect the APB's proposed change in accounting for investment tax credits which had aroused the ire of many corporate executives, accountants, and the government. What the opinion did make effective—most importantly, the principle of comprehensive tax allocation, which relates to timing differences between book and tax report-

---

Author's note: For his counsel during the preparation of this article, I should like to express thanks to Walter F. Frese, Professor of Business Administration at the Harvard Business School and a member of the Accounting Principles Board when it was formulating Opinion No. 11.

---

ing—is significant not so much in its immediate application but in its cementing of a trend toward making corporate earnings genuinely responsive to management performance and less vulnerable to accounting manipulations.

If the APB extends the opinion's accounting treatment to areas still exempt from the new accounting requirement, this could materially reduce the profits of many corporations, including those with foreign subsidiaries, and companies in the oil, life insurance, savings and loan, and shipping industries.

The opinion, which took effect on January 1, 1968, also serves to:

- Ensure continuance of practices whereby a company can choose the accounting policy that best reflects its particular circumstances.

- Provide a framework allowing management to make financial accounting policy decisions independently of tax accounting strategy. (All too often in the past, tax accounting considerations have caused poor decisions from the financial accounting point of view.)

- Encourage, in its implicit move toward the sources and uses of funds approach, the aim of corporate executives and CPAs to find ways to make more understandable a number of items on the balance sheet which cannot be explained satisfactorily to stockholders by the more traditional accounting concepts.

The APB decided in favor of *comprehensive* allocation despite tremendous pressure, chiefly from corporations, to sanction the *partial* allocation and flow-through methods of treating tax deferrals.

The Board underwent even greater pressure to reverse the position it took on investment tax credits in the "exposure" draft of Opinion No. 11, which was circulated earlier last year. In that draft the Board favored the deferral method, which takes the credit into income over the life of the asset that gave rise to the credit, in preference to the flow-through method, which boosts current earnings by the amount of the credit. Bowing to the widespread opposition, which made it more aware of the transitional and political problems, the Board finally agreed to delay its decision until later this year. In the meantime it is permitting either method to be used. Whichever treatment the APB eventually adopts, many corporations will be obliged to switch their way of handling investment credits.

Theoretically, companies need not follow the Board's opinions. But in any audited corporate report the CPA is required to disclose, either in the footnotes accompanying the statement or in the auditor's opinion, all material departures from APB opinions. Furthermore, the SEC and the major stock exchanges look with disfavor on such departures. So businessmen are under strong pressure to follow APB rulings.

In this article I shall discuss the delayed investment tax credit decision. First, however, I shall explore, with simple examples, the impact on the profit and balance sheets of the most important part of Opinion No. 11, comprehensive allocation of deferred taxes. (Other issues covered in the ruling include accounting for loss carry-forwards and loss carry-backs, tax allocation within a period, and classification of deferred tax accounts.) I shall also examine the opinion's potential effect on some basic accounting concepts underlying financial statements and discuss the opinion's implications for measuring management performance.

Handling Deferred Taxes

Comprehensive allocation proponents base their arguments on the generally accepted accounting concept that profits result from matching revenues and related costs. They argue that tax expenses should be recorded in the same accounting period as that in which the related revenue and expense items are recognized. When there is a timing difference between the recognition and payment of taxes, the logic of the debit-credit mechanism requires a deferred balance to be placed on the appropriate side of the balance sheet. This item, they argue, is *only* a "residual" entry and as such does not have all of the usual characteristics of a liability or an asset.

In recent years many businessmen, public accountants, and government officials have become increasingly critical of the comprehensive allocation method, which before Opinion No. 11 was required for most—but not all—major items giving rise to deferred taxes. They urged its replacement by either the flow-through or the partial allocation treatment.

Those who argue for the flow-through approach to deferred tax accounting claim that the income tax expense for a period should be limited to the tax payments actually assessed for the period by the government.

The partial allocation approach is a modification of the flow-through concept. Its supporters maintain that the balance sheet should show the amount of deferred taxes which the company actually expects to pay in the foreseeable future—say, within four or five years. Postponement of tax payments indefinitely, they claim, amounts to avoiding or reducing taxes; and it is then misleading to show the full tax deferral as a liability, since it does not represent a legally enforceable claim by outsiders on the company's assets. In short, they state, the deferred tax item appearing on the right-hand side of the balance sheet does not in most cases meet traditional criteria for liabilities.

The Board, after considering these objections, nevertheless decided to continue with greater emphasis and wider application its support of the comprehensive allocation approach. Its conclusion was summarized as follows:

"Interperiod tax allocation is an integral part of the determination of income tax expense, and income tax expense should include the tax effects of all revenue and expense items included in the determination of pretax accounting income."

The profit implications of the APB's decision against flow-through accounting are enormous. For example, one study of 100 major corporations for the years 1954–1965 indicates that 57 experienced timing differences between their book and tax handling of transactions. When the comprehensive allocation, rather than the flow-through, approach is applied to these situations, the resulting charges to income lead to an average earnings reduction of 6.5%; the total dollar reduction is almost $1 billion.[1]

Situations where an accounting transaction can be reported for financial accounting purposes in one period, but entered in a different period into the calculation of income taxes on the company's tax return, include:

- Recording profits on installment sales at the time of sale for accounting purposes, but reporting them on the seller's tax returns when the collections are received.

- Use of accelerated depreciation for tax purposes and the straight-line method for calculating book profits, or a longer asset life for book purposes than for tax purposes.

- Capitalization of research and development costs for financial accounting purposes and expensing them as incurred for tax returns.

- Recording profits from long-term contracts for tax purposes on a completed contract basis, but using the percentage-of-completion method to report financial results to stockholders.

Case of Retailer Smith

The profit implications of the opinion's deferred tax decision and the rejected alternatives can be illustrated by an example. (Depreciation and capitalization of expenses are more common instances of this situation in business, but I shall use installment sales here for simplification.)

In early January 1968, retailer Smith sold a freezer for $360 on an installment sale basis. The installment sales contract called for no down payment and 36 payments of $10 per month plus interest on the unpaid balance. The retailer's gross margin was 20% of the sales price. (The interest and any carrying charges related to the installment payments can be ignored in this discussion.)

According to a December 1966 APB decision, the retailer must use the so-called accrual method of handling the transaction on his books, rather than the installment method, since the circumstances of the sale were such that the collection of the sale price was reasonably assured. Therefore Smith will

---

[1] Price Waterhouse & Co., "Is Generally Accepted Accounting for Income Taxes Possibly Misleading Investors?" (New York, July 1967). p. 16.

how a pretax profit of $72 during 1968. If he had been able to use the
istallment approach, he would have shown a $2 before-tax profit at the time
ach $10 installment payment was received. The two methods are compared
1 *Exhibit I*.

Exhibit I. Accrual vs. Installment Treatment of Pretax Profit

ear	Accrual method	Installment method
968	$72	$24
969	–	24
970	–	24
Total	$72	$72

First-year taxes: For calculating his tax payments, however, the retailer
till has the option of using either the accrual or the installment method. If,
n order to conserve his cash, Smith decides to use the installment method for
ax purposes, he creates a tax deferral situation. He has recorded on his books
he full $72 profit at the time of sale, but for tax purposes he defers the actual
payment of taxes on this profit until it is time to meet the collection.

The after-tax profit consequences of using the accrual method for book
purposes, and the installment basis for tax purposes, depend on whether
Smith uses the flow-through treatment for handling the tax deferral or the
comprehensive allocation method recommended by the Board:

▼ The flow-through approach records for book purposes the current
year's tax payment actually shown on the retailer's tax return. If we assume a
50% tax rate, its application in this case would lead to the incremental effect
on profits shown in *Exhibit II*.

▲ The comprehensive allocation approach leads to a pretax profit of $72
on the company's books in the year of sale, and $36 after taxes. This treat-
ment puts the profit effect of the installment rate on the same basis as an
equivalent cash sale. The difference between the $36 tax expense shown on
the books and the actual tax of $12 paid to the Internal Revenue Service in
1968 is set up as a deferred tax account of $24 on the right-hand (liability)
side of the company's balance sheet. This account is reduced incrementally
each subsequent year by the amount of taxes paid on the profit from the
installment payments received during that year. So, in my example, the
deferred tax account would be reduced by $12 each year over the remaining
two-year installment payment period. (Incidentally, how to describe the
nature of this balance sheet deferral has been one of the most controversial
aspects of deferred tax accounting.)

A comparison of the results obtained from applying the flow-through
and the comprehensive allocation methods, when Smith uses different book

Exhibit II. Flow-through Tax Accounting Illustrated

Year	Pretax profit	Tax*	Net profit
1968	$72	$12	$60
1969	–	12	(12)
1970		12	(12)
Total	$72	$36	$36

*50% of the 20% profit included in the installments collected.

and tax income recognition timing, is shown in *Exhibit III*. (The cash flow effect of this sale depends on whether the retailer sells for cash or on an installment basis, and on the method he chooses to use on his tax return to recognize the profit from the sale. The financial accounting handling of the deferred tax, if any, does not change his cash flow.)

Second-year taxes: In addition to realizing a first-year profit differential of $24, the flow-through approach provides an opportunity to avoid the $12 reduction in second-year profit (see *Exhibit III*). Smith can accomplish this by making a similar $360 freezer installment sale in 1969. Again, the after-

Exhibit III. Flow-through vs. Comprehensive Tax Accounting: Tax Treatment for Book Purposes

Year	Flow-through	Comprehensive	Differential
1968	$60	$36	$24
1969	(12)	–	(12)
1970	(12)	–	(12)
Total	$36	$36	0

tax profit differential between the flow-through and comprehensive allocation treatment would be $24. But he would offset this amount with the second-year $12 profit reduction associated with the 1968 sale. So the net profit in the second year would be $12. This effect is illustrated in *Exhibit IV*.

If the retailer in this example is using the comprehensive allocation approach, the deferred tax item appearing on the balance sheet at the end of the first year would be $24. This deferral would rise to $36 at the end of the second year (the $24 difference between the tax payment recognized by the second-year sale handled on an accrual versus an installment basis, less the $12 reduction for taxes related to the first-year sale's actual tax payments made during the second year). If Smith sells one freezer each year on a three-year installment sale basis, his deferred tax will remain at $36. If he increases his installment sales volume, the deferred tax item will increase. It is this "permanent" deferral that the partial allocation and flow-through advocates claim should be included in earnings.

Thus, if the option to use flow-through accounting were available, the retailer could establish on a long-term basis a profit differential between himself and other retailers making similar installment sales who are using the accrual method for book purposes and the installment method for tax purposes, but are handling their tax accounting on a comprehensive alloca-tion basis. This differential of course would be proportionately greater if the retailer's installment sales volume were growing.

Accounting anomalies: My illustration in *Exhibit IV* raises the anoma-ous possibility that if the flow-through method had been approved by the

Exhibit IV. Flow-through vs. Comprehensive Tax Accounting: Tax Treatment of Second Sale for Book Purposes

Year	Flow-through	Comprehensive	Differential
1968	$60	$36	$24
1969	48	36	12
1970	(24)	–	(24)
1971	(12)	–	(12)
Total	$72	$72	0

APB, a sale on the installment basis (laying aside the carrying-charge effect) could lead to greater profit after taxes than would similar sales made for cash. In an expanding installment sales situation, this possibility can arise simply by arbitrarily choosing to use the accrual method for reporting pur-poses and the installment method for tax returns. This result of sanctioning flow-through is unacceptable, in my opinion, because it is contrary to the common-sense proposition that a cash sale should be no less profitable than a credit sale (ignoring financing charges, of course).

So far we have looked only at a profit on sale situation. Let us go back to the original one-freezer sale illustration and lay aside for the moment the Board's earlier 1966 accrual basis decision. If the retailer handled his install-ment sale in exactly the opposite way to the previously assumed method—that is, if he reported the sale on an accrual basis for tax purposes and on an installment basis for book purposes—the sale would have the after-tax effect on book profits shown in *Exhibit V*.

In this unlikely situation (which I am using solely for illustrative purposes), if comprehensive allocation were applied, the deferred tax item would show up on the asset side of the balance sheet, since the first-year profit recorded for taxes would be greater than the profit recorded for finan-cial accounting purposes. In a sense, the company has overpaid, or prepaid, some taxes.

Exhibit V. Flow-through vs. Comprehensive Tax Accounting: After-tax Book Profits

Year	Flow-through	Comprehensive	Differential
1968	$(12)	$12	$(24)
1969	24	12	12
1970	24	12	12
Total	$36	$36	0

Opinion No. 11 requires the disclosure of such deferred taxes. Before issu
ance of this opinion, the extent of deferred tax assets was not always dis
closed, since they were often netted against the related deferred profit bal
ance. Now, however, the deferred tax "asset" arising from such transaction
as the following must be disclosed:

■ Gains on sales of property leased back which are reported for tax pur
poses in the period of sale, but deferred for accounting purposes and amor
tized over the lease period.

■ Profits on intercompany transactions recorded on a subsidiary compa
ny's income tax return and deferred for financial reporting purposes in
consolidated statements until the assets involved are transferred outside the
intercompany group.

■ Rents, fees, and royalties reported for tax purposes as received, but
deferred for book purposes to the later periods during which they are earned

Questions for the Board

The APB now has clearly established a preference for comprehensive alloca
tion. I should mention, however, that in five important areas the Board
postponed deciding whether the opinion's conclusions should be extended
The companies that would be affected oppose this, with some justification
arguing that the tax deferrals are "permanent" because of special Interna
Revenue Code or business considerations. The areas in question, which in
most cases are the subject of special industry studies by the Board, are:

● Undistributed earnings of subsidiaries, particularly foreign ones.

● Intangible drilling costs on productive oil and gas wells.

● General reserves of stock savings and loan associations.

● Amounts designated as policyholders' surplus by stock life insurance
companies.

● Deposits in statutory reserve funds by U.S. steamship companies.

Unfortunately, Opinion No. 11 does not adequately describe in busines
terms the nature of the deferred tax item appearing on the balance sheet as a
result of applying the comprehensive allocation method. Consequently, the

opinion leaves the Board open to further criticism from supporters of the partial allocation and flow-through approaches. The continuing dispute will not lessen corporate executives' difficulties in trying to explain to readers of their financial statements the deferred tax entry, which in many companies runs into hundreds of millions of dollars.

Opponents of comprehensive allocation argue that the deferred tax items shown on the right-hand side of the balance sheet are not liabilities in the conventional sense. The liability cannot be reduced by sending a creditor a check; there is no legal liability to pay the amount, since the government's claim for taxes extends only to those on a company's tax return, which are computed by relating costs and revenues in accordance with tax code provisions; and if a company went out of business, the taxes previously deferred would not necessarily have to be paid.

The APB readily admits that deferred taxes do not have all the usual characteristics of debt. The opinion describes them as balance sheet residuals resulting from an effort to associate tax effects with the book expenses or revenues to which they relate. But this is hardly a satisfactory answer for businessmen to give their stockholders. Moreover, it has made many businessmen apprehensive that securities analysts and other users of financial statements—recognizing that deferred tax credits are not debt in the usual sense, but not knowing what they are if not debt—might indiscriminately include them as liabilities when computing debt/equity, working capital, and similar ratios.

Because of these circumstances, the opinion is encountering understandable resistance from some businessmen and users of financial statements who otherwise might support it. Furthermore, unless a better rationale for deferred taxes is forthcoming, the comprehensive allocation opponents' "nonliability" argument may gain greater strength, and confusion on the nature of the deferrals may increase.

Fortunately, the opinion does contain a possible answer to the problem, since it indicates that deferred taxes should not be considered payables in the usual sense. It is a pity that the APB did not push this notion further and develop a rationale describing deferred taxes that would have put the opinion on firmer ground.

Source of Funds Concept

In the past the deferred tax issue has revolved around the question of whether the deferral should be treated as a liability, in the traditional accounting sense. But if the right-hand side of the balance sheet is regarded as presenting the current status of a company's source of funds obtained externally, then this argument becomes irrelevant. The question should be: Is the deferral a significant enough source of funds to be disclosed on the right-hand side of the balance sheet? By its support of comprehensive allocation, the Board has indicated that this is a meaningful source of capital and that it is misleading to include it in earnings.

This funds approach, which several of the Board's earlier opinions also implicitly developed, can be extended to explain satisfactorily a number of other items appearing on typical balance sheets for which traditional accounting concepts provide no adequate answer. These might include self-insurance reserves charged to earnings, deferred profits on sale-and-lease-back arrangements, and various other items in the deferred income category that represent funds received but not yet earned.

Many current trends support this funds-flow orientation. Increasingly, users of financial statements seem to be demanding that companies meet the standard of meaningful and fair disclosure of sources and uses of invested capital. In response, modern financial reporting practice has elevated the funds flow statement to equal importance with the income statement and balance sheet. The Board's own opinions on such entries as gains on sales-and-leasebacks, without being explicit, seem increasingly to regard the accounting records of a company as maintaining a continuing record of the capital invested in the business.

Finally, a number of contemporary finance texts explicitly view assets as funds invested within the business, and liabilities and net worth as financial resources obtained from sources external to the company. Looked at from the viewpoint of the standard of meaningful and fair disclosure, the comprehensive allocation approach provides a mechanism for disclosing separately a significant source of capital in our present economic environment—the capital retained in the business by postponement of tax payments.

The favorable timing differences allowed by the federal government between tax returns and income statements have a cumulative beneficial impact on financial position and related funds flows. They allow management to have interest-free funds available indefinitely as the company continues postponement of tax payments through the recurring differences between book and tax profit. However, increased earnings will emerge only from putting this additional capital to work.

Misleading methods: By separately identifying as a "source of invested capital" the capital retained in the business through postponement of income tax payments, the comprehensive allocation approach avoids what, to me, are dangerously misleading implications of the complete flow-through and the partial allocation approaches—when considered by the standard of meaningful and fair disclosure of invested capital.

The complete flow-through approach indiscriminately mixes capital retained by postponing tax payments with "earnings," since no deferred tax item is set up. In terms of earnings as a measure of management performance, this gives the same significance to the deferred tax payments as it does to the results of decisions on the use of capital in operating activities. In my opinion, by current standards of fairness of disclosure, this is clearly "unfair" and misleading, not only to stockholders and other users of financial reports, but to management itself.

In some respects the partial allocation approach could be said to compound the felony. It singles out for identification on the balance sheet as a "source of capital" only those transactions where the related deferred tax item will be paid in the near future. This treatment can easily create the illusion that management has separately identified the postponed tax payments as a source of capital and is not taking credit for them as earnings, when, in fact, a significant portion of what is reported as earnings from year to year may be attributable to this factor.

Management Judgment

The Board's support of comprehensive allocation over flow-through treatment eliminates the danger that a management can, by arbitrarily adopting different accounting procedures for tax and book purposes, increase earnings by the profit difference between the two methods, plus an additional amount equal to the tax rate times this difference. If the opinion had approved flow-through accounting for tax deferrals, as many business and government leaders desired, it would have presented companies with many opportunities to do this through the method they used to handle such major accounting items as research and development and other intangible assets, depreciation, long-term contracts, and installment sales.

Business executives operate in a competitive world, where great emphasis is placed on earnings per share. If flow-through accounting for deferred taxes had been approved, it would have been difficult for a manager to resist improving his profits by bookkeeping decisions, even if he honestly thought that the realities of his company's situation did not justify the accounting practice he eventually adopted for public reporting purposes. For example:

■ An executive who believed his plant should be depreciated on an accelerated basis for accounting purposes would have been very tempted to use straight-line depreciation for book purposes and accelerated for tax purposes *if* his competitors were doing this to improve *their* earnings. In fact, if the manager did not grasp this chance to further increase profits, some might have said he was not acting in the most responsible way toward his company's owners, especially since the criteria for selecting one depreciation method over another are not precise.

Furthermore, once a manager starts bookkeeping his way to profits, it is difficult to stop, especially if he has trouble making his profit objectives through operations. The flow-through type of accounting, once adopted, could have encouraged such managers to seek additional timing differences so as to keep their tax income from getting ahead of their book income. For instance, retailer Smith of course wanted to increase his installment sales for additional profit and other reasons. But he might have had another motive—to avoid the profit-depressing effect of tax expenses without corresponding pretax income (observe his experience in 1969 and 1970 in *Exhibit II*). If he did not succeed, he might have been tempted to resort to such bookkeeping devices as changing his depreciation accounting.

For similar reasons, corporations sometimes find it expedient to switch accounting practice, like capitalizing rather than expensing such items as R & D. If they do this, under any accounting procedure they realize the profit difference between the two methods they are using. Under flow-through accounting they obtain an additional 48% (or whatever the tax rate is) of this profit. If the Board had sanctioned flow-through, the lure of this windfall would have made it difficult for some managers to choose objectively the accounting methods that best suit their companies.

There are two other aspects to the role of management judgment in tax accounting which I want to mention:

1. Proponents of partial allocation are willing to recognize a deferred tax item and the associated tax expense up to the estimated amount of postponed taxes that might be drawn down during, say, the next five years. Determination of this amount, they insist, must be left to management's judgment. While it is desirable to have management judgment reflected in financial accounting decisions whenever possible, I find it hard to see why the determination of the extent to which deferred taxes are shown as a source of funds should be left to management judgment, especially since the deferred tax impact can be calculated for every decision.

2. Comprehensive allocation provides a framework for separating the tax return accounting decision from the financial accounting decision. This gives management wider latitude in applying judgment to the financial accounting area than is the case with flow-through approaches, where the tax return decision influences the financial accounting decision. Comprehensive allocation leads to the same after-tax profit irrespective of what accounting alternative is used for tax purposes, while, as we have seen earlier, under flow-through methods the amount of the book profit is tied directly to the tax return accounting decision. From the point of view of measuring corporate profits, this is usually an undesirable result, since the goals of the tax and financial policies are very different. The usual objective of tax policy is to minimize current tax payments, whereas financial accounting policy's goal is to gauge managerial performance.

Opinion No. 11 will not put an end to the deferred tax accounting controversy. The opinion's failure to deal adequately with the balance-sheet nature of these deferrals leaves what is essentially a sound procedure open to an unwarranted amount of controversy and opposition. Unless this flaw is corrected in the near future, the opposition will continue.

Investment Tax Credit

The flow-through proponents view the investment tax credit as being in substance a selective reduction in taxes which otherwise would have been payable and which are related to the taxable income of the year in which the credit is granted. Consequently, they do not consider the credit as being related to the cost of using assets but, rather, to taxable income. Also, they say, it is not relatable to, or dependent on, future revenues, so they maintain that the credit is earned during the period in which it is obtained.

The advocates of deferral believe that an investment tax credit should be put on the balance sheet as deferred income and reflected in earnings as a separately identifiable item as the related asset is used and depreciated. In its original support of the deferral approach, the APB rejected the flow-through approach principally on the ground that the credit does not enhance the integrity of the earnings figure if earnings can be increased simply by buying an asset.

If the Board had stuck by this preliminary conclusion, its opinion would have had two potential effects on profit:

1. It would have reduced the attractiveness of seeking short-term after-tax profit through buying assets.

2. It would have enabled some companies, by retroactively applying the decision, to take part of their past investment tax credits into after-tax profits a second time.

The first of these profit-improvement effects can be illustrated by a simple case example:

■ In 1968 the Hampton Company bought a new piece of equipment costing $100,000. The expected life of the equipment was 10 years. Consequently, the company qualified to receive an investment tax credit of $7,000. Handling the credit on a flow-through basis would have improved 1968 after-tax profits by the full $7,000, but on a deferral basis by only $700. So the Board's original decision would have removed an opportunity for the Hampton Company to boost its 1968 after-tax profits by a further $6,300.

As noted, the exposure draft of Opinion No. 11 would also have permitted companies to apply its pronouncements "retroactively to periods prior to the effective date in order to obtain comparability in financial presentations for the current and future periods." To illustrate this proviso:

■ Let us assume that the Hampton Company had bought the machine in 1964, rather than 1968, and had accounted for the full $7,000 investment tax credit on a flow-through basis then. To apply the exposure draft's decision retroactively, the company would have had to reconstruct its past financial statements as if it had adopted the deferral approach in 1964. To do this, the company would in essence take the following steps:

1. Reduce the 1968 begnning retained earnings balance by the credit of $7,000 previously included in 1964 after-tax earnings.

2. Increase the 1968 beginning retained earnings balance by the $2,800 after-tax profit which would have been included in after-tax profits for the

years 1964 through 1967, if the item had originally been accounted for on a deferral basis.

3. Include in 1968 income a $700 credit related to the 1964 purchase.

4. Show the remaining $3,500 credit as a deferred item on the balance sheet, to be taken into income during the 1969–1973 period.

So the Hampton Company would be able to run $4,200 of its original credit through the income account twice. At the end of 1968, however, the company's retained earnings will be $3,500 less than they would have been if the retroactive accounting change had not been made. (It is important to note that regardless of how a company accounts for the investment tax credit, its cash flow is not affected.)

The Board's eventual decision on the investment tax credit is important to many industries and the users of their products. For example, one letter to the Board from an investment banking firm claimed that adoption of the deferral approach would reduce the airline industry's profits and retained earnings by about $1.5 billion over the next decade. The reduction in retained earnings, the letter claimed, would impair the industry's ability to borrow capital to finance expansion; and, as a result, more expensive equity capital would have to be used, and the carriers would have to raise fares to cover this extra cost.

Clearly, the investment tax credit is available to all companies on the same basis. Consequently, there is little rational justification for the APB to condone two very different methods for handling it. Eventually, the Board will have to settle on either the flow-through or the deferral approach. In my judgment, if the APB eventually throws its support to the flow-through method, this will represent a backward step in the Board's efforts to relate corporate profit figures more closely to the operating efficiency of businesses and make them less a function of accounting decisions.

An analogous situation, with ominous overtones, is the Board's withdrawal in January 1968 of its ruling that companies recognize that the conversion privilege of convertible debt has specific value and should be accounted for as a charge against earnings over the life of the bond. The Board decided that the matter needed further study after accountants and their clients had difficulty in placing a value on the conversion feature. Again the APB backed down from an earlier decision (1966) which would have made corporate earnings figures better reflect the consequences of managerial actions.

Conclusion

Opinion No. 11 is perhaps the most significant opinion issued by the Accounting Principles Board. Its principal focus, accounting for tax deferrals due to timing differences, affects many accounting and tax policy decisions, since in numerous situations companies can create timing differences between pretax accounting income and taxable income. The opinion also improves the integrity of corporate profits. Even if the price paid for this benefit is reduction of corporate profits, it will be well worth it, since it makes profit figures more realistic.

On the other hand, the APB's failure to develop fully the source of funds aspect of deferred taxes, or some similar rationale, leaves the opinion open to continuing criticism. But the opinion's brief, undeveloped acknowledgement that deferred taxes should not be regarded as payables in the usual sense opens up a new possibility for explaining many items in financial statements which cannot be satisfactorily described by traditional accounting conventions.

Given the many practical reasons expressed in the many objections the Board received to its proposed deferral approach for handling investment tax credits, the action delaying this decision was wise. Since the credit affects all companies in the same way, it seems reasonable to expect the Board to settle on one procedure eventually. This will not be an easy decision, since there are persuasive arguments for both the deferral and the flow-through alternatives.

The controversy preceding and following issuance of the opinion has done much to interest management in the APB's work. Now many executives seem to realize that they share a joint responsibility with the Board for establishing what constitute "generally accepted accounting principles." This commitment is encouraging, for without it the Board's purpose of making the financial reports of U.S. corporations more useful and meaningful might not be accomplished. Opinion No. 11 represents a major step toward achieving this goal.

As the Board searches for an answer to the investment tax credit question, and the many other unresolved accounting issues, it is hoped that the business community will participate in its deliberations and will support its decisions. If business fails to do this, the determination of corporate accounting practices could well pass to some government agency.

Lawrence Revsine is Assistant Professor of
Accountancy at the University of Illinois.

Some Controversy Concerning "Controversial Accounting Changes"[1]

Lawrence Revsine

The Accounting Principles Board of the American Institute of Certified Public Accountants in its recent *Opinion No. 11*[2] recommended comprehensive income tax allocation procedures whenever material, non-permanent differences exist between pretax accounting income and taxable income. Reported ". . . income tax expense should include the tax effects of revenue and expense transactions included in the determination of pretax accounting income. . . . The resulting deferred tax amounts reflect the tax effects which will reverse in future periods."[3] The nature of the deferred tax accounts which originate as a consequence of income tax allocation has been the object of much dispute in the accounting literature.

In its *Opinion* the Board did not attempt to dispel the controversy surrounding the nature of the deferred credit. The Board's reluctance to buttress its *Opinion* with theoretical justification is unfortunate for two reasons. First, it gives rise to otherwise avoidable speculation, such as Professor Hawkins', concerning the nature of the absent theory underlying the *Opinion*. Second, it prolongs the relegation of accounting practice to the status of an "art" at a

---

[1] David F. Hawkins, "Controversial Accounting Changes," *Harvard Business Review*, (March–April, 1968), pp. 20–41, reprinted in abridged form in *The Journal of Accountancy*, (May, 1968), pp. 63–66.

[2] Accounting Principles Board, "Accounting for Income Taxes," *Opinion No. 11*, (American Institute of Certified Public Accountants, 1967).

[3] *Ibid.*, p. 169.

Reprinted by permission of the author and publisher from *Accounting Review*, Vol. XLIV (April, 1969), pp. 354–58.

time when most business disciplines are moving towards the "positive science" approach.[4]

The purpose of this short paper is to critically examine Professor Hawkins' attempt to explain the nature of the deferred tax credit which arises as a consequence of the ruling in *Opinion No. 11*. The Board itself admitted that "deferred charges and deferred credits . . . do not represent receivables or payables in the usual sense. . . . "[5]; yet this was the only explanation for the nature of the credit which was in consonance with other aspects of the Board's recommendation. Since no theoretical justification for including the deferred tax account in the balance sheet had been proposed, Professor Hawkins advanced his own explanation in the hope that it would provide the needed justification:

> Looked at from the viewpoint of the standard of meaningful and fair disclosure, the comprehensive allocation approach provides a mechanism for disclosing separately a significant source of capital in our present economic environment—the capital retained in the business by postponement of tax payments.[6]

Professor Hawkins thus suggests that while the deferred tax credit may not share any of the external characteristics of liabilities, it does have one internal characteristic in common with them; the deferral, like liabilities, is a source of funds.[7] Furthermore, according to Hawkins, the Board itself implicitly shared his view of the credit as a source of funds:

> This funds approach, which several of the Board's earlier opinions *also* implicitly developed. . . .[8]

Fallacies in the Funds Flow Definition

Insufficient Justification Criterion

The essence of the issue *Opinion No. 11* sought to decide was whether the tax expense account ought to relate to book or taxable income. The balance sheet implications of each approach differ. If reported tax expense is to relate to

---

[4] For a description of this approach see Milton Friedman, "The Methodology of Positive Economics," in *Essays in Positive Economics* (The University of Chicago Press, 1953), pp. 3–43. Friedman develops his argument using John Neville Keynes definitions of a positive science (". . . a body of systematized knowledge concerning what is . . . ") and an art (". . . a system of rules for the attainment of a given end . . . ").

[5] Accounting Principles Board, *op. cit.*, p. 178.

[6] Hawkins, *op. cit.*, p. 30.

[7] "I admit that this approach is difficult to accept if one defines funds narrowly as actual cash flows. But this difficulty is removed if funds flow are viewed in their broader sense of changes in all financial resources." David F. Hawkins, "Letters to the Editor," *Harvard Business Review* (July–August, 1968), p. 164. Later in this paper we will contend that this approach is difficult to accept irrespective of the definition used.

[8] Hawkins, *op. cit.*, p. 30. (Emphasis supplied.)

book rather than taxable income, the difference between the reported tax expense and taxes actually payable must be debited or credited to a deferred tax account in the balance sheet assets or liabilities section. Alternatively, if reported tax expense is to relate only to taxable income, the deferral which arose in relating the expense to book income will not again materialize; it will not be separately disclosed but rather will "flow through" and be buried in the retained earnings account in the balance sheet. Thus, the sole implication of allocation versus flow through for the balance sheet is whether the difference between taxes computed on book income and taxes computed on taxable income ought to be separately disclosed in the assets or liabilities section or buried in equity.

Professor Hawkins' source of funds explanation is essentially an attempt to support the Board's conclusions by the use of a balance sheet argument which describes the nature of the controversial deferred credit. Logically, to be valid corroborating evidence, Hawkins' explanation should satisfactorily support the Board's position and support no other. Hawkins says:

> By its support of comprehensive allocation, the Board has indicated that [the deferred credit] is a meaningful source of capital and that it is misleading to include it in earnings.[9]

It is not evident from Professor Hawkins' statement why it would be misleading to include the impact of the deferral in earnings (and thus in the equity section of the balance sheet). Are not earnings also a "meaningful source of capital"? Couldn't advocates of the flowthrough approach support the balance sheet effect of their position using the same funds flow argument advanced by Hawkins in favor of allocation? Because both questions can be affirmatively answered, it appears that the source of funds justification for the nature of the deferred credit is an insufficient justification criterion; it serves to explain equally well both sides of the controversy.

Circularity

Accountants have always strongly objected whenever depreciation is referred to as a source of funds. Such references are understandable, however, since depreciation is usually prominently displayed in a funds statement under the caption "Sources of Funds," or "Funds Provided," or some other similar designation. This treatment of depreciation as a source of funds is essentially artificial in nature. It is necessary because depreciation which is itself not a use of funds is treated as if it were by virtue of its inclusion, with other expenses, in the uses of funds section of the statement. Thus, depreciation is added in the sources of funds section in order to negate the effect of treating depreciation as a funds outflow in the uses of funds section.

[9] *Ibid.*

While it is true that if the recommendations of *Opinion No. 11* are implemented the net change in the deferred tax credit account must be included in the funds statement as a source of funds, technically speaking, the change in the deferred tax credit account is no more a source of funds than is depreciation. The reasoning which supports this position is analogous to that of the depreciation explanation above. The amount of income tax liability shown on the tax return is, of course, a use of funds. Were there no difference between pretax accounting income and taxable income the entire amount actually due for taxes would, as income tax expense, be included as a use of funds in the funds flow statement. However, where accounting income exceeds taxable income, the amount of income tax expense recognized on the books will, pursuant to *Opinion No. 11*, exceed the amount actually owing for taxes. Under this circumstance, the tax expense included as a use of funds in the funds flow statement will exceed the amount of actual funds outflow. If no correction is made in the statement, uses of funds will be overstated by the amount of the divergence between tax expense and taxes actually payable. Therefore, to rectify this overstatement of the outflow, the deferred tax credit (which precisely equals the divergence between tax expense and taxes actually payable) is treated as a source of funds in the funds statement. Together then, the overstatement of the outflow coupled with the compensating inclusion of the deferral as an inflow result in a net outflow in the funds statement equal to the taxes actually payable.

Thus it is apparent that the deferred tax credit is an artificial adjustment; it is not a source of funds. But Professor Hawkins contends that the implicit justification for the Board's recommended balance sheet treatment of the deferral is its status as a source of funds. If this source of funds concept was implicit to the Board's recommendation (which I doubt) it would have then been relying entirely on circular logic to justify its balance sheet treatment of the deferral. That is, the deferral is a "source of funds" because the Board's reporting recommendations require a charge to tax expense which exceeds the cash outflow necessary to settle the firm's obligation to the government. To then justify the balance sheet existence of the deferral because it is a source of funds, while it is a "source of funds" only because of the nature of the Board's recommendations, is certainly circular.

Implicit Comparison

There is another facet to Professor Hawkins' proposed explanation of the nature of the deferred tax credit which should be examined. He states:

> The favorable timing differences allowed by the federal government between tax returns and income statements have a cumulative beneficial impact on financial position and related funds flows. They allow management to have interest-free funds available indefinitely as the company continues

postponement of tax payments through the recurring differences between book and tax profit.[10]

Thus, he contends that extant permissive tax regulations themselves result in a funds flow benefit to the firm. Obviously, however, a tax payment is itself a cash outflow; an outflow is hardly a funds flow benefit. The only justification for this favorable flow contention relies on an implicit comparison between the tax payments due under more "permissive" tax regulations and the payments which would be due under a law less liberal in its deduction allowances. It is certainly true that a firm is in a more favorable cash position when it is allowed certain tax return deductions not yet taken on the books than it would be were such deductions denied to it. But this cash benefit materializes only when we compare a firm's cash position after it utilizes these permissive regulations with its hypothetical position were it to ignore such opportunities.

This comparison implies choice of procedure. That is, it is assumed that the firm has benefited, cash-wise, because of its adroit choice of tax policy. But this choice is more apparent than real. Regarding tax policies of this genre, management actually has little discretion. Its primary function in tax planning is to avail itself, to the maximum legal extent, of all permissive opportunities in the law. In the typical situation, therefore, management has no logically defensible reason for not using the most liberal write-off provisions available under law.[11] There is no legitimate basis for comparing the cash position of a firm operating under a permissive tax law with the cash position of a firm subject to a stringent tax law since rational managements are confronted with no such real choice. Since the favorable cash effect (or source of funds) argument depends upon such an implicit comparison, this argument appears to be specious. In reality, management is seen to have taken the only logical tax determination policy available, and this policy has resulted in a minimum funds outflow and not a funds inflow.

Furthermore, admitting such implicit comparisons into the income determination process (as must be done to justify the funds flow explanation of the deferral) runs counter to established, traditional accounting theory. Arms-length transactions themselves, rather than some conjectural "might have beens" dictate the appropriate valuations which are entered into the accounts. Implicit comparisons of the type necessary to validate Professor Hawkins' funds flow explanation of the deferred credit are not admitted to the traditional accounting model.

---

[10] Ibid., pp. 30, 32.

[11] See, for example, Sidney Davidson, *The Meaning of Depreciation*, Selected Papers, No. 2 (The University of Chicago Graduate School of Business, 1962), p. 4:
"Any management that fails to take depreciation as rapidly as legally permissible to minimize the present value of tax payments is remiss in its responsibility to stockholders. This is something that must be done, and, in fact, I would say that any management that does not seek to maximize the present value of this stream of depreciation deductions is suspect in a sense and that we must look for the exceptional circumstances that justify this sort of procedure."

A Suggested Alternative

Professor Hawkins' paper itself reveals the existence of a real dilemma arising from the conclusions contained in *Opinion No. 11*. The recommendations of the Board give rise to a balance sheet deferred tax credit which defies classification. By the Board's own admission this account does not possess the normal characteristics of a payable. Nor can this account balance legitimately be considered to be a source of funds. The account arises as a consequence of implementing the belief of the Board that ". . . income tax expense should include the tax effects of revenue and expense transactions included in the determination of pretax accounting income."[12] Professor Hawkins strongly agrees that the primary purpose of the *Opinion* is to develop a more realistic after-tax profit figure whenever timing differences between book and tax deductions exist. The *Opinion* results in a ". . . cementing of a trend toward making corporate earnings genuinely responsive to management performance and less vulnerable to accounting manipulations."[13]

Since the deferred tax credit account is merely an adjunct which results from the Board's desire to represent after-tax profit more fairly and is not itself an integral part of this objective, the question arises whether it is possible to simultaneously achieve the Board's income statement objectives without introducing an artificial deferral whose claim to balance sheet status appears tenuous. The answer to this question seems to be yes. By treating the income tax allocation portion of the entry as a reclassification rather than as an adjustment it is quite easy to develop an income figure which is insensitive to management manipulation without introducing a "fictitious" deferral into the balance sheet. The following entry accomplishes this objective:

DR	Income Tax Expense	XXX
	CR Income Tax Payable	XXX
	CR Retained Earnings	XXX

The charge to income tax expense would, in accordance with the recommendation of the Board, relate the tax expense to reported pretax accounting income and thereby eliminate the possibility of management manipulation of reported profit. The credit to income tax payable would reflect the actual tax liability of the enterprise and would be wholly non-controversial. Only the treatment of the "deferral" is altered. Rather than treating this disparity between tax expense and taxes payable as a questionable liability account, the disparity is credited to retained earnings. This treatment retains the desirable income statement effect which was the primary objective of the Board without introducing an esoteric and inexplicable balance sheet account.[14] Actually, the "deferral" is denied any balance sheet impact.

---

[12] Accounting Principles Board, *op. cit.*, p. 169.

[13] Hawkins, *op. cit.*, p. 20.

[14] Robert K. Jaedicke and Carl L. Nelson, "The Allocation of Income Taxes—A Defense," *The Accounting Review*, (April 1960), pp. 278–281, suggest a similar treatment. They would, however, separately disclose the "deferral" in the equity section.

Unfortunately, this proposed alternative treatment appears to be at variance with the Board's

In conclusion, one would hope that future Accounting Principles Board opinions would attempt more adequate theoretical justification for the proposals advanced. The Board's failure to rigorously examine the nature of the deferral which arises as a consequence of its recommendation invites controversial speculation such as that of Professor Hawkins'. The Board's inability to adequately justify its conclusions should have served as a caution against a hasty pronouncement. Unfortunately, it did not.

---

guidelines in *Opinion No. 9* regarding direct charges to retained earnings. [Accounting Principles Board, "Reporting the Results of Operations," *Opinion No. 9*, (American Institute of Certified Public Accountants, 1967.)] To eliminate this inconsistency the divergence between tax expense and taxes payable would have to be credited to some income statement account rather than to retained earnings as I suggest. Doing so, however, would reintroduce the undesirable income statement impact of nonallocation which the Board sought to eliminate. Therefore, it seems preferable to broaden the guidelines in *Opinion No. 9* to facilitate such direct charges to retained earnings whenever income tax allocation procedures make such entries necessary.

G. Edward Philips is Professor of Accounting at the Pennsylvania State University.

Pension Liabilities and Assets

G. Edward Philips

The fact that employers commonly provide pensions for retired employees creates accounting problems. A central problem is determining the appropriate times to record the employer's pension expense. The purpose of this paper is to outline an accounting theory approach to this problem. in the proposed approach, the expense timing problem becomes a problem of asset and liability measurement.

The conclusions reached here do not necessarily suggest changes in the recommendations and rules set forth in ARS No. 8 and APB Opinion No. 8.[1] These AICPA publications imply the existence of certain assets which are netted against liabilities. By making these explicit, it is hoped that this study will contribute to developing a more consistent theory of accounting for pensions.

Pension Assets and Liabilities

We shall define "pension liability" as the value (at that point in time when we are measuring the liability) of the employer's obligation to make future pension payments to current and retired employees. This includes the obligation to make future payments based on or "related to" services yet to be

---

[1] Ernest L. Hicks, *Accounting for the Cost of Pension Plans, Accounting Research Study No. 8*, (AICPA, 1965), and *Accounting for the Cost of Pension Plans, Opinions of the Accounting Principles Board No. 8*, (AICPA, 1966).

---

performed (unearned benefits) but excludes anticipated pension payments to those to be employed in the future.

This definition is only one of several possible definitions of pension liability. It cannot be demonstrated to be a "true" definition, as accountants have never agreed what constitutes a "true" liability. Yet, as will be seen, this definition is analytically useful. It corresponds to the actuarial concept of "present value of benefits to be paid," and is relatively easy to measure.

We shall define "pension asset" as the value (at that point in time when we are measuring the asset) of the expected future employee services for which part of the pension liability has been incurred.

When an individual is employed, a pension liability arises immediately. There arises at the same time a pension asset, which may normally be supposed to equal the pension liability. At the time when an employee retires, the pension liability will have grown larger because of the time value of money, but the pension asset will have decreased to zero.

This can be illustrated with an example in which we will assume the non-existence of actuarial uncertainties. Suppose an employee retires at age 65 after 40 years of work, collects a pension of $5,000 a year for 20 years, and the relevant interest rate is 4%. The aggregate pension obligation of the employer is $100,000 ($5,000 times 20). The value of this obligation is the pension liability, which increases over the 40 working years from $14,154 at initial employment to $67,952 at retirement.

Given the interest rate and other actuarial factors (such as life expectancy, employee turnover, and vesting provisions), the value of the pension liability can be measured precisely at any point in time. In our simplified example the pension liability is determined by the interest rate and the amounts and the time of the future pension payments. Thus $14,154 is the present value, at 4%, of the $100,000 future pension payments discounted to the hiring date; and $67,952 is a similar present value at the retirement date. In order to make a comparable measurement of the pension asset, it would be necessary to estimate the amounts (value) and the time of the expected employee services. This is much more difficult than estimating the amount and time of future pension payments.

Pension expense, for any period of time, is the algebraic sum of the net changes in the pension liability and the pension asset. Pension expense is determined when the asset and liability have been measured at the beginning and end of a period of time. Since the liability is relatively easily measured, the crucial problem in accounting for pensions is an asset valuation problem.

Funding, Pension Expense, and Interest Expense

The theory proposed here is a theory of "total income," determined by changes in net assets. An analysis of income into components—various types of revenues and expenses—is a problem outside the scope of this theory. Accordingly, we shall not attempt to settle the question as to whether a distinction should be made between (a) pension costs as employee compensation and (b) interest income and expense. Accountants are not agreed on the necessity for this dichotomy. The APB opinion does not make the split,[2] while Moonitz and Russ emphasize the distinction between employment costs and financing costs.[3]

However one resolves this problem, a clear understanding of the relationships among (a) funding, (b) actuarial calculations, and (c) accounting for income and net assets is nonetheless necessary. These relationships can be illustrated by expanding our earlier example.

"Funding" involves setting aside funds to provide for future pension payments. The appropriated funds may be held by a trustee or insurance company. Additionally, a pension plan may be fully funded, overfunded, or underfunded. A fully funded plan is one in which the employer has set aside funds in an amount equal to the excess of the pension liability over the pension asset. An overfunded plan is one in which the funds exceed this amount, and an underfunded plan is one in which the funds set aside are smaller than this amount. An extreme case of overfunding would be "initial funding," in which the entire pension liability for a given employee is funded at the date of hiring. In our example this amount would be $14,154. No further employer outlays would be required, since this amount would accumulate at 4% interest to provide for the $100,000 pension payments. At the other extreme, with no funding at all, the employer outlays would be $100,000. Funding at retirement (known as terminal funding) would require setting aside $67,952. This would result in underfunding during the 40-year working period and full funding during the retirement years.

In our example, suppose there is no funding, so that total outlays are $100,000. Total expense will also be $100,000 (possibly divided between pension cost and interest cost), and will be recorded prior to these outlays be making accruals. Following the APB opinion, we would accrue one liability and charge one type of expense. This nets the pension asset (expected services) against the pension liability, combines the "interest liability" with the "pension compensation liability," and combines "interest expense" with "pension compensation expense."

If the $100,000 expense is split into pension cost and interest cost, the former will accrue over the 40-year working period while the latter will accrue over this period and also the 20-year retirement period. The expense (all of which is interest) during the retirement period is $32,048, the excess of retirement payments of $100,000 over the value of the pension liability at retirement, $67,952.

---

[2] *APB Opinion No. 8*, p. 83.

[3] Maurice Moonitz and Alexander Russ, "Accrual Accounting for Employer's Pension Costs," *Journal of Accounting Research* (Autumn, 1966), pp. 155–168.

The expense over the working period is $67,952. Any pattern of assignment of this expense to each year of the 40 years implies a valuation of the pension asset. A very conservative procedure would be to value the pension asset at zero. This would result in a charge to pension expense of $14,154 when the employee is hired. The $53,798 remainder of the $67,952 would accrue over the 40 years as interest on the liability at 4%. Such a procedure would undoubtedly be rejected as too conservative—it results in premature expensing by undervaluing assets.

Suppose we conclude that pension expense should be charged in equal amounts over the 40 working years, and that interest expense (possibly not recorded separately from pension expense) should be accrued at 4% of the accrued liability. The result would be an annual accrual of approximately $715 of pension expense, aggregating approximately $28,604 over the 40 years. Interest expense would be $39,348 over the 40 years. Interest expense would increase each year because of the $715 annual addition to the liability and because of compounding.

One way of looking at this is to suppose that in exchange for pension compensation the employee renders service, the value of which is equal in each of the 40 years. The value of the pension asset when the employee is hired, then, could be viewed as the present value, at 4%, of $715 worth of services per year for 40 years. This would be $14,154. This value would decline to zero over the 40 years. If the asset is netted against the pension liability and only the net pension liability recorded, then the interest expense on this net liability will amount to $39,348. If the asset were recorded separately and amortized by the annuity method,[4] each year's net income would not be affected, but interest expense would be greater. The higher interest expense would be offset by recording interest income on the asset.

If the plan is to any extent funded, the accounting is complicated by interest actually received on the amounts set aside. The same questions arise as to whether this is to be netted against interest expense or even netted against pension expense.

Funding has the effect of reducing aggregate outlays. In our example, they become smaller than $100,000. The total charges to expense will become less than $100,000 if the earnings on funds set aside are netted against pension and/or interest expense. Such an offset is commonly accomplished by the employer simply not recognizing earnings of funds held by a pension trustee. If the employer in our example funded approximately $715 per year for 40 years, he would simply charge these amounts to expense, an aggregate of approximately $28,604. The difference between this and the $100,000 received by the employee during his retirement would come from interest on the funds held by the trustee.

---

[4] For an outline of the annuity method of asset amortization, see Maurice Moonitz and Louis H. Jordan, *Accounting, An Analysis of Its Problems*, Vol. 1 Rev. ed., (Holt, Rinehart and Winston, Inc., 1963), pp. 387–389.

In the context of a theory of revenue and expense measurement, this procedure for recording pension cost might well be considered incorrect, since it offsets interest earned on funds set aside against interest expense (the growing liability). During the 40-year working period it also offsets the pension asset (and implicit interest earnings on this asset) against the pension liability (and interest expense on the liability).

If, however, our theory is concerned primarily with total income and not its composition, these offsets would appear acceptable. We will judge the results on the basis of their measures of net assets and total income. The test of accuracy of an income measure is whether it results from an accurate measure of assets and liabilities. A $715 annual charge to expense will be judged correct if the pension asset and liability measures implied by this charge are judged correct.

Actuarial Cost Methods

An actuarial valuation of a pension plan determines the amounts to be set aside by the employer to fully fund the plan. This involves two distinct steps. The first step is measuring, by actuarial calculations, the amount of the pension liability, the second step implies a measurement of the pension asset by applying an "actuarial cost method."

The first step is relatively noncontroversial. It is necessarily an estimate, since there is no direct market measure of the liability, but the estimation process is well established. The figure arrived at is calculated as "the present value on the valuation date of benefits to be paid over varying periods of time in the future to employees after retirement (plus any other benefits under the plan)."[5] This involves actuarial assumptions (such as life expectancy and employee turnover), selecting an appropriate interest rate, and the provisions of the pension plan. The accountant will almost always leave this calculation entirely to the actuary.

The second step involves a choice among a number of actuarial cost methods, which can give widely varying results. An actuarial cost method contains a specification of the time periods in which employees "earn" pension benefits. The effect is to split the pension liability into two segments, earned and unearned. When the pension fund equals the earned segment, the plan is fully funded. This division of the pension liability is equivalent to measuring the pension asset. The value of the "unearned" pension liability is logically equal to the value of the expected services to be received i.e., the pension asset. The "earned" pension liability is equivalent to the pension liability less the pension asset.

Given that the actuary can satisfactorily measure the pension liability, an accounting solution is possible if we can measure the pension asset. There is no market in which such assets are exchanged, to which we could look for a

---

[5] *APB Opinion No. 8*, p. 89.

direct approximation of value. Nor is it possible to objectively estimate the future services to be rendered and discount them to a present value, as we discount future pension payments in estimating a pension liability. The best we can do is to make assumptions as to the times and amounts in which the value of this asset changes.

The situation is strikingly parallel to the accountant's problems in fixed asset valuation. At acquisition, we can assume the asset value is equal to cost. (The cost of the pension asset is the amount of the pension liability at the date of hiring.) We can also reasonably predict both the asset value at disposition and also the time of disposition. (The pension asset has a zero value at retirement date.) But between acquisition and disposition, the pattern of change in asset value is difficult to measure. Accordingly, it would appear that choosing an actuarial cost method is similar to choosing a depreciation method.

It has been pointed out that an actuarial cost method based on equal pension expense charges over an employee's working years, has an effect on income equivalent to depreciating the pension asset by the annuity method.[6] In general, projected-benefit cost methods result in level pension expense charges.

The accrued benefit cost method charges pension expense with increasing amounts over an employee's working years. In applying this method in our example, we would assume that in each of the 40 years of service the employee earns one-fortieth of his future pension. The pension expense each year is the amount necessary to fund this fractional pension earned. Thus pension expense in any year is the present value, at 4%, of a 20 year annuity of $125 (1/40 of $5,000) from the retirement date. Under this method pension expense is approximately $354 the first year, $1,699 the fortieth year, and the aggregate amount is $35,322. This total is larger than under a level expense method ($28,604) because of the relative postponement of the liability accrual. The postponement reduces interest expense and increases pension expense.

The accrued benefit cost method yields an effect on income which is the same as using an annuity depreciation method in which the asset services are assumed to be increasing amounts, rather than level. In our example, we get the strange result that the implied pension asset value *increases* over the earlier working years. The pension asset value is reduced each year by the amount of current services rendered and increased by the interest factor. The value of the first year's services is taken to be only $354, while interest increases the asset $566 (4% of $14,154).

---

[6] We disregard here the possible income effects of capitalizing in inventory some types of expense (depreciation, employment costs), but not others (interest). "Pension expense charges" refers to the employee service compensation portion of total pension cost and thus does not include interest.

Some actuarial cost methods charge expense at a level percentage of payroll. If an employee's yearly earnings increase over his working years, but less than in proportion to the expense increase under the accrued benefit cost method, then these methods yield values between level charge methods (projected benefit) and the accrued benefit method. To get an income result equivalent to straight-line depreciation of the pension asset, it would be necessary to devise an actuarial cost method which gives declining pension expense charges.

The best actuarial cost method is that which most accurately reflects changes in the value of the pension asset. This is not necessarily the same method for all employers or all circumstances. APB Opinion No. 8 permits employers to choose among various methods. It would be desirable to have a basis for judging whether one method is better than another. While we cannot get a direct measure of the value of the pension asset, we can study the probable pattern of employee services for which the pension is compensation. Knowledge of this pattern over an employee's working years would permit an estimate of the pension asset at any point in time. We can begin by assuming that in each working period an employee receives compensation which is equal in value to the services he renders in that period.[7] This compensation is paid currently in part (salary or wages) and deferred in part (pension benefits), although the employee does not render two sets of services. We can measure current salary and wages, but in order to know current pension compensation, we must know the amount of total services. Establishing a figure for current pension compensation implies a valuation of current services and vice versa.

Current salary (or wage) is likely the only objective indication available as to the value of current services. It follows that the most reasonable assumption is that total current compensation is proportional to current salary. The best actuarial cost method, then, is that which reflects pension compensation proportional to salary. When this is done, the pension asset is implicitly valued as the present value of a series of future services the time pattern of which is proportional to the time pattern of future salary.

On this basis, we would reject a level charge method (projected benefit funding) because the expectation is that the average employee's earnings in salary or wages will increase over time, rather than remain constant. On the other hand, the accrued benefit method probably increases the pension charge such that it is more than in proportion to the salary increase. The

---

[7] We accept this as the most reasonable assumption, but it is not unchallengeable. The aggregate compensation over an employee's working life may be more or less than the aggregate value of his services. Even if the two are equal, the time pattern of services may differ from that of compensation. It may commonly be the case that earnings increase gradually over an employee's working life, but the value of services is a curve which first rises and then falls or levels off. If this is the case, some of the early compensation is an investment in expected future services, while in the later years, some compensation is a "pension before retirement."

extent of increase in the pension charge under the accrued benefit method depends on the length of the service period (working years) and on the interest rate. In our example, the 40th year's charge is approximately 4.8 times the first year's charge ($1,699/$353).

Comparable ratios for various lengths of employment service and interest rates are as follows:

Length of Service (Years)	Interest Rate			
	2%	3%	4%	6%
40	2.2	3.2	4.8	10.3
30	1.8	2.4	3.2	5.7
20	1.5	1.8	2.2	3.2
10	1.2	1.3	1.5	1.8

At an interest rate of 3% and a service period of 25 years, the expense approximately doubles over the employee's service period. Higher rates and longer periods will substantially more than double the annual expense over the service period. This is likely too large an increase.

Although the accrued benefit method is likely to result in recorded pension compensation which increases more than wages over an employee's service period, this is not necessarily unreasonable. If the pension is interpreted to be more a reward for long service than for specific services rendered, then such an increase may be appropriate. In general, we cannot be certain that the pattern of wages reflects the pattern of total services.

Some actuarial cost methods employ a level percentage of payroll rather than a level charge. These may be the methods which best conform to the theory proposed in this paper.[8]

Past Service Cost

When a pension plan is adopted, part of the pension liability is sometimes identified with past employee services, giving rise to problems of accounting for past service costs.[9] The crucial problem again proves to be one of asset valuation. In this case, however, it is more difficult to establish the reasonableness of an assumption that an asset exists.

Returning to our example, let us now suppose that the pension plan is instituted after the employee has completed 20 of his 40 years of service. He will still get a $5,000 pension for 20 years, and the 4% interest rate applies. At the time the plan is instituted (end of year 20) the pension liability is $31,013. The portion, if any, of this pension liability that is a past service

[8] Hicks describes the use of a level percentage of payroll as a "departure of practice from theory," but the "theory" he has in mind is level pension expense over an employee's service period. ARS No. 8, p. 128.

[9] We use the term past service cost to refer to both past service cost (on adoption of a pension plan) and prior service cost (arising with an amendment to an existing plan).

liability depends on the actuarial cost method used. A level (projected benefit) method which yields $715 per year of pension compensation over the 40 working years will result in a $21,294 past service liability. The remaining $9,719 of the $31,013 pension liability is, then, a "future service liability." The accrued benefit method results in approximately $14,900 past service liability and $16,113 future service liability.

The Accounting Principles Board is unanimously of the opinion that past service liability should be charged against subsequent income, not prior income.[10] This implies that a "past service asset" exists at adoption or amendment of the plan, and that this asset is at least as great as the past service liability.

The position that such an asset exists appears to contradict the assumptions of the actuarial cost method which established the amount of past service liability. An actuarial cost method reduces the pension liability to a net pension liability (pension liability minus pension asset) by assuming the pension liability can be assigned to periods of employee service. The past service liability is that part of the pension liability assigned to *prior* service. It is inconsistent to assert the existence of a corresponding *future* service asset.

We can escape this contradiction by assuming the existence of some other type of asset. that some asset is likely to exist, in respect to past service, is supported by the notion that an entity will not ordinarily make a large expenditure (or incur a liability) without obtaining a corresponding benefit. Current practice implies that some asset exists. When we omit past service liability from the balance sheet (as in accounting practice generally and as approved by APB Opinion No. 8), the income effect is the same as if the liability and corresponding asset were recorded. Given the actuarial cost assumptions employed, subsequent changes in the amount of the liability are readily measurable. The income measurement problem, then, is essentially an asset valuation problem. The income of periods after adoption or amendment of a pension plan is determined by the manner in which we amortize the asset.

The asset which we implicitly recognize by omitting past service liability from the balance sheet is strikingly similar to purchased goodwill. If such an asset exists it must be an expectation of improved future earnings—perhaps reflecting such things as improved morale, less likelihood of strikes, and greater employee productivity. We face the same kinds of problems in valuing (amortizing) this asset as we face in valuing goodwill generally.

A strong case could be made that, at least in some circumstances, no such asset exists. The incurrence of a large past service liability may indicate only an increased employee claim on entity assets, with no new assets created. Perhaps a labor union victory has increased the employee share of the corpo-

---

[10] *APB Opinion No. 8*, p. 73: "All members of the Board believe that the entire cost of benefit payments ultimately to be made should be charged against income subsequent to the adoption or amendment of a plan. . . . "

rate "pie," which is no larger than before. If this is so, the liability should be recorded as a loss, just as would a major lawsuit victory against the firm. If it is concluded that the liability should have been gradually accrued in the past, a correction of prior earnings, rather than a current loss, might be reported.

APB Opinion No. 8 requires, in effect, that the past service asset be amortized over not less than 10 years nor more than 40 years.[11] This permits considerable leeway and does not require justification for the write-off selected within this range. This rule appears defective in not providing for a faster write-off when the circumstances indicate small likelihood of asset value. Perhaps a general rule should be developed to cover all difficult to measure assets, including goodwill and other intangibles. The crucial problem of accounting for past service costs essentially is that of asset valuation. Only if we can specify circumstances which permit reasonable estimates of the value of "past service assets," can we hope to develop a rule for accounting for past service costs which requires the procedure followed to conform to the circumstances.

Summary and Conclusion

In this paper the accounting objective has been taken to be obtaining accurate periodic measures of net income by accurately measuring net assets. This makes it possible to avoid having to determine the appropriateness of netting or combining different "types" of assets and liabilities, revenues, and expenses. In ascertaining the effects of pensions on employer's net income, the crucial question is one of net asset valuation.

The "pension liability" is relatively easy to measure by calculating the present value of expected future pension payments to past and present employees. If this entire liability is not charged to expense as it is incurred, the effect on income is the same as if an asset had been recorded.

Assets are implicit in presenting accounting practice (and in APB Opinion No. 8) in two different ways. One of these assets offsets the portion of the pension liability which the actuarial cost method has "assigned" to future employee services. The other offsets the portion of the pension liability which the actuarial cost method has "assigned" to services prior to adoption of the plan (past service cost).

Both these assets are difficult to measure. The "future service" asset poses problems very similar to those of fixed asset depreciation. The "past service" asset, if it exists, poses problems similar to those of goodwill amortization. The pattern of amortization of the "future service" asset is established by choosing an actuarial cost method. A method which records pension expense in proportion to employee earnings may result in the most accurate asset and

---

[11] *Ibid.*, pp. 73–74.

income figures. the "past service" asset is as difficult to value as goodwill. It may be desirable to develop one rule to cover all such difficult-to-measure assets.

David Solomons is Professor of Accounting at the Wharton School, University of Pennsylvania.

Accounting Problems and Some Proposed Solutions

David Solomons

We have left far behind us the classical concept of "the firm" as an entrepreneurial unit controlled by its profit-maximizing owner or owners, operating in a geographically restricted area, and supplying a single product in response to a given demand. The modern corporation bears little resemblance to this simple picture. It operates on a world-wide scale; it markets thousands of products; and it does not accept demand as given but creates and controls it, within limits, through marketing expenditures.

Its diversification is one of the most striking respects in which the large modern corporation differs from the classical model of the firm, and the trend in this direction shows no sign of slowing down. Indeed, to the extent that it is reflected in the number of mergers and acquisitions which are reported, it seems to be gathering momentum. There were 2,377 mergers reported in 1966, while 1,416 were reported in the first half of 1967, with a predicted total for the year of 2,600. Many of these mergers undoubtedly have diversification as their main motive, both as regards products handled and geographical areas served.

While it is easy to distinguish conceptually between diversification of the evolutionary type, where new products or businesses are added as natural developments of the old, and diversification through the acquisition of unre-

David Solomons, "Accounting Problems and Some Proposed Solutions" in Alfred Rappaport, Peter A. Firmin, and Stephen A. Zeff, *Public Reporting by Conglomerates: The Issues, the Problems, and Some Possible Solutions,* © 1968. Reprinted by permission of Prentice-Hall, Inc., Englewood Cliffs, N.J.

lated businesses, it is not so easy in practice to say whether a particular addition falls into one category or the other. The expansion of the Columbia Broadcasting System and its affiliates is a case in point. The line from CBS radio to Columbia records, and hence to the Columbia Record Club seems natural enough, and so does the line between television and films. Broadcasting and musical instruments are not wholly unrelated, so the acquisition in recent years of companies making violin strings, guitars, and drums can be explained. The Columbia Record Club's mailing list might reasonably explain the group's recent move into the mail-order business through the acquisition of Sunset House. But can the acquisition of Holt Rinehart be regarded as a natural development on the ground that broadcasting and publishing are both concerned with communication? And is the acquisition by CBS of the New York Yankees natural because they are both in the entertainment business? It is just as easy to answer Yes as No to these questions.

Definition of Conglomerate Unnecessary

Though it seems commonly to be thought that the true conglomerate, resulting from a series of acquisitions, presents a more acute and urgent problem of financial reporting than does the other case, which might be called "volutionary diversification," in fact it is much easier to legislate for it. It is clear that the less closely related the various activities of a corporation are, the easier it is to account for each of them separately. The difficult problems are those relating to the allocation of common costs and of shared assets and the treatment of inter-divisional transactions. Obviously the more disparate the activities of the divisions are, the fewer costs and assets they will share, and the fewer transactions they will have with each other. Fortunately, therefore, the investor's most acute need—the unscrambling of the results of the substantially unrelated activities of the true conglomerate—is also the easiest to meet, as the Chairman of the SEC recognized in his statement, in September 1966, to the Senate Subcommittee on Anti-Trust and Monopoly.

Unlike some of those who gave evidence before the Senate Subcommittee,[1] or who have discussed the matter since, I see no reason to attempt to define a conglomerate, or to distinguish in any clear-cut way between the two types of diversification. It surely cannot be contemplated that any new disclosure requirements would be imposed on the conglomerates but not on other diversified companies. The investors' needs are much the same, however diversification comes about; and in any case, after a few years, acquired subsidiaries are just as much "part of the family" as new ventures which are developed internally. Any new disclosure requirements, it seems to me, must

---

[1] For a discussion of this evidence, see A. A. Sommer, Jr., "Conglomerate Disclosure: Friend or Foe?," *supra*, pp. 1–16.

be drafted in general terms, so as to apply to all companies; but different companies would be differently affected by them, according to their degree of diversification and, as I shall suggest, their internal structure.

Objectivity vs. Relevance

Other participants in this symposium will have weighed the benefits and costs of reporting financial results by company segments. In considering the methods by which such reporting may most effectively be done, it is important to keep before us the main purpose to be attained, namely, the enhancement of the predictive value of accounting information which is likely to result when the past and current performance of each segment of a business is known rather than just the overall results. If some of the resulting figures (e.g., some expense allocations) are not completely objective, this is no reason for denying the usefulness of the results. The trade-off between objectivity and relevance in accounting is going on all the time, and there is nothing unusual in the discovery that to increase the relevance of reported company results there has to be some sacrifice of objectivity.

Some writers in this field seem to be concerned, too, at the absence of "generally accepted accounting principles" relating to segmental reporting. But if this were to be considered fatal, accounting would have to stagnate, for if new developments had to await general acceptance before they could be introduced, most of them would be still-born. Let us get on and resolve the problems of segmental reporting, for out of the ferment, the general acceptance of some solutions as being better than others may be expected to result.

A Question of Equity

There is a question of equity between companies which calls for early recognition, for it has a bearing on the solution of the problems under discussion. Mr. Manuel Cohen drew attention to one aspect of it, in the statement to which I have already referred, when he pointed out that a percentage test as to what constituted a segment the results of which must be separately stated might allow a large division of a very large company to escape disclosure because it was a small part of the whole, while a much smaller division of a smaller company might be required to disclose its results because percentage-wise it formed an important part of its company's business. Issues of equity also arise in connection with the information which it is decided shall

---

[2] Cf. Professor Robert K. Mautz, in his article, "Conglomerate Reporting and Data Reliability," *Financial Executive*, 35, No. 9, September 1967, p. 31. "There are at present no generally accepted principles of accounting related to the allocation of common costs among segments of a company ... if management, in allocating common costs, has used assumptions entirely appropriate to its purposes, on what basis does the independent accountant find them faulty? ... until 'generally accepted principles' of allocations for external reporting are established, how does he show the impropriety of what may be quite rational assumptions?"

be disclosed. For instance, if companies were required to leave central administration and research expenses unallocated, as a pool of expense to be covered out of divisional contributions to overhead and profit, companies which had delegated most functions to divisions would show relatively small divisional contributions as compared with those who had delegated fewer functions and who had large corporate administrative and research staffs. The divisional "profits" of these latter companies would look relatively high. This result is not always palatable to the companies concerned, as the pharmaceutical industry, with its heavy basic research expenditure, will testify.

The fact is, of course, that a grave inequity is perpetrated by *not* requiring the reporting of segmental results, for companies making a narrow line of products may feel at a disadvantage compared with more diversified companies. A good example is Maytag, specializing in home laundry equipment. Its principal competitors are no more than subdivisions of the major appliance division of companies like General Electric, Westinghouse, and the Frigidaire Division of General Motors. Maytag's results are of considerable interest to the home laundry subdivisions of these companies, wheras Maytag can learn little from its competitor's accounts.

It is doubtful, of course, whether any product-line reporting which is likely to be required of its competitors in the foreseeable future would benefit Maytag, because even if G.E., Westinghouse, and the others disclose figures for major appliances, home laundry equipment will probably be merged with dishwashers, refrigerators, ranges, and other appliances. Except for a prospective entry into the dishwasher market, Maytag does not handle these other appliances.

Behind these questions of equity between company and company lie the two fundamental questions which call for answer:

1. What is the reporting unit to be, for which diversified companies must separately disclose results? What is the relevant segment that we should like to isolate?
2. What information is to be disclosed?

Neither of these questions admits of easy answer, and most of the discussion hitherto has been more concerned with asking questions and pointing out difficulties rather than with offering solutions. It is more fun to ask questions than to give answers. But perhaps by now we have enough questions and should turn to look for the answers.

Segments of Various Kinds

Bearing in mind that the purpose of requiring the reporting of company results by segments is to put investors in a position to make better informed investment decisions, it can be argued that any aspect of a business, separate information about which would materially influence an investor, ought to be the subject of separate reporting. There is no logical reason for being satisfied with divisions or product lines as the sole basis for segmental reporting. *Where* a company does business is of great concern to its stockholders and potential stockholders, also, especially when an important part of its business is done abroad. Reporting earnings by geographical source is an accounting service which investors should welcome.

Geographical segments of a business are as difficult to isolate as any other kind of segment. The problems of shared expenses and assets and of intersegmental transactions are always with us. But though entirely satisfactory solutions to these problems have not yet been found and perhaps finally cannot be, an increasing number of companies are already distinguishing in their financial statements between the results of domestic business and overseas business. As recently reported by Professors Berg, Mueller, and Walker, of the University of Washington,[3] in an admittedly small and statistically non-random sample of large U.S. companies having a substantial amount of foreign business, only two out of twenty companies gave no financial information about their international business. Fifteen of the twenty gave either dollar figures for net sales abroad or the percentage of total net sales made in international markets; and twelve gave either dollar figures for foreign net earnings or the percentage of total net earnings derived from international markets. The authors report considerable lack of uniformity in defining these terms and in arriving at the reported results, the differences of practice relating principally to the treatment of export sales from the U.S. and the way in which the activities of non-consolidated international subsidiaries were handled. However, the important point is that the investor's interest in the geographical source of his present and prospective dividends is recognized by most of these companies, and his need for something more detailed than total consolidated earnings is on the way to being met. A more detailed geographical breakdown than that between the U.S. (or in some cases North America) and the rest of the world is only the next step, and one already taken by some companies.

There is one troublesome aspect of this type of segmental reporting which differentiates it from product-line reporting and which was much discussed in Britain during the recent debates over the new Companies Act there, in connection with the Act's requirement that companies shall report the value of goods exported.[4] In Britain the main motive seems to have been to give publicity to companies which were making a full contribution to the improvement of the balance of payments situation. More rationally, one could argue that investors should know how their company's fortunes are likely to be affected by developments in various parts of the world. The difficulty is

---

[3] "Annual Reports Go International," *Journal of Accountancy*, August 1967, pp. 59–64.

[4] Companies Act 1967, sec. 20.

that a company may be exporting *indirectly*, without knowing it, by selling material to another company at home which then exports it in the form of a manufactured product or otherwise.

The British solution was to require direct export sales to be reported, leaving companies free to give additional information about indirect exports, if they were able to and so wished, in the directors' report to stockholders or the Chairman's speech. This seems a sensible procedure. Thus a hotel chain, with no direct exports, might well report how many visitors from foreign countries it had accommodated, and what it thought its earnings from them had been. The stockholders could hardly fail to be better informed as a result.

Yet another type of segmental reporting which investors might find useful would be between business transacted by a company with private customers and business transacted with public authorities at local, state, and federal levels. One obvious reason for wanting such information would be to assess a company's dependence on defense activity, and to estimate the impact which an outbreak of peace might have on it. Unfortunately again, as with export sales, sales to public authorities might be made at one or more removes, as a sub-contractor rather than as a prime contractor, and perhaps without the company even knowing to what use and to whose use its products were being put. It would be easy enough to require companies to report separately sales which they know to be destined directly or indirectly for public use, and earnings thereon. For the reason already mentioned, complete objectivity and precision, even in reporting sales, would not always be possible; but even if only direct sales to the public sector were reported, the investor would surely be better informed than if such figures were not disclosed.

To anyone who thinks that divisions or product groups are the only kind of sub-entity worth bothering about for reporting purposes, this discussion will look like a digression. However, the point should be emphasized that there are many dimensions to the question of reporting sub-entity results, and information which may be useful to the stockholders of one company may not be useful to those of another. However, it is probably safe to say that if satisfactory ways to report divisional results can be found, some of these other problems will be solved as by-products. For instance, work on defense contracts by large companies tends to be concentrated in a small number of divisions, and though some government work may be found in all divisions, the bulk of it will be found in a few. Thus the disclosure of divisional results will also show where the impact of government activity falls most heavily.

How Is the Reporting Unit to Be Defined?

The first question about divisional reporting to be settled is how the reporting unit is to be defined. Should the financial statements presented to the

SEC and to stockholders be allowed to follow a company's own organizational structure, reporting as a division (or, in the case of some very large companies, a group of divisions) whatever the company calls a division or group? The Chairman of the SEC does not (or, at least, did not) think so for he said, in his statement to the Senate Subcommittee, "Clearly the unit indicated on a corporate organization chart will not always be acceptable." The only alternative I have seen suggested is that companies should be required to report their results in accordance with some more or less broad standard classification such as the Standard Industry Code of the Census Bureau. The main argument for this proposal is, of course, that it would facilitate inter-company comparisons, segment by segment.

I do not like this suggestion. I think that a company should be free to choose whatever divisional or departmental structure it thinks most suitable to its circumstances, and having chosen it, it is natural that the accounting statements prepared for the guidance of management should follow and reflect this structure. If these statements, as we must presume, are the best that management can produce to guide their own decisions, then there is an initial presumption that the same statements, or less detailed versions of them, are likely best to serve the investor in making his investment and disinvestment decisions. Whether the same can be said about labor unions and government agencies, in the use they make of a company's financial statements, is perhaps doubtful. But our focus, in this discussion, had better be on the interests of the stockholders, at least initially.

The use of the Standard Industrial Code or anything like it as a basis of financial reporting to stockholders is unattractive for several reasons. It would represent a major departure from any existing practice for, as Mr Cohen points out, the Code is applied for statistical purposes by the Census Bureau to individual plants, not to companies, and in any case it is used only as a classification of output, not earnings. It bears little or no relation to the way that most companies keep their own accounting records, so that to adopt it as a basis for external reporting would mean that companies would have to choose between a non-preferred basis of cost and revenue classification and keeping duplicate records, one for SEC purposes and one for their own. Neither alternative is desirable. Moreover, unless by accident the standard classification corresponds to a company's own divisional organization, or unless the SEC is to be content with the reporting of gross margins on product lines, leaving all overhead unallocated, then a reporting system which departs so radically from the company's own internal structure must call for a proliferation of arbitrary expense allocations. In the result, therefore, there might be a gain in inter-company comparability; but the results being compared would have lost significance in the process.

The inclusion of "always" in Mr. Cohen's statement makes it impossible to disagree with it *in toto*; but I should hope that there would be few instances where the company's own organization could not be accepted as the basis for financial reporting. However, this view carries with it the corollary that the company has an obligation to explain its organization and to describe the activities of its divisions. The better annual reports to stockholders already do this. Companies could also be required to certify that the classifications used in their financial statements correspond with the principal centers of profit responsibility recognized in the company's internal structure, and this certificate could be corroborated by the auditors, who would naturally have become familiar with the company's structure in the course of their duties.

Whatever definition of product line or division is chosen, there will be problems. The question has been asked whether General Motors would be expected to report sales and earnings separately for their five passenger car lines because these cars are marketed by separate divisions, or whether the relevant category would be passenger cars as a whole.[5] If the Standard Industrial Code were used as the basis of accounting, no distinction would be drawn between one General Motors brand and another. This is one example where following the company's organization chart relentlessly would lead to more detailed financial reporting than would the use of a standard statistical classification, and perhaps more detailed reporting than stockholders would find useful. Of course the number of vehicles sold by each division of the major automobile manufacturers is already made known publicly each quarter, in any case. The General Motors case perhaps suggests the need for a company to be able to apply to the SEC for some relaxation of the rule I have put forward, that the classifications used in the company's financial statements should correspond with the principal centers of profit responsibility which it recognizes, where this would call for an unreasonable degree of disclosure. It would be most regrettable if any accounting regulations, because of their inflexibility, were to lead a company to change its internal organization and control procedures simply in order to avoid a degree of disclosure it thought unwarranted.

Another related question which Mr. Cohen asks is "how important a particular division must be in the overall picture of a company before separate earnings figures should be required." His reasons for regarding a percentage test alone as unsatisfactory have already been mentioned. The answer seems to be to use a two-prong test based on net sales. Any division which had net sales of more than $X *or* whose net sales to outside customers represented more than Y% of the company total would be required to be separately reported, with the net earnings therefrom. Companies would of course be left free to use lower limits, with consequently more detailed reporting. Presumably the SEC is only concerned with *minimum* standards of disclosure. But this would still leave a loophole for companies which would like to avoid reporting divisional results, for we have not yet defined

---

[5]Sommer, *loc. cit.*, p. 11.

the distinguishing characteristic of a division. If sufficient heterogeneity in a division's activities is allowed, the whole concept of a divisional structure becomes eroded; and if a very high degree of homogeneity is demanded (so as, for instance to split an electric lamp division into two, one making incandescent lamps and the other the fluorescent variety), then by means of a finer and finer breakdown, all "divisions" could become small enough to swim through the net of reporting requirements. It would be a mistake to try to legislate for this too closely. Few companies surely would seriously distort their managerial structures merely to evade some reporting regulations; and assuming this to be so, it seems enough to rely on the directors' certificate, already suggested, to the effect that the financial statements (with attached notes and schedules, of course) reflect the principal centers of profit responsibility recognized by the company's management structure. But to backstop this arrangement, let the SEC have powers to question the correspondence between the financial reports and the management structure, and as a last resort, if it is not satisfied, let it have the power to require that the company present its financial report in accordance with some approved standard classification. This sanction should be enough to keep companies in line.

Accounting Procedures for Segmental Reporting

The SEC has always shown a commendable reluctance to impose particular accounting methods on companies or to veto methods it did not like if it could avoid doing so. It is to be hoped that it will continue to take this approach to the problem of determining divisional sales and especially divisional profits. The emphasis should be on seeing that companies disclose the accounting procedures they have used in arriving at the results reported, rather than on dictating what those procedures should be.

In accordance with this approach, which would permit wide latitude in the choice of accounting method at the price of full disclosure of what has been done, it is unnecessary to prescribe, for example, whether and in what way central research or administrative expenditures are to be allocated to divisions, so long as a company makes clear how it has handled these expenses. Most discussion of the difficulties of segmental reporting has centered on this question of the allocation of corporate expenses, without much regard to their quantitative importance. In fact, they do not often represent more than 5 percent of a company's total expenditures; but even so, they may constitute a substantial proportion of a division's net income, and certainly enough to change the picture of a division's profitability.

Many different ways of handling these non-divisional expenses can be devised. A uniform basis for allocating them in total, to be used by all companies, could be laid down by the SEC; or a different uniform basis for each category of expense could be imposed on all companies; or uniform bases for each category of expense could be laid down, industry by industry, with a different set of bases for each industry—if anyone can devise a way of assigning a conglomerate to an industry; or any allocation in external reports could be prohibited, leaving divisional net earnings to be shown as contributions to corporate expenses and net profits; or companies could be left free to choose their own way of presenting the facts of the situation, as they see them, on condition, of course, that they explain clearly what they have done. I have already expressed my own preference for the last of these courses. I am also optimistic enough to think that, before long, good methods of handling this problem will drive out bad, and a large measure of uniformity will be secured without the need for regulations.

Besides the treatment of corporate expenses, there is quite a list of items, in fact, which will need to be the subject of explanatory notes. A few of these items will be mentioned shortly. But even taking a latitudinarian approach such as is advocated here, there is a need to prescribe one or two rules in the interest of uniformity. We can leave a broad area for individual freedom and yet stop well short of anarchy.

Inter-Divisional Transfers

One such rule would relate to inter-divisional sales. There are at least three possibilities as to how divisional sales might be reported. One is to report total sales by divisions, combining sales to outside customers and to other divisions. A second is to report inter-divisional sales and outside sales separately. The third is to eliminate inter-divisional sales, reporting only sales to outsiders. It is equally easy to adopt any one of these alternatives, but the best procedure seems to be to eliminate inter-divisional sales from reports to stockholders. This is really equivalent to saying that all materials or products transferred between divisions shall be transferred at cost, including a proportionate share of overhead. The result will be to leave each division to bear the cost of goods sold to outside customers, and it would report sales to outsiders and the costs thereof.

As a consequence of this procedure, important divisions which work mainly or perhaps wholly for other divisions of the company—the Fisher Body Division of General Motors might be an example—would disappear from the financial report, except to the extent that they had sales to outside customers. All earnings would be attributed to the divisions which market the final products. The result would be the same as if all stages of making the final product were carried on in the end-product division. For the purposes of financial reporting to stockholders, this is not at all an unsatisfactory result, whatever may be thought about it from a managerial point of view. It brings together in one place the profit which the company has extracted from a particular market—the market for Chevrolets, for instance, or all passenger cars, depending on how closely the financial statements follow the organization chart—without regard to the way the company has chosen to organize the manufacturing facilities used to serve this market.

If at first sight this appears to be inconsistent with the view put forward earlier, that the reporting regulations should conflict as little as possible with the accounting needs of the company's own management structure, a closer look will show that transfers only exist because products are made by one division and marketed by another. Only if all transfers could be valued at market prices established in perfectly competitive markets would it be possible to set up an external reporting system which gave the stockholder objective figures of divisional earnings which were consistent with the way that the company organized both its production and its marketing activities. But since such a basis for transfer prices is not always available, a choice has to be made. Pricing transfers at cost has the effect of attributing all profits to marketing activities, so the reporting system is made to conform closely to at least that side of the company's profile.

Where transfers of services take place between divisions, these should also be accounted for at cost. This is already an almost universal practice, and enforcing this as a rule for external reporting purposes should not give rise to any problems.

Pricing transfers at cost (including divisional overhead) means, of course, pricing them at average cost. To the extent that a division's cost of goods sold includes transfers from other divisions, therefore, it cannot be said that the division's profit—or even its gross margin—represents the diminution in corporate profit which the company would suffer if the division were closed down, nor will its results, by simple extrapolation, indicate the effect on corporate profitability of an expansion or contraction of the division's operations. The reason for this is that, since the cost of transfers charged to the transferee division includes costs which are fixed from the point of view of the transferer division and therefore from the corporation's point of view as well, the company's total costs will not increase proportionately with an increase in the volume of transfers taken by the transferee division.

This conclusion may be disappointing to those who think that it is easy to provide investors with measures of divisional contributions to corporate profitability. It is not easy, for this and for other reasons which will be referred to later. But there is no cause to be unduly discouraged merely because divisional results are subject to the same limitations as are the corporate results. No one expects corporate net profits to bear a constant relationship to sales, and therefore to be capable of prediction from a simple extrapolation of sales. At the most, the use of average cost for pricing transfers to a division simply extends to the measure of divisional results the limitations which already apply to the corporate results.

It is worth adding that, in the majority of diversified companies, interdivisional transfers are small in amount when compared with sales to outside customers, and it is easy to exaggerate the difficulty which they put in the way of measuring divisional performance. There are many companies in which the whole question could be forgotten without any serious distortion of the accounting results; and the broader the company segment which is chosen as the reporting unit, the more likely is this to be so.

Taxes on Divisional Earnings

Another matter about which it seems more appropriate to prescribe a procedure rather than simply to require disclosure as to a company's own choice of procedure is the treatment of taxes on divisional earnings. Stockholders are interested in having an approximation of the contribution which each division makes to the company's fortunes, so that it is divisional after-tax earnings which should be shown. It is not enough to divide up the corporate tax bill between divisions in proportion to their before-tax earnings, unless the same relationship between accounting profits and taxable profits exists for all divisions. If it does, there is no need to allocate taxes to divisions. If it does not—if, for example, some divisions attract depletion allowances and others do not—then taxes should be charged to divisions as nearly as possible in accordance with the amounts they would bear if they were separate businesses; and if a division shows a net loss, the tax relief which the company will enjoy as a result should be credited to it.

It has been pointed out to me that most divisions which attract depletion allowances are likely to be divisions making intermediate products for transfer to other divisions. This is probably true. If inter-divisional sales are eliminated from the financial statements, as was suggested above, then the income-tax charges or allowances relating to these intermediate divisions will have to be charged or credited to the divisions which market their products, in proportion to the value of transfers taken by each end-product division. This treatment seems to be consistent with the rationale of the treatment of inter-divisional transactions already proposed, in that it brings together in one place all of the profit extracted from a particular market, regardless of the manner in which the company chooses to divide up the responsibility for its production and marketing activities.

Other Matters to Be Disclosed

Perhaps there are other matters relating to divisional accounting for which procedures should be prescribed by the SEC; but it is to be hoped that the list of rules could be kept to a minimum. The price to be paid for this relative freedom from regulation is maximum disclosure as to the bases used in arriving at divisional sales and earnings. The need for an explanatory note about the treatment of central administrative and research expenditures has already been mentioned. Other matters which need to be explained to stockholders if the significance of divisional earnings is to be understood include the following:

1. Any charges which have been made by corporate headquarters to divisions for services, interest on capital, occupancy of premises or the like, and how any such charges have been computed.

2. If the recommendation made above that inter-divisional transfers should be accounted for at cost is not adopted, it will be necessary to explain how they have been valued and charged for. Generally, where transfers are not made at actual cost, the basis used will be either at market price, where one exists, or at market price less the selling expenses saved on internal sales, or at standard cost or some variant thereof. Occasionally incremental cost is used, but this is rare. The explanatory note on transfer prices may have to be somewhat lengthy, unless uniform procedures are used throughout the company, not an entirely common situation. This reinforces, perhaps, the case for eliminating transfers from the financial reports by accounting for them at cost.

3. The treatment of all non-operating gains and losses, such as gains and losses on the disposal of fixed assets, fairly attributable to particular divisions should be explained, especially if they have not been credited or charged thereto.

It will be said that to leave so many accounting matters to be decided by a company's management will greatly increase accounting disuniformity and impair comparability between companies, and to some this seems to outweigh everything else.[6] This I believe to be a short-sighted view. The most important quality in an accounting statement is the degree of correspondence between the picture it presents and the facts of the situation it represents. Comparability with other statements is a secondary, not a primary quality, and it will no doubt develop as we gain experience of segmental reporting. So long as each company discloses its methods and follows them consistently, investors cannot fail to be better informed, even if uniformity between companies suffers in the short run. In any case, the serious consequences of disuniformity flow from the failure of companies to disclose their accounting methods rather than from the differences among the methods themselves.

Reporting Divisional Investment

The demand for divisional or product-line reporting does not stop at the reporting of sales and earnings. Investment or capital employed in each

---

[6] This seems to be the view, for instance, of Mr. Keith Goodrich, as expressed in his article, "Executive's View of Corporate Reporting Responsibilities," in *The Financial Executive*, 34, No. 12, December 1966, esp. p. 20.

division must also be shown if stockholders are to be informed about the rate of return on investment from each division. Here again, companies have a good many choices open to them as to how divisional investment is to be computed, and the important thing is that the particular set of choices which have been made should be explained. Most fixed assets can be allocated directly to divisions, leaving usually only the corporate office building and the central research facilities, which are best left unallocated. Inventories and receivables are usually capable of direct allocation also. The company's cash balance is a function of many considerations, some of them unrelated to divisional behavior. It can well be left unallocated, as should any outside investments held by the company.

In computing the investment base for *corporate* Return on Investment calculations, a choice has to be made between using stockholders' investment or total investment. Whatever choice is made for corporate purposes, in comparing *divisional* rates of return it seems best to use total divisional assets as the investment base. In any case, the treatment accorded these matters in the company's financial statements needs to be explained.

There is one respect in which it is easier to compute the investment base for external reporting purposes than it is when the purpose is management appraisal. When top management uses Return on Investment as a measure of the performance of divisional management, the distinction between the expenses and assets which are controllable at divisional level and those which are not is important, and it is not always an easy distinction to draw. For the purposes of external reporting, however, it is the performance of a division's business, not of its management, which is of primary interest, and controllability at levels of management below the top is not a relevant consideration.

The Impact of Divisions on Each Other

It is the impact of divisions on each other which gives rise to some of the subtlest problems of performance measurement in a divisionalized business, problems which in the present state of the art are more often sidestepped than solved. For instance, a division produces a material both for its own use (or for sale to outside customers) and for another division. The quantity taken by the transferee division enables the producing division to spread its overhead and reduce its average unit cost. If transfers are made at cost, there will be no routine accounting measure, in the accounts of either division, of the benefit to the producing division from the economies of scale resulting from the production it transfers to the other division.

Inter-divisional benefits flow, too, when one side of a company's business brings revenue to one of its other activities. We have seen this exemplified recently in the scramble by the airlines to acquire or build hotels in countries which they serve. The ownership of Intercontinental Hotels by PanAm and of a large number of Hilton Hotels by TWA are the best known examples of this kind of integration. There is no doubt that some of the income generated for the group by the airline will show up in the accounts of the hotels, and some of the income generated by the hotels will take the form of increased sales of airline tickets. Some of these benefits of integration will no doubt remain with the division that generates them through commissions charged by one division to another on business brought in. But it is also certain that there will be more indirect benefits which will not be traced to their source.

Many other examples of this kind of integrated diversification could be cited. The Hilton Hotel Corporation is said to be considering going into the automobile rental business. Bell & Howell, already important in the field of visual aids for education, is going into educational publishing. The New York Central Railroad has recently expanded its hotel interests. There will be inter-divisional benefits from these developments for which no precise accounting is likely to be possible in the foreseeable future.

Conclusion

I draw attention to this matter to deflate any exaggerated hopes that divisional or product-line reporting will give stockholders accurate information about the contribution which each segment of a company's business is making to its fortunes; and the same point has already been made in connection with the pricing of inter-divisional transfers. To recognize this limitation is not to surrender the case for reporting segmental results. If we were to be satisfied with nothing less than perfect accuracy in the field of profit measurement, we should have to abandon the task altogether. But with all its shortcomings, no one can doubt that the investing public, though sometimes misled by accounting failures, is on balance immeasurably better off with the financial reports which it gets than it would be without them. And so it will be when segmental or divisional reporting becomes the rule rather than, as now, the exception.

5. NEW DIMENSIONS TO ACCOUNTING THEORY

In earlier sections of this book an attempt was made to point out the numerous branches of accounting theory currently being developed. This section presents some new dimensions which pervade all branches of accounting theory development and verification. The articles selected for this section provide the reader with some idea of the impact these new dimensions are making on accounting.

We have identified four specific areas for our purposes here: (1) the measurement of social change, (2) the relationship of the behavioral sciences to accounting, (3) empirical verification of accounting theories, and (4) efficient markets theory. Each of these topics is destined to appear often in future literature. These readings should provide a basis for dealing with the topics as their influence on accounting theory increases.

The first article, by C. West Churchman, discusses the measurement problems associated with decisions involving social change. He builds his arguments and discussions around the question of whether to build an airport runway in the place of an old historic church. One cannot help better understanding this significant problem of measuring social change after reading the article.

The second reading, from a report by the AAA Committee on Behavioral Science, Content of Accounting Curriculum, is related to the scope and content of the behavioral science areas and their relationships to accounting. The committee curriculum suggestions have been omitted, and their review is recommended for a better understanding of the report. The accounting profession is just beginning to appreciate the relationship of the behavioral sciences to accounting.

The third article, by Thomas H. Williams and Charles H. Griffin, compares the verification methodology of accounting theory with that developed in the physical and social sciences. They direct their attention to the accounting theory that is to be verified and the procedures and propositions that are currently being subjected to empirical verification.

The final article in this section is by Nicholas J. Gonedes. It demonstrates the possible use of the efficient markets hypothesis to evaluate and prescribe accounting outputs. The article includes a commentary on the efficient markets model and a discussion of aggregate market behavior with respect to both accounting and nonaccounting data.

*C. West Churchman is Professor of Business
Administration and Research Philosopher at
the University of California, Berkeley.*

On the Facility, Felicity, and Morality of Measuring Social Change

C. West Churchman

In a recent unpublished paper entitled "Questions of Metric," Stafford Beer cites some letters to the *London Times* addressed to a question of social change. The issue concerned the seven hundred years old Norman Church of St. Michael of Stewkley, which stands square in the middle of a possible runway of a possible Third London Airport—not by design surely. A cost benefit analysis had been made by a commission for each alternative site of the proposed airport. In the instance of St. Michael's Church, the commission had used the extant fire insurance policy on the church as the base. This method of analysis caused considerable anger among antiquarians throughout the United Kingdom. A Mr. Osborn suggested instead that one should take the initial investment, say 100 pounds in 1182, and discount it at 10 percent per annum to 1982; the approximate result is a one followed by 33 zeros—a mere decillion pounds. As Beer points out, if you adopt either cost-benefit strategy, you automatically decide the issue. If you use the fire insurance approach, the church is virtually an irrelevant consideration in the decision of where to build the airport; whereas if you use the discount

This paper was presented on August 18, 1970 at the annual meeting of the American Accounting Association in College Park, Maryland. This research was supported in part by the National Aeronautics and Space Administration under General Grant #NGL 05-003-012 under the University of California.

Reprinted by permission of the author and published from *The Accounting Review*, Vol. XLVI, January, 1971, pp. 30-35.

approach, the church is all that matters: it is inconceivable that one should build the runway there.

What I found most significant about this story of measuring proposed social change was the ease with which both the commission and Mr. Osborn were able to assign numbers. The facility is clearly a product of the history of enterprising accountants and economists, people who have spent their lives assigning numbers to social changes. So facile has the process become that so long as there is a hint of reasonableness, the numbers themselves carry the conviction of their accuracy. And both the commission and Mr. Osborn seem to have a plausible viewpoint. The commission might argue as follows: evidently, people do value St. Michael of Stewkley, in the sense that they are willing to pay a price for its value in the event that it is destroyed. This value is clearly represented by the amount of fire insurance they are willing to subscribe to, because the only reward for paying the premium is the expectation of a return provided the church is destroyed. Mr. Osborn, on the other hand, might argue that an investment was made in the year 1182, which could instead have been deposited in the yet-to-be Bank of England. Cashing in on the investment in 1982 would be like "cashing in" on the church to build a runway in 1982; assuming rational decision making, the total imputed value of the investment cannot be greater than the current value of the church.

My main point is that the facility of assigning numbers means that only a modicum of plausibility is needed to convince people that the numbers represent reality. In both of the cases cited, just a little more thinking would have ruined the case. All one has to do is apply Immanuel Kant's moral law, which, paraphrased, says that if a particular principle is used to measure social change for policy making, then this principle should be universally applied. The principle, of course, may contain reasoned exceptions and stipulations, but once it is enunciated, it ought to be applicable to all instances, or else it is basically unfair, i.e., immoral. Now the commission's principle seems to read as follows: whenever there is a positive value (benefit) to destroying an object X, then the cost of destruction is to be computed by using the extant fire or life insurance as a base. The commission's policy, if universalized, would neatly solve the population problem. There is surely a value in not having all the people which the demographers predict will be here in the year 2000 if nothing is done to prevent it. So—merely calculate the benefit of eliminating X and compare it with X's life insurance! The result is that only the best will survive—the Kennedys and the Onassises. Mr. Osborn's principle, on the other hand, is very nice for old criminals and professors: the investment in their birth for hospitals, nurses and doctors discounted to age 70 would make the decision to execute or retire unthinkable.

The two examples, then, are silly. So why mention them? Why, just to challenge any number assigners to come up with a better method, based on a principle which will pass Kant's test. More to the point, the examples clearly show how number assignment is based on very strong value and reality assumptions.

Suppose for the moment that we look at the reality aspect of measuring social change. We'd surely like to say that a measurement should reflect what really occurs. But what does this stipulation mean? We could make its meaning clear if somehow or other we could get outside the measuring system and what it is trying to measure. If we could do this, then we'd say to ourselves, "There's reality R in its box, and when R changes it sends a message or impulse to the measuring system M in its box. Since we're outside all this, and can observe it accurately, let's see if the numbers generated by M accurately correspond to the changes in R." We'd certainly have to fuss over the criteria of accurate correspondence, but that would be a technical matter we could hand over to some of the brilliant minds who like to fuss with these matters.

But of course this way of describing reality doesn't work at all, as any auditor knows. It isn't sufficient to stipulate that a good audit has occurred if a second party testifies that the auditor's numbers correspond to reality, because the second party may belong to the auditor's firm, or a competitor's firm, or the broad class of the inexperienced. To make any sense at all of this way of defining reality, we have to set down the stipulations of the competent, disinterested observer,[1] which as experienced auditors know, is no easy task. To accomplish the task we need a fairly elaborate theory of competence and honesty. So here is the same theme again: to know that we are measuring real change we need to have a strong theoretical base.

But suppose now that we do succeed in finding a satisfactory basis for assessing competence and honesty. Would we then want to say that M is measuring real social change if a sufficiently large class of competent, disinterested observers agree that it is? *Why* should agreement imply that reality is being measured? Here I'd like to introduce a pragmatic principle at least as old as William James. If I tell you that the last book on the top shelf of my study's bookshelf is red, and I present affidavits of color competent observers which certify my account, have I described reality to you? No, said James, because the description makes no difference whatsoever in your behavior relative to your practical goals. To be real for you is to make a difference for you. If I'd said that the red book is that set of dull platitudes of Chairman Mao, then some of you might report me, or admire me more, or whatever, and then reality comes into being.

Suppose we go back to Stewkley where the British Division of the Cleveland Wrecking Company is about to smash a priceless glass window of St. Michael's. We want to measure this social change. "There goes 3,000

---

[1] "Independent" in CPA language.

pounds," says the commission, and could hardly care less. "There goes a decillion pounds," says Mr. Osborn, and could hardly care more. But what has really happened? If we employed the method suggested earlier, we would bring in our disinterested observer to decide which number accurately maps reality. He would say things like "20 windows were broken, each 700 years old," or, "it took two weeks to haul St. Michael's away at an expense of 1,472 pounds and a sixpence."

Such a disinterested observer, in fact, would be very like many experts who today are measuring social change. Consider, for example, the issue of population. Here beyond a doubt is social change. In Paul and Ann Ehrlich's *Population Resources Environment*,[2] we are told that the doubling rate of the world's population around 1970 is about 30 to 35 years, in 1930 was 45 years, in 1850, 200 years. The book contains a number of other numbers: food production, pollution production, and so on. All of these numbers say something about social change, but you will note that they are all very much like the disinterested observer of the smashing of St. Michael's. No doubt in both cases the reports may be a bit shocking, and in this sense they "make a difference." But the difference may have no pragmatic import whatsoever. The Ehrlichs have much to say about the number of people who will starve if things go on as at present. This is much like telling us that the round ball will break St. Michael's window unless its basic policy of motion is changed. Another disinterested observer, also using numbers, could tell us how many people felt sad and for how long when they learned about St. Michael's or the starving children of Biafra.

It is really astonishing how many crisis-numbers are being thrown at the public these days. They all describe what programmers call the rate of activity in a certain sector of society. Since often the rate of activity-pollution or poverty or information-spread yields uneasy or horrible feelings, people and politicians are apt to conclude that something must be done to lessen the rate, or even to make it negative. But even if the disinterested observer is telling us about real impending disaster provided an activity continues to increase, it by no means follows that he is telling us about real social change in a pragmatic sense. The reality question is, "So what?" Only when we can measure in such a way that we know what to do about the result, only then will we measure social change.

The point I am trying to make is that the amount of change in some property of society or its environment by itself does not "measure" social change. What is needed besides is the basis of decision making which shows how the amount of change makes a difference. A good illustration is the so-called "protein gap," which very much interests the nutritionists these days. We are told,[3] for example, that a pregnant woman who lacks a sufficient

---

[2] W. H. Freeman and Co., San Francisco, 1970.

[3] See *International Action to Avert the Protein Crisis* (United Nations, New York, 1968).

amount of protein in her diet may well give birth to a deformed baby. We are also told that the amount of protein (note, again, the amount theme) in certain areas of the world is seriously deficient. What can be called the Fallacy of Filling the Gap immediately infers that we should produce and distribute more protein. Perhaps we should, but the protein gap by itself does not imply any such action. Besides a knowledge of the gap, we need to assume that the crisis warrants certain expenditures, that policies of making more protein will not introduce concomitant gaps and inequities in other areas, e.g., by changing the ecology of fish life. It so happens that protein is used as calories in calorie deficient diets, so that filling the protein gap by no means solves the nutritional problem. And so on.

Of course a profession may adopt a separatist philosophy to avoid the tremendous responsibility of measuring real social change in a pragmatic sense. The profession of accounting may say the same thing that many demographers say: "Look, we can't tell you what to do about the activity rate, but we can tell you what the rate is. We're like the speedometers on automobiles which measure changes in the car's velocity. The driver must decide what to do about a reading of eighty miles per hour." But the analogy doesn't work, for a very obvious reason: it's perfectly clear to both driver and auto designer that velocity is a critical aspect of the driving experience, and the method of correcting for too much or too little is also obvious. Given that we ought to drive automobiles if we want to, the speedometer is a great help and accurately measures social change. But the critical question is still there: ought we to drive automobiles? The speedometer is silent on this point. Given that we ought to reduce population by forcing every lady to take the pill, then the expert can or soon will tell us how to do the job. But the demographer is silent on the question whether we should so force pill taking.

The fallacy of the separatist philosophy is the one I mentioned earlier: once you begin to emphasize some aspect of real change by putting numbers on it, you may divert attention from the real issue. Consequently, I can't help but feel that the professions which try to place numbers on social change have the responsibility to go the entire way—to understand why the numbers make a difference and why the difference they make is the right difference.

For example, I believe the accounting profession should become deeply involved in helping society to measure the most critical aspects of social change—of pollution, population, information, whatever. But to do so, I think the profession will have to change some important traditional attitudes. It is to these social changes of the profession that I'd like to address the concluding remarks.[4]

In recent years, we have heard a great deal about how accounting and economics need to be enlarged to include "social indicators" or "social accounting." But I don't think the need is for more numbers, at all. The need

---

[4] To be sure, some changes have already been suggested.

is for the basis of justifying the numbers—the model or world view which tells us what difference the numbers make.

Decision-oriented accounting is quite different from accounting's traditional role in the private sector. Often the service which accounting has given is essentially comparisons: the accounts tell us how this period's costs, inventories, turn-over, profit, etc., compare with last period's. Comparative accounting is much like the rate-of-change of an activity mentioned earlier. It is useful if we know that the comparison makes a real difference in decision making, useless otherwise. Hence one basic change of attitude is towards finding a model for decision making. Of course, what I am saying is that the professions of operations research and accounting need to form a long-overdue alliance. But I think both professions will have to give up one cherished attitude—namely, the assurance of the expert. The "model" to which I referred is by no means easy to create, nor can any of us feel assured that a candidate model represents social reality. No longer can we call upon the disinterested, competent observer to settle our issues. There is no "outside" which can observe the "inside" trying to depict reality.

Returning to Stewkley once more, both the commission and Mr. Osborn had a model; there is no competent, disinterested observer to tell us which is right, if either. But is this so? Why not say as before that if a sufficiently large group of sufficiently competent experts agree, or—via the Delphi technique[5]—converge on agreement, then the model can be taken as representing reality? The answer, of course, is that to assume that a convergence of agreement of experts represents reality is to presuppose a fairly elaborate theory of the relationship between reality and expert knowledge, as well as a theory about how expert opinion is to be ascertained. Also assumed is our old friend the value judgment. Experts may tell us that in so-and-so many years we can expect brain-to-computer linkages and genetic engineering. This is like telling us that the population will double, the protein source will shrink, the air will be dangerously polluted. To repeat, what is left out of the expert's opinions is all we really need to know: what to do about it if they accurately portray a real trend.

No, if we are to serve society by measuring social change, I think we'll have to do so in an entirely different mode from the traditional one of being the separate, disinterested, and objective observers. These stipulations seem clear (to me):

1. We are not the only or even the basic methodology of assessing social change. There are other equally forceful methods: aesthetic, religious and political are three good examples.

2. We are not objective in the old-fashioned sense of "being apart," and "nonbiased." Our bias is based on our conception (world view) of how social reality works and what "makes a difference."

---

[5] Olaf Helmer, *Social Technology* (New York, Basic Books, 1966).

3. (My own bias.) In Beer's paper mentioned earlier, which has a very similar theme to this one but a radically different approach, Beer argues for a "meta" measuring system, one that measures the "eudomonia," or "prosperity," which is flowing through the social system. Beer approaches the problem in this manner because he likes to see the world as a flow, with feedbacks and other cybernetic devices. My bias is to look for the fiber of the system, the structure that ought to hold it together. This approach amounts to saying that we require an explicit moral base for measuring social change. Far more important than "agreement of experts" is the moral prescription which says that our measure should be based on a policy of moral universality—everyone to count as an end—and not a means only—a deep analysis of how people are affected by the difference the measure will make.

For example, Mr. Osborn was nearer to being right than the commission, but for the wrong reasoning. The point is not whether to discount from the past—but whether to discount into the future. I can see no moral justification in our saying that the numerical reward (joy, aesthetic pleasure, inspiration) of some future viewer of St. Michael's must be discounted back to present value, much as a future insurance premium would be—though I have some feeling-deficient friends who say just this: "The hell with the values of a generation as yet unborn, or at least 10% the hell per annum." So if we paint our world view with the Third London Airport as a temporary value for, say, thirty years of use and then no value thereafter, but St. Michael's will always bring joy to some thousands or so, then the cost number to be assigned to smashing the church is very large, because no future joy is to be discounted to present value on moral grounds.

Now there is no authority for my moral law, and many may disagree with it. Indeed, many should disagree with it, because the essence of moral discourse should be debate, not agreement. Anyone like myself who takes part in measuring social change must on the one hand declare and argue for his moral position, but should never on pain of displaying hubris, assume that he is the authority. So I declare and argue for the position that every social policy needs not only a cost-benefit number, but that the basic theory of assigning such a number should be revealed and assessed for its moral implications—i.e., whether if generalized it would imply a world where people are treated as ends rather than means only.

4. As number assigners we must be stubborn but not necessarily humorless. We will insist that the value of a life can be numbered and compared, no matter what our enemies say. So the population scarers may horrify us, but let us number the cost of a human starved to death. Of course, we can't be all that deadly serious about it, either. We should take on a lesson from Kenneth Boulding, who suggests that each citizen be assigned 22 deciles of a child, which he can sell on the open market place. This way the population will remain stable, assuming no bootlegging operations occur. You see, once we

give up the silly notion that numberers have the final answers, we can really enjoy ourselves now and then.

5. I hope the accounting profession will join other professional associations in looking at today's problems of society and suggesting some ways of assigning numbers to social change that make a difference—with all the humility, humor and purposefulness possible.

Report of the Committee on Behavioral Science Content of the Accounting Curriculum

The charge of this committee was to formulate a statement indicating the general scope of behavioral science material which should be included in the accounting curriculum and to suggest methods of incorporating such material into the curriculum. In developing this report, the committee operated within the context of two fundamental assumptions. First, it was assumed that accounting is action oriented; that most accounting reports are intended to provide information for decision-making. Unless accounting reports have the potential to influence decisions and actions, it is difficult to justify the cost of their preparation. For example, the standard of relevance as discussed in *A Statement of Basic Accounting Theory* requires that information ". . . must bear upon or be usefully associated with the action it is designed to facilitate or the result it is desired to produce. This requires that either the information or the act of communicating it exert influence or have the potential for exerting influence on the designated actions."[1] To state the matter concisely, the principal purpose of accounting reports is to influence action i.e. behavior. Additionally, it can be hypothesized that the very process of accumulating information, as well as the behavior of those who do the accumulating, will affect the behavior of others. In short, by its very nature, accounting is a behavioral process.

Our second assumption was that accounting education must provide some minimum awareness and knowledge of the behavioral implications of ac-

---

[1] Committee to Prepare a Statement of Basic Accounting Theory, *A Statement of Basic Accounting Theory* (Evanston, Ill.: American Accounting Association, 1966), p. 9.

Reprinted by permission of the publisher from *The Accounting Review*, Vol. XLVI, Supplement, 1971, pp. 247–260.

counting. This assumption is, of course, directly related to our first assumption. If accounting is, in fact, a behavioral process, then accounting education, by definition, should include appropriate attention to behavioral considerations. We doubt that this can be accomplished merely by requiring courses in those academic disciplines (psychology, sociology, etc.) usually identified as behavioral science. Though important in providing general background in behavioral theory, such courses cannot be expected to focus on the specific issues which may be most significant for accounting. Rather, relevant behavioral concepts and methods should be introduced and discussed within the accounting curriculum itself.

The foregoing assumptions provide the basis for the two major sections of this report. The first section presents a brief discussion of the scope and content of some behavioral science areas considered by the committee to be especially relevant to accounting. This discussion is not intended to provide either an extensive or intensive analysis of behavioral science topics. Its only purpose is to identify certain concepts which we believe should be of interest to accountants and to suggest an embarkation point for those readers who are interested in learning more about behavioral science. (Appendix A contains a bibliography which should be of assistance in this regard.)

The second section of the report contains examples of behavioral science materials which might be integrated into specific portions of the accounting curriculum. Again, we have not attempted to be all-inclusive but only to provide illustrations of how important behavioral concepts might be integrated into existing courses. Accounting instructors with some previous exposure to behavioral science will undoubtedly have their own preferences concerning the selection of such materials. But, it is our hope that those teachers who are relatively new to the area will find our suggestions helpful as a first step in incorporating behavioral concepts into their courses. Additionally, the appendices contain extensive bibliographical materials which should be useful for both teaching and research purposes.

Scope and Content of Behavioral Science

Behavioral Science Defined

The term *behavioral science* is of relatively recent coinage. The concept is so broad that it is desirable at the outset to attempt to delineate its scope and content. Behavioral science encompasses any field of inquiry that studies, by experimental and observational methods, the behavior of man (and the lower animals) in the physical and social environment. To be considered a part of behavioral science, research must satisfy two basic criteria. First, it must ultimately deal with human behavior. The primary aim of behavioral science is to identify underlying regularities in human behavior—both similarities and differences—and to determine what antecedent conditions give rise to them and what consequences follow from them. Second, the research must be accomplished in a "scientific manner." This means there must be a systematic attempt to describe, interrelate, explain, and hence predict some set of phenomena; that is, the underlying regularities in human behavior must be observable or lead to observable effects.

Fields or disciplines differ in the degree to which they deal with a body of knowledge obtained through objective, replicable and reliable measurement, and sound logic of inference. Whether a field is part of behavioral science depends on the methods by which human behavior is studied. The differences between the deliberate research activities of the behavioral scientist and the casual observations and conclusions of the sophisticated layman are mainly matters of procedure or method. They have to do with how clearly and precisely a person formulates his concepts, how carefully and systematically he makes and records observations, and how rigorously he reasons from data to conclusions.

The objective of behavioral science is to understand, explain and predict human behavior; that is, to establish generalizations about human behavior that are supported by empirical evidence collected in an impersonal way by procedures that are completely open to review and replication and capable of verification by other interested scholars. Behavioral science, thus, represents the systematic observation of man's behavior for the purpose of experimentally confirming specific hypotheses by reference to observable changes in behavior.

Alternative Methods of Classification

Notice that we have not defined behavioral science in terms of content areas but in terms of method and outlook. Descriptions of behavioral science often focus on the fields of anthropology, psychology, and sociology. Behavioral science, as discussed above, however, would include both more and less than what is traditionally included in these disciplines. It would include less in the sense that such specialized areas as physiological psychology, archaeology, technical linguistics, and most of physical anthropology would be excluded. It would include more in the sense that social geography, some psychiatry and the behavioral elements of economics, political science, and law would be included.

Recognizing the interdisciplinary and heterogeneous nature of behavioral science, what method of organization can be used to classify its scope and content? Several alternatives can be considered. One possibility is to distinguish subfields by reference to the *kinds of behavior* they focus on in their investigations. Linguists, for example, investigate aspects of speech behavior; political scientists concentrate on governmental processes; and economists, on market place behavior. This approach, though helpful, may not be an adequate guide. Many processes of behavior are interrelated to such an extent that it would be difficult to know where to draw the line.

Another alternative is to specify subfields in terms of *level of organization.* Various levels such as individuals, plurals, groups, institutions, and the like can be identified and used as a basis for specifying subfields. Problems arise, however, because biologists and physical anthropologists, though dealing with the individual organism, also deal with the laws of genetics governing races and species. Similarly, psychologists, though tending to focus on the individual, also deal with social interaction. Thus distinctions between subfields in terms of levels of organization may at best be only tentative and in need of constant reappraisal.

Another alternative is to distinguish subfields by their *research techniques*—field inquiry, laboratory experimentation, survey research, simulation, and so forth. Similar techniques, however, are becoming widely used by various fields. Statistical and polling techniques, for example, are now common in psychology, political science, sociology, economics, and anthropology.

Recognizing that the content of behavioral science is heterogeneous and does not fall very neatly into subareas, the approach adopted in this report is to focus on certain *problem areas* in which various kinds of behavior, levels of organization, and research techniques are interrelated, and in terms of which hypotheses and explanations may be drawn in conjunction with different subfields of behavioral science. Moreover, we have selected those problem areas which we believe to be especially relevant for accounting. The areas to be discussed are perception, motivation, anxiety and conflict, and attitudes and attitude change.[2]

Selected Behavioral Science Areas

Perception Perception is concerned with the problem of correspondence between the nature of the physical world and the character of sensory experience. It refers to the link between the actual reception of energy through the sense organs, which is called *sensation*, and such mental processes as judgment, reasoning, and memory. The task of perpetual studies is to define the properties of experience or response, on the one hand, and the properties of stimulation, on the other, and to specify the correspondence between these two sets of variables.

What a given individual will perceive in a given stimulus depends on many physiological and psychological factors such as sensory acuity, learning rates, and prior learning levels, as well as on properties of the stimulus patterns which are the objects of perception. Perception is an active process. Human beings put meaning into stimulus patterns; they do not just recognize meanings which are inherent in those stimuli. For example, the symbols of language that stand for objects, ideas, and so on do not have *intrinsic* meanings but come to have meanings by a process of social consensus. A

---

[2] This listing is based on T. W. Costello and S. S. Zalkind, *Psychology in Administration, A Research Orientation* (Englewood Cliffs, N.J.: Prentice-Hall, Inc., 1963).

language provides a classification of objects, events, and experiences which is a basis for our "reality." A single word may be used to denote a certain set of objects which will tend to be perceived as alike for the people who use that language. A different language may use one word for a certain subset of those objects and a different word for another subset. For the persons who use this second language, the whole set of objects will contain two kinds of things. In this way, the language we use determines what similarities and differences we are equipped to perceive. A language is learned. Similarly, our perceptions of the world and our beliefs about it are also learned.

Under some conditions, we tend to perceive what we want to perceive, not necessarily what is actually present in the stimulus pattern. The reason this is so is that the perceptual process operates to aid in the satisfaction of man's needs. We attend to and actively search for particular stimulus patterns. We perceive selectively and selection is related to what we care about. Moreover, the extent to which factors in the perceiver—his expectations, motives, attitudes—affect perception depends on how strong these factors are and how strong or compelling the stimulus pattern is. The more clear-cut or structured the stimulus pattern, the less it is amenable to perceptual distortion. Conversely, the more ambiguous the stimulus pattern, the more leeway there is for factors in the perceiver to operate in determining what is perceived. For example, perceptions are sometimes affected by a person's unconscious searching for objects related to strongly aroused motives. A study has shown that subjects who had not eaten for many hours were better able to detect food and food-related objects in a set of pictures which systematically obscured objects to the point of ambiguity as the hours of starvation increased up to a point of twelve hours after which the number of food associations decreased.[3] Another study found that hungry subjects "saw" more food-related objects even when no stimulus patterns were projected on a viewing screen.[4]

Perception has also been shown to be affected by persistent attitudes. For example, a research experiment asked children to match a spot of light to the size of several different coins by manipulating a knob that would vary the size of the light.[5] All children tended to overestimate the size of all coins but poorer children overestimated more than children of wealthy families, especially for coins of larger denominations. Presumably, the poorer children had more intensive positive attitudes toward money; it was literally more valuable to them than to the wealthier children. Thus, our motives, our attitudes, and even our social position can all affect our perceptions.

---

[3] R. Levine, I. Chein, and G. Murphy, "The Relation of the Intensity of a Need to the Amount of Perceptual Distortion, A Preliminary Report," *Journal of Psychology*, (1942), pp. 283-293.

[4] D.C. McClelland and I.W. Atkinson, "The Projective Expression of Needs: I. The Effect of Different Intensities of the Hunger Drive on Perception," *Journal of Psychology*, (1947), pp. 33-14.

[5] J.S. Bruner and C.C. Goodman, "Value and Need as Organizing Factors in Perception," *Journal of Abnormal and Social Psychology*, (1947), pp. 33-44.

We can summarize some of the general findings of studies of perception as follows. First, the perceptions of the individual—his ideas about persons and things—are selectively organized, only certain objects enter into his conception of the external world. Moreover, this selective organization of perception is determined not only by stimulus factors which derive from the nature of the stimulus object, e.g., frequency and intensity, but also by personal factors which derive from the characteristics of the perceiving individual, e.g., his wants, emotions, and mental sets. Second, the separate perceptions of the individual about objects and persons develop into *systems* of perceptions such that the properties of a given perception depend in part upon the particular nature of the inclusive system. The "same" perception may be embedded in different systems and therefore have different properties. In some cases, the perceived characteristics of an object may be exaggerated in one direction or another depending upon its relation to the inclusive system.

A study reported by Dearborn and Simon will serve to illustrate these two general findings.[6] Dearborn and Simon investigated the selective organization of the perceptions of industrial managers by using a group of 23 executives enrolled in an executive training program. The departmental affiliations of the executives were as follows: sales (6); production (5); accounting (4); miscellaneous(8). The executives were asked to read a standard textbook case, the "Castengo Steel Company," which gave a great deal of factual detail about the organization and activities of the company. Before discussion of the case, the executives were asked to indicate in a brief written statement "what they considered to be the most important problem facing the Castengo Steel Company—the problem a new company president should deal with first."

The findings revealed that five of the six sales executives (83%) mentioned sales as the most important problem facing the company. In contrast, only five of the remaining 17 executives (29%) mentioned sales. Moreover, of the 5 non-sales executives who mentioned sales, three were in the accounting department in positions that involved the analysis of product profitability. Similarly, organization problems were mentioned by 4 of the 5 production executives (80%) and by only 4 of the remaining 18 executives (22%). Only 3 executives mentioned human-relations problems; these were executives in the public relations, industrial relations, and medical departments of their companies. Thus, industrial executives, looking at exactly the same information, selected for emphasis those aspects of a complex problem which related to the activities and goals of their particular departments, suggesting that the selective organization of perception may shape organizational planning and policy.

A third general finding is that changes in perception may be brought about by either a blockage of want satisfaction or by a change in the individ-

---

[6] D. C. Dearborn and H. A. Simon, "Selective Perception: A Note on the Departmental Identifications of Executives," *Sociometry*, (1958), pp. 140–144.

ual's information. The degree and manner in which changes in wants and information produce changes in perception depend upon the characteristics of the pre-existing systems of perception and upon the characteristics of the person within whom the systems of perception reside. Our perceptions of the personalities of people, for example, tend to be unified and our first impressions of people tend to resist future change. New information may be accommodated in such a manner as to maintain the consonance of our pre-existing perceptions.

To illustrate, Haire and Grunes presented two groups of college students with the following description of a certain working man:[7]

To group I: "Works in a factory, reads a newspaper, goes to movies, average height, cracks jokes, intelligent, strong, active."

To group II: "Works in a factory, reads a newspaper, goes to movies, average height, cracks jokes, strong, active."

The two descriptions were identical except that for group I the man was characterized as intelligent. The students were asked to describe in a paragraph what sort of person they thought the worker was.

The typical description given by group II was summarized by the investigators as follows:

> Virtually every description would fit into the pattern of a typical American Joe: likable and well-liked, mildly sociable, healthy, happy, uncomplicated, and well-adjusted, in a sort of earthy way, not very intelligent, but trying to keep abreast of current trends, interested in sports, and finding his pleasures in simple, undistinguished activities.

The introduction of the term "intelligent" created difficulties for group I. This was, for many of the students in the group, inconsistent with their set of beliefs about factory workers. Most of them, however, managed to overcome this nonbelonging quality by protecting their original systems of perceptions regarding factory workers: Denial of the quality: "He is intelligent, but not too much so, since he works in a factory." Modification of the quality: "He is intelligent, but doesn't possess initiative to rise above his group." Denial of group membership: Some students denied the man was a worker by promoting him to a foreman. Recognizing the incongruity, but maintaining the original perception: "The traits seem to be conflicting . . . most factory workers I have heard about aren't too intelligent."

Perception is important to accountants because the impact of accounting processes and reports can be significantly affected by differences in perception. Perceptual differences can, and will, occur *within* the group of non-accounting individuals who use, or are subject to, the accounting system, as

---

[7] M. Haire and W. F. Grunes, "Perceptual Defenses: Processes Protecting an Original Perception of Another Personality," *Human Relations*, (1950), pp. 403–412.

well as *between* accountants and non-accountants. Financial accounting, for instance, emphasizes the information needs of the readers of financial statements. However, very little research has been devoted to determining the extent, if any, that the perceptions of the "reader" relative to the financial reports coincide with the intentions of the accountants who prepare the reports. Similarly, in management accounting, it is possible that substantial differences exist between the manner in which the accounting process is viewed by accountants and the way it is viewed by managers and workers. From the standpoint of actions taken as a result of the operations of accounting and control systems, *the only effective views* are those held by the (usually non-accounting) individuals who actually manage and perform the work of the organization.

The behavioral science area of perception has a crucial relationship to the impact of accounting on the users of accounting information as well as others who are in some way affected by the operations of an accounting system. Research on perception might be directed towards answering such questions as: How do various individuals and groups perceive accounting processes and reports? Do these perceptions differ from those of accountants? If so, why do they differ? What is the effect of such differences in terms of the behavior actually produced as compared with the behavior that may have been anticipated or desired by the accountants?

Motivation Motivation theory is concerned with understanding why individuals choose certain actions and reject others, and why they persist in a chosen action, even in the face of difficulties and obstacles. Investigation of the direction and persistence of action has traditionally focused on the growth and change in man's needs and goals and, also, on the nature and development of individual personality. In this section we summarize some of the general findings that have evolved out of the study of motivation.

One finding is that the thought and action of an individual reflect his needs and goals, but the relation is both complex and transitory. Similar actions may reflect different needs and different actions may reflect the same need. Needs and goals continuously develop and change as a result of changes in the physiological and psychological states of the individual. Needs may assume new forms through the fusion of originally distinct needs. Also, the degree to which needs are regularly satisfied or chronically frustrated determines the strength and primacy of these needs and the readiness with which other needs may emerge. For any given need there may be many different appropriate goals. If fully appropriate goals are lacking, the individual may develop substitute goals or sustain prolonged action toward remote goals by achieving intermediate goals.

A second general finding is that needs and goals become organized around an individual's personality. Personality plays a crucial role in motivation—organizing the needs and goals that have to do with self-enhancement and self-defense. Moreover, personality, which is a product of social interaction, tends to be defined in terms of group membership. Self-evaluation consists mainly of comparisons of self with groups to which the person belongs, as well as those to which he aspires to belong, and depends heavily upon achievement of goals which reflect group values. The standards of performance (i.e., aspiration levels) on which self-evaluation is based are determined in part by the relative status of the individual—higher status leads to higher levels of aspiration, lower status to lower levels of aspiration. Also, the high-status individual is more likely to receive cues from other people that serve to further reinforce his high self-evaluation.

A third general finding is that the arousal of a particular set of needs depends upon the momentary physiological state, environmental situation, and perceptions of a person. Most of the many needs of an individual are inactive or latent; at any given time, only a particular set of needs is active in directing and sustaining behavior.

These general findings can be examined within the context of contemporary theories of motivation. Maslow's theory of personality and motivation, for example, assumes that man is motivated to reach a certain goal because he has an internally generated need to reach it.[8] The Maslow theory is based on five sets of human needs which are categorized and ranked into a conceptual hierarchy beginning with certain primitive and urgent physiological needs and ranging upward to the need for self-actualization. These are:

> Need for self-actualization
> Need for esteem
> Need for belongingness and love
> Safety needs
> Physiological needs

The physiological needs refer to food, warmth, shelter, and other bodily needs. The safety needs include actual physical safety, as well as a feeling of being safe from injury, both physical and emotional. The need for belongingness and love represents a social need. It is the need to feel a part of a group or the need to "belong," suggesting the need both to give and to receive love. The need for self-esteem is based on the belief that a person has a basic drive for self-respect and the esteem of others. Finally, the need for self-actualization is an attempt to describe the process whereby an individual realizes the real self and works toward the expression of the self by becoming all that he is capable of becoming.

Maslow's hierarchy of needs underscores the fundamental point that until one set of needs is fulfilled, a person's behavior is generally not motivated by higher level needs. Also, once a set of needs is satisfied, it no longer motivates. The needs appear in sequence as a person grows from infancy to

[8] Abraham H. Maslow, *Motivation and Personality* (New York: Harper and Row, Inc., 1954).

adulthood. The pattern may be repeated, however, as new experiences are encountered at various times in life. Thus, an individual can be characterized as being primarily at an observable level on the hierarchy at a given time or in a given set of circumstances.

Whereas the first four levels represent *deficit needs* (because their satisfaction is so much a part of the natural development of a normal personality that they are stimulated only in the absence of their fulfillment), self-actualization is a *growth need*, the determinants of which are the individual's own peculiar set of potentialities and the internally defined goals he sets for himself. Self-actualizing people are motivated to become involved in types of creative expression that they themselves find gratifying. By its very essence, it is a self-perpetuating, ongoing, and never ending process. It implies that each new involvement of the self begets further involvement, that a person is never "self-actualized" but is always in the process of finding new goals and new means of expression.

Three important principles underly Maslow's theory of motivation. First, a similar need may lead to different responses, both in different individuals and in the same individual at different points in time. Second, the same need may be met by different satisfiers. One individual may seek to satisfy his need for status, or for acceptance by others, through a promotion within the formal organization, whereas another individual may seek satisfaction of this need through informal influence in the work group or even outside the organization. Third, similar behavior may be based on the operation of different needs. Because we are not able to see people's needs directly, we tend to judge their needs by their behavior. However, it is easy to make erroneous assumptions about the particular need or level of needs which produced the behavior. For example, an individual might be very productive in his work because he seeks the admiration and respect of others or because he is attempting to meet the standards he has set for himself.

Herzberg's theory of motivation, sometimes referred to as the "motivation-hygiene" theory, is illustrated by his research of the job attitudes (or job opinions) of 200 accountants and engineers.[9] Herzberg and his colleagues asked subjects to describe in detail when they felt exceptionally good about their jobs and when they felt exceptionally bad about their jobs. Analyses of the responses showed that the subjects most often mentioned good feelings related to job *content* factors and bad feelings related to job *context* factors. Herzberg classified the job content factors as "satisfiers" and context factors were called "dissatisfiers." Satisfiers include such factors as achievement, recognition, the work itself, responsibility, advancement, and growth. Dissatisfiers include company policy and administration, supervision, working conditions, interpersonal relations, salary, status, job security, and personal

---

[9] F. Herzberg, *et al, The Motivation to Work* (New York: John Wiley and Sons, 1959), and F. Herzberg, *Work and the Nature of Man* (Cleveland: World Publishing Company, 1966).

life. The satisfiers, which are all related to the job itself, were called *motivators*, since other findings in the study suggested that they were effective in motivating the employee to greater performance and productivity. The dissatisfiers were called *hygiene factors* and were viewed primarily as preventive and environmental in nature.

Herzberg stresses that the factors which truly motivate are "growth" factors, those that give the individual a sense of personal accomplishment through the challenge of the job itself. Real motivation is seen as resulting from involvement in successfully performing an interesting task and from feelings of accomplishment. The dissatisfiers are classed as deficit needs. Good working conditions, for example, were rarely named as contributing to job satisfaction, but bad working conditions were frequently named as sources of dissatisfaction.

The important feature of Herzberg's theory of worker motivation is the contention that the "satisfiers" and "dissatisfiers" are separate, distinct, discrete factors, rather than opposite poles of the same factor. The fact that something does not dissatisfy cannot be interpreted to mean that it satisfies. Herzberg's charge to management is to recognize this disparate nature of motivators and hygiene factors.

From the standpoint of formal organizations, the essential question concerning motivation is how to create a situation in which an individual perceives that his personal needs can best be met by working toward the accomplishment of the goals of the organization. Since organizational goals and accomplishment are often stated in accounting terms, and since individual performance is often evaluated by accounting measures, the implications of motivation theory for accounting are perhaps greater than those of any other behavioral area. We need to consider such questions as: What kinds of motivations are produced by accounting systems and reports? How does accounting influence aspiration levels? How effective are accounting indicators of performance (such as "net income" and "return on investment") in motivating individuals to accomplish the goals of the organization? How do accounting measurements influence the satisfaction of needs at *all* levels of Maslow's hierarchy? Do accounting systems assist individuals in achieving maximum fulfillment of their job-related needs, particularly when they are making their maximum contribution to the organization? To what extent is accounting a hygiene factor, as defined by Herzberg, rather than a motivator?

Anxiety and Conflict Not all behavior results in the satisfaction of needs. Some behavior occurs because individuals *fail* to satisfy their needs. The study of anxiety and conflict is concerned with what happens when the accomplishment of goals is, for some reason, blocked. An individual's response to conditions that hinder his satisfaction of needs is complex. In some cases, he may mobilize more energy for goal striving. In other cases, he may direct energy toward reducing unpleasant tensions.

Frustration occurs when energy has been mobilized for some action but circumstances either prevent the act or block the individual from goal attainment. The term *anxiety* is often used to describe the feeling or state experienced by an individual when some external threat exists to his feelings of self-esteem. The term *conflict* refers to the behavior of groups that may be pulling against each other, rivalries between individuals, and subjective uncertainties within an individual. These three terms overlap in many of their meanings. A person experiencing conflict, for example, may be frustrated in his desire to achieve some goal to the point where the frustrations threaten his feelings of self-esteem, thereby creating anxiety which, in turn, can produce conflict both internally and in his relations with others.

An individual's response to a disturbance or strain in the environment (stress) will vary with its degree and duration, its nature, the quality of leadership available, the characteristics of the individual, and the group to which he belongs. The initial response to even moderate stress is often one of shock and resistance, followed by recovery and perhaps over-compensation. Stress may increase the variability of behavior and reduce its consistency. Whereas moderate stress may tend to produce some performance improvements, severe stress will usually result in disorganized performance. If the stress is extreme, or continues over a long period of time, lowered performance and, ultimately, collapse or breakdown may result.

As long as an individual under stress can draw additional energy or can use alternative paths to his goal, his behavior will remain goal-oriented and performance may improve. At some point, however, the individual may internalize his sense of frustration. The point at which this will occur is dependent, in part, on the resources and characteristics of the individual and, in part, on the duration and intensity of the frustrating stress. When it does occur, the focus is no longer on the frustrating situation but on a frustrated individual who begins to respond more to the unpleasantness of his feelings of frustration than to his previous goal.

One reaction to frustration is aggression. When goal-striving is blocked by a barrier of some kind, aggression is one technique for removing the barrier. Generally, the violence of the aggression will be a function of the strength of the motivation; the mode of aggression will depend on the perception of the barrier; and, the expression of the aggression will be related to expectations concerning the probability that it will be met with punishment. Frustration elicits aggression only if the goal is perceived as attainable. If the goal is not perceived as attainable, no further energy will be mobilized to seek it. In fact, when a goal is perceived to be totally unattainable, apathy rather than aggression is likely to be manifested.

Anxiety involves the feeling of uncertainty and helplessness one experiences in the face of danger. The effect of anxiety on an individual's behavior is related to his level of aspiration and to whether he tends toward high need achievement or failure avoidance. People vary in their characteristic level of anxiety from highly anxious, almost continuously worried individuals, to those who show anxiety only under the most stressful conditions. Some persons are success seekers and thus are willing to set high levels of aspiration. Others are failure-avoiders and set low levels of aspiration.

Behavior in achievement situations differs significantly depending upon whether the individual is oriented principally toward attainment of success or toward avoidance of failure. Those who have strong "avoidance of failure" tendencies tend to be more anxiety prone in situations in which their performance will be evaluated by others. People who have strong "need for success" tendencies, on the other hand, often show little anxiety in such situations. Moreover, differences in the quality of performance have been observed between high and low anxiety groups in achievement situations. Generally, high anxiety people do better than those with low anxiety *if* they can be protected from feeling threatened. Thus, when the emphasis is on the task rather than the person's ability to perform the task, anxiety seems to aid performance. Low anxiety people have been found to do better than high anxiety people when the achievement situation aroused a sense of threat. The implication is that if attention is focused on the task the increased drive of the anxious individual will motivate him towards superior performance. If, however, the focus is on the person and his possible failure, the anxiety may bring about conflict, excuse making, and lower performance.

Internal conflict represents a state in which the individual is being pulled in opposite directions by forces within himself. Conflict can arise both prior to action and after a decision has been made. Conflict prior to an action involves the tensions leading to, or resulting from, an inability to make a decision. Sometimes, facts from different sources, or represented by the views of different people, are inconsistent. Faced with this situation, an individual can try to ignore the inconsistencies, cut himself off from their source, or surround himself only with people who are in harmony or consonance with his thinking. Festinger, in his discussions of cognitive dissonance, indicates that conflict resolution is a strong motivating force in human experience.[10] Dissonance is unpleasant and we are usually motivated to eliminate it. Festinger describes some situations in which dissonance produced behavior that would have been considered irrational if viewed from the standpoint of commonly accepted motives. For example, he reports a study of a religious group that had predicted a catastrophic flood which would overwhelm most of the world on a certain date. This prediction was held to have been given to these people directly by their gods and was an integral part of their religious beliefs. When the predicted date passed uneventfully, considerable dissonance developed in these individuals. They continued to believe in their gods

---

[10] L. Festinger, "Cognitive Dissonance as a Motivating State," in Costello and Zalkind, *op. cit.*, pp. 170–179.

and in the validity of the communications from them, but at the same time they knew that the predictions had been wrong. At first, the social support of the group tended to reduce individual dissonance so that members did not discard their beliefs or their commitments to them. Later, as the dissonance became stronger, the group which had previously been disinterested in publicity became avid publicity seekers. Presumably, if more people could be convinced to believe in the messages, the dissonance between the belief and the knowledge that the messages had not been correct could be reduced.

Conflict between individuals and groups occurs when the respective parties perceive that the satisfaction of their needs and accomplishment of their goals are being blocked by others and action is taken to reduce the threat. Some behavioral scientists believe that conflict in itself is not necessarily undesirable for an organization. Whether such conflict will improve performance or result in undesired actions depends on its nature, extent, and severity as well as on the structure, climate, and leadership patterns of the organization.

The relationship of accounting to the behavioral areas of anxiety and conflict is complicated by the fact that, as suggested above, these conditions may be either functional or dysfunctional for an organization. Argyris has provided a classic description of dysfunctional anxiety and conflict brought about by the misuse of accounting and budgeting controls.[11] Stedry has argued that budgeting practices must be tailored to the aspiration and anxiety levels of the individual being budgeted and, since individuals differ in these respects, control systems should not treat all people "equally."[12] Research findings on anxiety and conflict, and their impact on organizations, is still relatively limited. Nevertheless, it seems clear that awareness of such research will assist accountants in gaining new insights into the effect of accounting on people and organizations. Questions that might be investigated include the following. Do certain accounting techniques and reports contribute to excessive conflict? Why? How can they be changed to reduce conflict? Is it possible (and desirable) to consider individual differences with regard to frustration and anxiety levels when designing and operating accounting systems? To what extent does the behavior of accountants in their relations with others create anxiety and conflict?

Attitudes and Attitude Change As an individual develops, his perceptions, feelings, and action-tendencies with respect to various objects become organized into enduring systems called attitudes. Knowledge of the attitudes of people is an important aid in predicting and influencing their behavior. Anyone who is seeking to affect the behavior of others—whether these others

---

[11] C. Argyris, "Human Problems with Budgets," *Harvard Business Review*, vol. 31, No. 1 (Jan.–Feb., 1953), pp. 97–110.

[12] A. C. Stedry, *Budget Control and Cost Behavior* (Englewood Cliffs, N.J.: Prentice-Hall, Inc., 1961).

are subordinates, superiors, or colleagues in his own organization, or those he deals with in other organizations—soon becomes aware of the importance of their attitudes.

Definitions of attitude emphasize the interrelatedness of various components: a *perceptual* component which consists of the beliefs of the individual about the object of the attitude; a *feeling* component which refers to the emotions connected with the object—the extent to which the object is felt to be pleasing or displeasing, liked or disliked; and an *action-tendency* component which includes all of the behavioral intentions or readinesses associated with the attitude. If an individual holds a positive attitude toward a given object, he will be disposed to help or reward or support the object; if he holds a negative attitude, he will be disposed to harm or punish or destroy the object.

Attitudes differ in their effects on social action according to their primary characteristics. An attitude may always be described as either favorable or unfavorable, but it is usually not enough to describe only the direction or sign of an individual's attitude toward a given object. Rather it is often necessary to derive a quantitative measure of the degree of favorability or unfavorability. In addition, a given attitude may incorporate highly favorable beliefs about its object, but only mildly favorable feelings, and perhaps only slight tendencies to take favorable action with respect to that object.

There may also be extensive variations in the number and kind of elements making up the components. The perceptual component may include an exhaustive set of beliefs about the object; the feeling component may be relatively simple and undifferentiated; and the action-tendency component may be highly complex in that the individual is prepared to take many and varied sorts of actions. Further, an individual's various attitudes may differ in the degree to which they are isolated from one another or are interconnected with each other. Few attitudes exist in a state of complete isolation, rather they form clusters with other attitudes.

Attitudes develop in the process of need satisfaction, i.e., in response to problem situations involving attempts to satisfy specific needs. However, an individual's attitudes tend to be enduring systems, they remain with him and may be used by him to solve a number of different problems. Thus, any given attitude may serve various goals, and different needs can give rise to the same enduring attitude.

The attitudes of a person are shaped by the information to which he is exposed. An individual who has strong needs that must be satisfied by the development of appropriate attitudes will undertake a wide search for the necessary information. However, he may not be in a position to obtain reliable, factual information himself and, in some cases, he may have to invent facts in order to develop an important attitude. Individuals are often at the mercy of various authorities for much of the content of their attitudes.

Through ignorance or intent, these authorities are sometimes unreliable. All of this suggests that the nature of our attitudes (as well as the incidence of certain superstitions, delusions, and prejudices) is related to the reliability of the authorities we depend upon, the range of experiences to which we have been subjected, and the degree to which our major needs are adequately satisfied.

Many of the attitudes of an individual have their source and their support in the groups to which he gives his allegiance. However, even though his attitudes tend to reflect the beliefs, values and norms of his groups, the individual does not passively absorb the prevailing attitudes in the various groups with which he affiliates. Attitudes, like perceptions, develop selectively in the process of need satisfaction. Each person tends to pick and choose, from the attitudes available to him, those which are need satisfying for him. Thus, the effect of group influences on the formation of attitudes is both indirect and complex.

An individual tends to accept as his own those specific attitudes which are consistent with his personality. The personality of the individual, however, is not a perfectly integrated system and he may adopt attitudes that are inconsistent or contradictory because of different teachings of his accepted authorities in different areas, conflicting group affiliations, and conflicting needs.

Several general findings have evolved out of the study of attitudes and attitude change. One is that the modifiability of an attitude depends upon the characteristics of the specific attitude, the attitude system in general, and the personality and group affiliations of the individual. Therefore, attitudes once formed, differ in their modifiability. To a certain extent, attitude modifiability is a function of the extremeness, consistency, interdependence, need-serving, and value-relatedness of the attitude. Attitude modifiability also depends on the level of intelligence of the individual, his general susceptibility to persuasive communications, and his readiness to accept change. Moreover, attitudes which have strong social support through group affiliations are difficult to change, especially if they are endorsed by a group in which membership is highly valued.

Another finding is that attitude change can be induced by exposure to additional information; changes in group affiliations; enforced modification of behavior; and from procedures which change personality. The direction and degree of attitude change induced by additional information is a function of situational factors and of the source, medium, form, and content of the information. The effectiveness of new group affiliations in inducing attitude change depends upon the characteristics of the group and the nature of the individual's membership in it. The effectiveness of enforced modification of behavior is a function of the circumstances of the enforcement. The effectiveness of personality change techniques in modifying a particular attitude depends on the appropriateness of the techniques relative to the total personality of the individual.

The relationship of accounting to attitudes and attitude change can be illustrated by the following quote:

> Involvement and participation in the planning, collection, analyses and interpretation of information initiate powerful forces for change. Own facts are better understood, more emotionally acceptable, and more likely to be utilized than those of some "outside expert." *Participation in analysis and interpretation helps bypass those resistances which arise from proceeding too rapidly or too slowly.*[13]

In general, it can be hypothesized that the more accounting is viewed as a closed system, the less positive will be its impact on an organization. Accountants may need to consider the development of a whole series of ongoing techniques for involving concerned non-accountants in meaningful participation with respect to accounting and control processes in order to create more favorable and open-minded attitudes about accounting systems and the organizations which they serve. Specific questions that should be investigated by accountants include: What are the attitudes created in various users of accounting information by the reports that they receive and the context in which they receive them? How do these attitudes affect the performance and interpersonal relations of the users? Do certain accounting processes and techniques contribute to undesired attitudes within an organization? What happens when accounting reports provide information that is inconsistent with the attitudes of the receivers of the reports? To what extent does accounting information reinforce or change existing attitudes?

---

[13] Reported in F.C. Mann, "Studying and Creating Change: A Means to Understanding Social Organization" in Costello and Zalkind, *op. cit.*, p. 325.

*Professors Williams and Griffin are Professors
of Accounting in the Graduate School of
Business, The University of Texas at Austin.*

On the Nature of Empirical Verification in Accounting

Thomas H. Williams and Charles H. Griffin

Since the formulation by Paton and Littleton of a relatively logical, well-articulated 'theory of accounting,' researchers have devoted a substantial portion of their efforts to modification of this classical cost theory and to independent formulations of entirely new object theories.[1] The appearance of a formally structured set of propositions also stimulated interest on the part of some accounting researchers in the problems associated with theory construction and verification. This latter interest has manifested itself in diverse forms, ranging from somewhat casual statements, seeking to identify the relationship between accounting theory and accounting practice, to more abstract metaphysical and philosophical musings. However, only minimal attention has been given to the question of *verification*, or *theory validation*. Some conveniently surmise that accounting practice and verification of theory are essentially synonymous. But no serious attempt has been made to identify that which constitutes verification. That this is a significant deficiency is evident from Professor Machlup's outline of the wide variety of possible modes of verification:

---

[1] The new object theory formulated by Professor R. J. Chambers in *Accounting, Evaluation and Economic Behavior*, Englewood Cliffs 1966, is probably the most comparable to the Paton-Littleton theory in terms of scope and logical rigour; other significantly different expositions, such as *A Statement of Basic Accounting Theory*, (American Accounting Association), are generally more parochial in scope or less well articulated.

Reprinted by permission of the authors and publisher from *Abacus*, Vol. 5, December, 1969, pp. 143–156.

> Verification in research and analysis may refer to many things, including the correctness of mathematical and logical arguments, the applicability of formulas and equations, the trustworthiness of reports, the authenticity of documents, the genuineness of artifacts or relics, the adequacy of reproductions, translations and paraphrases, the accuracy of historical and statistical accounts, the corroboration of reported events, the completeness in the enumeration of circumstances in a concrete situation, the reliability and exactness of observations, the reproducibility of experiments, the explanatory or predictive value of generalizations.[2]

Whichever of these forms, if any, verification in accounting assumes, it depends essentially upon a metatheoretical or metaphysical concept of truth. It is our purpose to examine the process of determining what is truth in a variety of different contexts and disciplines and to speculate upon, or roughly sketch, its special relevance to, and application in, accounting.

In view of the exploratory nature of this study, we shall ignore the more subtle or paradoxical validation disputes in other disciplines (e.g., the Eisenberg uncertainty principle in physics and the Gödel results regarding consistency in mathematics), as these would seem to possess the potential for promoting new insights only when a relatively firm and widely accepted understanding of the general verification process is common.

Pure and Physical Geometry: The Classical Distinction Between Truth Criteria

The question of truth, or theory verification, has been painstakingly researched by scholars concerned with the philosophy of science. Their work has focused primarily on mathematics and the physical sciences. This is natural in view of the long, parallel history of rigorous theory construction in these disciplines. In addition, the extensive use of mathematics in the development of scientific theories suggests a strong affinity of interests and objectives. Yet mathematics concerns itself with the purest abstractions, while the physical sciences deal with the concrete, the real world. In view of these antithetical positions, the question arises: are there different truth criteria for the two disciplines, or is there some single way of establishing the validity of the theoretical propositions of both?

Euclidean geometry is a classical illustration of the dilemma. On the one hand, this mathematical structure is a highly-developed axiomatic formulation depending ostensibly only upon the rules of logic for its validity. On the other hand, the theory has been interpreted by many mathematicians—and physical scientists—as the description *par excellence* of the universe, confirmation of which emerges from its highly-successful application to physical

---

[2] Fritz Machlup, 'The Problem of Verification in Economics,' *The Southern Economic Journal,* July 1955, p. 1.

phenomena. It has been established, however, that two separate and unique theories with distinctive truth criteria exist. Hempel describes this distinction in the following terms:

> The nature of the peculiar certainty of mathematics is now clear: A mathematical theorem is certain *relative* to the set of postulates from which it is derived; i.e., it is necessarily true *if* those postulates are true; and this is so because the theorem, if rigorously proved, simply re-asserts part of what has been stipulated in the postulates. A truth of this conditional type obviously implies no assertions about matters of empirical fact and can, therefore, never get into conflict with any empirical findings, even of the most unexpected kind; consequently, unlike the hypotheses and theories of empirical science, it can never suffer the fate of being disconfirmed by new evidence: A mathematical truth is irrefutably certain just because it is devoid of factual, or empirical content. Any theorem of geometry, therefore, when cast into the conditional form described earlier, is analytic in the technical sense of logic, and thus true *a priori*; i.e., its truth can be established by means of the formal machinery of logic alone, without any reference to empirical data.[3]

.   .   .   .   .

> When the physicist uses the concepts of point, straight line, incidence, etc., in statements about physical objects, he obviously connects with each of them a more or less definite physical meaning. Thus, the term "point" serves to designate physical points, i.e., objects of the kind illustrated by pinpoints, cross hairs, etc. Similarly, the term "straight line" refers to straight lines in the sense of physics, such as illustrated by taut strings or by the path of light rays in a homogeneous medium. Analogously, each of the other geometrical concepts has a concrete physical meaning in the statements of physical geometry. In view of this situation, we can say that physical geometry is obtained by what is called, in contemporary logic, a semantical interpretation of pure geometry. Generally speaking, a semantical interpretation of a pure mathematical theory, whose primitives are not assigned any specific meaning, consists in giving each primitive (and thus, indirectly, each defined term) a specific meaning or designatum. In the case of physical geometry, this meaning is physical in the sense just illustrated; it is possible, however, to assign a purely arithmetical meaning to each concept of geometry; the possibility of such an arithmetical interpretation of geometry is of great importance in the study of the consistency and other logical characteristics of geometry, but it falls outside the scope of the present discussion.[4]

In brief, there is a difference between the logical truth of mathematics and the factual truth of the physical sciences.

Perhaps, a few comments respecting mathematics as a separate discipline are relevant. While the mathematician may gain inspiration from the obser-

---

[3] Carl G. Hempel, 'Geometry and Empirical Science' in *The World of Mathematics*, James R. Newman (ed.), New York 1956, p. 1638.

[4] Hempel, p. 1642.

vation and interpretation of selected physical phenomena, his theory *as a mathematical theory* is independent of any particular referents. Verification of the theory lies merely in establishing that all of the results (theorems) have been derived from the postulates in accordance with logical principles. The axioms, or postulates, are not self-evident truths, because they do not contain statements about which truth or falsity can be predicated. They merely provide the basis, along with the primitive terms, from which a series of conclusions can be derived. A 'quasi-verification' process is, however, sometimes superimposed on this metatheoretical conception of theory validation. In certain instances, mathematical theory attempts to generalize from, or on, several existing theories of mathematics. The validity of such a generalized theory may then be established by interpreting it in terms of some other mathematical entity (e.g. the set of natural numbers). If the theory yields results which are the same as those already 'known' about the numbers, the mathematician may be encouraged to believe that his more abstract and general theory has been verified. Yet within the context of the previous discussion, this is an unusual type of verification, since the objects of verification themselves purport to be independent of reality. Thus, it may be more appropriate to assert that methodologically the mathematician has merely *illustrated* an instance of his theory *within mathematics*, rather than having confirmed it or established its truth. At best, he has obtained only indirect evidence that the logic of his theory, which is the ultimate criterion for truth in mathematics, is correct.

It may be argued that the comments regarding the nature of physical geometry can be generalized to all physical sciences. A theory in the physical sciences is established by establishing the correspondence between the results of the theory and phenomena experienced or observed. Yet, the confirmation process is not based upon a one-to-one correspondence between each element of the scientific theory and some phenomenon in the real world. Rather, the theory exists in a manner much like that in mathematics, wherein concepts, interpreted concepts, are linked through definitions and logical transformations. The fundamental assumptions of theory are thus not applied to the real world and justified on the basis of self-evident truth. Rather, they are the source of a series of conclusions; the assumptions and the conclusions together constitute the theory; and the theory *per se* is given greater or less credence depending upon the correspondence between the conclusions and the real world. Hempel summarizes this process as follows:

> A scientific theory might therefore be likened to a complex spatial network: Its terms are represented by the knots, while the threads connecting the latter correspond, in part, to the definitions and, in part, to the fundamental and derivative hypotheses included in the theory. The whole system floats, as it were, above the plane of observation and is anchored to it by rules of interpretation. These might be viewed as strings which are not part of the

network but link certain points of the latter with specific places in the plane of observation. By virtue of those interpretive connections, the network can function as a scientific theory: From certain observational data, we may ascend, via an interpretive string, to some point in the theoretical network, thence proceed, via definitions and hypotheses, to other points, from which another interpretive string permits a descent to the plane of observation.

In this manner an interpreted theory makes it possible to infer the occurrence of certain phenomena which can be described in observational terms and which may belong to the past or the future, on the basis of other such phenomena, whose occurrence has been previously ascertained. But the theoretical apparatus which provides these predictive and postdictive bridges from observational data to potential observational findings cannot, in general, be formulated in terms of observables alone. The entire history of scientific endeavor appears to show that in our world comprehensive, simple, and dependable principles for the explanation and prediction of observable phenomena cannot be obtained by merely summarizing and inductively generalizing observational findings. A hypothetico-deductive-observational procedure is called for and is indeed followed in the more advanced branches of empirical sciences: Guided by his knowledge of observational data, the scientist has to invent a set of concepts—theoretical constructs, which lack immediate experiential significance, a system of hypotheses couched in terms of them, and an interpretation for the resulting theoretical network; and all this in a manner which will establish explanatory and predictive connections between the data of direct observation.[5]

Thus, depending upon the particular assumptions adopted, a set of theories purporting to explain the same physical phenomena may exist. Perhaps the best illustration is again in the area of physical geometry. Several non-Euclidean geometries have been developed, basically through modification of the postulate of parallels. Each of these alternatives is a logically consistent mathematical geometry. Of these, Riemann's generalization of his elliptical geometry has a *physical* interpretation which for certain purposes (viz., application of Einstein's general theory of relativity) corresponds more closely with observed results than does Euclidean geometry. Conant has observed that 'a theory is only overthrown by a better theory, never merely by contradictory facts';[6] we are inclined to add that the use to which a theory is put may also generate evidence for the choice of one theory or another.

Clearly then, distinctly different truth criteria exist for mathematics and physical science. For mathematics, truth is synonymous with logical consistency; appeals to other mathematical entities merely provide indirect assurance to the theorists that the canons of logic have been satisfied. On the other hand, in the physical sciences, the truth criterion is correspondence with observables. Significantly, however, it has been noted that the physical scientist does not argue about the truth or falsity of his assumptions, but rather

---

[5] Carl G. Hempel, 'Fundamentals of Concept Formation in Empirical Science' in *International Encyclopedia of Unified Science*, Vol. II, No. 7, Otto Neurath, Rudolf Carnap, and Charles Morris (eds), Chicago 1952, pp. 36–7.

[6] James B. Conant, *On Understanding Science*, New Haven 1947, p. 36.

about the correspondence of derived results with the real world. Different assumptions merely produce different theories; the predictive or explanatory content of these different theories thereafter indicates their appropriateness or relevance to the real world. Henry Margenau incisively states this meta-theory of the physical sciences as follows: 'Processes of validation, when conjoined with the metaphysical requirements ... [on constructs], create scientific knowledge. It is this purgatory of validation which removes from constructs the figmentary stigma which their epistemological genesis first attached to them.'[7]

Truth Criteria for Theories in the Social Sciences

Since the social sciences consist of a more heterogeneous group of disciplines than do the physical sciences, we shall first examine the truth criterion used in economics. Thereafter, the specific conclusion regarding verification of economic theory will be considered in the context of the broader perspective of the social sciences as a whole.

Economic theory deals with a number of different objects of inquiry, among which are the various individuals and organizations specific to mi-croeconomics, macroeconomics, welfare economics, international econom-ics, etc. All of these objects of interest and investigation, however, are charac-terized by their independence of the investigator; i.e. the economist de-scribes, explains, and/or predicts the behaviour of certain variables (people, goods, dollar measures, etc.) over which he exerts no direct control. In this sense, the investigative problem appears to be essentially analogous to that experienced in the physical sciences. Two of its major distinguishing charac-teristics are the introduction of the human element into the object theory and the difficulty, if not the impossibility, of controlled and reproducible experi-ments.

With these similarities and differences in mind, let us examine the econo-mist's characterization of his truth criteria. Admittedly there is no single conception of the empirical verification process in economics; different econ-omists take different positions, ranging from a mathematics-like *a priorism* at one extreme to an eighteenth-century empiricism at the other. However, as we are examining the metatheory of economics merely as a source of ideas for accounting and not as an object in itself, a position which represents the view of many economists has been selected.

Machlup describes verification in economics in various ways. At one point he says:

> ... verification in the sense most relevant to us—the testing of generaliza-

---

[7] Henry Margenau, *The Nature of Physical Reality*, New York 1950, p. 105. The reader may be interested in Margenau's more subtle analyses of the processes of identifying and measuring objects in the real world, and the meaning of such processes (Ch. 6).

tions—is *a procedure designed to find out whether a set of data or observations about a class of phenomena is obtainable and can be reconciled with a particular set of hypothetical generalizations about this class of phenomena.*[8]

Machlup develops a schematic representation of the verification process which appears in Figure 1. This schematic model is explained as follows:

The design for the model was suggested by the usual metaphors about an analytical "apparatus," "machine," or "engine of pure theory." Something goes into a machine and something comes out. In this case the input is an assumption concerning some "change" occurring and causing other things to happen, and the output is the "Deduced Change," the conclusion of the (mental) operation. The machine with all its parts furnishes the connection between the "assumed cause," the input, and the "deduced effect," the outcome. The main point of this model is that *the machine is a construction of our mind, while the assumed and deduced changes should correspond to observed phenomena, to data of observation, if the machine is to serve as an instrument of explanation or prediction.* In explanations the analytical machine helps select an adequate "cause" for an observed change; in predictions it helps find a probable "effect" of an observed change.

The machine consists of many parts, all of which represent assumptions or hypotheses of different degrees of generality. The so-called *fundamental assumptions* are a fixed part of the machine; they make the machine what it is; they cannot be changed without changing the character of the entire machine. All other parts are exchangeable, like coils, relays, spools, wires, tapes, cylinders, records, or mats, something that can be selected and put in, and again taken out to be replaced by a different piece of the set. These exchangeable parts represent *assumptions about the conditions* under which the Assumed Change must operate. Some of the parts are exchanged all the time, some less frequently, some only seldom. Parts of type A, the Assumed Conditions as to "type of case," are most frequently exchanged. Parts of type B, the Assumed Conditions as to "type of setting," will stay in the machine for a longer time and there need be less variety in the set from which they are selected. Parts of type C, the Assumed Conditions as to "type of economy," are least exchangeable, and there will be only a small assortment of alternative pieces to choose from.[9]

This conception of the verification process generally supports our previous observation that verification in economics may well be a reasonable analogue of verification in the physical sciences.

Perhaps the major reservation expressed by Machlup and other economists regarding the verification procedure in economics *vis-à-vis* that used in the physical sciences is the uniqueness of events and non-reproducibility of experiments. It is argued that unlike the controlled laboratory experiments that are performed by the physical scientist, the economist is unable to repeat the unique conditions specified in his model. The actual conditions of 'Ex-

[8] Machlup, 'The Problem of Verification in Economics,' pp. 1–2. The diagram is from p. 13.
[9] Machlup, p. 12.

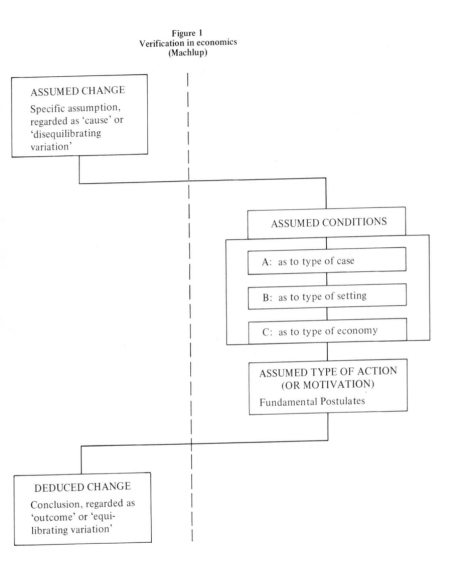

Figure 1
Verification in economics
(Machlup)

ASSUMED CHANGE

Specific assumption,
regarded as 'cause' or
'disequilibrating
variation'

ASSUMED CONDITIONS

A: as to type of case

B: as to type of setting

C: as to type of economy

ASSUMED TYPE OF ACTION
(OR MOTIVATION)

Fundamental Postulates

DEDUCED CHANGE

Conclusion, regarded as
'outcome' or 'equi-
librating variation'

**A Model of the Use of an Analytical
Apparatus**

On the right side is the 'machine of pure
theory', a mental *construction* for heuristic
purposes; on the left side are assumptions of
independent and dependent variables whose
correspondence with data of observation may
be tested.

periment 2' cannot be exactly the same as the conditions of 'Experiment 1.' However, this circumstance leads only to a reservation concerning the conclusiveness and the confidence one feels in the product of the verification procedure.[10] We might well conclude that we have *not* distinguished a situation in which a different truth criterion is applied; essentially the same procedure used in the physical sciences is also applied in economics.

Other social sciences, such as psychology and sociology, appear to possess essentially the same characteristics as economics—in respects pertinent to this inquiry—and thus, to the extent that relatively rigorous theories exist in these disciplines, the same testing or confirmation procedures would seem to apply. The major characteristic connecting the disciplines is, for our purposes, the existence of theoretical propositions about variables in the real world which are not subject to the influence of the investigator. Perhaps the degree of conclusiveness in these disciplines is less than that in economics; yet, as previously indicated, this does not alter our conclusions, since it is the nature of the truth criterion, and not the degree of corroboration afforded by present testing procedures, that is relevant to our investigation.

In summary, we conclude that there exist but two distinctive truth criteria. Truth of a mathematical theory is predicated upon logical consistency. Truth of a theory in the physical and social sciences is based upon correspondence between deduced results and observable phenomena. We have taken the position in the latter case that the fundamental assumptions or hypotheses are not testable propositions; rather they are the source of unique theories, each of which is subject to empirical test. In respect of disciplines in which the tests are less conclusive, the choice of a particular theory for a given application becomes more subjective; accordingly, it is subject to applicational validation rather than metatheoretical investigation.

What Is the Accounting Theory That Is to Be Verified?

A purely abstract accounting theory, independent of the impingements of the atmosphere of business, would seem to be inconsistent with the origins of accounting and its role in the business world. Most accountants would contend that the concepts of accounting theory have real world referents. As we have shown, if that is to be the case the validity of an accounting theory is not dependent upon its logical consistency alone. It should therefore be possible to identify the referents in the real world which correspond with certain of the deduced results in accounting theory, or in particular accounting theories.

---

[10] One is tempted to conjecture at this point that Machlup and other economists overstate the absolute reproducibility of the experiments in the physical sciences, and thus understate the degree of confirmation of empirical tests in economics. However, this subtlety is more relevant to a development of the metatheoretical properties of economics rather than an exploratory study of its general properties for use in reflecting upon an accounting metatheory.

The identification of real world referents is not as easy as it might appear at first glance. Several classes of phenomena are candidates. First, one might take the ultra-empiricist (perhaps now behavioural) view, that accounting is merely what accountants do. Here the object of attention is the person of the accountant as he engages in his 'art.' This choice lacks appeal for a variety of reasons, the most important of which is that the study of accountants *as accountants* falls more properly within the domain of the sociologist. Even if this objection were disregarded, however, to adopt as the referent of accounting theory 'accountants as actors in the business environment' does not seem to provide a basis for a reasonably general, and pregnant set of accounting constructs.

Another possible referent for accounting theory is the business enterprise. That it is a candidate for choice is suggested by the dominant and converging attention given to it—both in accounting theory and in procedural pronouncements of the AICPA. An important instance of this attention in theory construction is the use of expected or normative behaviour patterns of the enterprise in arguments about the usefulness of particular accounting constructs, or sets of constructs. For example, arguments advanced on behalf of current cost and replacement cost often cite the opportunities available to the enterprise and the behaviour pattern it is expected to exhibit regarding the replacement of inventory or the replenishment of fixed assets. To take another case, Chambers' argument for current cash equivalents is based upon the position that this measure of resources reflects the options open to the enterprise (or the manager of the enterprise). In all these instances, however, characteristics of the enterprise appear to be adduced in arguments about a different referent (e.g. the real world referent of the construct 'value measure,' whatever this might be). The enterprise *per se* is not the primary referent.

A third possible referent is the user of accounting data. In a manner analogous to the use of the behaviour of the business enterprise or manager in support of a particular proposition, reference to users would (and does) provide a basis for advocating the superiority of one possible accounting construct over another. As will be argued later, we believe that the needs of the recipient of accounting information play an important role in the attempt to relate accounting to the business world, but the recipient himself does not appear to be the *specific* object of inquiry about which accounting theorists assert propositions.

Finally, we might posit that the referent of accounting theory is neither individuals nor organizations, but rather some abstraction having defined attributes; thus accounting is merely what it is defined to be.[11] In particular, accountants are concerned with wealth, both in dynamic and static contexts,

---

[11] An extreme form of this conception, which seems to leave accounting with little, if any, empirical or deductive content, is found in the following statement:

and wealth is an abstraction that must be defined and thereafter measured. This position is essentially the one taken by Professor Myron Gordon who, while allowing the possibility of a larger domain of accounting theory, says that 'the literature that may be designated as accounting theory deals with (1) the choice among alternative definitions of income, and (2) the measurement rules that follow from and implement or that supplement a definition.'[12] Accordingly, the objects of accounting theory are the referents that we define; they do not exist in a tangible form in the real world.

If an abstract entity as defined by the accountant is the referent of accounting theory, what determines the defined attributes and the kinds of proposition which will be generated?

Several characteristics or conditioning influences are of interest. First, the products of accounting are statements; the theory of accounting will therefore concern itself with the conditions under which statements are interpretable—the problem of communication. Second, the products of accounting are quantitative statements; the theory of accounting will therefore concern itself with measurement procedures. And of course there must be a set of constructs, related however abstractly, to the recipients and subjects of statements and measurements.

As for the kinds of proposition which may be generated, there is at present a manifest lack of a clear distinction between descriptive and normative propositions. The technical literature of accounting is overloaded with statements claiming that this or that phenomenon, construct or point of view is of

---

'There appear in the practice of life certain expressions which are empiricist in character but not suitable for use within scientific analysis. They may be regarded as a kind of old folklore, as speech customs which are related to the transfer of certain institutions. One speaks of the "cost" of a production and goes on using this expression not only in our bookkeeping departments but also in social analysis.... Accountants handling the profit reckoning of firms, ministers of finance handling taxes and customs of whole countries, evolved certain rules for their respective activities which could be written down and taught to the younger clerks and undersecretaries. One of the main points has been the reaching of a fair "difference" between certain "positive" and certain "negative" items recorded in their books. Expressions such as "cost," "profit," and "investment" are plausible results of bookkeeping and reckoning in money. This business is comparable with a chess player's notes of his moves or a railroad manager's notes on transport timetables and similar items of his enterprise. The transfer of chess-playing or railroad administration in a systematized way may be executed, as it were, scientifically, as far as consistency is concerned; but the important point is that the apprentice does not learn the behavior of human beings in general or the making of games or of railroads in general but only the handling of given institutions. It is a long story how economics became a discipline which appeared to be more than an administrative instruction to bookkeepers, ministers of finance, politicians, and other people who wanted to use some historically given institution such as money, taxes, or customs.' Otto Neurath, 'Foundations of the Social Sciences,' Vol. II, No. 1 of the *International Encyclopedia of Unified Science*, pp. 38-9. We hope to demonstrate that while this is closer to the truth than most of us would like to accept, it does invoke an extreme, indeed emotive, argument in order to make a distinction between different empirical disciplines. Strangely enough, this commentary on accounting is in fact an indictment of the fundamental basis of economics.

[12] Myron Gordon, 'Scope and Methods of Theory and Research in the Measurement of Income and Wealth,' *The Accounting Review*, October 1960, p. 606.

interest to accountants, and exhorting the reader to accept the writer's prescriptions. Thus, rather than attempting to validate proposals or conclusions, attention is focused on the way in which the descriptive constructs, what is said 'should be done' can be done. It might be said, of course, that most propositions within the object theory are descriptive in nature; and that the normative propositions relate primarily to the accountant as a producer of information and to the users of the information supplied. But because of the importance of these latter considerations to the acceptance of certain propositions and the rejection of others it seems appropriate, and we hope it will be fruitful, to reflect upon how they affect or condition our conception of the verification processes of accounting.

If defined entities, whose properties are measurable and measurements of which occur in communications to interested recipients, measurement and/or communication theory seem to provide appropriate analogues for accounting. If there are in the real world no such entities as those defined, then any accounting theory relating to them is not amenable to the type of verification adopted in the physical and social sciences. On the other hand, a concern with communication of information and 'meaningful' measures of defined quantities establishes some significant difference between accounting and mathematics. This is not to gainsay the possibility of creating very abstract formulations of segments of the accounting process. For example, if accounting is viewed as a measurement process, its technology, abstractly conceived, might be expressed in terms almost identical with the following description of a general measurement model:

> The process of measurement may be described *formally* as follows: Let $P = \{p_1, p_2, \ldots\}$ denote a set of physical objects or *events*. By a measurement A on P we mean a *function* which assigns to each element p of P an element $b = A(p)$ in some mathematical system $B = \{b_1, \ldots\}$. That is, to each element of P, we associate an element of some abstract system B. . . . The system B consists of a set of elements with some *mathematical structure* imposed on its elements. The nature of the set P and the actual mapping into the abstract space B comprises the operation of measurement. The mathematical structure of the system B belongs to the formal side of measurement theory. The structure of B is dictated by a set of rules or axioms which states relationships between the elements of B. [13]

Although they are not as abstract as this, the mathematical formulations of the accounting process by Mattessich [14] and Ijiri [15] are examples of theoretical

---

[13] C. H. Coombs, H. Raiffa, and R. M. Thrall, 'Some Views on Mathematical Models and Measurement Theory' in R. M. Thrall, C. H. Coombs, and R. L. Davis (eds), *Decision Processes*, New York 1954, p.25 (emphasis added).

[14] Richard Mattessich, *Accounting and Analytical Methods*, Homewood, Ill. 1964.

[15] Yuji Ijiri, *The Foundations of Accounting Measurement*, Englewood Cliffs 1967.

expositions which rely for their validation on the truth criteria of mathematics—namely, logic. However, we suspect the predominant thrust of most work on accounting theory might be more closely related to the following proposal by Gordon:

> An accounting theory may accordingly be defined as a set of statements: (1) the objective of a firm is to maximize the variable X; (2) the decision process by which the firm seeks to realize the objective is Y; (3) Z_1 and Z_2 are two alternative definitions of income, wealth, etc.; and (4) Z_1 results in a larger value for X given Y than Z_2.
>
> The task of the theorist is to arrive at such sets of statements and demonstrate by deductive and empirical evidence the validity of the conclusion. The fact that X will vary depending on Z and not merely with Y presents logical difficulties that are more apparent than real. The real task is to systematize and generalize our Z-type statements, take advantage of the work of economists and psychologists in arriving at X and Y type statements, and master the methods of research for proving statements about relations among variables.[16]

This description seems to embrace many of the essential features of the measurement and communications aspects of the accounting discipline. However, our analysis also suggests that segments of accounting theory may be different in character, and that each may have its own unique type of confirmation.[17]

What Accounting Theory Is Now Being Verified?

The previous discussion has approached the problem of the nature of empirical verification in accounting by reference to the nature of the theory to be verified. Since our purpose in this study was primarily to obtain initial insights, we now propose to direct our attention to the procedures and propositions which are currently being subjected to 'empirical verification' in an attempt to deduce a description of the accounting theory to be verified. In this appraisal we do not propose to consider surveys of practice and compendia of procedures such as are found in *Accounting Research Study No. 7* or in *Accounting Trends and Techniques*. While these documents are well organized and are useful as compilations of facts concerning what is being done

---

[16] Myron J. Gordon, 'Scope and Methods of Theory and Research . . . ', p. 618.

[17] For example, the set of theories employing abstract mathematical formulations would rely on logic for their truth criteria; those aspects of theory which are isolated as essentially a measurement process might approach the problem of empirical verification in a manner suggested by Kermit D. Larson, 'Descriptive Validity of Accounting Calculations,' *The Accounting Review*, July 1967. Finally, other aspects of accounting theory might be treated solely as communication problems, requiring different validation procedures, many of which would probably come from psychology.

in practice, they do not purport to provide the substance, or the means, of *verifying* any related theoretical proposition.[18]

Attempts to verify propositions about accounting are a comparatively recent theoretical and empirical exercise, particularly if one looks for research proposals stated in the strict form of hypotheses. Indeed, most of the examples are dated within the last five years. An indication of the general nature of the investigations recently completed, or currently in process, is given in the Appendix, a classified summary of empirical research projects reported in the literature. We have classified the projects as follows:

   I. Effect of Accounting Measurements on Users (Internal and External)
  II. Relationship between Accounting Measurements and Selected Dependent Variables
 III. Behaviour Patterns of Accounting Measurements
 IV. Effect of Users on Accounting Measurements
  V. Miscellaneous Research Projects.

A brief commentary on each of these classes may be helpful.

I. The first class embraces a variety of propositions. This work seeks to determine whether or not accounting data enter into the decision processes of the user, whether different types of measurements produce different decisions (which, of course, presupposes a positive answer to the previous question), and lastly, which selected measure of a given variable is the most desirable. Accordingly, this class of projects focuses on the communication aspects of accounting and draws its inspiration from the desire for establishing normal or uniform rules. It is also consonant with the Gordon scheme outlined in the previous section. II. The second class is explicitly independent of user influences. It relies on measured associations between accounting measurements and, in most cases, independently determined business or economic variables. Yet, in some instances, an association presumes a user acting as an intermediary between the dependent and the independent variable. For example, if there is a relationship between measures of income and stock prices, there is probably a presumption that this relationship exists due to the fact that the accounting measures have been communicated to interested investors and, using this information, investors have engaged in market transactions. In other instances, this implicit introduction of the user does not exist. III. The third class embraces analytical studies of accounting measurements under different environmental conditions or policy circumstances.

---

[18] The exclusion of such studies may indicate bias. If 'accounting is what accountants do,' then such inventories and compendia may be prime sources of inductive generalizations; however, since most accounting theorists do not seem to accept this position, and further because its adoption would seem to generate a rather sterile verification requirement, we have chosen to eliminate it from our consideration.

This type of research provides insight into the limiting values that the measured quantities may assume under the conditions which are postulated, and is thus more strongly related to the measurement aspect of accounting. IV. The fourth class is a variation on the first. In Class I, the researcher attempts to discover whether accounting data influence or affect the user and in what manner. In the fourth class, however, the researchers seek to discover whether or not the user influences the types of accounting measurements that are produced. To the degree that there is evidence of such influence, some measure is provided of indirect confirmation for Class I type projects, since it may be assumed that at least the individuals influencing measurements must believe that resulting measurements affect the recipients of accounting data. V. The final category is a miscellaneous one, consisting primarily of studies designed to gain some understanding of the nature of the practising profession. In some instances, the character of these studies approaches that of the surveys of practice which, as we said earlier, we have excluded from our set of admissible research projects.

The summary statement of types of research reported appears to support the position reached in the preceding section. Emphasis is placed upon the reporting of measurements as a descriptive process, and on the problem of choosing what shall be communicated to users in the context of some stated objective.

One additional point of interest which emerges from the empirical research projects cited in the Appendix is the range of methods of confirmation or testing. Three distinct categories can be identified:

1. Statistical tests of data (data analyses),
2. Laboratory experiments, and
3. Simulation.

The statistical tests of data rely to a large extent upon a presumed connection between a reported amount or statement proposition and a real world action or event. This connection is mediated by a 'black box.' How the reported amount or statement gives rise to a change in the course of affairs and how other concurrent affairs affect the dependent event are not describable; but the analyses purport to indicate whether or not there is a significant connection by measures of association. The laboratory experiments are mainly applications of methods of psychological inquiry so structured that they deal with accounting or related matters. Generally they produce only reasonably plausible conclusions. A recurring objection to laboratory work of this kind is the difficulty of knowing whether the subjects are 'representative.' Interestingly enough, this difficulty is mentioned both by independent critics of 'confirmed' results and by researchers 'explaining' unconfirmed hypotheses. Finally, the simulation technique is a new and interesting approach to confirmation which assumes many different forms. It may involve a man-machine interaction; the computer simulates some aspect of the economic environment and reacts continuously to human decisions.[19] In other instances, there is no human element in the exercise and the simulation consists merely of the working out of a probabalistic counterpart of the real world.[20] Finally, a simulation may be used as a strictly analytical device to investigate the behaviour pattern of a given variable under various postulated conditions.[21] The degree of confirmation given by simulation exercises appears to be an unresolved question in all empirical sciences; however, we would speculate that it will prove to be one of the most useful and widely applicable forms of the verification process in accounting.

[19] Recent efforts to use the Carnegie-Mellon business simulation for research purposes are illustrative of a more complex form of this approach; a study by Professor Bruns, 'The Accounting Period Concept and its Effect on Management Decisions,' is a more constrained form of this type of analysis.

[20] The study by Bonini, *Simulation of Information and Decision Systems of the Firm*, is illustrative of this type of simulation.

[21] The McCosh project, 'Accounting Consistency—Key to Stockholder Information,' reflects this type of use of the simulation technique.

*Nicholas J. Gonedes is Assistant Professor of
Accounting, Graduate School of Business at
the University of Chicago.*

Efficient Capital Markets and External Accounting

Nicholas J. Gonedes

The purpose of this paper is to present a framework that should be useful in making evaluative and prescriptive statements about accounting, developing *testable* hypotheses, and interpreting the results of hypothesis tests. For reasons that will subsequently become evident, attention is restricted to accounting numbers that are (or can be) made available given the current technology (which includes existing accounting procedures). Throughout, the accounting process will be treated as a production process, the outputs of which are numbers that possess potential informational content.

The discussion that follows pays particular attention to the implications of capital market *efficiency* for accounting. The discussion will be confined to accounting numbers transmitted to capital-market transactors viewed as an *aggregate*.[1] (Considering only *aggregate* capital market behavior will be

An earlier version of this paper was presented at the Annual Meeting of the American Accounting Association, University of Maryland, August, 1970. I am indebted to Ray Ball, Eugene Fama, David Green, Larry Revsine, Roman Weil, E.E. Williams, and, in particular Robert Officer and Nicholas Dopuch for their comments on earlier drafts.

[1] The phrase *in the aggregate* needs to be emphasized. Ignoring differences between *aggregate* behavior and *individual* behavior, as I sometimes did in *Accounting for Common Stockholders* (University of Texas Press, 1969), may induce unnecessary or erroneous propositions relative to the tasks at hand. A useful discussion in this regard appears in Fritz Machlup, "Theories of the Firm: Marginalist, Behavioral, Managerial," *American Economic Review* (March 1967), pp. 1-33.

Reprinted by permission of the author and publisher from *The Accounting Review*, Vol. XLVII, January, 1972, pp. 11-21.

justified below.) Thus, the entire discussion will pertain to "external accounting" rather than "internal accounting."

The dichotomization of accounting into "external" and "internal" accounting may be distasteful to some. It seems that the dichotomy is unnecessary in developing a general perspective of accounting, e.g., a producer of numbers that possess potential informational content. The perspective is equally applicable to, say, the income numbers transmitted to the capital markets and the numbers generated via mathematical programming tools for purposes of managerial decision making. On the other hand, the dichotomy may be quite fruitful in defining issues of interest and formulating research strategies, among other things. The latter proposition is predicated upon the (seemingly trivial) observation that the relationship between an accounting process and those within a firm differs from the relationship between an accounting process and the capital markets. In addition, the applicability of normative statements (regarding users' behavior) with respect to internal accounting does not appear to be the same as in the case of external accounting. (The rationale underlying this statement will appear below.)

The major argument of this paper is quite simple (though, I hope, not simple-minded): observations of the market reactions of recipients of accounting outputs should govern evaluations of the actual information content of accounting numbers produced via a given set of procedures and the informational content of accounting numbers produced via an alternative set of accounting procedures. As will be indicated below, if accounting numbers do not reflect inside information at about the time that they are made publicly available, then one should expect these market reactions to be anticipatory reactions (assuming that the numbers do have informational content). After my major argument is developed, I shall attempt to respond to some major counter-arguments, such as: (1) that observations of recipients' reactions should not govern evaluations of accounting numbers and procedures because recipients may have been "conditioned" to react in a particular manner, and (2) that recipients may be reacting to numbers regarding which they (a) "should not" be reacting or (b) "should not" be reacting in the manner in which they are reacting.

Many of my statements are based upon the theory and evidence regarding the efficient markets model, so I shall begin with a brief commentary on the latter.[2]

---

[2] A very extensive recent review of this material appears in Eugene F. Fama, "Efficient Capital Markets: A Review of Theory and Empirical Work," *Journal of Finance* (May 1970), pp. 383–417. See also Eugene F. Fama, "The Behavior of Stock Market Prices," *Journal of Business* (January 1965), pp. 34–105; Benoit Mandelbrot, "The Variation of Certain Speculative Prices," *Journal of Business* (October 1963), pp. 394–429; Benoit Mandelbrot, "Forecasts of Futures Prices, Unbiased Markets and Martingale Models," *Journal of Business* (January 1966), pp. 242–55; Paul A. Samuelson, "Proof that Properly Anticipated Prices Fluctuate Randomly," *Industrial Management Review* (Spring 1965), pp. 41–49; and Richard Roll, "The Efficient Market Model Applied to U.S. Treasury Bill Rates," unpublished Ph.D. thesis, University of Chicago, 1968.

A Brief Commentary on the Efficient-Markets Model

There exists a relatively large (and quite reliable) body of evidence that is consistent with the proposition that the market for securities is an efficient market in the sense that: (1) market prices "fully reflect" all publicly available information and, by implication, (2) market prices react instantaneously and unbiasedly to new information. The empirical implications of these assertions can be made concrete by supposing that they are true and, in addition, by supposing that market equilibrium can be described in terms of expected rates of return measured (for example) via the Sharpe-Lintner[3] asset-pricing model which relates asset-returns to asset-risk.

Let $E[\tilde{r}_{it+1} \mid \Omega_t]$ be the expected rate of return on the ith security at $t+1$ given all publicly available information, Ω_t, at a time t. The statements that (1) market equilibrium may be described in terms of expected rates of return and (2) market prices fully reflect all publicly available information, Ω_t, imply that one cannot on average earn "abnormal" returns by using the components of Ω_t, i.e.,

(1)
$$E[\tilde{Y}_{it+1} \mid \Omega_t] = 0, \ t = 1, 2, \ldots$$

where:

$$\tilde{Y}_{it+1} = \tilde{r}_{it+1} - E[\tilde{r}_{it+1} \mid \Omega_t].$$

In other words, the rate of return series, $(\tilde{r}_{it+1})$ is a "fair game" relative to the information series (Ω_t).

Recall that (1) is derived by assuming that efficiency conditions prevail. In order to test the efficient markets model, (1) is used as a basis for testable implications. For example, one obvious component of the series (Ω_t) is the series of observed rates of return. Hence, one test of the fair game property is a test of whether trading systems based upon observed rates of return (or prices) permit one to consistently earn "abnormal" rates of return. Another

---

[3] William F. Sharpe, "Capital Asset Prices: A Theory of Market Equilibrium Under Conditions of Risk," *Journal of Finance* (September 1964), pp. 425–42; John Lintner, "The Valuation of Risk Assets and the Selection of Risky Investments in Stock Portfolios and Capital Budgets," *Review of Economics and Statistics* (February 1965), pp. 13–37. Also see William F. Sharpe, "A Simplified Model for Portfolio Analysis," *Management Science* (January 1963), pp. 277–93; William F. Sharpe, *Portfolio Theory and Capital Markets* (McGraw-Hill, 1970); John Lintner, "Security Prices, Risk, and Maximal Gains from Diversification," *Journal of Finance* (December 1965), pp. 587–615; John Lintner, "The Aggregation of Investors' Diverse Judgments and Preferences in Purely Competitive Security Markets," *Journal of Financial and Quantitative Analysis* (December 1969), pp. 347–400; Jan Mossin, "Equilibrium in a Capital Asset Market," *Econometrica* (October 1966), pp. 768–83; Eugene F. Fama, "Risk Return and Equilibrium," *Journal of Political Economy* (January–February 1971), pp. 30–55; and Eugene F. Fama, "Risk Return and Equilibrium: Some Clarifying Comments," *Journal of Finance* (March 1968), pp. 29–40.

test involves examining the estimated serial covariances of the "fair game" random variable, $\tilde{Y}_{it+1} = \tilde{r}_{it+1} - E[\tilde{r}_{it+1} \mid \Omega_t]$ since for a fair game random variable, the expected values of these estimates equal zero, for all lags. (Note, that zero serial covariances are necessary, not sufficient, conditions.) Results from and discussions of these types of tests are readily available.[4]

As noted earlier, the efficient markets model implies that market prices adjust "instantaneously" and unbiasedly to new information. Hence another method of testing the model involves examining market reactions to new information that is publicly available, such as earnings announcements, stock-split announcements, and dividend announcements. Studies that employ this approach include those by Ball and Brown, Beaver, Fama *et al.*, Scholes, Waud, and Ball.[5]

Another type of test is concerned with the extent to which efficiency conditions prevail. The tests described above focus upon efficiency conditions defined relative to *publicly available* information. Suppose, however, that the rate of return series ($\tilde{r}_{it}$) fully reflects *all* available information. This implies that no individual or group of individuals can consistently earn "abnormal" rates of return because of "monopolistic" power over some kind(s) of available information. This type of finding would greatly extend the applicability of the efficient markets model. Tests conducted with respect to this issue examine the performance of those who might have potential "monopolistic" power over some available information, e.g., stock exchange specialists, mutual funds, and corporate insiders. Evidence regarding this issue was provided by Jensen, Niederhoffer and Osborne, Sharpe, and Scholes.[6]

---

[4] See, e.g., Fama, "The Behavior of Stock Market Prices," pp. 34–105; Eugene F. Fama and Marshall E. Blume, "Filter Rules and Stock Market Trading," *Journal of Business* (January 1966), pp. 226–41; M.C. Jensen and G.A. Bennington, "Random Walks and Technical Theories: Some Additional Evidence," *Journal of Finance* (May 1960), pp. 469–82; Roll, "The Efficient Market Model," 1968; and the articles in: *Journal of Financial and Quantitative Analysis* (September 1968), a special issue devoted to the Random Walk Hypothesis; and Paul H. Cootner, *The Random Character of Stock Market Prices* (The MIT Press, 1964).

[5] Ray Ball and Philip Brown, "An Empirical Evaluation of Accounting Income Numbers," *Journal of Accounting Research* (Autumn 1968), pp. 159–78; William H. Beaver, "The Information Content," *Empirical Research in Accounting; Selected Studies 1968*, Supplement to the *Journal of Accounting Research*, VI, pp. 67–92; Eugene F. Fama, L. Fisher, M.C. Jensen and Richard Roll, "The Adjustment of Stock Prices to New Information," *International Economic Review* (February 1969), pp. 1–21; Myron Scholes, "A Test of the Competitive Market Hypothesis: The Market for New Issues and Secondary Offerings," unpublished Ph.D. thesis, University of Chicago, 1969; Roger N. Waud, "Public Interpretation of Discount Rate Changes: Evidence on the 'Announcement Effect,'" *Econometrica* (March 1970), pp. 231–50; and Ray Ball, "Changes in Accounting Techniques and Stock Prices," unpublished research in progress.

[6] M.C. Jensen, "The Performance of Mutual Funds in the Period 1945–1964," *Journal of Finance* (May 1968), pp. 389–416; M.C. Jensen, "Risk, The Pricing of Capital Assets, and the Evaluation of Investment Portfolios," *Journal of Business* (April 1969), pp. 167–247; Victor Niederhoffer and M.F.M. Osborne, "Market Making and Reversal on the New York Stock Exchange," *Journal of the American Statistical Association* (December 1966), pp. 897–916; William F. Sharpe, "Mutual Fund Performance," *Journal of Business* (January 1966), pp. 119–38; and Scholes, "A Test of the Competitive Market Hypothesis."

In general, the efficient markets model has held up quite well. The strongest support is provided by those studies that examine the "fair game" properties of the model relative to observed rates of return (or prices). Evidence provided by studies that deal with market reactions to new information is also consistent with the model though, admittedly, these kinds of tests have not yet been applied to all possible types of new information. The evidence provided by the few tests that focus upon transactors that may have "monopolistic" access to available information is, primarily, consistent with the model; yet some of these tests provide some interesting contradictory evidence. For example, the work of Niederhoffer and Osborne[7] suggests that specialists on the New York Stock Exchange may possess and exploit monopolistic access to information. The results presented in Jensen[8] do not suggest that mutual funds never have access to "inside information." Also, Scholes' results[9] suggest that corporate insiders may have monopolistic access to information. He observed significant market reactions to large trades consummated on behalf of corporate insiders. (The price reactions seemed to be independent of the number of shares involved.) This result suggests that such transactions have information content and that the market reacts rapidly to this publicly available source of information. But the same evidence suggests that corporate insiders may occasionally have monopolistic access to existing information or "inside information." Operationally, "inside information" may be defined as information to which the market would react if it were available (or predictable). When, and if, the information ultimately becomes available, the market reacts rapidly to it. The fact that we observe market reactions at about the time the insiders' transactions occur (rather than, say, "anticipatory" reactions relative to these transactions) suggests that up to the time of the transaction, these corporate insiders may have had inside information and that this information (if it exists) is "received" by the market via the transactions rather than before the transactions (when the insiders may have acquired the information). Thus, Scholes' study provides evidence in support of the efficient markets model, when defined relative to all *publicly* available information, and it provides some evidence that is inconsistent with the model, when defined relative to all available information.[10]

A recent remark by Fama is a fair appraisal of the available evidence regarding the efficient markets model:

---

[7] Niederhoffer and Osborne, "Market Making and Reversal," pp. 897–916.

[8] M. C. Jensen, "Risk, The Pricing of Capital Assets, and the Evaluation of Investment Portfolios," *Journal of Business* (April 1969), pp. 167–247.

[9] Scholes, "A Test of the Competitive Market Hypothesis."

[10] Recognize however (as did Scholes) that some of the sample sizes used in his study were relatively small. Also, in this regard, one may want to consider the general normative issue of minimizing "abnormal returns" (if they exist) to "insiders" via alternative supply-of-information mechanisms.

The evidence in support of the efficient markets model, is extensive and (somewhat uniquely in economics) contradictory evidence is sparse. Nevertheless, we do not want to leave the impression that all issues are closed. The old saw, "much remains to be done," is relevant here as elsewhere.[11]

The theory and evidence regarding the efficient markets model have some important implications with respect to the context within which the accounting process functions. In particular, it appears that the accounting process— *qua* supplier of information—does not possess strict "monopoly power" over the supply of information pertinent to the valuation of a firm. Instead, it appears that the accounting process (*qua* supplier of information) functions within a competitive context. Some implications of these propositions will be considered shortly. First, however, an attempt will be made to clarify these statements and their underlying rationale.

On the Competitive Context of Accounting Numbers

The "fair game" model used above,

$$(2) \qquad E[\tilde{r}_{it+1} - E(\tilde{r}_{it+1} \mid \Omega_t) \mid \Omega_t] = 0,$$

states that the rate of return series ($\tilde{r}_{it+1}$) is a "fair game" in regard to the information series (Ω_t). Now, consider the types of events represented in (Ω_t) and the types of events represented by accounting numbers.

Presumably, the accounting numbers issued by any firm reflect events that impinged upon the firm's operations. Such events include (1) those that occur within the factor-input markets regarding which the firm is a transactor, and (2) those that occur within the output markets of the firm. These kinds of events may be specific to a particular industry or they may be economy-wide events. Finally, some of the events that influence a firm's operations may be specific to that firm. This perspective of a firm's operations is similar to that which underlies the "market model" (and its variants) for rates of return on common stocks,[12] namely, that the behavior of a given security's rate of return may be explained in part by general market (and possibly industry) factors and in part by factors affecting that particular security only. More abstractly, this perspective merely proposes the existence of cross-sectional dependence with respect to firms' operations, as measured by, for example, firms' income numbers, sales numbers, and so forth.

The preceding statements are not merely speculations. Evidence supporting them was provided by Brealey, Brown and Ball, Lev and Gonedes.[13]

11 Fama, "Efficient Capital Markets," p. 416.

12 See Benjamin F. King, "Market and Industry Factors in Stock Price Behavior," *Journal of Business* (January 1966), pp. 139–90 and the references in footnote 3.

13 R. A. Brealey, *An Introduction to Risk and Return from Common Stocks* (The MIT Press, 1969); Philip Brown and Ray Ball, "Some Preliminary Findings on the Association Between the

The information series, (Ω_t), also contains indicants that reflect economy-wide and industry-wide events. Such indicants include industrial-production reports, national income reports, reports on industrial prices, reports on stabilization policies (e.g., reports on the policies of the Federal Reserve Board), and forecasts that emanate from trade-group conferences, *inter alia*. All such items are obviously publicly available. Additionally—and more importantly for our purposes—they are competitive sources of information *vis-à-vis* accounting numbers because both kinds of information sources reflect the same types of events: economy-wide events and industry-wide events.

Evidence that is consistent with the existence of competing sources of information regarding a firm's operations was provided by Ball and Brown, Gonedes, Watts, and Fama, Fisher, Jensen and Roll.[14] In particular, the consistency is reflected in the "anticipatory" price movements that precede announcements of accounting numbers, such as accounting income numbers. If there were nothing competing with accounting numbers as sources of information, then (assuming that accounting numbers have some informational content) one would expect to observe rapid price movements at the time the accounting numbers are issued (officially). Under these conditions, one would not expect to observe price movements that begin to "anticipate" accounting numbers by several months or weeks. Under these (admittedly extreme) conditions, the informational content of accounting numbers would constitute "inside information" (as defined earlier); hence there would be no market reaction to the numbers until they were brought "outside" and made part of the publicly available information. Yet, the empirical results referenced above (footnote 14) do not support the existence of such a market reaction. Of course, if accounting numbers possessed no informational content, then one would expect to observe neither "anticipatory" market reactions nor sharp price reactions at the time the numbers are issued. Since the available evidence documents the "anticipatory" movements, the latter proposition is not supported.

Alternative indicants of economy-wide and industry-wide events are not the only potential competitors of accounting numbers *qua* sources of information. Additional potential competitors include, for example, statements

---

Earnings of a Firm, Its Industry, and the Economy," *Empirical Research in Accounting; Selected Studies, 1967*, supplement to the *Journal of Accounting Research*, VI, pp. 55–77; Baruch Lev, "Industry Averages as Targets for Financial Ratios," *Journal of Accounting Research* (Autumn 1969), pp. 290–99; and Nicholas J. Gonedes, "On Accounting-Based and Market-Based Estimates of Systematic Variability," and "Evidence on the Information Content of Accounting Numbers," Report No. 7115, Center for Mathematical Studies in Business and Economics, University of Chicago, March 1971.

[14] Ray Ball and Philip Brown, "An Empirical Evaluation of Accounting Income Numbers," *Journal of Accounting Research* (Autumn 1968), pp. 159–78; Nicholas J. Gonedes, "Some Evidence on Investor Actions and Accounting Messages, The Parts I and II *Accounting Review*, (April 1971; July 1971); Ross Watts, "The Informational Content of Dividends," Ph.D. thesis, University of Chicago, 1971; and Fama, Fisher, Jensen and Roll, "The Adjustment of Stock Prices," pp. 1–21.

made by corporate officials regarding their firms' operations, releases issued by brokerage firms, releases issued by market-newsletter services, reports filed with the S.E.C. on insider trading, reports on changes in a firm's management, registrations with the S.E.C. with respect to security flotations, information "leakages," and the outputs of prediction models, among other things. If such kinds of publicly available information reflect something that, *ex ante*, affects the value of a firm, then, according to the efficient markets model, their informational content will be impounded in the current market price.

One implication of the preceding remarks is that market transactors, in the aggregate, do not blindly accept and use only accounting numbers in establishing market prices. The market's reactions (if any) to accounting numbers suggest that the events reflected in accounting numbers, e.g., economy-wide and industry-wide events, affect the values of firms and, hence, the informational content of these numbers will be impounded in current market prices. But alternative sources of information also reflect these events; hence, the market is not constrained to use accounting numbers only as sources of information regarding these events. Additionally, if these alternative sources of information suggest that accounting numbers are "deficient" indicators of events that affect the values of firms, then the accounting numbers will not be blindly used by the market. That is, if accounting numbers have little or no informational content, alternative sources of information could be selected. Furthermore, the competitive context of accounting numbers will result in their not being used if they lose their informational content.

Since market transactors, in the aggregate, do not blindly accept and use accounting numbers only, the market's reactions to accounting numbers (e.g., the anticipatory reactions noted above) provide reliable indications of accounting numbers informational content.[15] If these reactions do exist, then the implication is that accounting numbers do reflect events that affect the values of firms (i.e., that they do have informational content). Observe that the above conclusion about market reactions as evaluators of accounting numbers' informational content is not dependent upon any particular accounting procedure or accounting definition (e.g., a definition of "income" or "cost"). Thus, for example, it is quite possible that the informational content of, say, accounting income numbers computed according to one procedure will be insignificantly, or no different from income numbers computed according to an alternative procedure, as revealed by the reactions of the market (in the aggregate) to these numbers (or predictive ability tests, discussed below). A similar remark may be applicable to alternative definitions of income (e.g., income before extraordinary items or after extraordi-

---

[15] This is the so-called Psychological Interpretation of accounting theory discussed by Sterling, "On Theory Construction and Verification," pp. 444–457. *The Accounting Review* (July 1970).

nary items). If so, then there may be no empirical support for dogmatic statements proclaiming that one procedure or definition is "better" than some other one, at least from the point of view of aggregate market behavior.

The preceding remarks emphasize *aggregate* market behavior. This emphasis is justified by the nature of the capital markets. To see this, first recall that an efficient market is a competitive market, a market within which each individual is a *price taker*. Within the context of such a market, market behavior is a result of the interactions among rival price takers. That is, within the context of such a market setting, achievement of a competitive solution (the establishment of competitive prices) is induced by the workings of the system as a whole, or *aggregate* market behavior, and not necessarily by individual "rationality." Rejection of this argument would seem to involve the familiar *Fallacy of Composition*, i.e., the argument that what is true for a part is necessarily true for the whole.

Of course, one might argue that the reliability of market reactions as evaluators of accounting numbers is suspect because the procedures used to produce the numbers may have induced market inefficiencies. This argument suggests that the market ought not be reacting the way it is reacting and, hence, that continuing to provide such numbers would be socially dysfunctional. Also, one might argue that the market is "conditioned" to react as it is reacting and, thus, market reactions do not provide evaluations of the informational content of accounting numbers. Instead, they provide indicants of the efficacy of conditioning processes. These arguments are considered in turn.

Some Counter Arguments

First, the preceding remarks on market efficiency and competitive sources of information suggest that the use of any alternative accounting procedure will not, taken by itself, induce market inefficiencies, e.g., *systematic* forecasting errors that induce *systematic* valuation errors. Suppose that the contrary were true, then an opportunity to earn "abnormal" profits by taking advantage of the market's systematic errors would exist. For some t^*, this opportunity's existence would be part of the availiable information, Ω_{t^*}. Hence, using the "fair game" properties of the efficient markets model, discussed above, one may conclude that the existence of this opportunity would lead to its own demise via market adjustments at t^*. Note that the detection of these systematic errors might be induced by observations of the errors themselves as well as the indications of sources of information that compete with accounting numbers.

Of course, one might argue that "nobody" aside from a small number of persons (e.g., persons trained in accounting) will recognize that an accounting procedure is inducing a market inefficiency. The argument must allow at least one person to recognize the induced inefficiency, or else how could one propose that there is such an inefficiency in the first place? If this situation prevails, then knowledge of the induced inefficiency is, operationally, "inside information" for the person(s) aware of the inefficiency. That is, all other persons would react to this information if they had it, and when (and if) the information becomes publicly available, the market will rapidly react to it. Now, consider the situation of the omniscient group. They are confronted by an opportunity to earn "abnormal" profits. So, they may take advantage of this particular opportunity by transacting in the market directly and selling information regarding the alleged inefficiency or attempting to sell "superior" portfolio management services by demonstrating their "superior" forecasting abilities. The omniscient group will be motivated to do these things in order to realize the expected "abnormal" returns. More simply, the group possessing the information need only publicize the information.[16] If this information is, in fact, inside information, the market will react to it. In either case (i.e., selling the information or merely publicizing it), the existence of the detectable accounting-induced inefficiency will, on average, lead to its own demise in the context of an efficient capital market.

Finally, one might assert that the existence of an inefficiency (induced by the choice of an accounting procedure) may be detectable, but the market may not be able to "correct" the inefficiency because the results of using the alternative accounting procedures may not be available. Hence, one may only be able to assert, say, that income is "overstated" because of a depreciation procedure, but the magnitude of the "overstatement" is not known with certainty because the results of using different depreciation procedures are not provided by the firm(s) under review. But in a world of uncertainty, few things are known with probability equal to one; most human actions must (explicitly or implicitly) be predicated upon nondegenerate probability distributions. And, decision-theoretic tools for constructing such distributions for the effects of alternative accounting procedures do exist.[17]

The preceding remarks merely recognize that (detectable) systematic forecasting errors induced by accounting procedures provide profitable opportunities for those who possess more accurate forecasts, e.g., sellers of more

---

[16] Thus, if academics are the possessors of the "inside" information, they may publish articles on the induced inefficiency, thus transforming the "inside" information to publicly available information.

[17] See, for example J.L. Livingstone, "Accelerated Depreciation and Deferred Taxes: An Empirical Study of Fluctuating Asset Expenditures," *Empirical Research in Accounting; Selected Studies, 1967,* supplement to the *Journal of Accounting Research,* VI, pp. 93–117; J.L. Livingstone, "Accelerated Depreciation, Cyclical Asset Expenditures, and Deferred Taxes," *Journal of Accounting Research* (Spring 1968), pp. 77–94; J.L. Livingstone, "Accelerated Depreciation, Tax Allocation, and Cyclical Asset Expenditures of Large Manufacturing Companies," *Journal of Accounting Research* (Autumn 1969), pp. 245–56; and Eugene F. Brigham, "The Effects of Alternative Depreciation Policies on Reported Profits," *The Accounting Review* (January 1968), pp. 46–61.

accurate forecasts or transactors who possess more accurate forecasts. On average, the actions of these persons will provide a basis for the opportunities' demise. In general, if expectations are "rational," as defined by Muth,[18] then any systematic effect(s) of something known on something predicted will be taken into account in forming the prediction.

Another argument that questions the reliability of market reactions as means of evaluating the informational content of accounting numbers is predicated upon the possibility of "conditioning" transactors so that they will react in a particular manner to accounting numbers.[19] A concise statement of this argument was provided by Sterling:

> If the response of receivers to accounting stimuli is to be taken as evidence that certain kinds of accounting practices are justified, then we must not overlook the possibility that those responses were conditioned. Accounting reports have been issued for a long time, and their issuance has been accompanied by a rather impressive ceremony performed by the managers and accountants who issue them. The receivers are likely to have gained the impression that they ought to react, and have noted that others react, and thereby have become conditioned to react.[20]

I shall assume that Sterling had in mind a kind of "conditioning" that may be observed (directly or indirectly). If this were not the case, his assertion would not be testable. As he suggested (via quotations from Hempel)[21] such an assertion would have no empirical import and, thus, "it cannot be significantly proposed or entertained as a scientific hypothesis or theory."[22]

Presumably, the "conditioning" argument is advanced in order to suggest that the market may not be doing what it "should" be doing with accounting numbers, i.e., that there may be systematic accounting-induced errors in forecasts predicated upon accounting numbers and, hence, systematic errors in the markets valuations. Note, first of all, that this argument ignores the impact of competing sources of information on the market's use of accounting numbers. As indicated above, if the information provided by these alternative sources suggests that accounting numbers are "deficient" indicators of events that affect firms' values, then the accounting numbers will not be used. Also, note that the arguments just advanced regarding alternative accounting procedures are applicable here as well. Suppose that the conditioning argument is valid, then at least one person is confronted by an

---

[18] See John F. Muth, "Rational Expectations and the Theory of Price Movements," *Econometrica* (July 1961), pp. 315–35.

[19] This perspective is evident in, e.g., R.J. Chambers, *Accounting Evaluation and Economic Behavior* (Prentice-Hall, Inc., 1966), Chapter 8; and Sterling, "On Theory Construction and Verification," pp. 444–57.

[20] Sterling, p. 453.

[21] Carl Hempel, Philosophy of Natural Science (Prentice-Hall, Inc., 1966).

[22] *Ibid.*, p. 30.

opportunity to earn, *ex ante*, "abnormal" returns. As before, suppose that information about the "conditioning" is "inside" information possessed by some group. Then, as before, the possessors of this information will be motivated to sell their information or sell their information along with "superior" portfolio management services. Alternatively, if they are altruistic, they may simply publicize the existence of the opportunity to earn, *ex ante*, "abnormal" returns.[23] If the opportunity did exist, its existence will, on average, provide a basis for its own elimination within the context of an efficient market.

The crux of my argument remains unaltered: the market's reactions (e.g., anticipatory price reactions) to accounting numbers provides reliable indicants of accounting numbers' informational content. It might be added that one who seeks a market based evaluation of accounting numbers' informational content need not use only direct reactions to particular accounting numbers, such as the reactions documented in Ball and Brown and Beaver[24] with respect to income numbers. One might also attempt to evaluate the informational content of accounting numbers by examining their predictive ability in regard to accounting numbers for which market reactions have been documented. For example, one might discover that several different accounting-number series provide unbiased forecasts of some accounting number that possesses information content. Yet, the statistical efficiency of the forecasts may vary across number-series. *Ceteris paribus*, the number-series that provides the more efficient forecasts would possess greater informational content, according to this indirect test. The use of predictive ability tests may be justified in terms of market efficiency and the theory of "rational expectations": The systematic relationship(s) between something known and something to be predicted will be taken into account in forming the prediction(s). When alternative "knowns" are available, the one(s) providing the "best" predictions will be employed. The criterion of predictive ability and some of its potential drawbacks were recently discussed at length by Beaver, Kennelly, and Voss.[25]

Clarifying Remarks

Some comments on what was not asserted and issues with which I have not dealt are in order. First, it was not argued that market transactors never

---

[23] If this actually occurred and if the market did not purchase the information or react to the mere publication of the information, the possessors of the information might conclude that the market is inefficient. But there is an alternative conclusion. The supposed "inside" information may not have been inside information!

[24] Ball and Brown, "An Empirical Evaluation," pp. 159–78; Beaver, "The Information Content," pp. 67–92.

[25] William H. Beaver, John W. Kennelly, and William M. Voss, "Predictive Ability as a Criterion for the Evaluation of Accounting Data," *The Accounting Review* (October 1968), pp. 675–83.

make "mistakes," in the sense of never having predictions disproved by subsequent actualities. The "fair game" model (see p. 341) is based upon expectations. It states that on average the rate of return series ($\tilde{r}_{it+1}$) is a "fair game" with respect to the information series (Ω_t). Since we are not dealing with degenerate probability distributions one should expect to observe transient deviations from the average. Additionally, it was not argued that each market transactor will use all existing sources of information or that the market (in the aggregate) is unaffected by the cost of obtaining information relative to the expected benefits associated with the information. Whether any individual will use a particular source of information and the extent to which any source of information is employed by the market (in the aggregate) depends upon the costs and benefits associated with that source of information. Not using a source of information that costs more than it is worth is not an indication of inefficiency. This phenomenon was described in picturesque terms by Stigler: "There is no 'imperfection' in a market possessing incomplete knowledge if it would not be remunerative to acquire (produce) complete knowledge: information costs are the costs of transportation from ignorance to omniscience, and seldom can a trader afford to take the entire trip."[26] Also, it was not suggested that the existing supply-of-information mechanism is, in fact, a globally optimum mechanism. And, clearly, nothing proposed in this paper rules out specialization in the production of sources of information, such as accounting numbers. In addition, the preceding discussion did not embrace comparisons between accounting numbers computed according to known techniques and numbers computed in accordance with yet-to-be-developed techniques. It did involve consideration of the informational content of numbers that are (or can be) made available given the current technology. The dynamical issues that attend technological innovations are, in principle, as relevant to the production of accounting numbers as they are to the production of other goods or services. But the existence of dynamical issues need not induce market inefficiencies. Note, also, that changes in the methods of production employed by the accounting process may affect other producers of information sources, i.e., such changes may be associated with externalities. The effects of competition amongst suppliers of information will not, however, be precluded by all kinds of externalities.[27]

Final Remarks

At an earlier point in this paper it was stated that the accounting process would be viewed as a producer of numbers that possess potential informa-

---

[26] George J. Stigler, "Imperfections in the Capital Markets," *Journal of Political Economy* (June 1967), p. 291.

[27] Pertinent discussions in this regard appear in Kenneth J. Arrow and Tibor Scitovsky, eds., *Readings in Welfare Economics* (Richard D. Irwin, Inc., 1969).

tional content. It was suggested that observations of market reactions to such numbers should govern evaluations of the actual informational content of these numbers and evaluations of procedures that are used to produce accounting numbers. If these numbers do not reflect inside information as of the time that they are made public, and if they do have some informational content, then one should expect these reactions to be anticipatory reactions. If my depiction of the accounting process and its competitive context is not wholly inaccurate, then the apparent implication for accounting is that it should devote itself to the production of numbers that have informational content, as indicated (directly or indirectly) by market reactions. It is not clear to me that, "The fact that receivers react is information to us and it is up to us to decide whether or not that reaction is pathological."[28]

It appears that an important task for accounting researchers is to design and conduct tests that will indicate the (market-determined) informational content of (1) accounting numbers produced via a particular set of procedures, and (2) accounting numbers produced via alternative sets of accounting procedures. As indicated earlier, these tests may involve direct use of market reactions or indirect use of market reactions via, e.g., predictive ability tests. (I am not suggesting that these kinds of tests are easy to design and conduct.) Moreover, some of these tests may involve what *appear to be* "purely statistical" issues, such as evaluating the descriptive validity of alternative distributional assumptions and alternative time series models. Yet, it seems that dealing with these kinds of issues is consistent with the role of producer of numbers with potential informational content. In order to design and conduct appropriate tests using these numbers, one may have to first consider such statistical issues.

In addition, one will often be forced to invoke presuppositions, or statements that are themselves not testable (or not tested within the confines of a given project) but which lead to testable statements.[29] In other words, some things will have to be taken as givens, or the unproblematic features of an inquiry. This, however, is not an uncommon trait of inquiries:

> Not everything is or can be problematic all at once . . . where all is problematic, nothing is left with which a problem can even be formulated, let alone solved. . . . We presuppose, in every inquiry, not only a set of data but also a set of generalizations, both about our materials and about the instruments by which they are to be transformed in the cognitive enterprise.[30]

---

[28] Sterling, "On Theory Construction and Verification," p. 454 (emphasis added).

[29] For example, one presupposition underlying the efficient markets model is that equilibrium conditions may be described in terms of expected returns, but this is, of course, not the only approach. A different approach is pursued in, for example: Roy Radner, "Competitive Equilibrium Under Uncertainty," *Econometrica* (January 1968), pp. 31–58, and "Problems in the Theory of Markets Under Uncertainty," *American Economic Review* (May 1970), pp. 454–60.

[30] Abraham Kaplan, *The Conduct of Inquiry* (Chandler Publishing Company, 1964).

Of course, one check on the "reasonableness" of such presuppositions is the consistency of observable phenomena with the testable implications under consideration and the consistency of one test's results with the results provided by alternative tests dealing with the same or related issues.